# A SOCIAL HISTORY OF BRITAIN IN POSTCARDS 1870–1930

# A SOCIAL HISTORY OF BRITAIN IN POSTCARDS 1870–1930

Eric J. Evans & Jeffrey Richards

LONGMAN
London and New York

LONGMAN GROUP LIMITED London

*Associated companies, branches and representatives throughout the world*

*Published in the United States of America by Longman Inc., New York*



*First published 1980*

BRITISH LIBRARY CATALOGUING IN PUBLICATION DATA

Evans, Eric J
A social history of Britain in postcards, 1870–1930.
1. Great Britain – Social conditions – 19th century 2. Great Britain – Social conditions – 20th century 3. Postal cards – Great Britain
I. Title II. Richards, Jeffrey
769′.4′9309141081 DA560 79–41449

ISBN 0–582–50292–6

Set in 11/12½pt Comp/Set Bembo
Printed in Great Britain by
Fletcher & Son, Limited, Norwich

TO JOHN MACKENZIE, POSTCARD SUPERSTAR

# CONTENTS

# PREFACE AND ACKNOWLEDGEMENTS

Although this book was conceived as a unity, Chapters 1, 2 and 3 are basically the work of E. J. E. and the introduction and Chapters 4, 5 and 6 the work of J. M. R.

Many individuals and institutions have been generous with their time, help and advice and we would like to tender our grateful thanks to the following:

*Annan Public Library; Atkinson Library, Southport; Barnsley Public Library; Birmingham City Housing Department; Birmingham Reference Library; Blackburn District Central Library; Blackpool District Central Library; Bolton Reference Library; Bury Library, local history section; Chesterfield Public Library; Cornwall County Record Office; Essex County Record Office; Ewart Library, Dumfries; Hastings Area Library; Huddersfield Central Library; Hull Central Library, Local History Department; Institute of Historical Research, University of London; Kent County Record Office; Lancaster University Library; Lancashire and North Staffordshire Miners' Welfare Convalescent Home, Blackpool; Leeds Library Services Department; Liverpool Record Office; Manchester Central Library, Local History Department; National Coal Board, Records and Registry Services; National Union of Mineworkers; Pontefract Public Library; St Helens Library, Museum and Arts Department; Scarborough Public Library; Sheffield Reference Library; South Humberside Area Record Office; Torquay Public Library; United Biscuits Ltd.; Warrington Borough Council; Whitechapel Bell Foundry.*

*Beatrice Bayley; Anna Benson, Assistant Keeper of Technology, Higher Hill Museum, Hilmshore, Rossendale; Messrs J. Delaney and A. Fusco, Strand Palace Hotel, London WC 2; Christine Evans; Mrs B. Hance, Company Historian, GEC Marconi Electronics Ltd; Brett Harrison, Cumbria County Record Office, Barrow; Elizabeth Leese; Marion McClintock; Mrs E. Newton, Personnel Officer, GEC Mechanical Handling Ltd, Spencer Works, Melksham; Leslie Richards; Elizabeth Roberts; Frank Bell; Michael Steyn.*

We owe special debts of gratitude to our friends and colleagues at Lancaster, John MacKenzie, John Walton and Michael Winstanley who have patiently answered many queries, criticized drafts and contributed many helpful suggestions. Hetty Evans kindly gave up considerable time to the unrewarding but vital task of checking certain references in not always immediately accessible places for which we are most grateful.

Helen Lea typed parts of the manuscript with much greater efficiency and imperturbability than E. J. E. typed other parts. We are most grateful also to Marian Jackson for much secretarial and administrative assistance.

We are indebted to all of the foregoing individuals and institutions. They have prevented many errors and misconceptions. For those which remain we must bear all responsibility.

All of the postcards used in the book are from the J. M. Richards Collection with the exception of cards 3 and 25 in Chapter 1 and card 5 in Chapter 2 which are from the J. M. MacKenzie Collection and appear by gracious permission. We have tried to select cards of good visual quality but sometimes historical importance and rarity has had to take precedence over clarity.

Eric J. Evans, Jeffrey Richards
*Lancaster, October 1979*

# INTRODUCTION

# THE PICTURE POSTCARD

When he made his celebrated *English Journey* in 1933, J. B. Priestley discerned three Englands. The first was 'Old England', the timeless, unchanging, historic landscape of Gothic cathedrals, medieval castles, Tudor manor houses and eighteenth-century coaching inns; the tourist's England, rural England, 'Merrie England'. The third was 'Postwar England', the England of unplanned ribbon development, of filling stations, super-cinemas, the palais de danse, chain stores, wireless and motor coaches, the consumer's England of rising democracy and declining privilege. The second was 'Victorian England', the England of Priestley's own roots and background, which he describes as

> *the industrial England of coal, iron, steel, cotton, wool, railways; of thousands of rows of little houses all alike, sham Gothic churches, square-faced chapels, Town Halls, Mechanics' Institutes, mills, foundries, warehouses, refined watering places, Pier Pavilions, Family and Commercial Hotels, Literary and Philosophical Societies, back-to-back houses, detatched villas with monkey trees, Grill Rooms, railway stations, slag-heaps and 'tips', dock roads, Refreshment Rooms, doss-houses, Unionist or Liberal Clubs, cindery waste grounds, mill chimneys, slums, fried-fish shops, public houses with red blinds, bethels with corrugated iron, good-class drapers' and confectioners' shops, a cynically devastated countryside, sooty dismal little towns and still sootier grim fortress-like cities.*

What he was describing was the England, or rather the Britain of the Industrial Revolution, the Midlands and North of England, South Wales and Central Scotland, the pulsing heart of the kingdom, the source of its wealth and might, the matrix of its class system, the wellspring and legacy of the technological inventions and commercial processes that had put Britain in the forefront of the world's nations.

This is the world captured forever in the photographic picture postcard, and its value for the social historian, as that world rapidly recedes from view, is the permanent record it provides of all the facets that Priestley describes. The word 'picture postcard' means to most people lurid coloured cartoons of fat ladies and weedy little men on the beach, captions like 'I've lost my little Willie' and messages no more illuminating than 'Having a wonderful time – wish you were here.' But in its golden age, the picture postcard was far more. The IPM (International Postcard Market) Catalogue, the postcard collectors' bible, lists some 1,500 different categories of card, including such diverse topics as scouting, the suffragette movement, Irish home rule, polar exploration, exhibitions, pageants, football, missionary activities and maritime disasters. One collector advertises regularly in the *Postcard Collectors Gazette* for cards depicting 'outdoor barbers, Hindu incinerations, ostrich farming, prostitutes, nomads, dancing bears, executions, death cages, dervishes, snake charmers, head hunters, plague scenes, etc.'

We are not concerned with the outré or bizarre here but the simple record of everyday life in the period between 1870 and 1930, which was the golden era of the postcard, both in the pictures and the messages on the back. It is easy enough to despise such ephemera; the traditional historian, geared as he is to examining such detailed documentary evidence as parliamentary records and court rolls, has been reluctant enough to admit the value of film for history, let alone the humble postcard photograph. But the medieval historian would give his eye teeth for postcards from the peasants and nobles of his era with whatever scraps of information they might contain about the pattern of existence.

In the postcard, the social historian possesses fragments of people's lives. He touches a hundred isolated moments, hears the echoes of voices long stilled, reaches out down the years to grasp at the day-to-day life of Everyman. To take just a few examples from J. M. R.'s collection: a public school boy writing to his friend (1907): 'Your school looks ripping – I suppose some of the buildings in the photo are houses. Remember me to your mater and pater.'; or a young Scottish lady to her cousin in Dalkeith (1909): 'Ask Uncle G. if he is coming to the 'Professional' Golf Tournament next month. Hope Aunt M. is quite well. Love to all. Yr. cousin Bella.'; or an army officer's wife to her husband (1909): 'Many thanks dearest for p.c. I hope you had no trouble with your men in London. Lt. Dunant said he hoped you had help. My thoughts have been at Liverpool St. station all day. This day week we shall be expecting you home. You will let me know which train'; or to Gertie from her brother: 'Now for the surprised [sic] that I am going to tell you about the wedding which weare [sic] having in our house and I am to be the best man for our Joe is getting married on Saturday but we are only having a party amongst ourselves.'; or on a postcard showing the station clock at the Lancashire and Yorkshire Railway Company's Bury station, this: 'Dear Jim, I wonder if you have forgotten this place. Well I never thought *you* would have treated me like this but I suppose we have to live and learn. I hate being fooled. If you dont want to write to me why not be honest and tell me and then I shall know what to do. If your mother does not wish it write and tell me.' From all classes and walks of life the postcards came, revealing speech patterns, standards of literacy, social attitudes, current preoccupations, fads and fashions. Arrangements for visits, requests for money, messages about sending and receiving parcels, attending church meetings and meeting trains, announcements of bereavements, congratulations on birthdays, weddings and anniversaries, exchanges of information on sport and leisure, romantic missives made all the more mysterious and intriguing by the use of mirror writing or the positioning of the stamp, each position having a particular epistolary significance, all make up a mosaic of everyday life. The postcard reveals for instance the extreme formality of address between relations ('your loving brother', 'your affectionate cousin'), something now almost extinct, the common practice of whiling away the time on trains and on stations by sending a postcard (From Preston in 1910: 'I'm on my way to Blackpool, but have to wait some time here for a train. I'm using the rotten pen of the young man at the book stall.'), and the fact that a trip to the cinema was sufficiently unusual and exciting an event to merit discussion in a card of 1910 and that the inability to hire a bicycle in a Yorkshire village was an occasion for surprise in 1904.

Sometimes the evidence presented by the message is more substantial and this became particularly true during the First World War when many families were split up and communicated extensively by postcard. For instance, Walt Charnley writes to his wife Kit in Liverpool en route for Woolwich Arsenal in 1914:

*Got my papers fixed up fine and am writing this in the 12 o'clock puff-puff for Woolwich from Lime St. There are 4 of us in the carriage. A parson in one corner, soldier in another, myself and a civilian. I saw Roskelly in town he is like me on Home Service, but they wont let him stay at his job, they told him he would have to report and go away. He is keeping his house on and Mrs Roskelly is living there alone. I had coffee with him and will tuck into my egg sandwidge* [sic] *in a little while. It is now 1.p.m. we are at Crew* [sic] *station and I have put my grub where it will never be seen again. 5.50 p.m. arriving at Euston station. Just going to get some tea and then report to Woolwich.*

Later he sends another card:

*I am just going back to barracks after being at the Arsenal to pass my trade test. I dont know how I have got on yet. . . they kept us in barracks all weekend. I never spent so long a weekend in my life. We have plenty of grub which is good and clean but not served up in style. . . the place seems full of soldiers. The barracks is packed out.*

On a 1917 picture postcard of Victoria station, Harry writes to his mother:

*I got back alright but not until this morning. I arrived at Euston at 12.10 and had dinner. Intended going by last train so went to the Empire and saw 'Hanky Panky', very good. Saw one of our men at Victoria, went and had a drink and missed the train, so did not get back till this morning. I got the transport officer to sign my pass at Victoria but have to go up before the Colonel on Monday but it will be allright. I got back at 9.40 this morning. There was an explosion on the destroyer in the harbour at 8.30 this morning, a torpedo exploded and killed 14, blew them to pieces, and smashed the windows in the town. An air raid on Folkestone between five and six yesterday afternoon, which resulted in great loss of life, 14 girls being killed in one shop.*

On a card of the Rose Tea Gardens, Watford Heath, dated 14 June 1916, a letter from a Quaker conscientious objector to his brother:

*Dear Tom, Just a few lines to let you know I am in the best of health . . . I am not in the ambulance section now I have transferred into the agriculter* [sic] *for a little while. I am working at Oxhey Grange now but I dont know how long for as I am going to a place called Wareham with 2 more chaps. We are sleeping in a loft here. We have our meals at the Rose tea gardens. I am cutting pea sticks in the wood next to the field where your lot was camped. There is no camp here now. Penrose seems a nice chap. We came here yesterday in the Motor Car it is only 14 miles from Jordan's. We start work at 6.30 a.m. and finish at 5.30 p.m. and at 1 o'clock on Saturday. I met a chap in Jordan's who was camped in the same tent here with you. I forget his name but he is coming to France on Friday with a few more chaps. They have got another hospital in London. No more this time. From Thy brother Jim.*

In the pictures on the cards, we have a record of buildings now demolished, vehicles now obsolete, costume no longer worn, customs fallen into disuse, the landmarks and signposts of a way of life, something to be preserved and cherished before it goes the way of all ephemera – into the waste basket and the dustbin.

This is not a history of the postcard. That function is already well served by several excellent works, listed in the Further Reading list at the end of this introduction. It is rather an examination of several aspects of the social history of Britain – work, shopping, leisure, transport, city life – which the postcards chart and illustrate. But it is necessary to sketch in briefly the story of the postcard in those years as background to this discussion.

The first postcard was issued in Austria on 1 October 1869, a plain card with a printed two-kreuzer stamp on one side and space for a message on the other. Exactly one year later in 1870 they were issued for the first time in Britain. They were rapidly taken up by the world of commerce and soon all the major commercial companies were using them to acknowledge receipt of goods, confirm appointments, despatch price lists etc. So widely were they used that there was strong pressure exerted to end the Post Office's monopoly of their production and in 1872, commercial firms were permitted to produce their own cards so long as they were not sold to the general public. From 1875 they could be sent abroad.

But the general public were also taking to the postcard for speed of communication. Considerable concern about their use was expressed in newspapers and periodicals, because of the lack of privacy involved in sending an open message, fear that the art of letter writing might be threatened and anxiety about the propriety of conducting correspondence by card. An Edwardian card in J. M. R.'s collection sent from a man to his cousin in Kidderminster observes: 'Excuse the p.c. They are so handy.' An etiquette book of 1890 advised: 'It is questionable whether a note on a postal card is entitled to the courtesy of a response.' Nevertheless the widely publicized fact that W. E. Gladstone and later George Bernard Shaw favoured correspondence by postcard gave them respectability. The sheer convenience ensured their success and by 1879 the Post Office had an annual turnover of 50 million postcards. Agitation for the legalization of private postcard production finally achieved success from 1 September 1894.

The main postcard development of the 1890s was the addition of pictures. Pictorial stationery had been in common use since the 1840s and there had been pictorial advertisement cards since 1870. But the first picture postcards seem to have emanated from the Paris Exhibition of 1889 and to have caught on rapidly.

By the time Edward VII ascended the throne, picture postcards were an accepted part of national life. They were given final boosts by the Boer War and the decision of the Postmaster-General in January 1902 to authorize the divided back postcard permitting both messages and address on the back, instead of the address alone which was all that was legally allowed before; in fact messages had long been written on the cards and the Postmaster-General was simply legalizing an existing practice. They began to be sold everywhere and by 1903 some 600 million postcards were being sent annually, ten times as many as were sent in 1871. By 1914, 880 million cards were posted. Collecting had also become a craze. Postcard-collecting clubs sprang up, with at least six specialist magazines in circulation, and many surviving cards bear the legend: 'Here is one for your collection', testifying to the enthusiasm for the craze. Production companies multiplied to meet the demand and Anthony Byatt has listed 278 different firms all over Britain.

Postcards were invaluable during the First World War in maintaining links between families and in the dissemination of propaganda. By 1917, the British Forces postal service was employing over 4,000 men handling 2 million letters and postcards daily. The role of the postcard in the First World War is covered in detail in the fine book *Till the Boys Come Home* by Tonie and Valmai Holt.

In 1918 when the cost of sending a postcard was doubled, to a penny, half the previous year's total of postcards was sent. In the years following the end of the war, the boom subsided. The growth of the telephone took much of the commercial business, and the new craze, popular snapshot photography, was advanced as the price of the new cheap, convenient box camera fell progressively. In 1920 five times as many cameras were sold as in 1914. The quality, volume and range of postcards declined and by 1930 the age of the picture postcard was over.

Although its golden age was essentially brief, 1902–18, the era of the postcard was longer, 1870 – 1930, particularly when it is realized that the photographic cards in which this book is mainly interested recorded not just the world of its own decade but the buildings and transport of a slightly earlier period.

The functions of the postcard in society were many and the social history of the postcard, as distinct from social history from postcards which we attempt here, has yet to be written. It is worth noting just a few of the postcard's functions. Advertising was from the outset a basic role of postcards. Pin-up and glamour cards proliferated, with the name of Gladys Cooper particularly prominent; she was photographed in a wide variety of outfits and poses. There were immediate news photographs; photographers were despatched to fires, wrecks, disasters of all kinds. The immediacy of their visual impact anticipates television. There was a strong and continuous propaganda use, with pictures of the Royal Family and royal events, portraits of politicians and party slogans, and, during the war, anti-Boer and anti-German atrocity pictures, portraits of victorious British generals, and scenes of Allied victories. The value of these cards for education must not be forgotten. Robert Roberts recalls in *The Classic Slum*, his evocative study of slum life in Edwardian Salford:

> *To a child avid for experience a newsagent's shop with a good display provided pleasure free and delightful. The picture postcard became a new aid to self-education as effective as any of his school lessons. Every great event of the day was reflected in illustration and explained in simple text. Through cards I remember the loss of the* Titanic *with awful vividness. Coloured photographs of Marie Studholme and later the young Gladys Cooper fixed the child's conception of womanly beauty. The scraps of lush verse that often went with them seemed to one far more 'poetic' than the stuff learned by rote at school.*

Some cards actually set out to be 'educational', reproducing scenes from Dickens, extracts from the poets and artistically composed shots of historic places.

Postcards in their range and richness were seen as a vital new source for the historian and we can do no better than echo journalist James Douglas who wrote in 1907;

> *When the archaeologists of the thirtieth century begin to excavate the ruins of London, they will fasten upon the Picture Postcard as the best guide to the spirit of the Edwardian era. They will collect and collate thousands of these pieces of pasteboard and they will reconstruct our age from the strange hieroglyphs and pictures that time has spared. For the Picture Postcard is a candid revelation of our pursuits and pastimes, our customs and costumes, our morals and manners.*

FURTHER READING

Byatt, A. *Picture Postcards and their Publishers* (Malvern, 1978)
Carline, R., *Pictures in the Post* (London, 1971)
Coe, B. and Gates, P., *The Snapshot Photograph: the Rise of Popular Photography 1888–1939* (London, 1977)
Hill, C. W., *Discovering Picture Postcards* (Princes Risborough, 1978)
Holt, T. and V., *Till the Boys Come Home* (London, 1977)
Holt, T. and V., *Picture Postcards of the Golden Age* (London, 1978)
Macdonald, G., *Camera: a Victorian Eyewitness* (London, 1979)
MacKenzie, J., 'Deltiology', *Lancaster Comment*, **73** (January 1977), pp. 12–15
*The Postcard Collectors Gazette*, passim
Priestley, J. B., *English Journey* (London, 1933)
Roberts, R., *The Classic Slum* (Manchester, 1971)
Scott, W. J., *All About Postcards* (Leeds, 1903)
Staff, F., *The Picture Postcard and its Origins* (London, 1979)

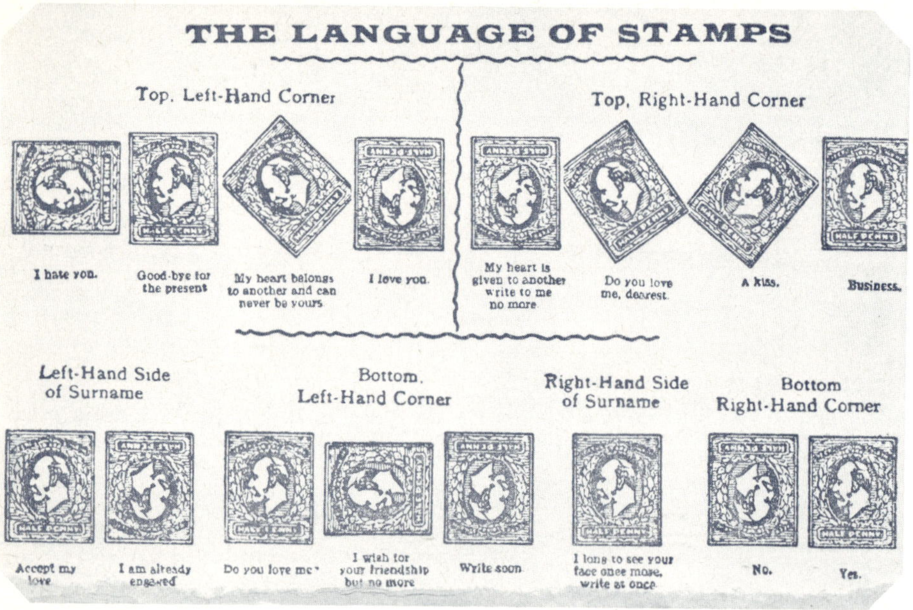


1. THE LANGUAGE OF STAMPS – EACH POSITION INDICATED SOME DIFFERENT ROMANTIC MESSAGE

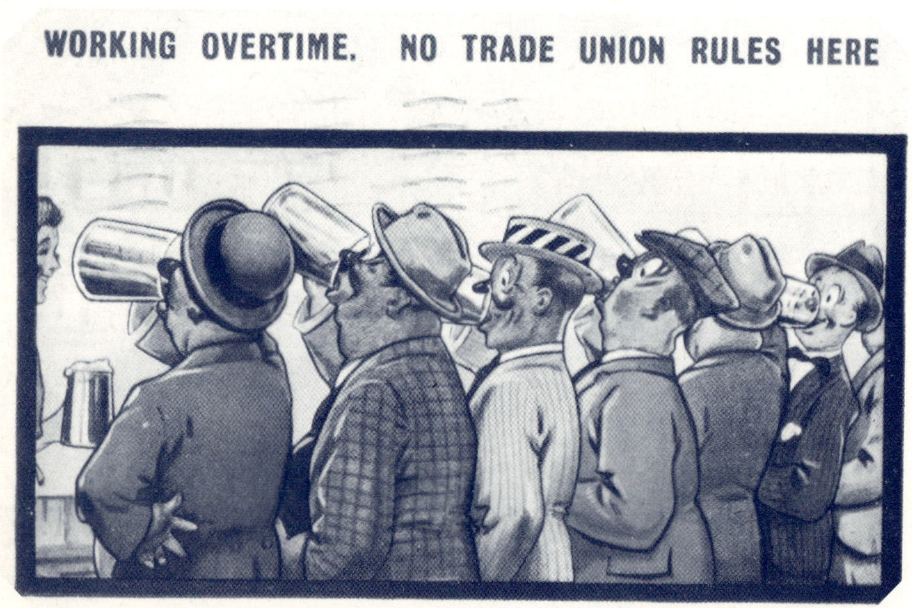


2. THE COMIC POSTCARD – HERE WITH POLITICAL OVERTONES

3. THE TOPICAL POSTCARD – SHOWING THE RESULTS OF A GERMAN AIR RAID

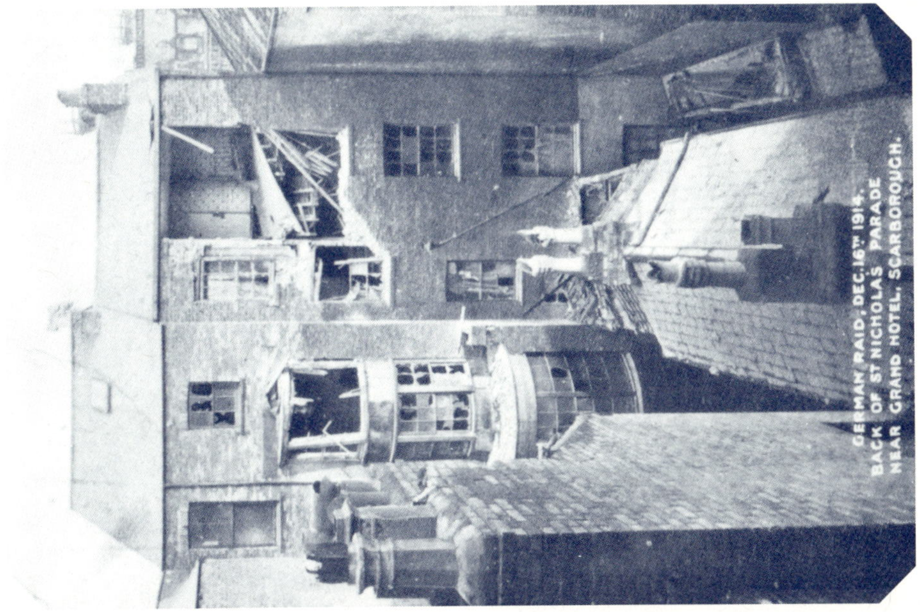


4. THE POSTCARD SHOP – THIS ONE IN SOUTH SHIELDS BOTH MANUFACTURED AND SOLD THE PROFITABLE COMMODITY

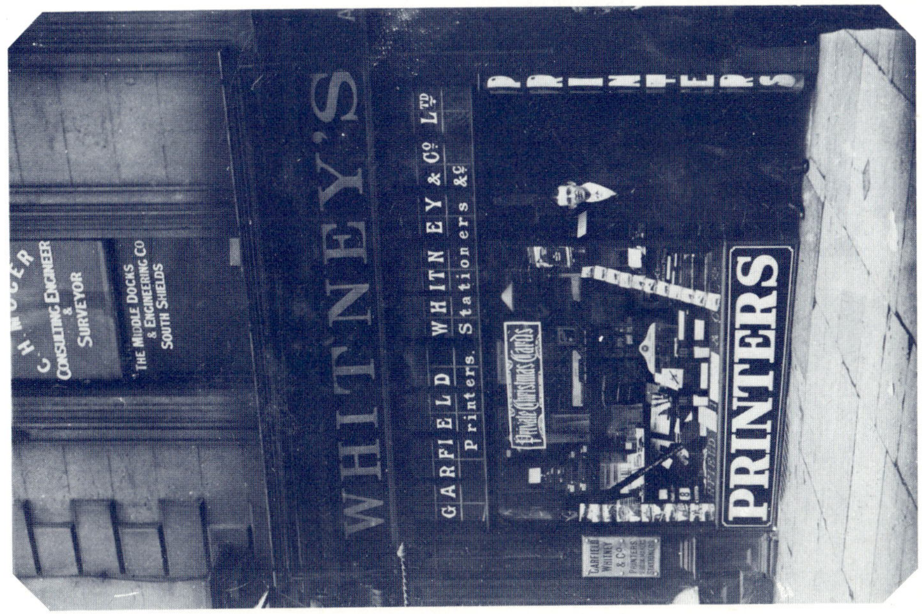

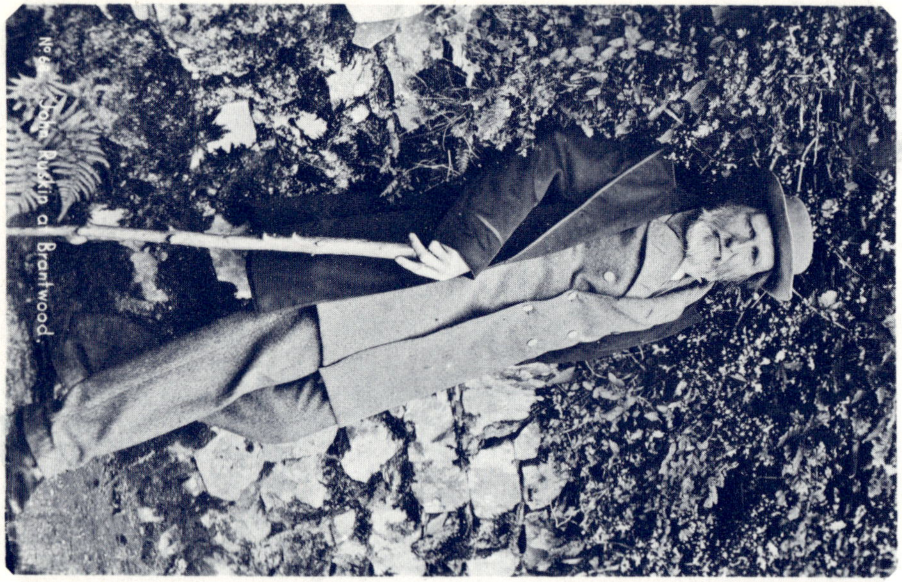


5. THE CELEBRITY CARD – JOHN RUSKIN IN EXTREME OLD AGE

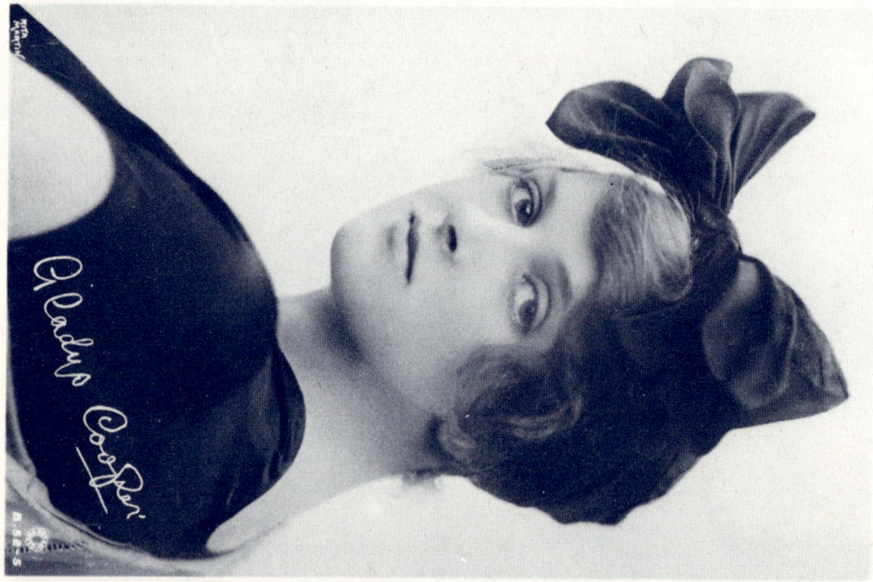


6. THE PIN UP – GLADYS COOPER, THE PARADIGM OF PULCHRITUDE

7. THE PROPAGANDA CARD (i) POLITICAL

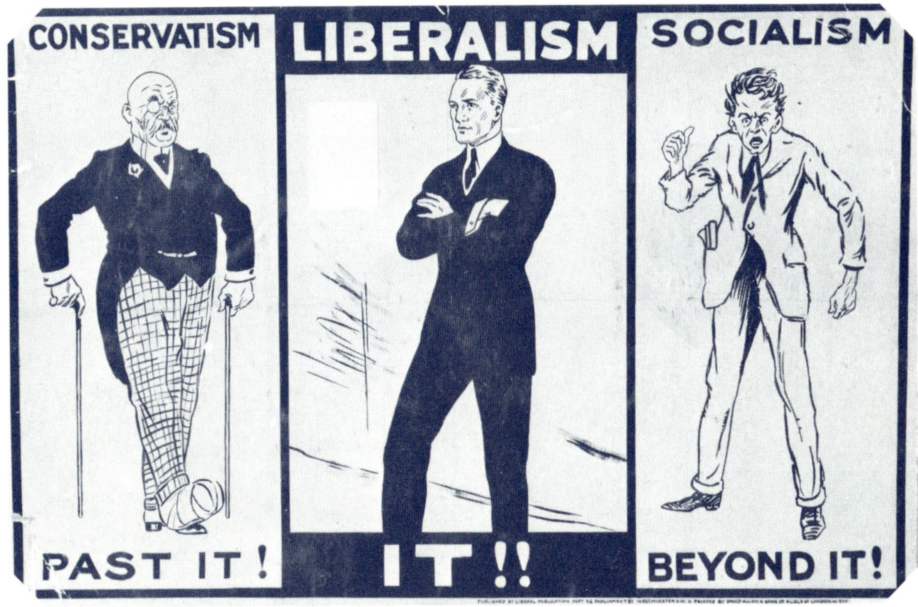


8. THE PROPAGANDA CARD (ii) ROYAL

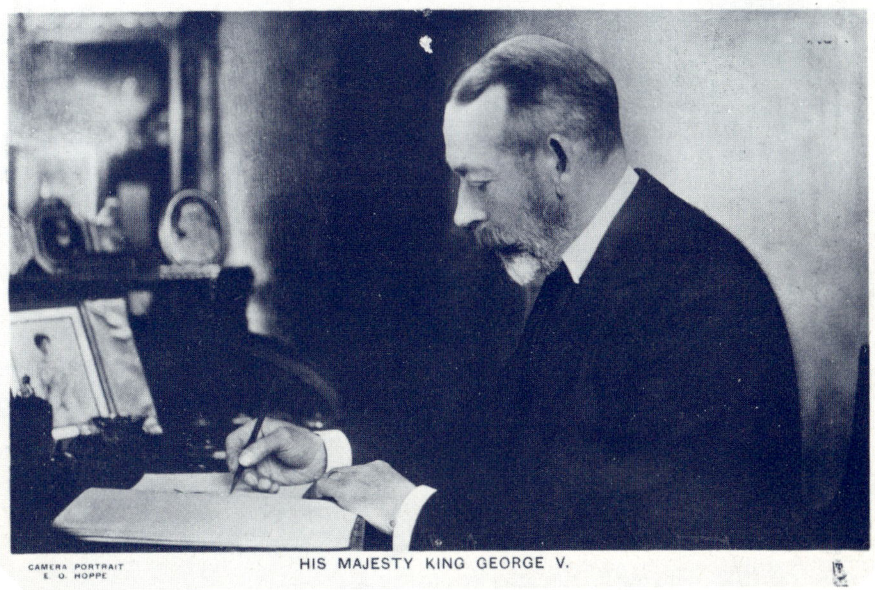

# CHAPTER ONE | URBAN LIFE

Victorian cities were at once the pride and the perturbation of their creators. Their presence, in all their profusion and diversity, was a tribute in brick and stone to the transforming vitality of industry and commerce. As early as 1880 no less than 80 per cent of Britain's population lived in towns, whereas in 1800 only 25 per cent had done so. London, by far the largest urban agglomeration in the world, accommodated 4½ million people at the end of Victoria's reign. More than 10 per cent of the population lived there. No fewer than 36 towns now had populations in excess of 100,000 against only ten fifty years earlier. Apart from London, there were four urban monsters with populations in excess of half a million – in descending order of size, Glasgow, Liverpool, Manchester and Birmingham. No town apart from London had topped 400,000 in 1851. Though the rate of population growth was slackening in the second half of the nineteenth century the pace of urbanization was quickening as factory production spread beyond the precocious textile industry.

Civic leaders took enormous pride in their creations. Town halls, built on the grand scale even in otherwise quite humble textile towns, gave splendid, if often derivative, scope to the architectural imagination. Cuthbert Brodrick's massive town hall in Leeds, opened amid maximum publicity and civic embellishment by Queen Victoria in September 1858, cost £130,000 to build and included one of the largest organs in Europe, weighing over 70 tons and incorporating 6,500 pipes. Not the least of Manchester's contributions to urban culture was the orchestra developed by Charles Hallé after 1858. The Hallé Orchestra, offering regular concerts in the Free Trade Hall, was the prototype of twentieth-century provincial symphony orchestras.

Food for the mind was an important priority for those who wished to make their cities great. Many took advantage of the 1850 Free Libraries Act to establish large collections for reference and smaller district lending libraries at ratepayers' expense. The most impressive of them was

Birmingham's central Reference Library opened in 1866 under the fervent patronage of the leading Baptist minister, George Dawson. Civic dignitaries thought it an appropriate way of perpetuating their names to donate land or buildings for libraries, institutes, technical schools, parks and other amenities. The gift by Archibald Walker, first Provost of the small Clackmannanshire town of Tillicoultry, of a drinking fountain to mark his retirement from office in 1900 is a small but pertinent example of the tradition of service to and identity with the urban community which marked town development in hundreds of different places. As some pointed out, local government and local amenities should not be merely functional; they grasped for a civic ideal. Dawson put it well when he opened the Birmingham Reference Library: 'A great town consists to discharge towards the people of that town the duties that a great nation exists to discharge towards the people of that nation.'

The ideal could even be worked out in the provision of sanitary amenities. Joseph Chamberlain's energy and drive as Mayor of Birmingham from 1873 to 1876 was in large part responsible for the corporation's taking over privately owned gas and water works in 1875–76. He launched a massive improvement scheme, closed numerous insanitary drinking wells after receiving health inspectors' reports and Birmingham's death rate was cut by 20 per cent in ten years. As much deserving of memory was Sir James Bazalgette's reconstruction, or more accurately, construction of much of London's sewerage system in the 1860s. This was a project on the epic scale in everything except, necessarily, public accessibility and approbation.

By the 1870s a distinctive urban ideal was emerging in British towns which encompassed service, identity and pride. Looked at from one angle they possessed in 1900 a confidence, an organizing structure and a sense of purpose quite belying the pragmatism and bewildering rapidity of their creation. The radical Liberal MP, Joseph Cowan, saw even in the growth of a heavy industry town like Middlesbrough an example of 'that irresistible and victorious civilization which has for its foundation, industry and freedom'. Speaking in 1881, he went on to assert that 'Our towns are the backbone of the nation. They give it strength, cohesion, vitality.'

But there was another side to the story. The expansion of the nineteenth-century town had been one of the wonders of the modern world but as the economic vicissitudes of the 1880s and 1890s induced in observers a more introspective and less expansive state of mind, so attention became fastened on more worrying facets. Towns had grown fast, too fast certainly for the provision of basic requirements for health. Edwin Chadwick had demonstrated as early as 1842 the differential death rates in village and town and between comfortable rural squire and factory worker. The social imbalance was exacerbated once manufacturers and the professional classes moved out either to residential suburbs designed to be exclusive or to surrounding villages which became, as the expansion of the railway system permitted it, almost extended prosperous suburbs of the industrial and commercial centres – though such a description would have sent *frissons* of horror through genteel Hyde, Wilmslow or Solihull. As the *Birmingham Daily Mail* put it when speaking of the once upper-crust area of Acock's Green in 1903: 'Those of the more wealthy residents who have loved the place for its quiet exclusiveness and pleasant detachment are moving further out . . . like the Arab, they are folding their tents and stealing silently away in the direction of Knowle or Solihull, when the octopus tentacles of expanding Birmingham are as yet in the distance.' A town like Bolton doubtless looked very different from the superior late Victorian villas laid out spaciously along Chorley New Road where dwelt Boltonian mill owners and professional men than from the crowded dwellings of Mill Hill or Springfield, near the town centre, where their employees lived. The general tendency in town development was for the more salubrious areas to be situated to the west so that the prevailing winds should not blow the smells of factory and the detritus of overcrowded lesser humanity in their direction.

This physical separation in many urban communities carried dangers. Many of those most wary of the uncivilizing effects of urban living deplored the exodus of those who had most stake in the community, since they left without leadership or moral example the deprived, the badly housed or the homeless, the physically infirm and the migrant workers. It was a rootless community and rootlessness carried dangers. Much labour was casual, badly paid and implied no permanence or attachment to the community. Men moved from job to job; whole families might move out to the countryside for haymaking or hop picking in the summer; myriad hawking or casual trading opportunities might offer and take a family away until the luck ran out. A general trek away from the biggest cities by much of their unskilled and casual labour force was noticeable during summer months – fortunately so, since without it death rates from infectious and enteric diseases would have been even higher in hot summers. Most wandered back as autumn turned to winter. In winter both town and countryside offered fewer jobs but the towns represented a safer haven with more soup kitchens and more shelter even in the hovels and insanitary tenements which most of the unskilled had to use as homes.

Henry Mayhew brought the deprived London masses vividly to life in the 1850s. As early as 1855 the Tory *Quarterly Review* drew attention to the presence in London of 'a class decidedly lower in the social scale' than the labourer 'whose utmost efforts do little more than maintain them in a state of chronic starvation', many of whose members are 'at open war with society, and professedly live by the produce of depredation or the wages of infamy'. The same point was emphasized in 1891 by Rev W. D. Morrison: 'There is a population of habitual criminals which forms a class by itself . . . not to be confounded with the working or any other class.' These were the elements characterized by Dickens in *Oliver Twist* with Fagin and his thieves' apprentices. They were increasingly referred to as 'the dangerous classes' and their danger was not just to individual person or property; it was to the fabric of society. Perhaps 10 per cent of London's population formed a criminally inclined sub-stratum owing no allegiance to the established order and living off it in a threateningly parasitic manner.

Whereas the mid-Victorian period concentrated on urban opportunity therefore, it became increasingly fashionable to refer from the 1880s to the urban menace. Many hitherto amorphous worries crystallized during the harsh winter of 1885–86 when on three days in February a mob of unemployed dock workers and building labourers from south and east London took to the streets and attacked property in Piccadilly, the heart of the city's clubland. Order was restored only with extreme difficulty and the chief commissioner of Metropolitan police, Sir Edmund Henderson, paid for his failure to preserve the peace of the smoking room and the gaming tables with his job. It is often said that Joseph Chamberlain's government Circular urging local authorities and poor law guardians to find temporary work for the destitute in paving streets, laying out cemeteries or extending sewerage works was motivated by fear of the mob. It was the first government initiative on unemployment and it was issued five weeks after the London riots.

The preservation of law and order, a task discharged usually with brisk and generally tolerant efficiency by the police gave rise to the image of the avuncular 'bobby'. Generalizations about the prevalence of crime are notoriously unreliable because of changing fashions in prosecution and the varying amounts of unreported and undetected incidents. Fears for law and order seem to have been especially high in the 1880s and 1890s, however, and prison sentences were particularly common. Fewer prosecutions were being brought for murder, woundings and theft by the 1920s and far fewer people were in prison in 1920 (35,000) compared with 1901 (149,000). This dramatic decline, however, rather reflects deliberate changes in sentencing policy, placing more emphasis on fines and less on prison. The successful imposition of such a policy depends on greater ability to pay fines, reflected in generally improved living standards. It is doubtful if the apparently popular image of the policeman was shared by organized workers. Complaints about excess of police zeal towards strikers were rife during the labour unrest of 1910–12 and 1926.

While the middle classes retreated to large semi-detached or detached villas built in huge numbers between 1880 and 1914 in London's Hammersmith or Dulwich, Birmingham's Edgbaston or Harborne and Manchester's Didsbury, therefore, what one author called the 'bitter cry' of the overcrowded and underprivileged was being heard not only through the modulations of the social investigators but with discordant major-key insistence by the unfortunates themselves. The resolution depended on increasing state intervention as the twentieth century began.

Between 1880 and 1930 social policy was revolutionized in an attempt to eliminate the horrors of city life and to realize for all the civilizing attributes of urbanization enjoyed by the mid-Victorian few. More hospitals were built, more schools established, more drains laid, more places of charitable resort – Salvation Army hospitals and working men's dining rooms – came into existence but the key to the whole business was housing. Speculative builders had created during the period of most rapid expansion high-density, low-quality accommodation for the working classes at minimum cost. Better homes did not pay; the over-riding need was to site workers as near as possible to their place of employment; environmental considerations were of no account. The major problem, thus, was to solve the housing crisis. The ready-built slums of early and mid-Victorian Britain, those 'pestilential human rookeries . . . where tens of thousands are crowded together amidst horrors which call to mind what we have heard of the middle passage of the slave ship' must be cleared.

Early efforts did not inspire confidence. Major rehousing involved the expenditure of funds which local authorities did not possess and which central government still regarded as quite outside its proper responsibility to provide. Permissive legislation, culminating in the Artisans' Dwelling Act of 1875 to permit the removal of overcrowded dwellings and the erection of sanitary, secure houses in their place, met with a patchy response. Less than one competent authority in eight made early use of the 1875 Act and Joseph Chamberlain's Birmingham, which did, paid much greater attention to the first part of the Act than the second. Birmingham cleared its city centre slums but only to replace them with far more profitable and prestige-laden buildings such as Corporation Street's banks and insurance offices in realization of Chamberlain's long cherished dream to make his city the acknowledged capital of the midlands distinguished by superior, or at least more, commercial and cultural amenities than any possible rival. Since the city was more than three times bigger than any other midland town the realization of this objective was not difficult. The city's housing policy, however, merely shifted the problem a mile or two from the city centre. By 1900 Birmingham was typical of many industrial cities in having a city centre with a defined commercial area around Corporation St, a burgeoning shopping development half a mile to the south centred on New St and its markets a little further south still around the famous Bull Ring. The working-class families displaced by redevelopment decamped to Vauxhall, Bordesley and Ladywood which formed a kind of inner circle of urban deprivation and overcrowding. All too often the problems were not solved, but merely removed to an adequate distance from the sight and smell of important visitors travelling into Birmingham by way of Snow Hill or New St stations.

Charitable organizations made close studies of housing deprivations and many palliatives were offered without ever attacking the root problem. It was characteristic that they insisted on prompt payment of rent for the dwellings they erected or refurbished with no backsliding and clear evidence of a 'respectable' attitude. Octavia Hill, who had many emulators in London for her policy of moral reformation through proper housing management and inculcation of the virtues of economy and self-discipline, had all the houses she took over in previously 'unrespectable' courts distempered and thoroughly cleansed. She also laid on running water. London's most famous private housing organization, the Peabody Trust, which had housed about 19,000 people by 1900, dealt only with those in regular employment. It could not help the plight of the casual labourers of the east end on such a basis.

The Royal Commission on Housing of 1884–85 provided massive evidence of the scale of the housing problem counterbalanced by its opinion that 'there has been a failure in administration rather than in legislation'. Local authorities were exhorted to take over the town's water supply, if still in private hands. Further featherweight housing legislation followed in 1885 and 1890 and a more ambitious Act of 1909 was vitiated by a slump in the building trade. The intractability of the problem and its only adequate solution was pointed out with brutal logic by the Whitehaven Medical Officer of Health in 1913: The crux was 'the deplorable overcrowding of houses on area'; authorities would remove the worst examples but 'The process necessarily reduces the number of available houses and imposes on the Town Council the obligation of providing houses to take the place of those demolished or absorbed'. State aid was needed to build on the scale required. Without it real progress could not be made despite valuable palliatives like the Reckitt garden village in Hull or the teetotal Cadbury creation of the Bournville estate for its Birmingham employees or the co-operative housing schemes like the Moor Park estate also in Birmingham. Before 1914 only the middle classes and skilled workers in steady jobs benefited significantly from houses with running water and inside lavatories. As late as 1939, 90 per cent of all houses in Stepney were still without baths.

The inter-war period brought a housing revolution with the advent of the state-subsidized council house. Three Acts, in 1919, 1923 and 1924, offered subsidies from the state to encourage council house building and local authorities took advantage of the long-delayed opportunity. Between 1919 and 1930 about 600,000 council houses were built in England and Wales; in Scotland more than two-thirds of all houses built were council-owned. It was not merely the numbers which signified; standards in the new dwellings were a dramatic improvement on those they replaced. Bleak and functional the designs may have been, imparting a uniform greyness to the suburbs in which they were located, but they were low-density houses with proper sanitary facilities, guaranteed repair facilities and an appropriate number of bedrooms for the families accommodated. The tenements and 'back-to-backs' began to disappear.

Social commentators in the 1920s remained rightly appalled by the intractability of the problem in the inner cities. On the Registrar-General's yardstick for overcrowding, 12¼ per cent of London's population, mostly living in the east end or immediately south of the Thames, remained overcrowded in 1930, 10½ per cent of Liverpool was similarly circumstanced and 8 per cent in Sheffield. In the old pit communities of County Durham, now wracked by depression, the figure even exceeded 20 per cent. Nor could it be denied that the housing boom of the 1930s, which imparted a recognizably modern look to our city suburbs, primarily benefited the lower middle classes and the settled worker able to borrow in depressed money markets at 2½ – 4 per cent on a solid three-bedroomed semi-detached costing somewhere between £250 and £550. Almost 900,000 private dwellings were built between 1914 and 1929. During the thirties a further two million were added and by the outbreak of the Second World War almost a third of all households were owner-occupied, compared with a mere 10 per cent in 1914. Prosperous suburbs, generally three to four miles from city centres, such as Birmingham's Erdington or King's Heath, Manchester's Davyhulme or Flixton and Sheffield's Bradway or Eccleshall, grew up, many of them erstwhile separate villages swamped now by the ever-rolling tide of urban development.

The housing record is patchy. It may be contended that those in poverty benefited least and that the city centres and the inner penumbra remained overcrowded and insanitary. Even here, however, things were far healthier in 1930 than in 1870. Much the same distinction could be made in the fields of health and medical care. A general, not to say decisive, improvement is discernible despite the continued absence of a national health service and many continuing areas of deprivation.

Death rates, in the low 20s per thousand of the population, remained fairly constant during the formative period of the industrial revolution before 1870. During our period the decline was steady and marked. The rate dropped below 20 for the first time in 1881 and had reached an average of 18.3 in the 1890s. This was reduced to 15.4 in the first decade of the new century and it stood at a mere 11.4 in 1930 following an average for the 1920s of 12.1.

Many reasons may be adduced to explain the decline. More stringent sanitary legislation was introduced from the 1860s with an emphasis on compulsory minimum provisions. A medical officer of health had to be appointed everywhere after 1872 and his annual reports were frequently a spur to the removal of dangerous and offensive 'nuisances' from city streets. Compulsory vaccination against smallpox helped, though not as much as contemporaries believed. Smallpox was declining in incidence and possibly in virulence throughout the nineteenth century and the compulsory provisions were a farce in many cities. Improved nutritional standards were far more important and these will be investigated in Chapter 3. A better diet, or simply more food, will not guard against infection but it is the best protection against its more debilitating effects. Quite simply, more people recovered from infections in 1920 than had done so in 1870. Lower-density housing also helped to check the spread of epidemics.

Hesitant steps were also taken to improve a medical service which was far too dependent on the poor law with all its hated associations in the popular mind with degradation. In 1891, of 113,000 available hospital beds, two-thirds were administered by the poor law; only a quarter were in the voluntary hospitals which were supported by subscriptions and benefactions while the remainder (a mere 9 per cent) were owned by local authorities. Even this does not tell the full story, for less than three poor law 'hospital' beds in twenty were in full poor law hospitals. The remainder were wards in workhouses disproportionately peopled by the aged destitute and quite inadequate with regard to both nursing and medical services.

The improvements in the first thirty years of the twentieth century were striking. By 1921 the number of beds was twice as large as in 1891 and a larger proportion – 47 per cent – were voluntary or local authority owned. Impressive research-oriented teaching hospitals like the London or St Bartholomew's were very much the exception, of course, but the new techniques they pioneered were gradually filtering down. In the last years before the poor law was finally dismantled in 1929 more poor law hospitals were built with a generally better nursing establishment.

The most important piece of legislation contributing to the rise in health standards was undoubtedly Lloyd George's 1911 National Insurance Act. For the first time compulsory sickness insurance was introduced with a basic weekly sickness benefit of 10*s* (50p) for the insured, though not his or her family. A range of reorganized medical services was also introduced, the most important of which was the 'panel' of general medical practitioners available for consultation and treatment. The new machinery, set alongside existing voluntary and poor law provision, represented a wastefully divided use of limited resources but it brought the state much more decisively into the field of medical care.

The system did not encourage preventative medicine nor, since fees continued to be involved for medical consultation, the seeking of an early diagnosis. The poorer sections of the community treated themselves with proprietary medicines or 'quack' remedies and regarded a visit to the doctor very much as a last resort. In consequence, physicians frequently saw poor patients only when they were beyond effective help. The death rate in London's east end in the 1920s was 50 per cent higher than in Bournemouth despite a differential age-structure which might seem to have favoured the capital. In the poorest areas, also, there was no surplus family income for health insurance schemes much patronized by families with steady work. But the advances of the first 30 years of the century could not be gainsaid. Average life expectancy in 1900 was about 45 years; by 1930 it had almost reached 60.

One reason for the sudden improvement was the decline in infant mortality. While death rates generally had been declining since the 1870s infant mortality had been intractably constant at about 3 infants out of every 20 live births dying in their first year. Indeed, in 1899 the figure for England and Wales had reached an unprecedentedly high 163 per 1,000. By 1910 it was down to 105, in 1920 to 80 and in 1930 to 60 (the present level hovers in the mid teens). Among causes of death diarrhoea and enteritis show a particularly sharp fall between 1900 and 1930 as do the main infectious diseases including measles, scarlet fever and whooping cough. This suggests that improved standards of hygiene and housing were having their effect, but it does not explain why infant mortality levels did not begin to decline until a generation after other death rates started to fall. Possibly better standards of education in mothercraft had an influence, though that subject did not have a high place on the curricula of most schools.

A final, important, feature of urban life in this period was the advent of compulsory elementary education. Contrary to popular belief this was not effected by the 1870 Elementary Education Act, designed to 'fill up the gaps' left by the voluntary system of education provided by nonconformist and Anglican churches, but by amending legislation passed in 1880. The emphasis was firmly on 'elementary' education. Children were to attend school compulsorily from the ages of 5 to 10. Not until 1918 was schooling mandatory until the age of 14.

The purpose of the elementary education provided divided the protagonists. A few saw it as the firm foundation to a life of enlightened pursuit of learning; far more were strictly utilitarian in their approach. Education for the lower orders, as conceived by virtually all the church schools and by many of the 'school boards' of locally elected worthies set up under the 1870 Act, was to equip young minds with information and skills appropriate to their station in life. Over-education was as dangerous and probably more unsettling than brute ignorance. Hence the regimented and unimaginative teaching methods concerned with the acquisition of factual information rather than broader understanding. Pupils were not encouraged to discover things for themselves. They were prepared for tests, on which the income of the school via a government grant partly depended, which similarly tested unimaginative rote learning of tables, rules of grammar or passages of scripture.

The numbers of new schools established between 1870 and 1900 is impressive. About 5,700 board schools were built and the Church schools, in a furious battle to compete with the secular newcomer, built an equivalent number to add to their pre-1870 stock of 9,000 or so. By the turn of the century about 4½ million children were being educated in elementary schools, many of them in the characteristically gaunt, functional and foursquare design favoured by schools architects. A marked penchant is detectable for high-set windows to discourage youngsters' idle peering when they should have been learning their seven times table or the precise details of David's struggle with Goliath.

Some school boards, especially in the big cities, showed an inclination by the 1890s to develop education beyond the confined limits of the elementary syllabus. The 'higher grade schools' which they promoted permitted children to stay on from 12 to 15 years. They offered some kind of threat to the existing grammar schools and in doing so threatened to upset the precise educational hierarchy. It had been assumed by those who promoted the 1870 Act that elementary education was the appropriate scheme of learning for the working classes; grammar schools trained the children of the lower middle classes while the public schools catered for the nation's future leaders in government and administration.

A Conservative government, worried alike by the pretensions of the 'advanced' school boards and by the manifest inability of the Church schools to stand the competition from them, passed an Education Act in 1902 which emphasized the hierarchical verities and also provided a quite unmerited lifeline for the Church schools, much to the anger of nonconformist Liberals. The School Boards were abolished and educational administration transferred to new local education authorities of the county and county borough councils. For the first time Church schools were to be maintained by ratepayers, whether they supported sectarian education or not. The local education authorities would provide compulsory elementary education. Additionally they might offer secondary education if they thought it desirable, but secondary education would not be free. Despite a Liberal amendment of 1907 which insisted that at least one-quarter of secondary-school places should be provided free of charge, the secondary system which developed decisively favoured the better off.

After 1902, education beyond the elementary level was a rare privilege accorded to the very able working-class child. Though authorities were administering over 1,300 secondary schools by 1930, their intake was overwhelmingly middle-class. The proportion of free places to them had also increased, to more than 40 per cent, giving a child about a 1 in 13 chance of winning one, but in the competition for free places middle-class children, not surprisingly, proved much more adept at winning the 'scholarships'. In 1927 – 30, for example, 11 per cent of elementary school children in Liverpool and Birkenhead went on to secondary schools, most having won free places to do so. In middle-class Wallasey nearby the proportion was 25 per cent.

Such a discrepancy can be explained in various ways, however. Middle-class families, then as now, prized education more highly than their working-class counterparts. Many of the 89 per cent of Liverpudlians not going on beyond the age of 14 would have been subject to fierce family opposition had they tried to do so. The concept of a working-class 'family' income remained a real one and a child staying on at school represented a delayed income and a continued burden. The children of those parents who had fought to outwit the school inspectors in the 1880s and 1890s on their tours to ensure compulsory attendance were themselves in the van of those parents who believed in the 1920s that the opportunity for a steady job at 14 was far more valuable than yet more irrelevant, if not disquieting, fact-grubbing. In many working-class areas, for a boy to have his head in a book was a clear sign of effeminacy.

City life was hard, generally bleak and often dangerous. Nevertheless between 1870 and 1930 urban man was in general benefiting from improvements to his lot. He was better housed and, whether he liked it or not, rather better educated in 1930 than in 1870. He also had access to a wider range of anyway more reliable medical facilities, though he still had to pay for them; his children were also more than twice as likely to survive their hazardous first year of life. A degree of levelling between the income and expectations of the working man and his professional counterpart was noticeable, though the gulf between them remained wide and cavernous where there was widespread unemployment. No one spoke any longer of the 'dangerous classes' which seemed to threaten Victorian towns. In spite of the remaining poverty and deprivation, few challenged the existing urban order by their very presence. By 1930 Britain was more or less fully inured to urban civilization.

## FURTHER READING


Abel-Smith, B., *A History of the Nursing Profession* (London, 1960)

Abel-Smith, B., *The Hospitals in England and Wales* (Harvard, 1964)

Briggs, A., *Victorian Cities* (London, 1963)

Coleman, B. I. (ed), *The Idea of the City in Nineteenth-Century Britain* (London, 1973)

Dyos H. J. and Wolff M., *The Victorian City* (2 vols., London, 1973)

Evans, E. J. (ed.), *Social Policy, 1830–1914* (London, 1978)

Fraser, D., *The Evolution of the British Welfare State* (London, 1973)

Gauldie, E., *Cruel Habitations: A History of Working Class Housing, 1780–1918* (London, 1974)

Gilbert, B. B., *The Evolution of National Insurance in Britain* (London, 1966)

Halsey, A. H., *Trends in British Society since 1900* (London, 1972)

Hurt, J. S., *Education in Evolution* (London, 1972)

Hurt, J. S., *Elementary Schooling and the Working Classes, 1860–1918* (London, 1979)

Lawson, J. and Silver, H., *A Social History of Education in England* (London, 1973)

Mowat, C. L., *Britain between the Wars, 1918–1940* (London, 1955)

Smith, F. B., *The People's Health, 1830–1910* (London, 1979)

Stedman Jones, G., *Outcast London* (London, 1976 ed.)

Stevenson, J., *Social Conditions in Britain between the Wars* (London, 1977)

Tarn, J., *Five-Per Cent Philanthropy* (London, 1974)

Thompson, P., *The Edwardians* (London, 1977)
Tobias J. J., *Crime and Industrial Society in the Nineteenth Century* (London, 1967)
Treble, J. H., *Urban Poverty in Britain, 1830–1914* (London, 1979)
Wohl, A. H., *The Eternal Slum* (London, 1977)

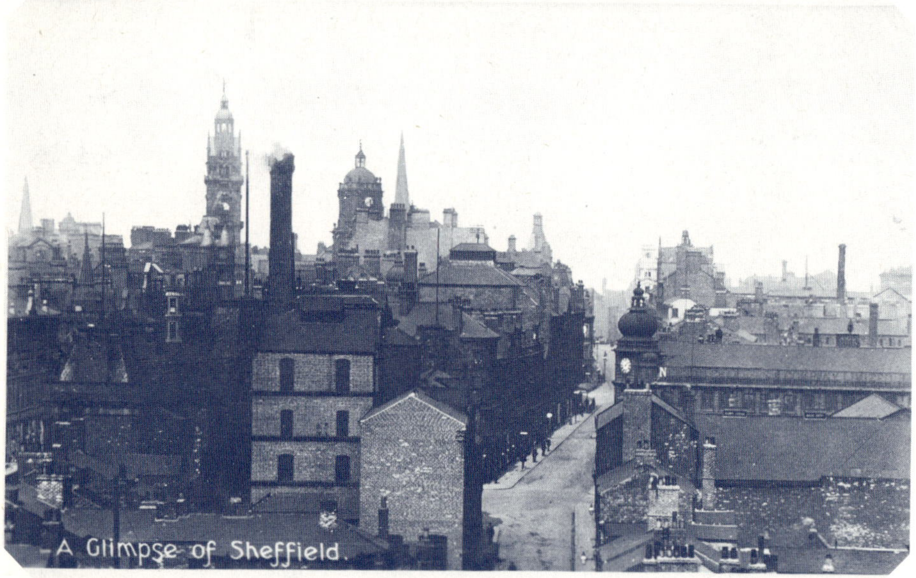


1. TOWN CENTRE

Sheffield immediately before the First World War. This card shows the cramped and largely unplanned development of Yorkshire's premier metal town. The photograph is taken from a street just off The Moor, looking north. The street in the centre is Union St and the clock in the foreground belongs to the Newton Chambers Company, colliery owners and coal exporters. The taller spire, centre left, is of St Paul's church, demolished in the 1930s; next to it is the tower and clock face of the Town Hall. The Athol hotel, Pinstone St, is just visible left-centre. The tall spire behind the town hall belongs to St Marie's Roman Catholic church, with the Cathedral spire just visible in the far left.

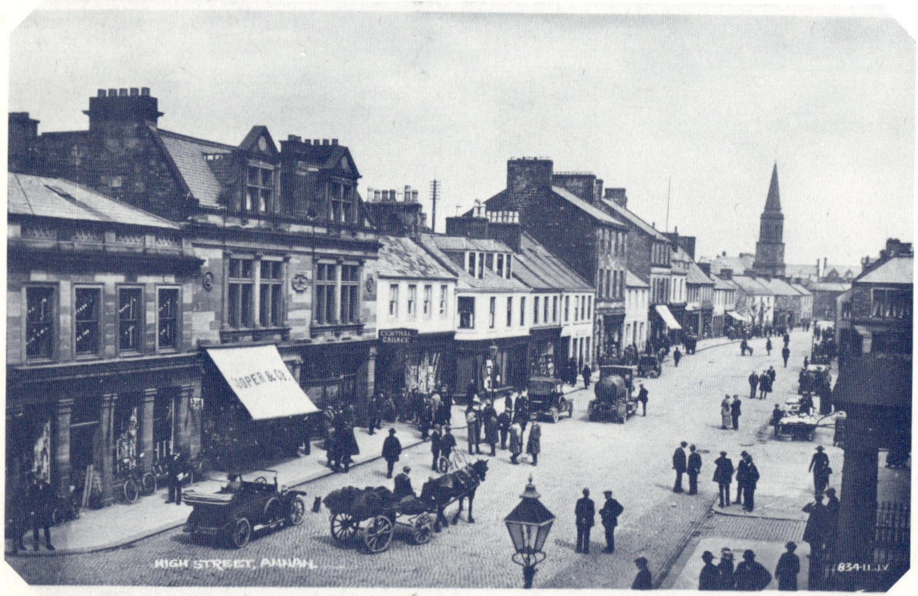


2. HIGH STREET

The main thoroughfare of Annan, Dumfriesshire, in the mid-1920s. Annan was a small Scottish market town with a population of 3,900 in 1921, when it also supported an engineering boiler works and a small shrimp fishing industry from the Solway estuary. Though some motor traffic passes along, pedestrians can still hold conversations in the middle of the road in perfect safety. Nor is the horse-drawn coal delivery cart inconvenienced as it makes its way down the still cobbled street. This card was sent from a homesick north Walian who found southern Scottish hospitality less than warm: 'Here's my address, dear Mother and please *avail* yourself of it just to cheer me up a little. The solitude is disquieting & the price of digs also (49*s*) [£2.45]. A real inharmonious [sic] Scotch Spinster the landlady'.

## 3. COMPANY TOWN

Barrow-in-Furness, like any new town in the nineteenth century, experienced great problems of housing in the early years. Its 'Barrow Island Huts' became a by-word for insanitary and verminous accommodation; many skilled workers even refused to move their families to them. In the 1880s the Furness Railway Company erected solid tenements on the Glasgow style to house shipbuilders and engineers, many of whom came south from Scotland. Here we see Ship Street, within 200 yards of the Vickers works – a part of these new 'Barrow Island Buildings'. Vickers themselves, at the end of the century, eased the housing shortage further by building the Vickerstown suburb. Tenements within the huge sandstone buildings of Barrow Island were rented at from 5*s* 3*d* to 7*s* 6*d* (26–37½p) a week for surprisingly spacious accommodation. Some tenements had three-bedroomed apartments. It was common practice for the Railway Company to lease an entire building to a particular ship's crew with separate accommodation for all from captain to deckhand. Gradations of hierarchy and status were not invariably demarked by geographical separation.

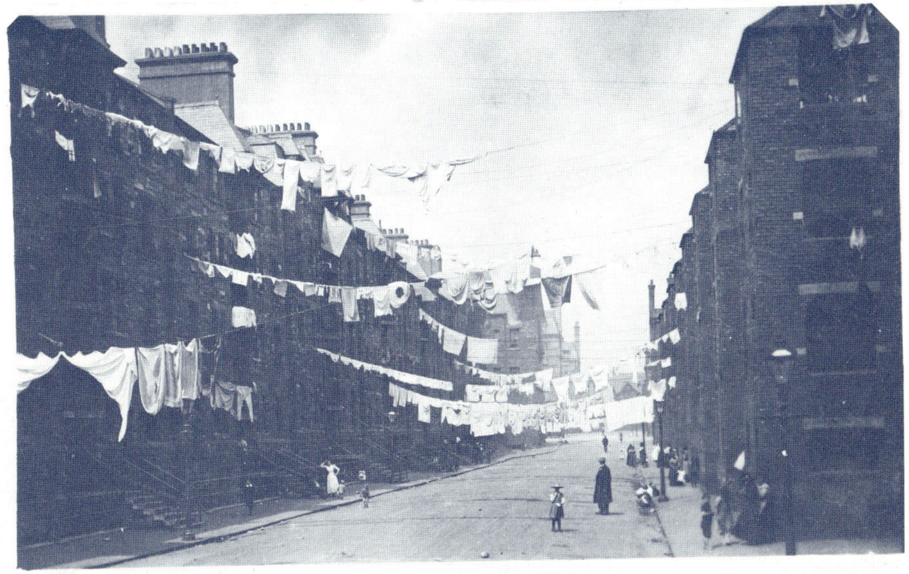

SHIP STREET, BARROW-IN-FURNESS.

## 4. WOOLLEN TOWN

Holmfirth, some 6 miles south of Huddersfield in west Yorkshire, was a fairly typical small woollen town with a population of 10,400 in 1921 – about the time this picture was taken. Water wheels, using the River Holme, still powered some of the mills. In 1925, fifteen woollen and worsted manufacturers and three yarn spinning firms were in operation here and there was also a foundry near the river and a chemical works. The shop on the extreme right is Kemp's hairdressers and next to it stands C. H. Smith, one of nine butchers in the town. Beyond the Church (Anglican despite the strikingly nonconformist design of its interior) stood a tailor and draper owned by a very old Holmfirth family of Quaker origin, the Battyes. Battyes drapers still survives and the ironmongery store then owned by H. B. Swallow still trades as such. The single-decker bus standing in Towngate belonged to the Barnsley & District Company; Towngate was the road leading out of the town towards Barnsley, 13 miles to the east.

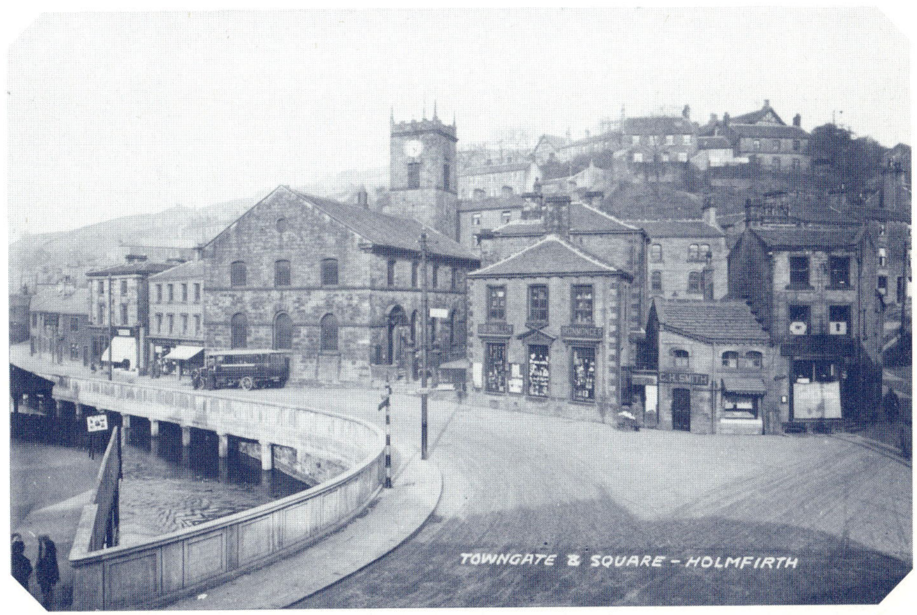


TOWNGATE & SQUARE – HOLMFIRTH

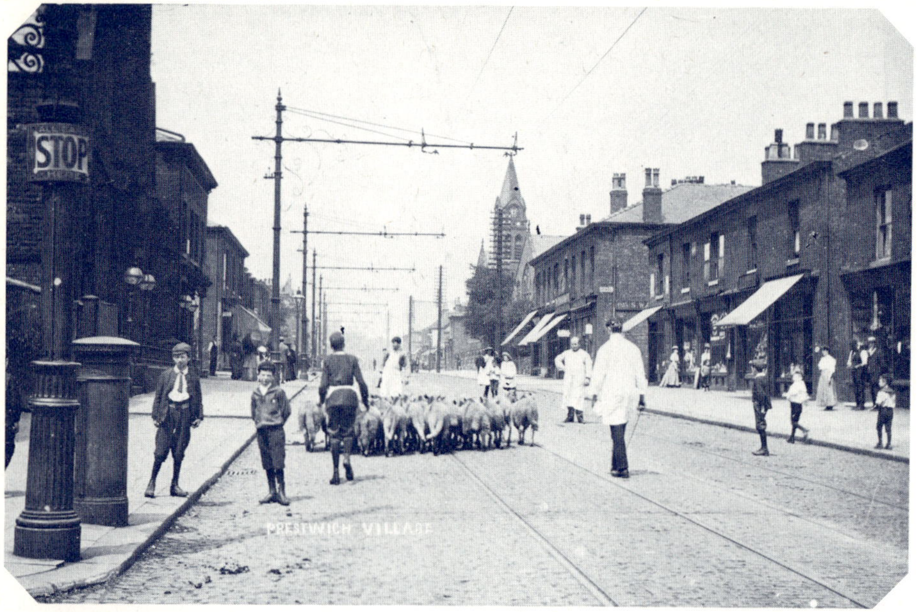


## 5. COTTON SUBURB

It was hardly justifiable to describe Prestwich, in south Lancashire, as a village in the Edwardian period, but this card does. It stands 3½ miles north-west of Manchester on the Bury road and, with its tram route and new shops, was being sucked inexorably into the greater Manchester conurbation. The scene here, however, qualifies as *rus in urbe*. Sheep are being driven along the road to slaughter before an interested audience of children. Careful scrutiny of such events was not always disinterested. Robert Roberts described what could happen in nearby Salford: 'It was not unheard of, when a large flock of sheep was passing our street end, for a drover and his dogs seemingly to mishandle them, so that a score or so would suddenly "hive off" down a certain entry. There a backyard door swung conveniently open. Two fewer sheep ran out to rejoin the mainstream. For the next few days lamb sold cheap about the streets.'

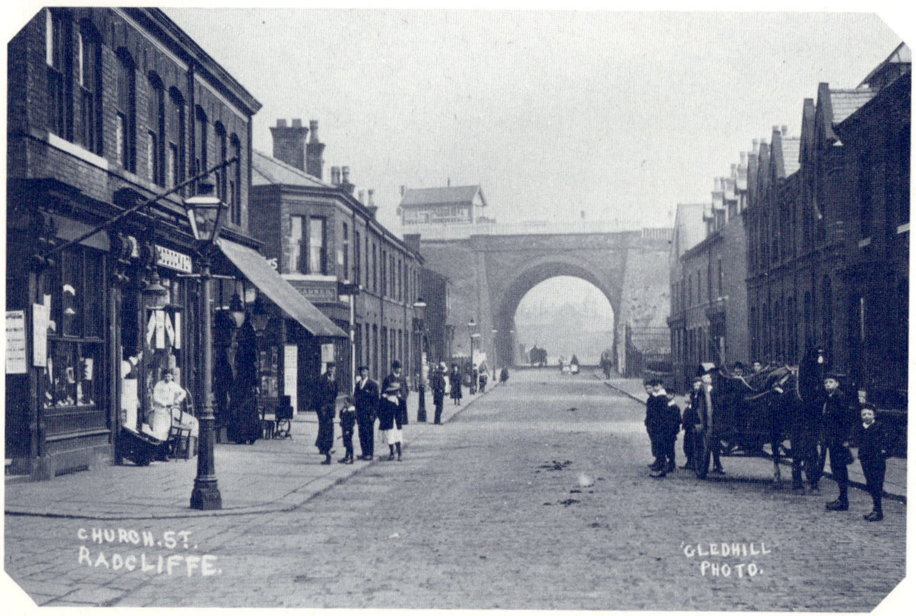


## 6. TWO VIEWS OF A COTTON TOWN (i)

Radcliffe, north of Manchester, had a population of some 13,000 when this photograph was taken in the first decade of the twentieth century. It is a splendid example of a cobbled street in a reasonably prosperous part of the town. Houses and shops intermingle and professional work was carried on from some of the houses. In the background is Radcliffe railway station, bestriding the road to Bury. The clutch of shops on the left includes a bookshop, owned by Henry Garner; bookshops were not found in the poorer areas. A grocer and his assistant stand outside the shop owned by George Braddock and the shop nearest camera was a hairdressing establishment owned by Thomas Williams. The notice outside his shop advertises entertainment at the Bury Hippodrome. The rate books for Radcliffe reveal the unusual fact that none of these shops changed hands in the decade 1904–14. Turnover among shopkeepers could be rapid, with stability more likely in the more prosperous areas.

7. TWO VIEWS OF A COTTON TOWN (ii)

An interesting contrast to the previous card. This one, sent in 1905, shows Radcliffe's main thoroughfare, Blackburn St, with working men in clogs leaning against a lamp post while two youths, one a delivery boy, pose for the camera. Radcliffe Bridge is in the middle distance; a tram is crossing it. The bridge spans the River Roche, one of two famous north-west industrial rivers which flow through Radcliffe, the other being the Irwell. The public house, the Bridge Inn (left foreground), is supplied by Seed's brewery, one of many small independent brewers which survived into this period. Note the male domination of this industrial scene. A single female, in authentic working-class shawl, can just be discerned crossing the bridge.

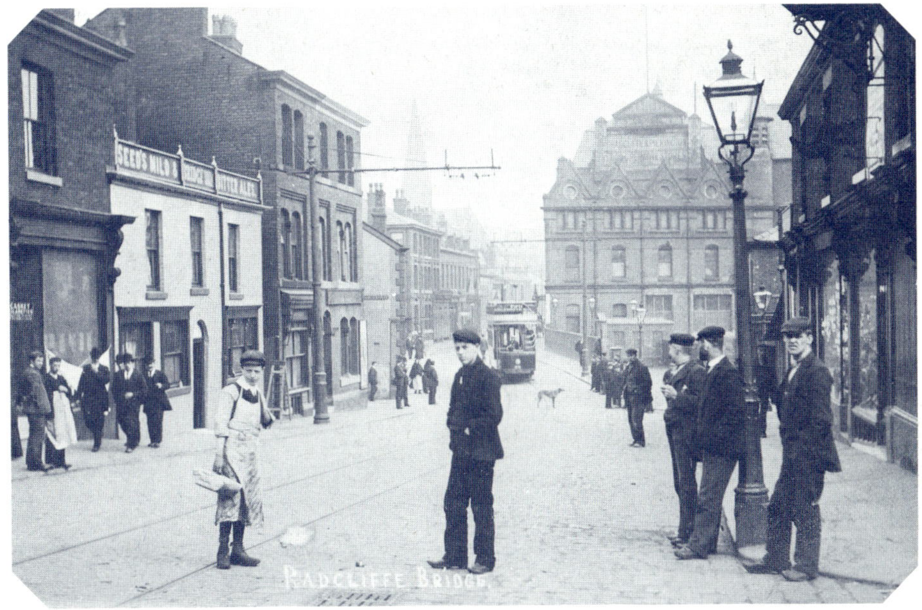


8. MIDDLE-CLASS SUBURB

This card shows nannies pushing prams along Clyde Road, Didsbury, one of Edwardian Manchester's most favoured suburbs. The recently built houses accommodated lawyers, doctors and managers. Nannies were an important part of middle-class family life. The custom in many upper-middle class families was for children to be seen by their parents only for an hour or so each day; for the rest they were given in charge to 'nanny'. Nannies bore a heavy responsibility and some discharged it with excessive strictness. Lord Curzon remembered many beatings. 'She established over us a system of terrorism so complete that not one of us ever mustered up the courage to walk upstairs and tell our mother and father.' The love and kindness of others quite eclipsed that shown by their parent. Sometimes this surrogate motherhood had damaging consequences in later life. Nannies were perforce socially isolated, so total were their responsibilities. In London's west end they would meet for walks and gossip in Hyde Park while they wheeled their charges; there was little opportunity for more exciting recreation.

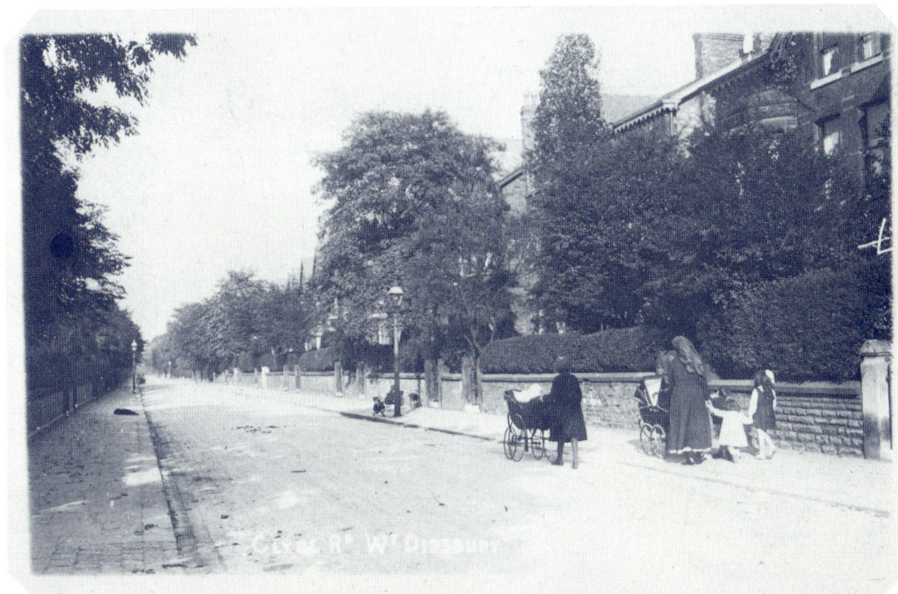

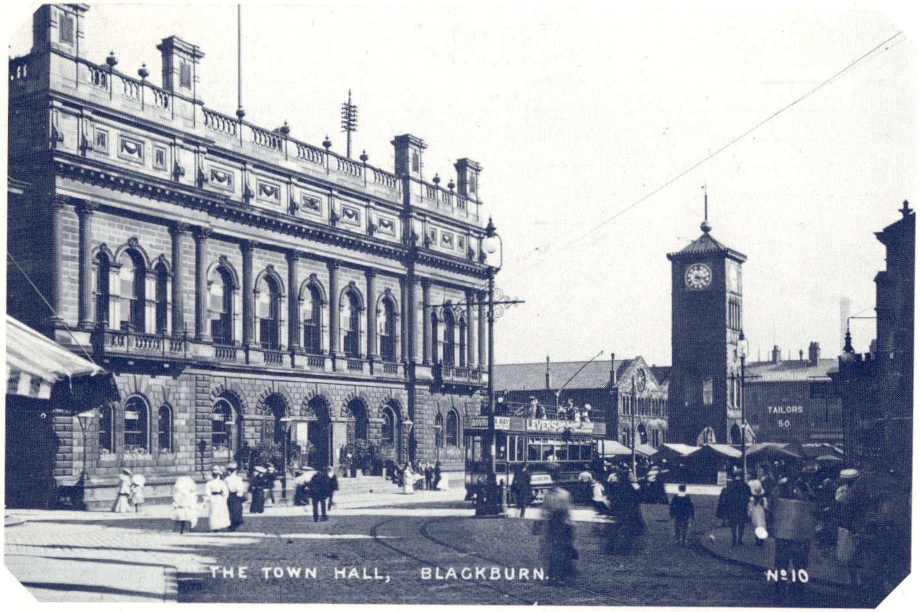


9. TOWN HALL

In general Victorian local authorities spent money with extreme frugality but town halls were an exception. They symbolized civic probity and a proper pride in urban achievement; hence there was to be no skimping. Architects were given almost a free hand to design appropriately weighty buildings; hence the profusion of adapted Greek designs, linking modern industrial and classical civilizations. Birmingham's Greek Temple of a town hall (1834) is well known, as are the enormous lion-guarded edifice opened in Bolton in 1873 and Rochdale's full-hearted celebration of the Gothic revival (1871). Blackburn town hall, shown here, is less grand than these but more typical. It was designed by James Paterson to include doric porches and corinthian columns and built between 1852 and 1856 at a cost of £30,000. The design included an assembly room 5,700 square feet in extent, able to house an orchestra. Across the Market Square stands an Italianate campanile and bell tower with orb and weather vane on top. This presided over Blackburn's central market area from 1853 until demolition and redevelopment in 1969. This card dates from 1910.

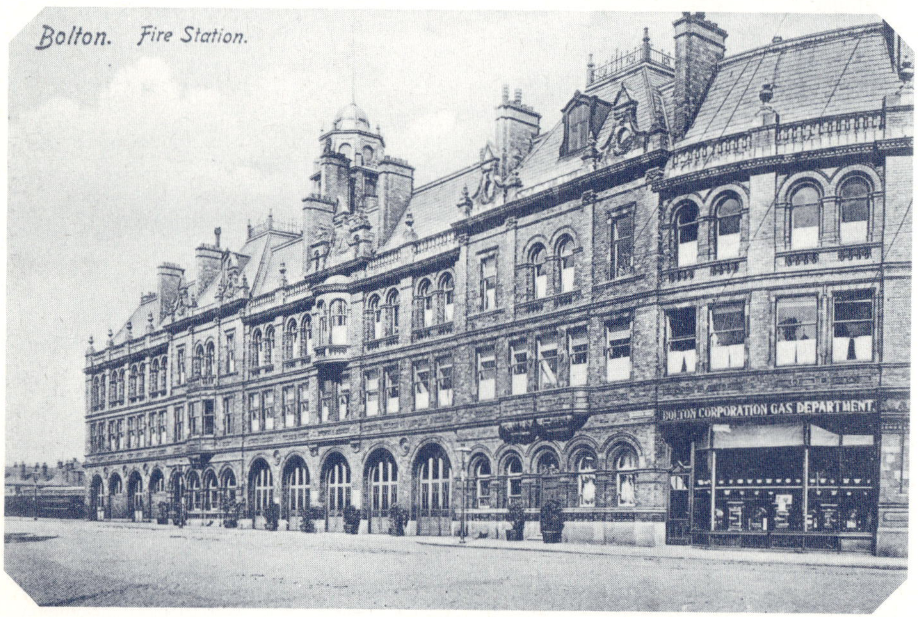


10. MUNICIPAL AMENITIES

Fire was an ever-present hazard of densely populated cities and all local authorities needed efficient brigades. This card was made soon after the Bolton fire brigade moved from Coronation Street to new and much larger premises in Marsden Road in 1899. For the first time living accommodation was provided for the permanent staff and their families. The Bolton force depended on horse-drawn fire engines or 'steamers' until a Leyland motor engine was delivered in 1913. These premises remained in use as the central fire station until 1971. On the right of the picture can be seen the premises of the corporation Gas Department. These were used as showrooms only from 1902; the main offices were in Hotel St. The town's gas had been supplied by the independent Gas, Light and Coke Company since 1820 but the corporation took it over in 1872 and ran it until the gas industry was nationalized in 1949.

11. COMMERCIAL BUILDING

If cotton was the king of the British industrial revolution then this building, Manchester's Royal Exchange, surely housed its court. The Exchange has changed much over the years. This, the third Exchange, was erected in the early 1870s and enlarged immediately after the first war to accommodate 12,000 members. Records of the day's prices and trading were prominently displayed above the clock in the huge central trading area which stretched to 4,405 square yards. Much of this imposing building was destroyed by bombing in 1940 and a fourth exchange was opened in the 1950s before conversion to a theatre symbolized the abdication of King Cotton.

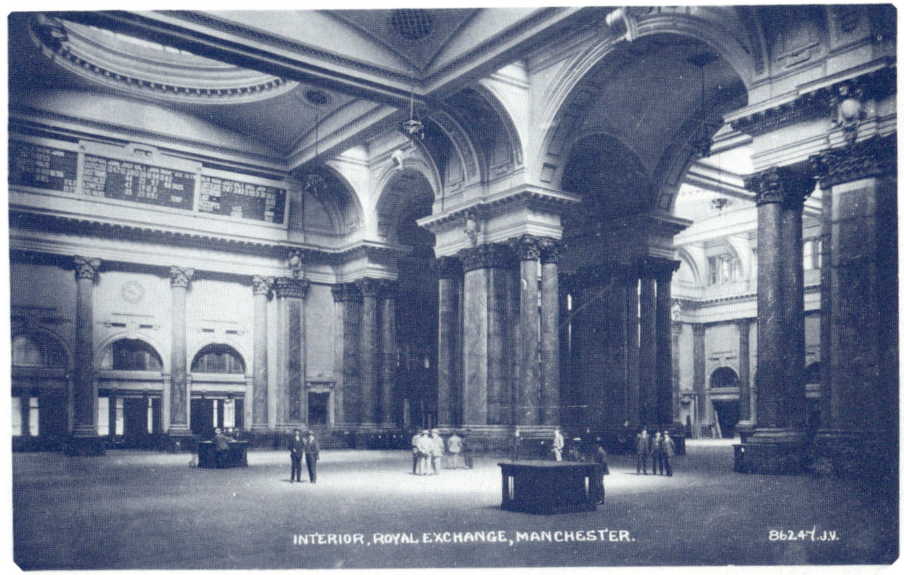


12. PUBLIC MONUMENTS (i)

The Queen Victoria Memorial, Derby Square, Liverpool. Though a decidedly unpopular monarch during her indulgently long years of seclusion from the public eye after the death of her beloved Albert in 1861, Queen Victoria was venerated as never before when she moved into old age between the golden (1887) and diamond (1897) jubilees of her accession. By the time of her death in 1901 she symbolized the glories of the British Empire during the years of its biggest expansion. Local authorities naturally sought to commemorate her passing by opening appeals for appropriate memorials. This monument was unveiled by Victoria's sixth child, Princess Louise, in September 1906. It stands on the site of the old Liverpool Castle. Public subscriptions raised £10,000 to which the city council added a further £6,000. The Queen is in full regalia and smaller sculptures above symbolize motherhood.

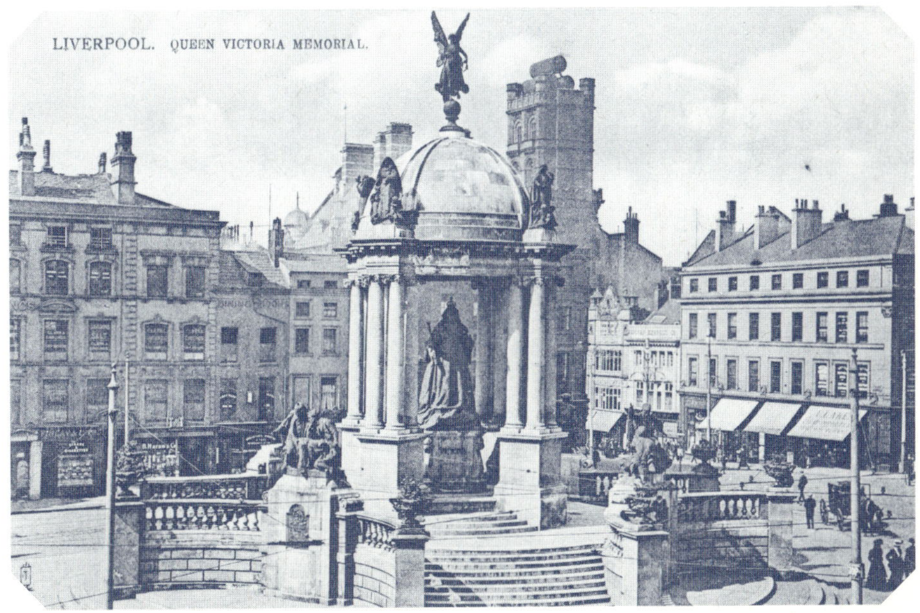

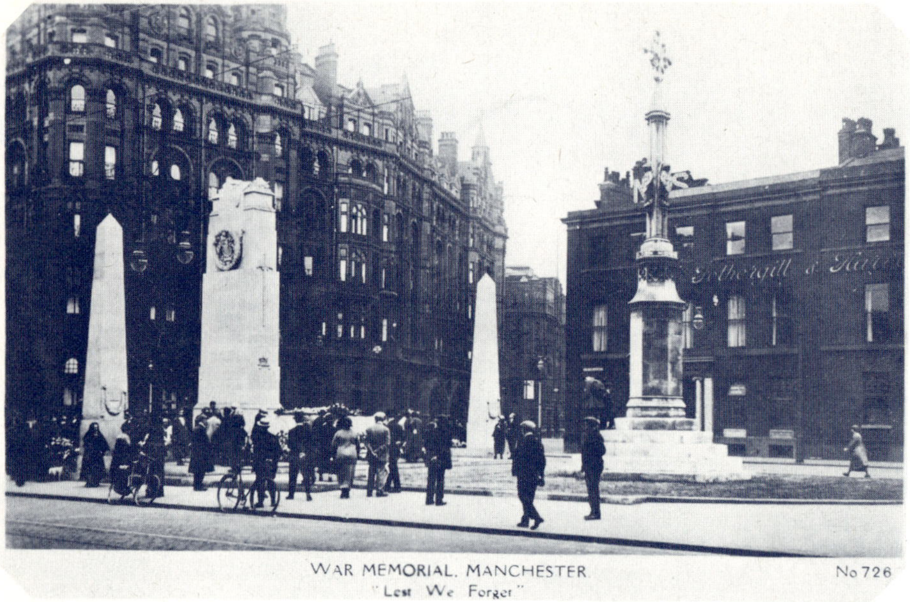


13. PUBLIC MONUMENTS (ii)
War memorials were erected in every town and city in the land to commemorate the fallen of the First World War. This card is somewhat misleading since Mancunians universally refer to it as their Cenotaph. Its pedigree is impeccable. Designed by no less an architect than Sir Edwin Lutyens, who had designed the Whitehall Cenotaph, this 36-ft monument in Portland stone was unveiled in July 1924 by Lord Derby, assisted by a Manchester mother who had lost three sons in the war. Like so many similar memorials it was financed by private subscription supplemented by local government aid. A correspondent to the *Manchester Evening News* described it as 'a hymn in stone to stir the heartstrings of every citizen whom the war robbed of a relative or friend.' The cross on the right-hand side of the picture is not part of the cenotaph but from a church which had stood in St Peter's Square until 1907. Within a few years the restaurant across the square had been demolished to make way for an imposing new central library.

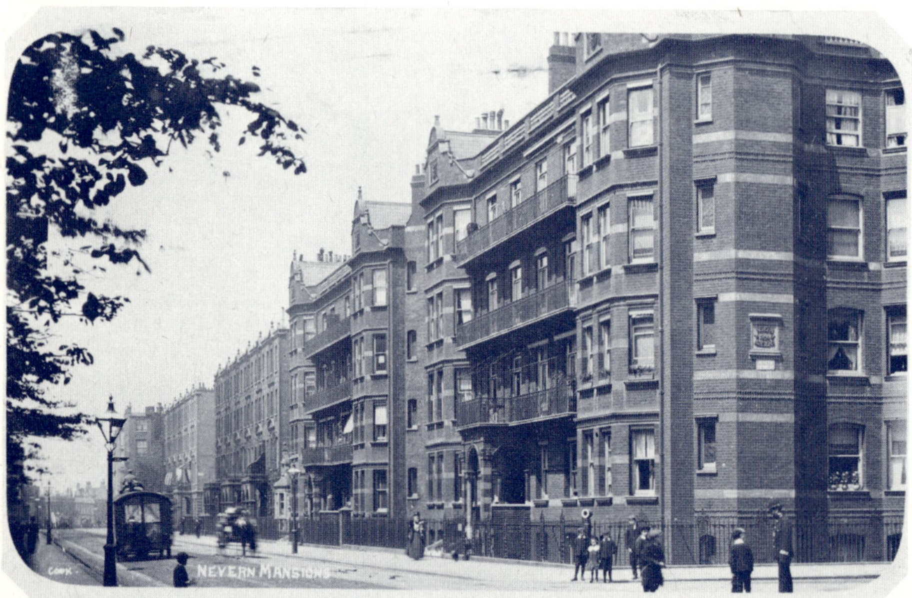


14. LUXURY APARTMENTS
The sleepy thoroughfare shown here, amazingly enough, is Warwick Road, Earls Court, which is now one of the curses of the commuter using the westward approaches to London. Nevern Mansions, constructed in 1890, was one of a large number of buildings in a then-exclusive area designed as town apartments for the well-to-do. In the 32 apartments occupied in 1902 could be found no fewer than three major-generals, two solicitors with offices in the centre of legal London, a prosperous merchant, a dried-fruit broker and a dentist. Mobility was high. By 1913 only four 1902 occupants were still in their original residence, though two more had moved within the building. Now only two mere majors and a naval commander could be boasted, but any military demotion was amply compensated by the arrival of Sir John McCall, Agent-General for Tasmania. This card was sent to a lady in Le Havre; the writer regrets that his 'Italian trip' has fallen through but refers to a successful regatta. Clearly, we have penetrated the upper crust.

15. PLANNED SUBURBS (i)
Various examples may be cited of housing schemes designed by entrepreneurs to improve living conditions for their employees. Lever's Port Sunlight and Cadbury's Bournville spring immediately to mind. None is more visually appealing than this Garden Village in Hull, the brainchild of the Quaker industrialist Sir James Reckitt. The project was begun in 1907 and Reckitt's objective, as *The Builder* reported in 1913, was 'to provide a house and a good garden – in fact a better house, if possible, and a garden attached – for the same rent as is now paid for inferior houses in terraces and interminable rows with no garden at all.' About 600 houses were eventually built on the 130-acre site all with hot-water systems and mostly in semi-detached pairs. Trees were planted along the roads to enhance the rural illusion. The social buildings, including this Village Hall opened in 1910, were provided out of Reckitt's own pocket. It acted as a social centre for religious organizations and the choral society. It was demolished after bomb damage but most of the village still survives, protected since 1971 as a conservation area.

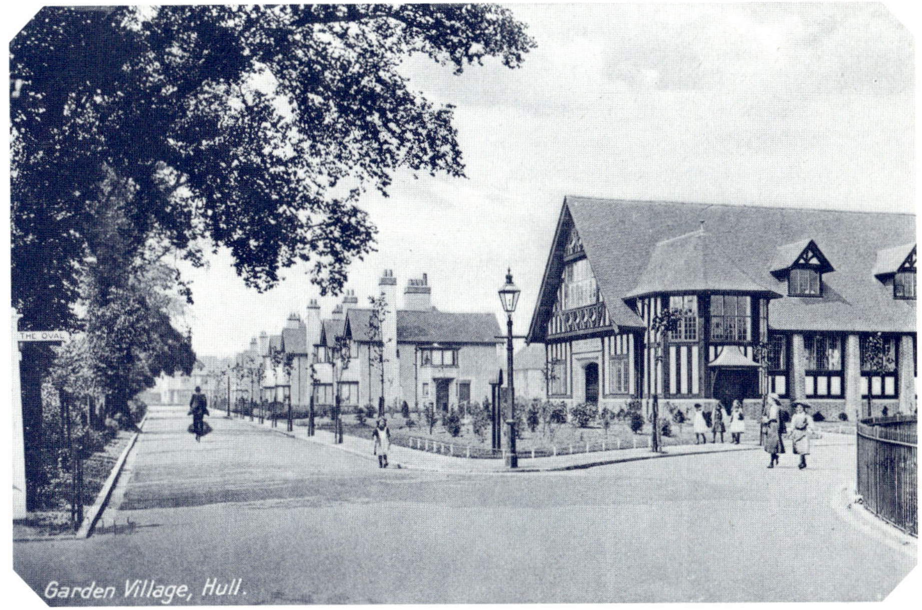


16. PLANNED SUBURBS (ii)
This co-operative project to provide working men with airy homes is now almost forgotten. The Moor Pool estate, two and a half miles south of Birmingham's city centre, was begun in 1907. It was managed by Harborne Tenants Ltd on the principle of co-partnership. Share capital was raised in lots of £10 with profits distributed among tenants in proportion to the rents paid released as further shares in the company until a member 'has invested an amount equal to the value of the house he occupies'. Rents varied between 4*s* and 15*s* (20–75p) a week and by 1912 500 houses had been built on 54 acres. When the scheme was initiated the Bishop of Birmingham, Charles Gore, declared the project's intention 'to make an Edgbaston for the less wealthy on that spot.' Low-density housing was the aim, with gardens and allotments available. A range of social amenities – bowling, lawn tennis, athletics and cycling – was established; even a newspaper, the *Moor Pool News*, appeared in 1910 informing tenants of housing progress and providing gardening hints, book reviews and local news.

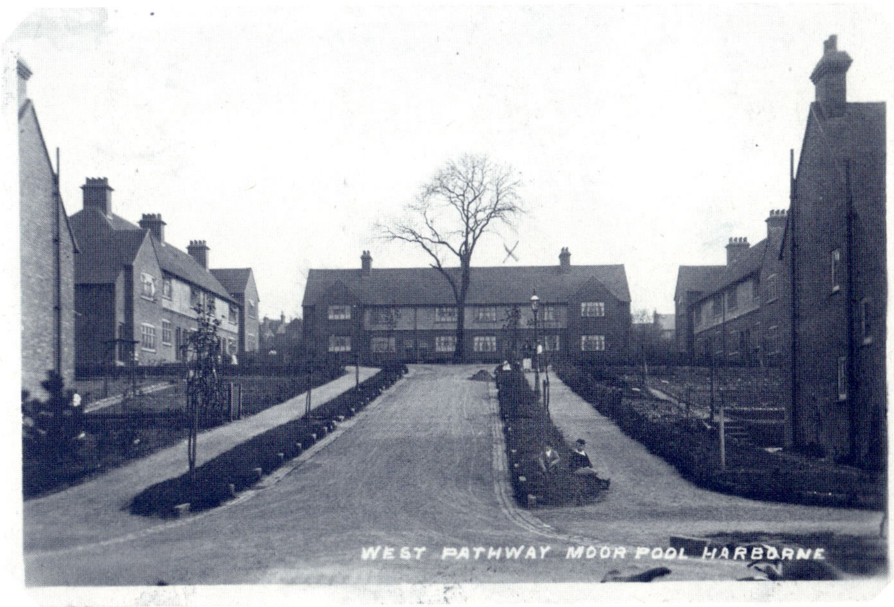

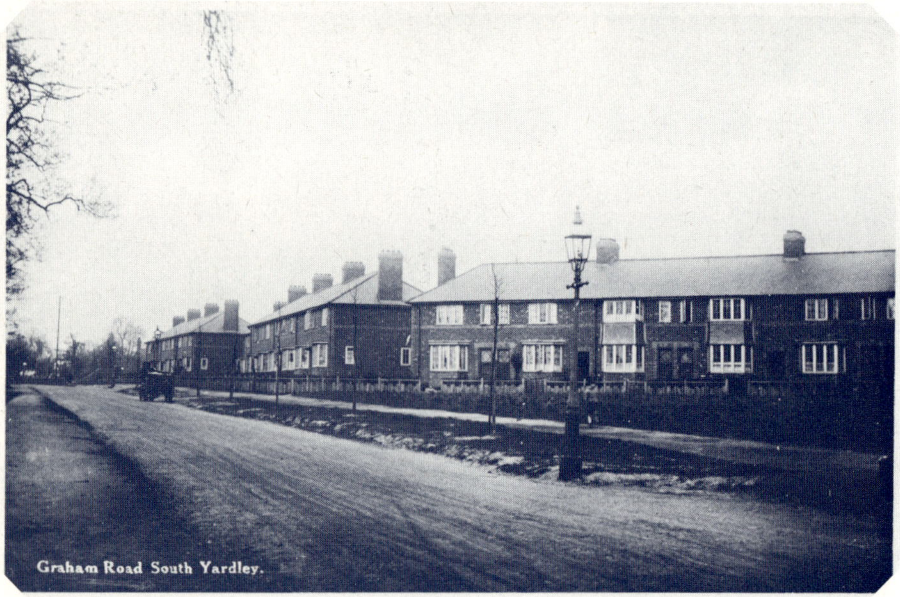


## 17. COUNCIL HOUSING

Only when local authorities built their own houses for rent by the poorer sections of society, which did not happen widely until 1918, did residual nineteenth-century problems of overcrowding, insanitary accommodation and consequential preventable disease begin to recede. Between 1919 and 1929 1.4 million new houses were built, of which 36 per cent were council houses. Birmingham contributed its full share to this total. Its 30,000th council house was ceremonially opened by the Labour Minister of Health, Arthur Greenwood, in July 1930. The houses shown here, just off Coventry Road, two and a half miles south-east of the city centre, provided three bedrooms and one or two living rooms and were built in 1925. In 1933 rents varied between 9*s* 9*d* and 16*s* 3*d* (48½p–81p) per week. The simple, functional design conceals generally high standards of workmanship and materials. Such houses have worn well over more than half a century.

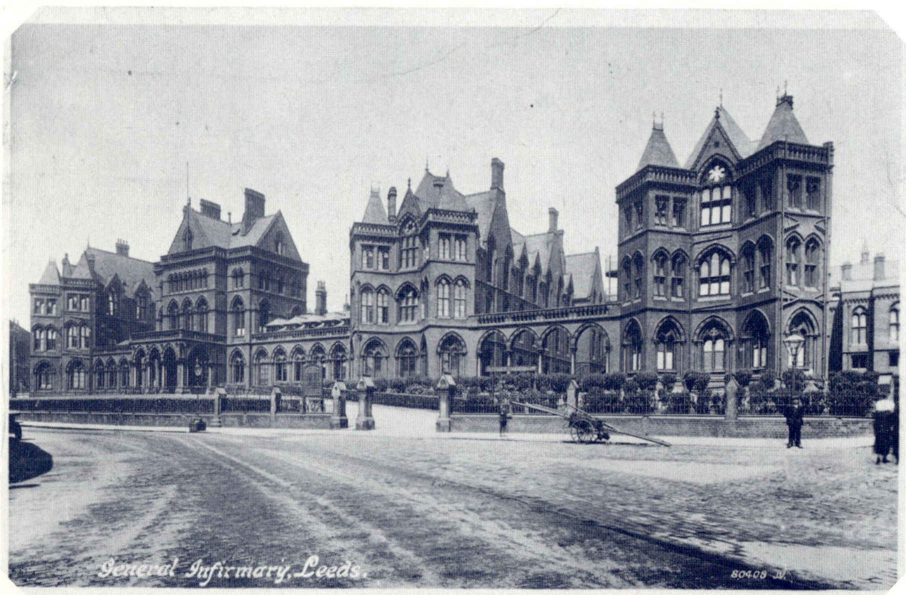


## 18. HOSPITAL EXTERIOR

Hospital building proceeded rapidly in the second half of the nineteenth century, spurred by the development of medicine as an organized profession and also by the now-acknowledged fact that death rates were higher in the new industrial towns than elsewhere. Poor law hospitals, voluntary general hospitals and hospitals for the treatment of particular diseases were all established, but there was, of course, no national health policy. Private subscriptions were still the most substantial source of income. The Leeds General Infirmary, pictured here, opened in 1869 and cost more than £120,000, which was raised privately and through established charities. It was extended in 1892 with the addition of an isolation block. By 1916, when this card was sent, further extensions provided accommodation for more than 500 patients. The design is characteristic and bears a striking resemblance to the Birmingham General Hospital in Steelhouse Lane, opened in 1897.

19. HOSPITAL INTERIOR (i)

This card is of the London Hospital on Whitechapel Road, the largest hospital in late Victorian Britain with 800 beds. It shows a pioneering treatment for tuberculosis of the skin. Partly because of the patronage of Edward VII's wife, Queen Alexandra, the hospital's President after 1904, the 'light machines' of a fellow Dane named Finsen, were installed. The patient received ultra-violet light in the treatment of one of the most disfiguring of the then common diseases. The new treatment brought marked success and in fact held the field until the introduction of the drug Calciferol in the 1940s. For some time before the First War the London Hospital was the only place where the treatment was on offer. Its chairman, Viscount Knutsford, reported, 'From all parts of England and from every corner of the globe miserable beings who had hidden themselves from the sight of their fellows hurried to "the London" in an endless stream. In a few days we had a waiting list for two whole years ahead.'

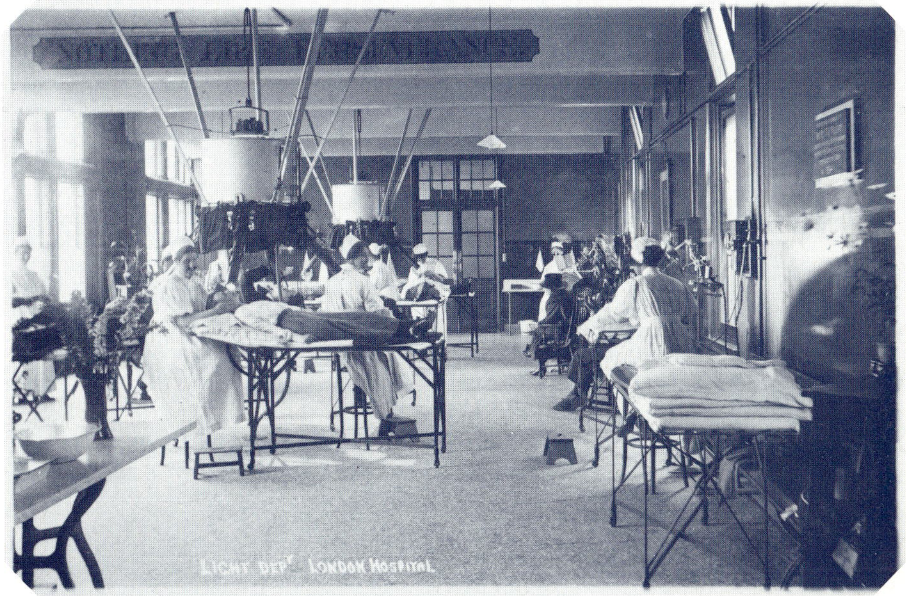

20. HOSPITAL INTERIOR (ii)

By the late nineteenth century care was at last being given to the hospital regime. This example unfortunately cannot be identified but, even allowing for the careful staging of the shot, standards of regularity, order, discipline and cleanliness may be discerned. Care has been taken over detail. The windows open for ventilation and have blinds. Flowers are permitted as are toys for the children in this mixed women's and children's ward. Such adornments may be overlooked but they represented an immense improvement on earlier hospitals serving as final, inadequate transit posts for the dying. Due in no small measure to the indefatigable efforts of Florence Nightingale, nursing reform was bringing basic medical and pastoral knowledge to what was emerging as a new profession. Her nursing school, opened at St Thomas's Hospital, London, in 1860, was influential in raising standards generally. Matrons were now trained nursing administrators; a system of probationer nurses was begun. Change came slowly, of course. In many poor law hospitals before 1914 'pauper nurses', with no more training and only slightly better health than the sick inmates they were supposed to tend, still provided what nursing there was.

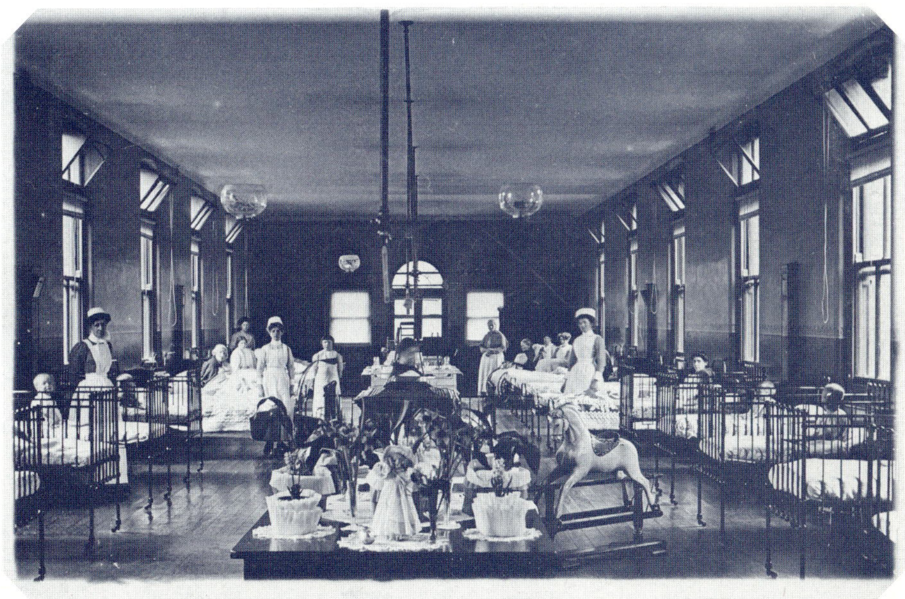

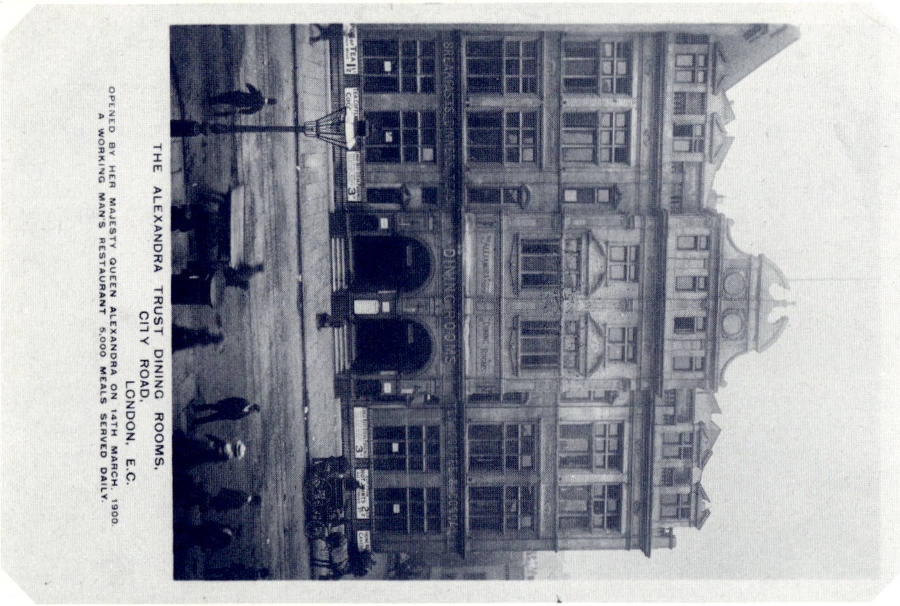


21. CHARITY DINNERS
Charitable benefaction was at least as important as the poor law in providing help for the destitute. The Victorians were great believers in the value of charity both to donor and recipient. The new generation of retailing plutocrats was no exception. Thomas Lipton, whose grocery stores had made him immensely wealthy, organized charity dinners for the London poor to celebrate Victoria's diamond jubilee. In 1898, he donated £100,000 to found a trust for the building of accommodation in the name of the then Princess of Wales to provide meals for the deserving poor. Lipton's knighthood followed the same year and this fine building, the Alexandra Trust Dining Rooms, was opened on City Road in 1900. Beefsteak puddings and 'hot joints' provided wholesome fare at very low prices. The building lay near the City of London Maternity Hospital and the Victoria Hall; it continued to function until just after the Second World War. The premises are now occupied by an Oriental carpeting concern.

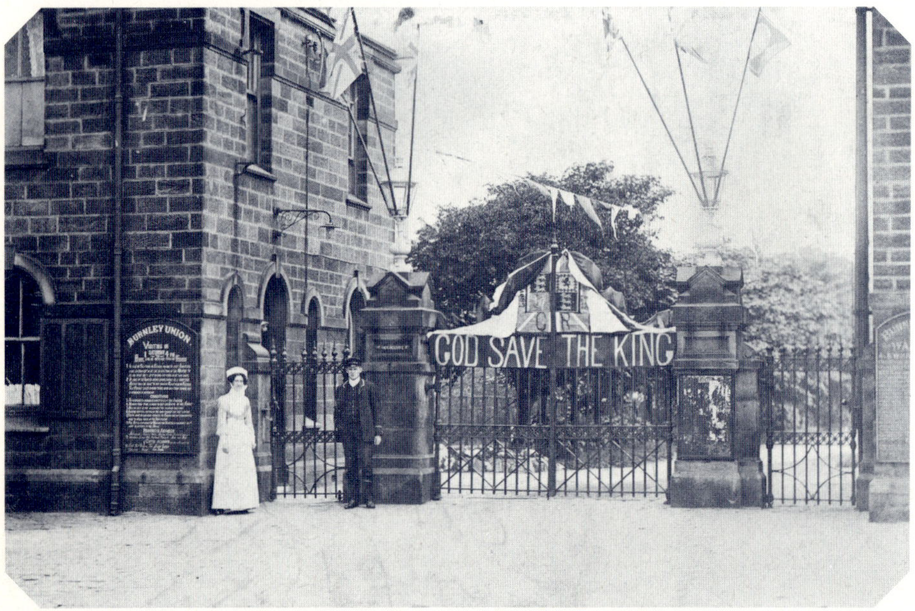


22. WORKHOUSE
Most workhouses for the orphaned and destitute were desperately unpleasant places. This was the intention; the Victorians wanted them inhabited by no shirkers seeking an easy existence at the ratepayers' expense. Here, however, we see a workhouse in rare festive mood, celebrating the coronation of George V in 1911. The local photographer must have worked with extraordinary speed. The coronation took place on 22 June; this card was posted five days later. The notice on the left of the picture contains strict conditions governing the weekly Saturday afternoon visits to this workhouse. It lists prohibited articles and gifts allowed. This Burnley Union workhouse in Briercliffe Road, Rake Head, was built in 1876 at a cost of £20,000. It could then accommodate 320 paupers but extensions between 1882 and 1895, including an infirmary, more than doubled this number. Most of the buildings still stand, incorporated now into the Burnley General Hospital.

## 23. LIBRARY AND INSTITUTE

Libraries, mechanics' institutes and technical schools held an honoured place in the late Victorian town. They provided facilities for self-education beyond the elementary level and represented, like town halls, a source of civic pride. Many were donated by leading businessmen and dignitaries whose names were perpetuated in the institute. The Gamble Institute, St Helens, the home of glass in the 1890s, resulted from a donation of £30,000 by Colonel David Gamble, son of the founder of the chemical manufacturing firm of Joseph Gamble & Son, and three times Mayor of the town. It was opened in 1896, resplendent in fashionable terra-cotta. A lending library was established on the ground floor together with a reference department and general reading room. Basement and higher floors were given over to manual and technical instruction ranging from cookery and laundry classes, through carpentry and hygiene to physiology and mathematics. The practical subjects were equipped with appropriate laboratories. David Gamble's later career was festooned with honours. He had been created baronet in 1894 and became Knight Commander of the Bath in 1904.

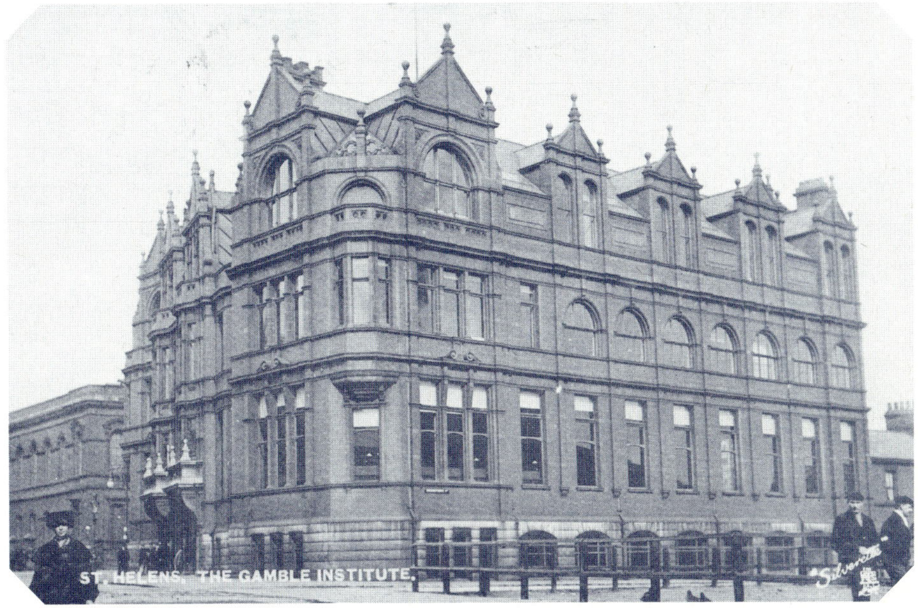

ST. HELENS. THE GAMBLE INSTITUTE.

## 24. LIBRARY AND BOARD SCHOOL

The library at Dalton-in-Furness was opened in 1905 by virtue of a gift from the Scottish-American steel magnate and educational philanthropist Andrew Carnegie. Salaries and other running costs were to be met by the ratepayers. The school outside which these uniformed boys are exuberantly posing is Nelson St, built in 1887 for boys only. It was administered by the Dalton School Board until 1902 and by the Lancashire County Council thereafter.

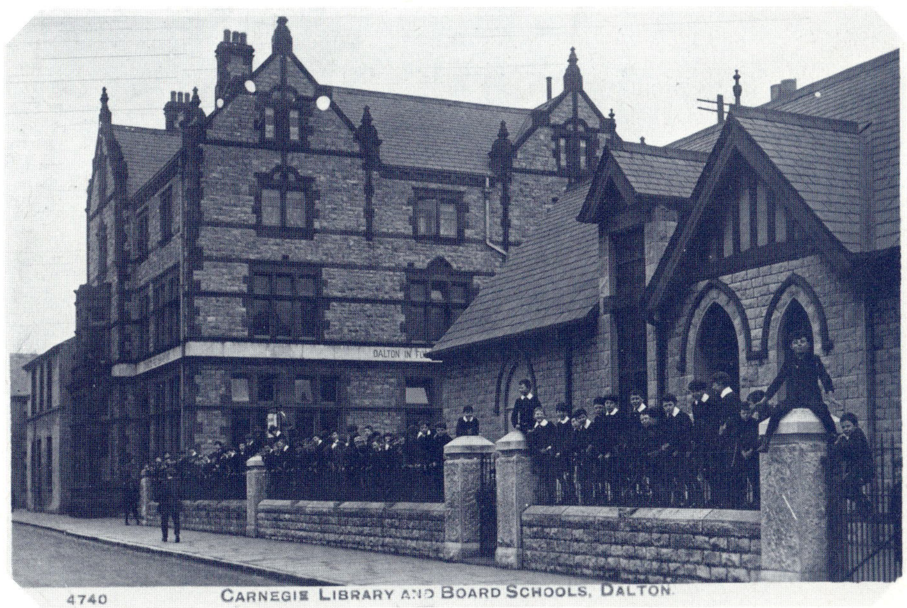

4740 CARNEGIE LIBRARY AND BOARD SCHOOLS, DALTON.

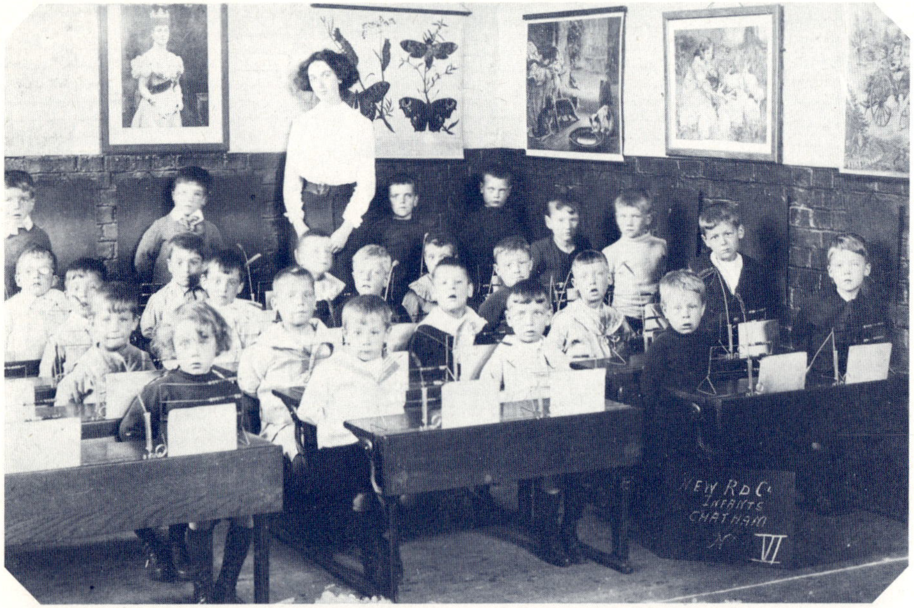


25. ELEMENTARY SCHOOL

This school, New Road Council School in the naval town of Chatham, is a good example of the bleak, functional buildings erected by school boards in the thirty years after the passing of the 1870 Elementary Education Act. It was built in 1890 to house 530 pupils and was in 1907 one of eight elementary schools in the town providing education for 4,000 children. All but two of these had been built since 1870. Four schools were denominational, one Roman Catholic and three 'National' (i.e. Church of England) at a time when such distinctions could be extremely important. Note here the stark brick walls in contrasting white and green. The photograph is of Queen Alexandra. The pupils, some of the boys appropriately sailor-suited, stare at the camera which many of them have evidently never seen before. In front of them are simple abacuses to help with their arithmetic. The teacher may well have been Miss F. A. Rees who was in charge of the infant school in 1907. Much elementary school learning was drearily factual in kind and repetitive in method.

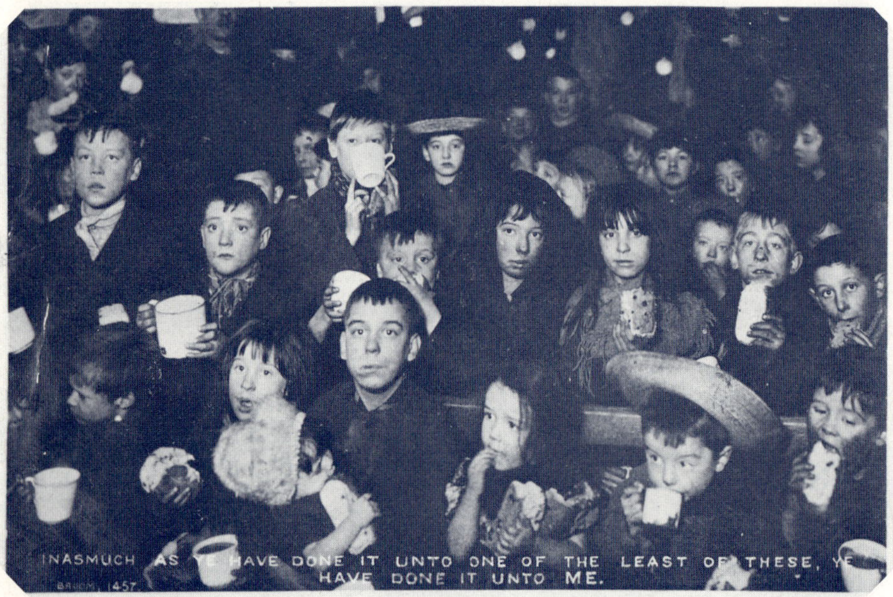


26. POOR CHILDREN'S TREAT

It is not possible to place this card precisely beyond saying that it was posted from London in February 1905. It shows a treat of buns and cocoa being given to poor children, probably from London's east end. They seem also to be watching some kind of entertainment which has been provided. The grubby faces are marvellously alive. As the writer of the card said in his only message: 'Hows [sic] this for a study in expression?' One wonders how much the cares of child-minding weigh on the boy third from the left on the front row as he nurses a younger sister. Childhood was soon over in working-class London.

27. OUTING

An altogether different class of treat from that in No 26. This shows some kind of school or Sunday school holiday. The children's clothes are respectable and many of the children are sitting demurely on the bank; the others are paddling or catching tiddlers in the Trent. Judging by the numbers of passers-by on Trent Bridge this shot was probably taken on a Sunday. The clothes would seem to support this conclusion. The card was sent from Nottingham to Girvan and the man writing it assures his female correspondent: 'You would like this almost as much as Girvan'.

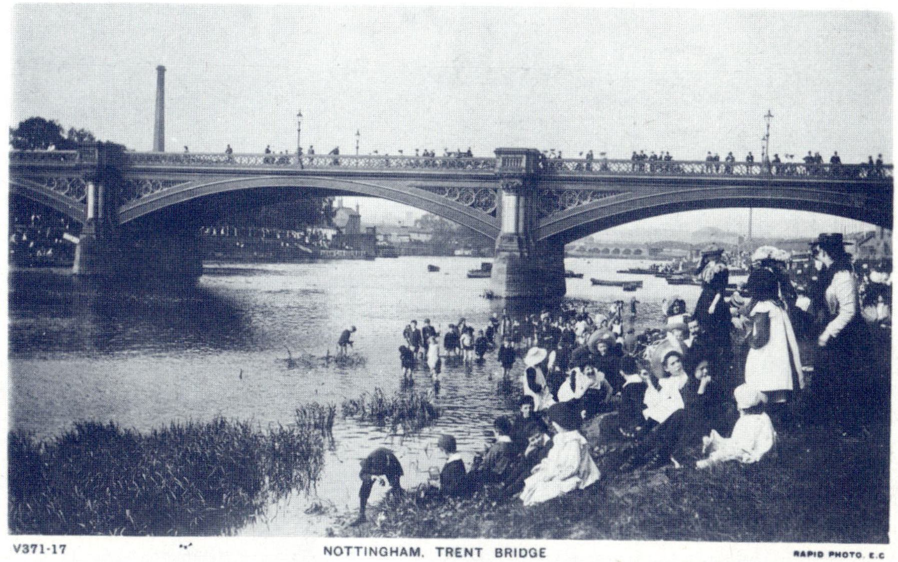


28. LOCAL FIRE

One of the attractions of Edwardian postcards is their immediacy. Here a local photographer has gone to the scene of a minor disaster and snapped it for its curiosity value. The little knot of inquisitive children in diverse dress is characteristic. Note, too, the firefighting equipment drawn by cart. This fire gutted the butcher's premises of Herbert Hickson of 74 Westbourne Grove, Hessle. The small Hessle brigade got the fire under control before the larger Hull force could arrive but, as the local newspaper reported, not in time to save the building.

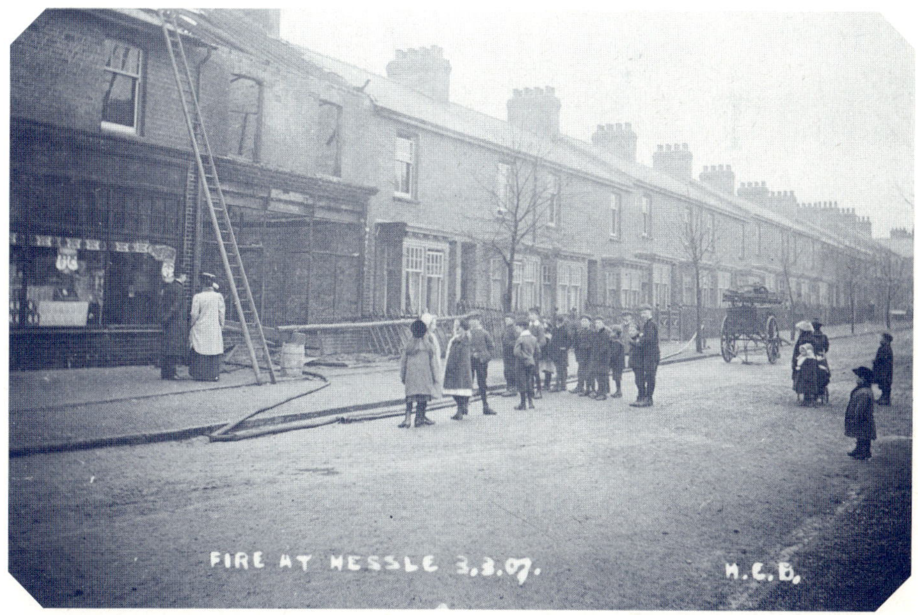

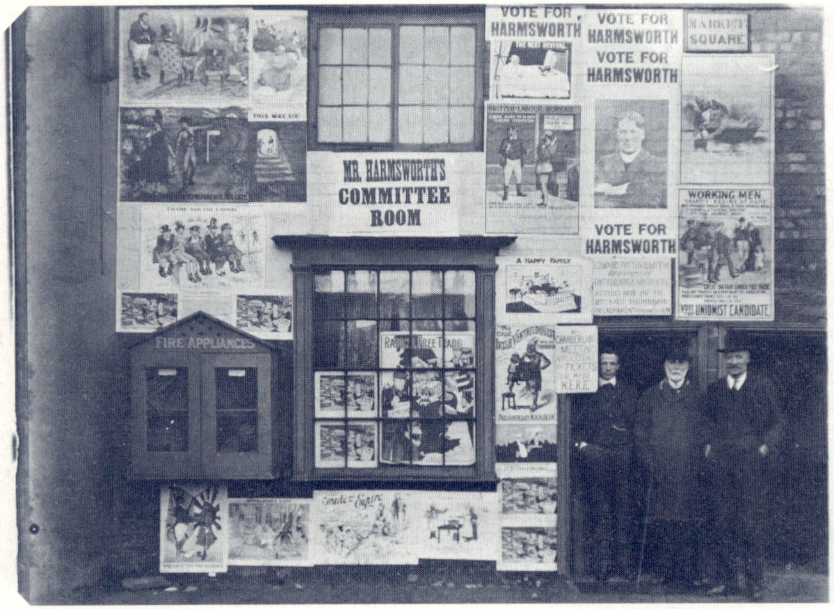


29. POLITICS

Political postcards are rare but this one gives the authentic flavour of battle in the 1906 election. The candidate in question was Hildebrand Harmsworth, fifth of the Harmsworth sons and younger brother of the press barons Northcliffe and Rothermere. Having lost Gravesend in 1900 as a Liberal Unionist, he campaigned vigorously for Joseph Chamberlain's policy of imperial preference against the concept of free trade which had been economic orthodoxy for almost a century. Free trade was the great issue in the 1906 election as the posters here show. They depict working men deprived of jobs by free trade and in need of a radical new direction, based on close trading links with the British Empire. Chamberlain spoke for Harmsworth in Wellington during his fight to gain mid-Shropshire for the Liberal Unionist protectionists in 1906, but to no avail. Harmsworth was defeated by 4,806 votes to 3,114 during the national pro-Liberal landslide. Harmsworth retreated from the hustings into the safer Northcliffe haven of journalism. Largely financed by his brother, he became sole proprietor of the *Globe* which continued to campaign for imperial preference in the two elections of 1910.

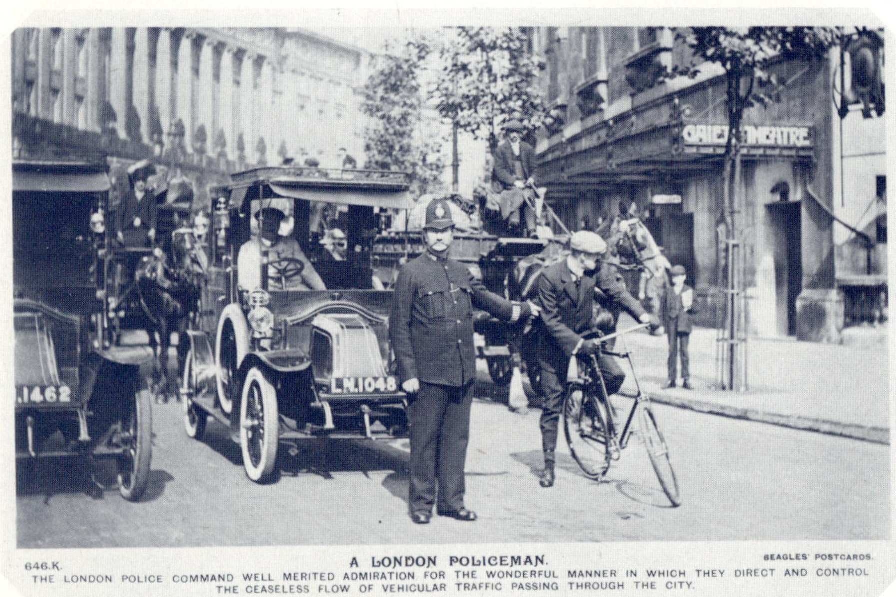


30. LAW AND ORDER (i)

A card offering the benevolent face of authority in the reassuring presence of the London bobby directing traffic as early as 1912–13. London's Strand at this time was a bewildering mixture of new-fangled motors, bicycles, horse-drawn carriages and horse-drawn delivery carts. Motor cars were in theory restricted to 20 mph but the law was often broken. Not pictured here but already an important part of London's traffic scene were the motor buses. The open-topped, petrol-driven London double-decker was introduced in 1910 and rapidly chased horse-buses from the highway; more than 1,000 were in service by 1914. The Gaiety theatre on the right was one of London's premier theatres for musical comedy at this time but underwent a sad decline. It closed as a theatre in 1939 and was demolished in 1957. It was replaced by the office of the English Electric Company.

31. LAW AND ORDER (ii)

A real curiosity card of convicts on the Isle of Wight taken by a local photographer, J. S. Coombe. It may be that he has deliberately darkened the faces of the convicts. Crime was an increasing worry in Edwardian England, perhaps a reflection of the squeeze on living standards brought about largely by rising prices after a long period of improvement. Not all working men, especially those on strike in the period of labour unrest between 1910 and 1913, would accept the avuncular image of the police suggested by the previous card. Between 1900 and 1910 the prison population of England and Wales increased by about 42 per cent from 14,739 to 20,904. This latter figure was not to be exceeded until the 1950s.

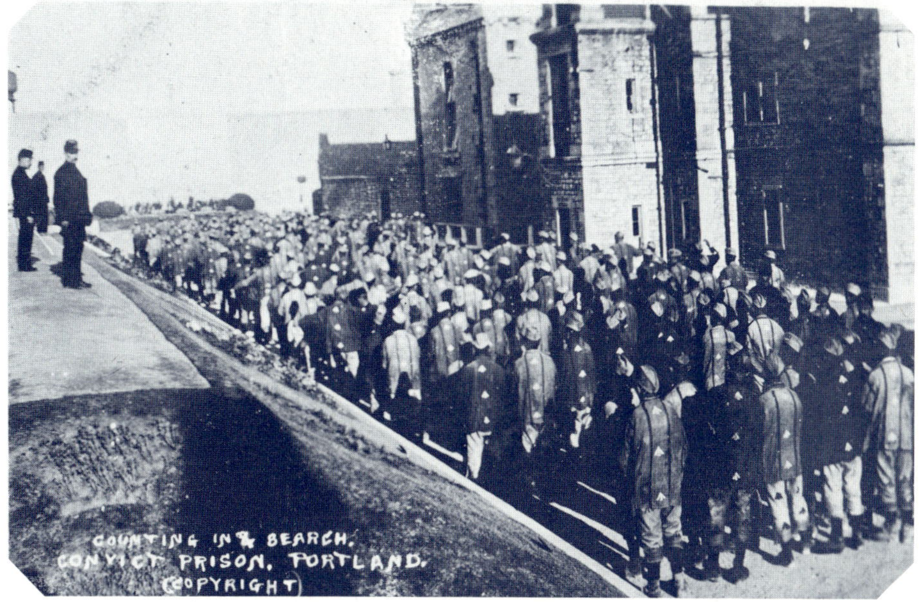

# CHAPTER TWO | WORK

Britain did not become fully industrialized until the second half of the nineteenth century. Although the industrial revolution is usually dated from the 1780s early development was most unbalanced, depending to a disproportionate extent on textiles. Large factories before the 1850s were effectively confined to Lancashire, parts of Yorkshire's West Riding and central Scotland. The coming of the railways in the 1830s and 1840s greatly stimulated the iron industry and coal production to fuel the trains. Revolutionary changes in iron and, particularly, steel technology in the 1850s accelerated the process and thereafter massive expansion in coal, metal working and shipbuilding was experienced. Only now did the heavy industries come into their own and Britain achieve industrial maturity.

One obvious characteristic of a mature industrial society is the contraction of the agricultural labour force. This did not happen until the later nineteenth century either. The highest recorded census figure for rural workers is 2,017,000 in 1851, representing 21.5 per cent of the entire labour force and 27.3 per cent of male workers. By 1871 the total had dropped to 1,769,000 and the proportions to 14.9 per cent and 19.9 per cent respectively. By the end of our period, in 1931, the land could claim only 1,353,000 workers (95 per cent of them men) or 6.4 per cent of the total workforce. The decline was inexorable. Rural workers were attracted by the higher wages which could be earned in factories and the beginnings of a national rail network in the 1840s made long-distance migration in search of profitable work feasible. During the last quarter of the nineteenth century as depression hit the corn-growing south and east of England the pace of departure from the land quickened.

In this period units of industrial production grew much larger. Even in the cotton textile factories of Lancashire, which had been the birthplace of the industrial revolution, about two-thirds of all workers were in mills employing fewer than 200 hands in the 1840s. Elsewhere small workshop and even domestic production remained the norm. Most master cutlers in Sheffield, one of Britain's leading workshop centres, employed fewer than a dozen men each, including apprentices. The early stages of the industrial revolution were typified by a huge expansion in the number of relatively small firms rather than by Blake's 'dark, satanic mills'. Thus, while Birmingham's population rose from 71,000 to 344,000 between 1801 and 1871 and Sheffield's from 36,000 to 80,000, neither became an industrial city in the modern sense.

Britain's workforce in the late nineteenth century was geared to export production. Amazingly, Britain in 1870 produced more than half the world's iron and almost half its steel; although these proportions were cut back in the years before the First World War as other nations, most notably the United States and Germany, industrialized, the country's trading success remained enormously impressive. Almost 85 per cent of British cotton textiles were exported, 57 per cent of her woollens, almost 40 per cent of her heavy engineering products including ships and almost one-third of her coal. These basic industries employed almost a quarter of Britain's occupied population of 18 millions in 1911.

This was the age of coal and steam. Engineering, railways and shipbuilding required far more power than the early textile mills and Britain was fuelled by coal. To the established mines in Northumberland and Durham and central Scotland were added new and increasingly profitable pits in the east Midlands, in south Yorkshire, in Kent and, most impressive of all, in south Wales. In the fifty years before 1914 the labour force in coal mines quadrupled to over a million. Relative stability in the later 1870s was followed by massive expansion in the 1880s and 1890s. Expansion was not accompanied by rationalization, however, and coal workings remained in a large number of very diverse hands. In 1913 no fewer than 1,589 separate undertakings owned the 3,289 collieries; often the owner was a single landowner. The 'average' miner worked in a pit employing 340 people. In the north-east and in south Wales particularly mining was closely integrated with primary industrial production, either metals or ships.

Shipbuilding was a massive growth industry. It is not generally realized that as late as 1870 seven times as many sailing ships were on register as steam ships. Heavy engineering technology revolutionized the industry in the next generation; 12,602 steamships were registered by 1913, four times the number available in 1870 and, in terms of tonnage, thirteen times greater than sail. British shipyards consumed a third of her entire steel production and a vast diversity of employment opportunities developed both for skilled men and labourers as the great amalgamated companies grew to the full height of their powers in the race to convey exports and imports: Palmers and Swan Hunter on Tyne and Wear; Cammel Laird on the Mersey; Harland and Wolff on the mouth of the Lagan at Belfast. In 1914 more than 200,000 men were shipbuilders.

Specialized engineering towns grew to cater for the railway network. The operating companies generally preferred reliance on their own specialist works to build and service their steam trains. Railway communities grew both in previously rural areas, like Ashford, Crewe, Swindon and Wolverton, situated on the main lines and in existing urban centres like Derby and Doncaster.

Iron and steel technology produced new communities too. The iron ore resources of places like Coalbrookdale on the banks of the Severn in Shropshire, which some consider the original site of the industrial revolution, were worked out and superseded by new towns like Middlesbrough. Middlesbrough had a mere 8,000 inhabitants in 1851 but pig iron production and the railway network stimulated its growth to 55,000 in 1881 and to 120,000 in 1914 at which point it was the 25th largest town in England and ahead of such more established places as Coventry, Preston or Stockport. Its success completed a north-eastern conurbation of second-generation industrial progress stretching more than 30 miles from Tees to Tyne and based on heavy engineering in iron and steel, ships and coal. The combined populations of Gateshead, Middlesbrough, Newcastle, South Shields and Tynemouth in 1911 exceeded 820,000, greater than both Liverpool and Manchester. The population of County Durham, further, was exceeded by only two other and much larger counties, Lancashire and Yorkshire. Meanwhile a similar concentration on the west coast of local iron workings, shipbuilding and railway access brought skilled men crowding from Scotland, Merseyside and the north-east to the Vickers yards at Barrow-in-Furness which grew from a mere hamlet of 500 people in 1851 to 19,000 in 1871 and to 64,000 in 1911.

The heavy engineering revolution not only created new towns but expanded and developed established metalwork centres of south Yorkshire and the west Midlands. About 460,000 engineering workers were employed in 1911 and an ever larger proportion were finding their way into large steam-driven factories, like Tangyes or Guest Keen and

Nettlefolds in Birmingham, manufacturing a wide range of machinery from humble screws to complex engines. Workshop production of certain specialized products survived and flourished, whether in fine cutlery around Sheffield or in the manufactures of Birmingham's 'gun quarter' around Snow Hill and Hockley or in chain making in that complex of industrial villages lying north and west of the city and known as the Black Country. The number of chainmakers in Staffordshire and Warwickshire, all in small workshops, more than doubled between 1861 and 1911 to accommodate increasing demand from steamships and elsewhere. In the east Midlands boot and shoe manufacture, traditionally a craft occupation for small workshops, was being steadily mechanized from the 1890s to meet the threat from American competition. Amalgamations took place in shoe machinery manufacture and Leicester and Northampton employed over 75,000 hands in the industry at the turn of the century.

The great new departure for the future, of course, was vehicle manufacture. The invention of the pneumatic tyre facilitated the development of bicycles and bicycle manufacture enabled Coventry to revive after its ribbon trade had declined in the middle years of the nineteenth century. Birmingham, Coventry and Nottingham became the country's leading centres for cycle production and this undoubtedly gave the midlands a head start in the race to build motor vehicles in the early years of the new century. The decade before the First World War saw a great expansion in opportunity for engineers and skilled craftsmen provided by the internal combustion engine. Though both Herbert Austin and William Morris groped towards it, mass car production had not arrived by 1914. No fewer than 393 motor car firms were then in operation with more than 120,000 vehicles registered. More than 100,000 workers were employed in the car and ancillary industries, mostly in the midlands from Wolverhampton in the north to Oxford in the south, though the American firm of Henry Ford had established a subsidiary company at Old Trafford, Manchester. The most successful ancillary firm was undoubtedly Joseph Lucas of Birmingham which had begun by making lamps for bicycles and graduated to mechanized transport with such success that it established hegemony in the supply of electrical equipment to the British trade. The early years of Britain's car industry emphasized variety of production and style to cater for a luxury market. Implicit in the choice of this road was a disproportionate early demand for craft skills, particularly in machine tools and the new skills of electronics. The mass market and the assembly line, which would confirm the west and south midlands as one of Britain's most prosperous areas, were to come in the inter-war years.

Textiles must not be forgotten since they provided more than a million and a quarter jobs early in the twentieth century, more than half of them in the production and finishing of cotton goods. In textiles, specialization, having started first, had proceeded furthest. With a decline in production in Scotland the cotton industry was more than ever concentrated in Lancashire. Within this area refinements were apparent; Bolton tended to handle the finer yarns and Oldham the coarser varieties, for example. Oldham also boasted the world's leading textile machine manufacturers, Platts. The irony of their situation was that, while they supplied customers all over the world with the most advanced textile technology, Lancashire firms, set in their ways and perhaps rendered complacent by the ease of their success when Britain was the only industrial nation in the world, were reluctant to re-equip their mills with ring spinning machines. This attitude may have been defensible in a period of uncertain markets during the late 1870s and early 1880s but it was less so when the market expanded in the 20 years before the war. King Cotton remained Britain's leading export earner but the crown was sitting uncertainly by 1914 with opportunities lost for productive reinvestment and rationalization to meet the challenge of more competitive world markets. The family firm still predominated. The mildly benevolent, paternalistic but autocratic and myopic millowner like Stanley Houghton's fictional Nat Jeffcoate in *Hindle Wakes* was an accurate enough characterization.

Across the Pennines, Yorkshire's great wool and worsted industries centred on Leeds and Bradford respectively were already feeling the effects of foreign competition by 1914. Whereas the numbers employed in cottons continued to rise until the first war (a rise of 28 per cent to 577,000 between 1870 and 1907) wool and worsted workers declined from a peak of 302,000 in 1890 to 261,000 in 1907. Yorkshire had expanding industries to compensate for the loss of jobs but the problems faced by one of the country's premier export industries was an important indicator for the future.

As is generally known, textiles were a major source of employment for women. They comprised 62 per cent of the workforce in cottons at the beginning of the twentieth century and 42 per cent in woollens. Among the unskilled workers the proportions were even higher. Women had been employed in the mills partly because they were allegedly more amenable to the harsh and unremitting discipline of factory work than men but mainly because they were cheaper. On average, they earned only a half to two-thirds the wages of their male counterparts. The use of women in textile mills was only a continuation of the tradition of family employment in clothing manufacture which long pre-dated the industrial revolution. Whereas in pre-industrial domestic employment women continued to contribute significantly to the total family budget, however, the tradition in mill communities was for women to give up factory work either on marriage or on the birth of the first child. The phrase 'the mill girl', therefore, is often precisely accurate.

Opportunities for female employment were by no means confined to northern mills. In 1871, women formed 31 per cent of the total occupied workforce; in 1901 29 per cent and in 1931 30 per cent. In view of the massive changes which took place during those 60 years these proportions are almost uncannily static. They also confirm what historians have long alleged: the female contribution to the national wage and salary bill was not dependent on new secretarial and administrative openings in the early part of the twentieth century, conveniently following the demise of the stereotype of an unemployed middle-class woman of the Victorian age.

The constant proportion conceals important shifts within the broad category of female employment. In the 1870s domestic service was far and away the most common occupation for women. In 1871 no less than 46 per cent of all women in paid employment were so employed and while the figure includes a proportion of daily domestic helps and chars the bulk of the 1,678,000 so categorized were resident, 'living-in', servants. A precise hierarchy existed from teenage girls occupied as kitchen, nursery or laundry maids through house and parlour maids and nurses on to the small number of cooks and housekeepers. Domestic service expanded very rapidly in the third quarter of the nineteenth century when the ranks of the middle classes were swollen by industrial and commercial expansion, and by the professions, of which a complex society had increasing need. Servants, both male and female, became almost an opportunity for conspicuous consumption: manuals existed advising on the number and categories of servants a given income was expected to sustain. Additionally, the fey and decoratively impotent role assumed by wives in polite Victorian society placed a premium on the acquisition of staff sufficient to cater for every domestic necessity.

During the last quarter of the century the total number of female servants continued to grow but the rate of acquisition slackened as many families began to feel the double pinch of higher wage bills and lower profits from their businesses. Compulsory education also kept young girls from the labour market for longer and when they reached it alternatives were beginning to present themselves. It had always been harder to recruit servants in industrial Lancashire and Yorkshire where girls preferred the higher wages, shorter hours and greater independence afforded by mill work. Now, as the economy expanded and diversified, the shortage spread south even to the servant-keeping citadels of London, the spa towns and the south coast. In 1881 there were 218 female domestic servants to every 1,000 families in England and Wales; by 1911 this had dropped to 170. As a prospective employer on Tyneside complained, there was 'an overflow of Shop Girls, Typists and Female Assistants of every description' but a 'perpetual cry for good domestic servants'.

Unmarried women and girls from the working class were finding increasing opportunities for work, some in factories, some as typists and secretaries, some in multiple retail outlets. For reasons which will be explained in Chapter 3, improved living standards at the end of the nineteenth century were attended by a retailing revolution and many girls now earned their first wages not as scullery maids but as shop girls. Another important characteristic of the mature industrial society – swollen service and administrative sectors in the economy – benefited women workers. A mere 2,000 women had been employed in commercial clerical tasks in 1861; by 1911 there were 157,000. In public administration the figures were 3,000 and 50,000 respectively.

Thus, the primacy of domestic service was under severe challenge even before 1914. The war accelerated the process dramatically. For the first time the total number of servants declined and all but the wealthiest had to do without domestic help. Around London the number of servants per 100 families fell from 24.1 to 12.4 between 1911 and 1921. During the war, as is well known, large numbers of women (900,000 by 1918) found unprecedentedly profitable employment in Lloyd George's munitions factories. Others took on tasks previously considered male preserves while conscription took able-bodied men to the front in droves after 1916. Bus conductresses, many of them previously in service, appeared; jobs in welfare and nursing, in education, even in heavy industry opened up. Widened horizons and fatter pay packets made a return to domestic service once peace returned doubly unalluring. Except in the upper echelons, it had always been regarded as low-status and low-wage work, acceptable only because easy to obtain. In the 1920s, more preferred clerical, educational or light industrial jobs. The increased range of employment opportunities was not accompanied by any perceptible improvement in status for women at work. Very few indeed challenged the primacy of men in professional occupations or in skilled jobs. Women remained relatively unskilled and underpaid.

It is notoriously difficult to generalize about both working hours and wage levels. Raw figures, when they exist, tell much less than the whole story. Wage data usually omit references to the value of 'in-kind' payments and perks. These might be relatively trivial, as with flagons of cider provided as lunchtime sustenance for harvesters or absolutely central as with bed and board for domestic servants. Nevertheless, a few observations may be hazarded in support of the contention that working conditions and remuneration alike improved between 1870 and 1914.

Working hours had been the subject of struggle throughout the nineteenth century. Governments consistently took the view that it was no part of their responsibility to interpose themselves between master and man to fix hours of work or rates of pay. Heads of household, so the theory ran, could bargain for optimum conditions in a free market. Since 1833, however, effective legislation had been on the statute book to protect women and children, who were not free agents, from exploitation – either by employer, husband or father. By 1870 no child could work under the age of 8; from 8 to 13 a maximum working day of 6½ hours was prescribed with provision for at least 10 hours' compulsory education in each working week. Women and children from 13 to 18 were forbidden to work more than 10 hours in a day or 58 hours a week; nor could they work after 6 p.m., or after 2 p.m. on Saturdays.

In many factory towns shift systems and work arrangements were such that curtailment of the working day for women and children effectively applied to men also. In less regulated, predominantly workshop trades, long hours, sometimes more than 12 a day, were still being worked in 1900, but not consistently. Many workers preferred the freedom to finish an order by a due date, working at leisurely pace early in the cycle then round the clock as deadlines approached. In some well-paid craft trades in metals, tailoring or woodwork the tradition of the 'Saint Monday' extra holiday remained into the new century. The Children's Employment Commission reported that as late as 1864 the observance of Saint Monday was 'general' in a city even of such diverse trades as Birmingham.

Few men worked more than 60 hours regularly by the 1870s unless they worked for themselves. Campaigns to institute a standard working day were organized by unions and other groups from the 1870s onwards. A Nine Hours League was formed by the Amalgamated Society of Engineers in 1871 and an engineering strike on Tyneside in that year won recognition of the 9 hour day from their employers, a conflict which opened the way for a general reduction of hours at least for skilled men during the 1870s and 1880s. The institution of Bank Holidays (see Chapter 7) further helped to consolidate the working week as one of 9 or 9½ hours on Monday to Friday with a half-day holiday on Saturday. Enormous variations were found, of course, and in the building trade, which expanded during a property boom in the 1890s, 'normal' working weeks were sacrificed to maximize the hazardous bounty of good weather for outside work. Piece-rate wages were a further inducement for the productive.

Campaigns for an 8 hour day during the 1890s met with frosty receptions from the employers, many of whom were now struggling to maintain profits during a period of falling prices and uncertain markets. Most craftsmen in Lancaster in the 1890s were working a week which varied between 50 and 55 hours. This situation was fairly typical, though the well-organized miners became the first group to win a statutory maximum shift in the Eight Hours Day Act of 1908. By the 1920s, though, working hours had been reduced in many trades to about 48 a week, more often still in 5½ days than in 5.

Living standards rose during the last quarter of the nineteenth century. For most skilled workers the benefits of industrial growth had been apparent earlier. Engineers had been in great demand to build and maintain the new machines in the first half of the century. It has been calculated that between 1850 and 1886, skilled workers' rates of pay rose by about 30 per cent. In the next 30 years more gains were made, particularly by skilled metal workers, railwaymen and some building craftsmen. Much of the widespread industrial unrest of the period 1908–14, as so often with strikes, was led by privileged groups of workers trying to consolidate gains already made and differentials successfully staked during a time of rising prices.

By the outbreak of the First World War the borderline of the 'aristocracy of labour' was a wage of about £2 a week, more often achieved by piece-rate workers. Many skilled men had to make do with 30–35*s* (£1.50–£1.75). Basic rates for most skilled men in Barrow in 1908 were between 30*s* and 38*s* (£1.50–£1.90), but overtime earnings could put them over the £2 mark. Between 1914 and 1920 acute labour shortage resulted in huge increases for skilled men. Railwaymen and printers did particularly well as differentials between the skilled and unskilled widened after a period of narrowing in the first years of the century. Money wages for the skilled virtually doubled between 1906 and 1924.

Wages of the unskilled and semi-skilled at the end of the nineteenth century seem to have varied between about 18*s* and 30*s* (£0.90–£1.50) a week, though periods of inactivity caused by illness and unemployment might push the average lower. Despite considerable fluctuations in the trade cycle and consequent unemployment, especially in the late 1870s, mid-1880s and early 1900s money wages remained remarkably stable, easing slightly upwards just before the war. The dramatic increase in living standards, arguably the first time that ordinary workers could show material benefits from industrialism, derived far more from falling prices. Food prices, especially of basic necessities like bread, cheese, sugar and tea, fell by 40 per cent or more. By a nice irony, that free-trade doctrine which had been the lodestar of British businessmen in the 1840s and 1850s brought an acceptable standard of living to the masses in the 1880s and 1890s as the great granaries of the United States were opened to the British consumer, much to the discomfiture of indigenous corn growers, many of whom slipped gravely into debt.

Living standards rose but we should not paint too rosy a picture. When Charles Booth and Seebohm Rowntree made their influential studies of London and York in the 1880s and 1890s they both concluded that, despite this new availability of cheap food, about 30 per cent of the populations they studied were living in poverty, bereft of resource against adverse economic circumstance, particularly unemployment. Rowntree calculated that in York 'the minimum weekly expenditure upon which physical efficiency can be maintained' was 21*s* 8*d* (£1.08½); many families earned less even in continuous work. The margin between penury and tolerability remained desperately narrow; 3 babies in every 20 still died in 1900 during their first year.

During this period the labour force became more highly organized. Before the late 1880s the only successful trade unions were of skilled workers, uniting as much to preserve their exclusivity from dilution by the unskilled as to put pressure on their employers. In the early 1880s there were perhaps three-quarters of a million trade unionists, about 8 per cent of the total male workforce; women were hardly organized at all. In a hectic three years between 1889 and 1891 new unions were established, many of them of unskilled and semi-skilled workers drawing inspiration from strikes by the gas workers and the London match girls. In those years union membership doubled to 1½ millions. The new 'general unions' symbolized the ending of organized labour on merely a craft and sectional basis but the contrast should not be overdrawn. Many of the unskilled unions, grand in concept, proved fallible in reality and failed to survive the adverse conditions of the early 1890s. Although membership of trade unions continued to rise and had reached 2 millions by 1900, only 10 per cent of members were unskilled.

The true period of massive expansion of unionism among the unskilled, semi-skilled and among women was the 1910s. Between 1910 and 1920 union membership increased from 2.57 millions to 8.35 millions with recruitment mainly among the unskilled. Indicative of this was the progress of the Workers' Union, a non-craft organization later amalgamated into the Transport and General Workers' Union. It had a mere 4,500 members in 1910 but by 1919, with 495,000 members, it was the largest union in the country. In 1920, membership of unions reached its highest point, about 45 per cent of all workers being members, and this was not exceeded until 1946. Wide variations existed among trades. Miners were massively organized, with 82 per cent of their workforce paying dues; transport workers were 58 per cent unionized, engineering and shipbuilding workers 51 per cent. By contrast, textile workers, with their large female element, were only 25 per cent unionized and the remainder of the clothing and tailoring trades only 15 per cent. Less than 1 woman worker in 5 was a member of a trade union.

Such an expansion of union influence was accompanied by some seismic shocks. From 1907 until the watershed of the general strike in 1926 there was much labour unrest and true industrial peace did not begin until the early 1930s. In addition to 1926, more than 10 million working days were lost to strikes in 1908, 1911, 1912, 1913, 1919, 1920, 1921, 1922 and 1923. The *modi vivendi* of the late nineteenth century, conciliation procedures and sliding wage scale agreements, broke down as a new phenomenon, national collective bargaining, became a reality. The process was facilitated by union amalgamations, beginning with the Miners' Federation of Great Britain in 1889 and consolidated by the formation of the Transport and General Workers' Union and the Amalgamated Engineering Union in the 1920s. Huge national unions could use collective bargaining to bring pressure not only onto employers but also, as in the First World War and during the early 1920s, onto the government. By the end of the 1920s government had been brought directly into the maelstrom of wage bargaining and trade unions, despite recent reverses, were being recognized, however reluctantly in some quarters, as one of the great economic and political institutions of the state.

Arguably, the British economy had to accustom itself to more fundamental change during the 1920s than in any previous decade. The world of work we have been analysing had become dependent on the old, staple heavy and exporting industries for a lead. These were the industries upon which Britain's pre-war industrial supremacy had been based. Now that supremacy came to an end and the main growth sectors in the economy shifted dramatically. Britain had to become much less reliant on the export of a small number of primary products, textiles, ships and coal in particular, and switched instead to light engineering, including cars, 'consumer' industries and to the provision of services. This structural change was accompanied by greater per capita productivity and, in most areas, rising living standards. The inter-war period still has what seems an indelible reputation as one of misery and depression. One can readily understand why yet the very sectors which thrived – building, electrical goods, vehicles for the home market, entertainments – could not have done so had the general trend not been one of rising living standards.

The speed and shift away from the 'primary' industries, even before the world slump began in 1929, is remarkable. During the 1920s the number of workers employed in mining went down by more than 20 per cent, in iron and steel by 34 per cent and in mechanical engineering and shipbuilding by 44 per cent. By contrast the labour force in food, drink and tobacco processing rose by 8 per cent, in building by 9 per cent in electrical goods by 11 per cent, in paper, printing and publishing by 12 per cent, in gas, water and electricity by 21 per cent and in vehicle manufacture by 36 per cent. Productivity in many of the old industries improved and the contribution they made to the economy remained important, but reliance could no longer be placed on them as a source of employment, as in the past.

Textiles, coal and shipbuilding were all hit by a collapse of export markets. Not only were they ill-equipped in most cases to meet the competition from other industrial nations – that had been going on at least since the 1870s – they were hit by hitherto underdeveloped countries learning the arts of fuel extraction and mass production. For example the emergence of an indigenous Indian textile industry had disastrous repercussions in Accrington, Oldham and Stockport. Cotton exports had earned an unprecedented £401 million in the boom year of 1920. By 1930, less was earned than had been in 1913 and by 1938 they realized a paltry £49.7 million. Coal, now challenged by the new exploitation of oil, had export earnings of £120 million in 1920 but only £49 million in 1930, though this represented, it is true, only a little less than the pre-war peak achieved in 1913.

As we have seen, employment in the old staple industries had been regionally concentrated. More than 80 per cent of the cotton industry was established in Lancashire and north Cheshire; more than half of Britain's ships were built either in the north-east or on Clydeside. Thus, when markets collapsed the results were catastrophic in particular areas. Worst hit were towns dependent on one heavy industry when the bottom dropped out of the world market. Textiles, though severely affected, could sell some of their wares to British consumers; shipbuilders could not. At the depth of the depression, therefore, 91 per cent of Saltburn's and 77 per cent of Jarrow's workforce was unemployed. In the north-east as a whole 30.6 per cent of the population was unemployed compared with a national average of 22.9 per cent and an average for London and the south-east of 13.1 per cent.

By the late 1920s Britain had reached a period of damaging transition. New light engineering, food processing, commercial and advertising organizations tended to look for space in the south and midlands, leaving the main urban areas of the north, south Wales and central Scotland either marking time or in disastrous decline. Slough boomed while Merthyr Tydfil stagnated; Luton, Oxford and Coventry were often crying out for skilled manpower while highly trained men in middle age whose skills had been rendered redundant by world trends they could barely comprehend and certainly not in the least degree affect congregated impotently on street corners in Barrow, Coatbridge or

Stockton. Though firms could be attracted to the larger northern cities if they offered industrial diversity, the old industrial primacy of the north had been surrendered, probably for ever. Young politicians like Harold Macmillan representing 'depressed areas' saw in the cruel twists of economic fortune the re-emergence of 'two nations' with interests and opportunities just as starkly contrasted as those discerned by Disraeli in the 1840s, and they feared for the social cohesion of Britain. The early experiences of privileged politicians of the Macmillan stamp probably did far more to put Britain on the road to 'demand management' and government control of the economy than did the economic theories of John Maynard Keynes. By the end of our period the majority of the population was enjoying higher real wages, better working conditions in the new, lighter, forms of industry or in office work and was beginning to taste the sweets of consumerism on which they, or their children, would fatten and gorge themselves under the same benevolent eye of Harold Macmillan in the 1950s. Meanwhile a minority in Wales, Scotland and the north of England waited hopelessly for the return of jobs which had gone for ever, reliant for mere existence on state doles rigidly and meanly means-tested by governments which did not understand the forces they were trying to control. Unemployment would eventually recede, of course, though not in the worst areas until preparations for the war against Hitler offered new uses for old industrial plant and derelict yards. The centre of industrial gravity, though, had moved irreversibly south, bringing to an inglorious conclusion 150 years during which the pulse of the nation could only be reliably felt north of a line from the Severn to the Humber.

FURTHER READING:

Aldcroft, D. (ed.), *The Development of British Industry and Foreign Competition, 1875–1914* (London, 1968)
Alford, B. W. E., *Depression and Recovery: British Economic Growth, 1918–1939* (London, 1972)
Allen E., Clarke, J. F., McCord, N. and Rowe D. J., *The North East Engineers Strikes of 1871* (Gateshead, 1971)
Anderson, G., *Victorian Clerks* (Manchester, 1976)
Ashworth, W., *An Economic History of England, 1870–1939* (London, 1960)
Bythell, D., *The Sweated Trades* (London, 1978)
*Fontana Economic History of Europe*, Vols. III and IV (London, 1973)
Horn, P., *The Rise and Fall of the Victorian Servant* (Dublin, 1975)
Kirby, M. W., *The British Coalmining Industry, 1870–1946* (London, 1977)
Lovell, J., *British Trade Unions, 1875–1933* (London, 1977)
Mathias, P., *The First Industrial Nation* (London, 1969)
Mowat, C. L., *Britain between the Wars, 1918–1940* (London, 1955)
Musson, A. E., *The Growth of British Industry* (London, 1978)
Pelling, H. M., *A History of British Trade Unionism* (London, 1963)
Reed, D. A., 'The Decline of Saint Monday, 1766–1876', *Past and Present,* **71** (1976), pp. 76 – 101
Roberts E., 'Working Class Living Standards in Barrow and Lancaster, 1890–1914', *Ec.H.R.*, 2nd. ser., **30** (1977), pp. 306–21
Stevenson, J., *Social Conditions in Britain between the Wars* (London, 1977)
Vaizey, J., *The History of British Steel* (London, 1974)
Wells, F. A., *The British Hosiery and Knitwear Industry* (Newton Abbot, 1972)

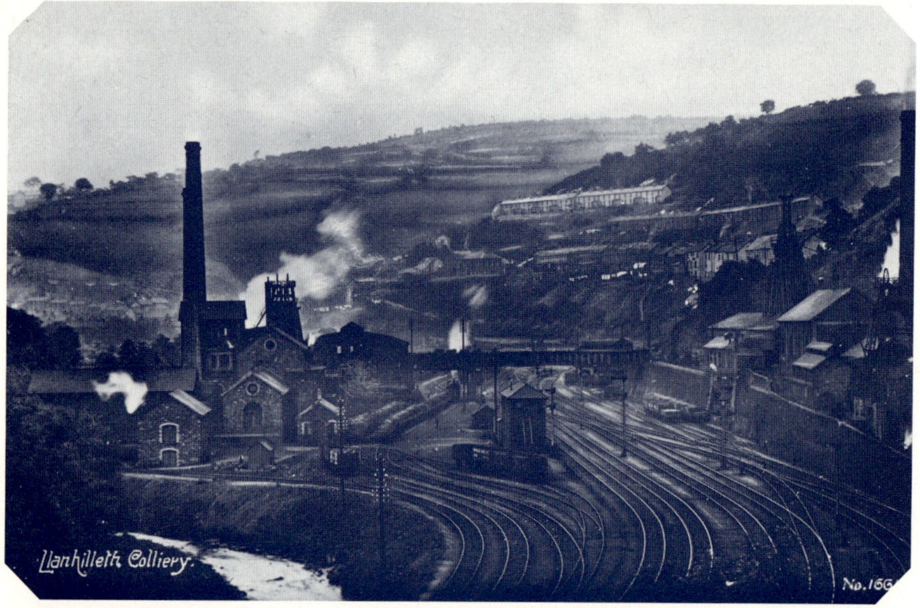


1. COAL MINING (i)

Llanhilleth colliery was a smallish pit in eastern south Wales, near Abertillery. Notice the pit cottages on the steep slopes rising from the River Ebbw. Originally two pits were sunk here, one for house coal in 1865 and one for steam coal in 1892. These were amalgamated by the owners Partridge, Jones & Paton of Newport. This mine also demonstrated the close working relationship between coal and steel in south Wales since it produced high volatile coking coals for the steel market. Almost 2,000 men were employed here in the early 1920s but depression brought a steady decline and Llanhilleth's reserves began to be worked out. The pit closed in March 1969.

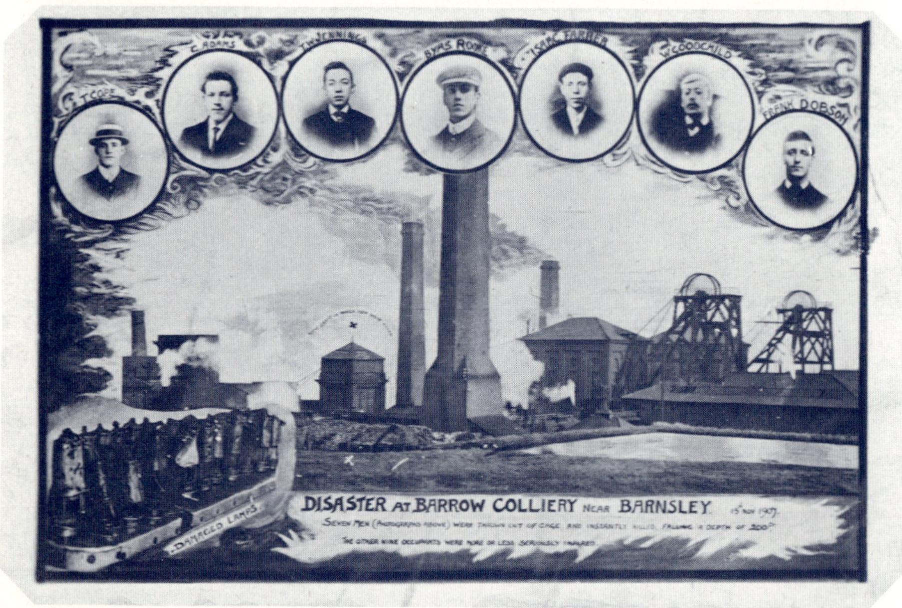


2. COAL MINING (ii)

Mining, of course, was one of the most dangerous of occupations. More than 1,000 miners were killed every year and the fatal accident rate in 1930 (107 per 100,000 employed) was higher than in 1920. This 1907 disaster at Barrow colliery, Worsborough nr. Barnsley, occurred because of incorrect fastening of the footplate on the cage taking men back to the surface after a shift. The seven men pictured here, aged 18–40, were killed. Goodchild left a widow and six children. It was to ease the financial loss from such disasters as these that the West Riding Miners' Permanent Relief Fund had been established in 1877. In 1907 it had 32,000 members and met claims arising from no less than 4,000 accidents a year. As the *Barnsley Chronicle* on 23 November 1907 reported, 'about one member out of every half-dozen meets with a casualty of some sort annually'. Widows of miners in the scheme who were killed at work received a lump sum of £5 then a pension of 5*s* (25p) a week, plus 2*s* (10p) a week for each child.

## 3. COAL MINING (iii)

More insidious hazards of pit life concerned permanent impairment of the lungs associated with work in 'the dust'. The dread words pneumoconiosis and silicosis do not appear in the mortality statistics for miners until later but 'diseases of the respiratory system' caused the death of 1 miner in 5 between the ages of 20 and 65 in 1921; tuberculosis killed 3 out of 20. For miners recuperating after illness the Lancashire and Cheshire miners provided this splendid convalescent home on the sea front in north Blackpool in 1927. The home has room for 150 men, most of whom stay for a fortnight of sea air, rest and quiet. Lancashire miners currently contribute 12p a week towards its upkeep. In 1976 the north Staffordshire miners sold their own convalescent home and merged with the Lancashire men to reduce running costs.

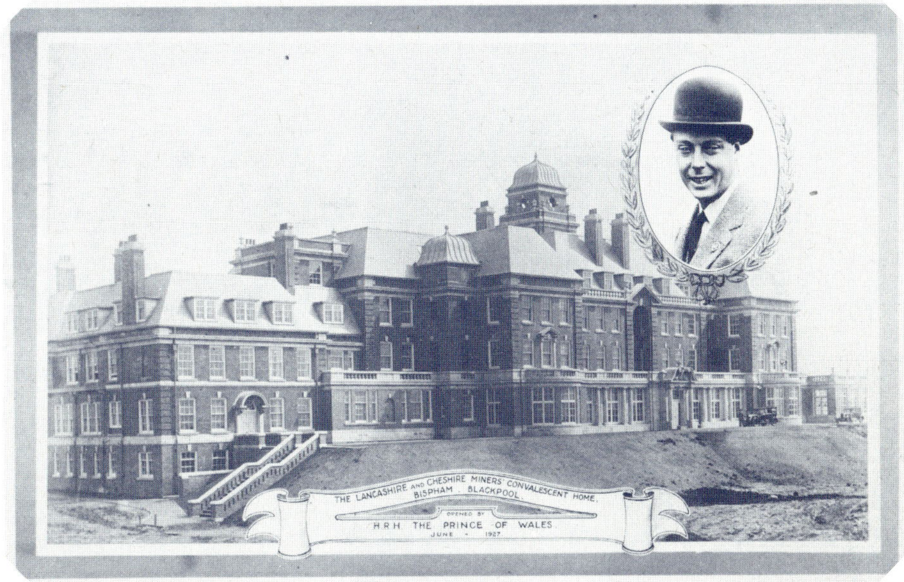


## 4. TIN MINING

Tin mining remained an important part of Cornwall's economy until the early twentieth century. The great days of the eighteenth century, when the Dolcoath mine pictured here was sunk, would not return, but as late as the 1860s 1,200 people were employed here and it reached deeper levels to search for tin beneath the exhausted copper reserves. American and Australian competition in both tin and copper hit Cornwall hard. By 1906 only 8,000 tons of tin were being drawn from the six large mines, headed by Dolcoath. Smaller concerns had already closed and this mine went out of productive existence in 1920.

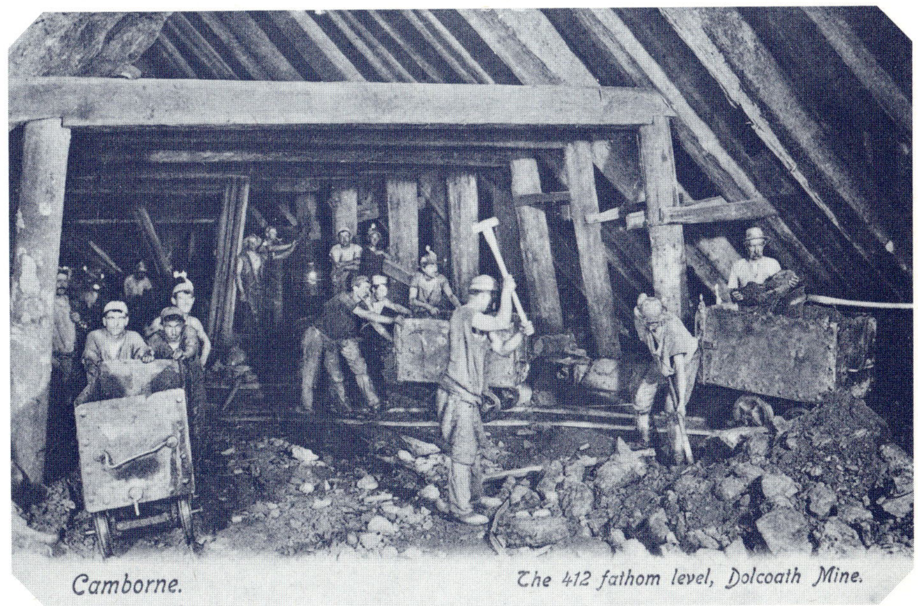

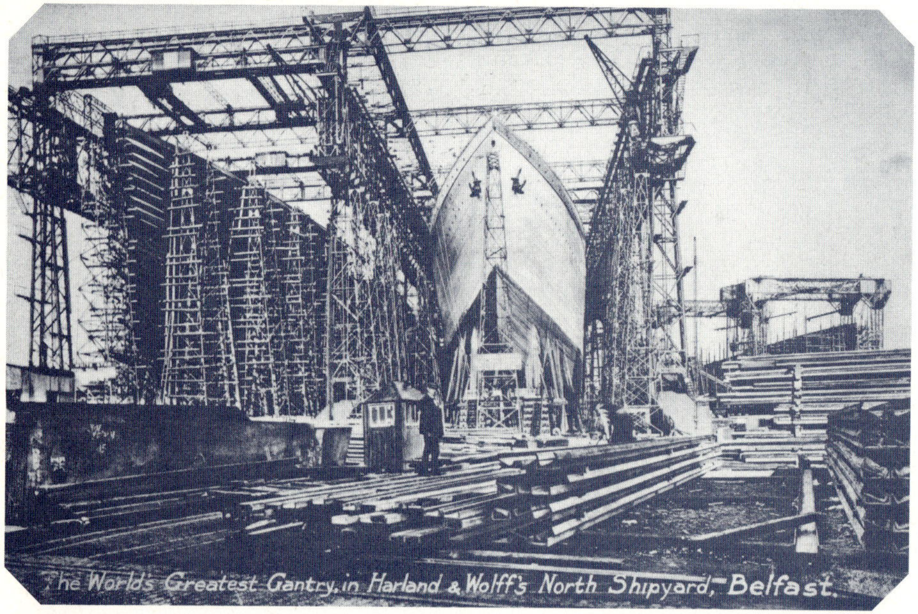


## 5. SHIPBUILDING

Benefiting from developments in steel technology, Britain easily maintained her shipbuilding supremacy before 1914. In 1913 60 per cent of the world's tonnage of new ships was launched from British yards, and British ships put £94 million onto the credit side of our trading ledger. The industry was to be severely hit by the loss of overseas markets after 1918, but the Harland and Wolff yard, pictured here, was less seriously affected than some. The Belfast shipbuilders, in which the Clydeside concern John Brown had acquired a controlling interest in 1906, remained the biggest builder of passenger liners and it dominated the market for vessels in the luxury class. Against the trend, Harland and Wolff was employing more men on building passenger liners in 1922 than in 1913. Here we see the White Star liner *Olympic*, sister ship to the *Titanic*, on the gantry and almost ready for launching in 1910.

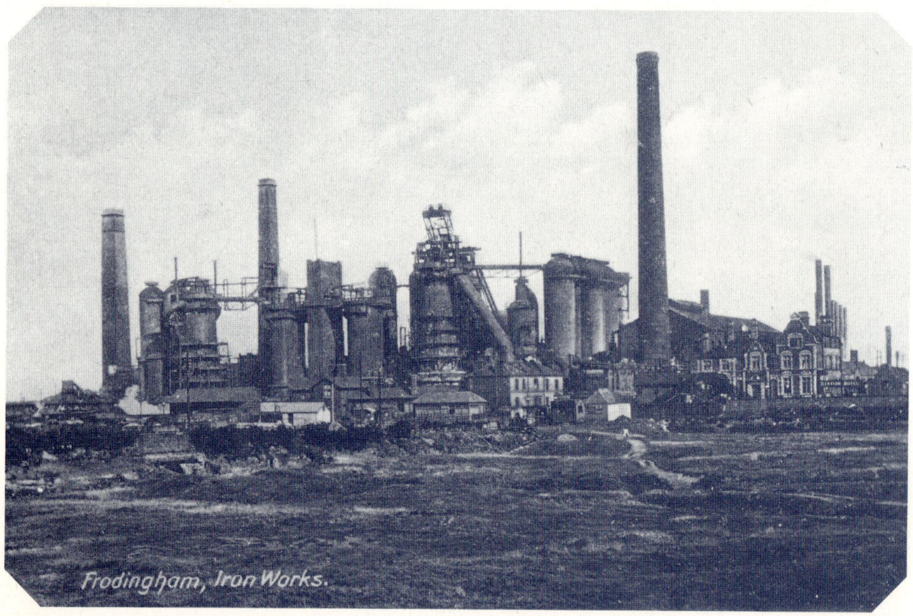


## 6. IRON WORKS

The Frodingham Iron Company, Scunthorpe, was founded in the 1860s soon after the discovery of ironstone in the town. It was built near the London and North Eastern railway line which can just be seen on the right of the card. Beside it, in the very shadow of the works, stood the Station Hotel. Steelmaking plant was not built here until 1888 with milling and a melting shop in operation by the mid-1890s. Scunthorpe was now established as a one-industry town. The Frodingham Iron & Steel Company was a large concern with issued capital of £500,000 in 1904. It was later taken over by a Sheffield firm and amalgamated into the United Steel Company which survived until nationalization. The plant is now incorporated into the British Steel Appleby–Frodingham complex.

7. FOUNDRY AND ENGINEERING WORKS

Spencer's Foundry, Melksham (Wilts.) is now incorporated within the enormous General Electric Company. It began in 1873 as a small engineering works founded by the teetotal son of a brewer. The firm employed over 60 men by 1880 but expanded rapidly thereafter as it moved into profitable port-handling equipment. By 1900 it had become a limited liability company with offices in London, Hull and Liverpool. New premises near the railway line for ease of transportation were built in 1903 when the workforce was about 350. Workers are seen leaving the factory in this card of 1906. The firm was diversifying in common ways, now producing car parts, electrical installations, elevators and conveyors for many different industries.

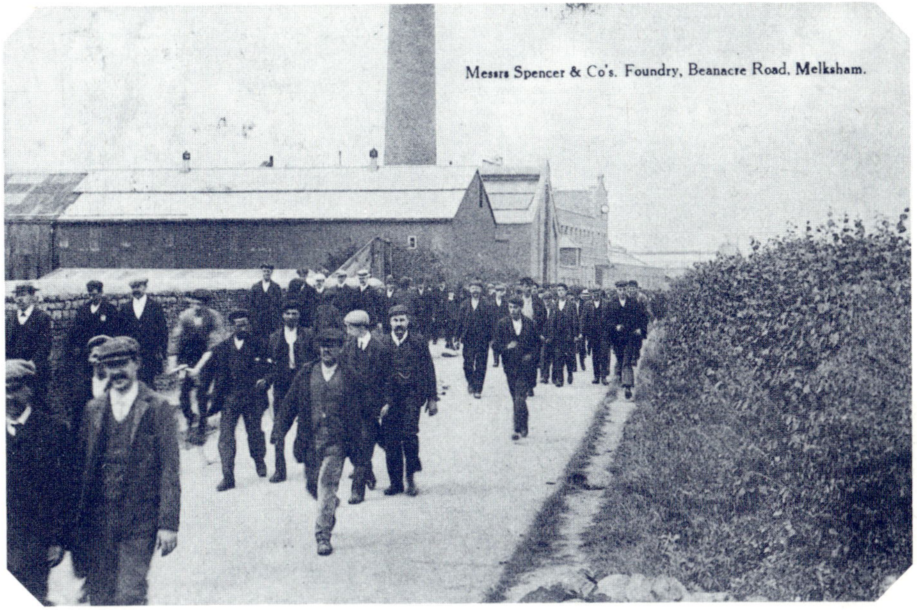


8. METALWORK

This card illustrates file manufacture, one of the lighter of Sheffield's multifarious steel trades. Files had been made in small workshops for centuries and machine filing took over only slowly. After forging the files required heat treatment for hardening. This card is unusual in that it was used by representatives to advertise their company. It was sent to a shipbuilding and engineering company in Hull by Flockton, Tomkin & Company, a small metal firm operating from Newhall Steel works, Burgess St, just off Attercliffe Road in the very heart of Sheffield's steel quarter on the banks of the much-polluted River Don. The firm advertised itself as 'manufacturers of best crucible cast tool, shear, spring & blister steel, files, hammers, saws etc.'

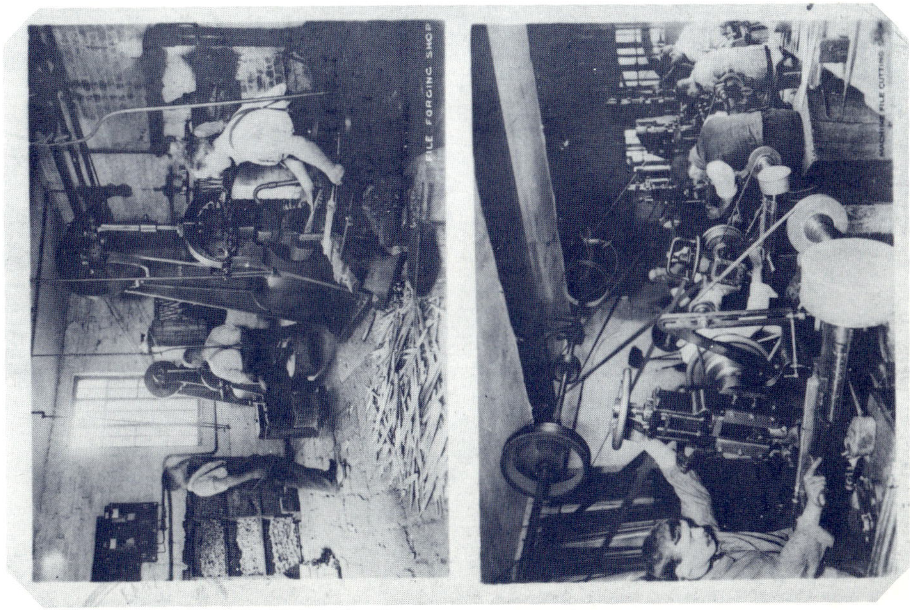

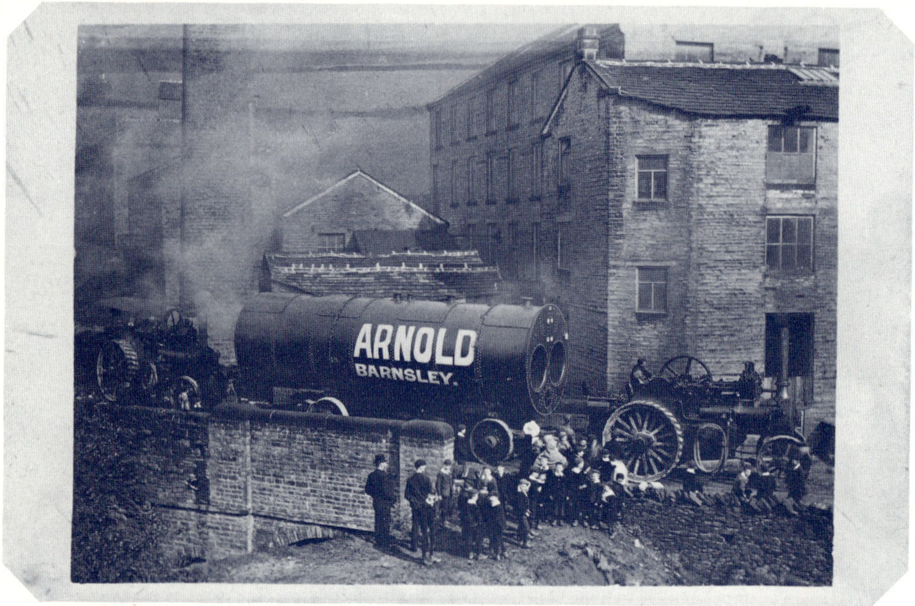


9. BOILERMAKERS

Wrought iron boilers for making steam in engines were essential components in a range of manufacturing industries. Boilermakers were among the elite of engineering workers and protected by a strong union; the boilermakers union in 1906 had 50,000 members and still functioned as an old-style association of craft workers. Here we see a new boiler on its way to delivery watched by an attentive group of children in best clothes. The firm responsible was William Arnold and Company of the Victoria Iron & Boiler Works, Stocks Lane, Barnsley – one of only three boilermaking firms in the town in 1902. The firm had been making boilers since 1842 and also carried out repairs for local collieries and mills. It went out of business in the 1920s.

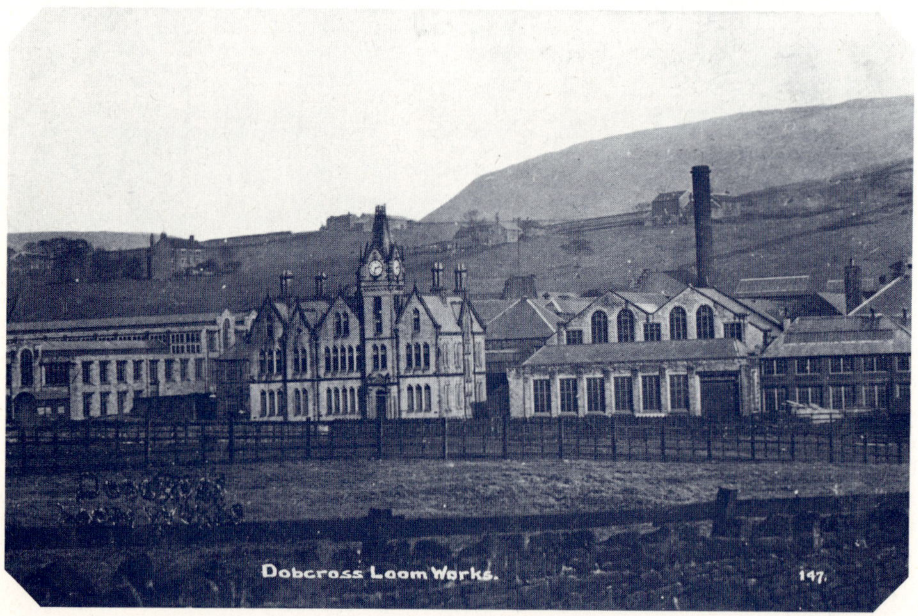


10. TEXTILE MACHINERY MANUFACTURER

The factory here belonged to Hutchinson, Hollingworth and Company, makers of the Dobcross loom which was in extensive use in the woollen and worsted areas of Yorkshire and which still survives in some mills. Dobcross stands high in the Pennines near Saddleworth and just into Yorkshire. The firm also made carpet looms and some preparatory weaving machinery. Skilled engineers and machinists were among the elite of the working class.

11 and 12. COTTON WEAVING

Handloom weavers had been among the best paid of all workers in 1800. Cartwright's power loom, adapted by Horrocks, was widely used by the 1820s and rendered nugatory the skills of the handloom men whose wages plummeted disastrously in the 1830s and 1840s. Their successors, the powerloom weavers, were never among the top wage earners. Despite a rapid expansion of the cotton trade just before 1914 when over 800,000 looms were in operation (compared with 530,000 in 1935) weavers rarely made more than 25*s*–27*s* a week (£1.25–£1.35) whereas fine mule spinners could make £2. Powerloom weavers were part machine minders, part skilled men. They had to replenish the supply of weft to the shuttle by hand since the fully automatic power loom, invented in the United States in the 1890s, made little progress in Lancashire. The men at the extreme left and right of Card No. 11 are both holding manual shuttles. Card No. 12 shows a weaver at his loom. The caption here 'Pulling Back O'wd Lad to save a fine' probably refers to the procedure necessary to correct a fault in the weave. The weft would be cut out past the fault and the warp pulled back to enable re-weaving to take place. Weavers were fined if they allowed faulty cloth to pass from their looms. Weavers suffered badly during the inter-war depression. No less than 54 per cent of all looms were standing idle in 1930.

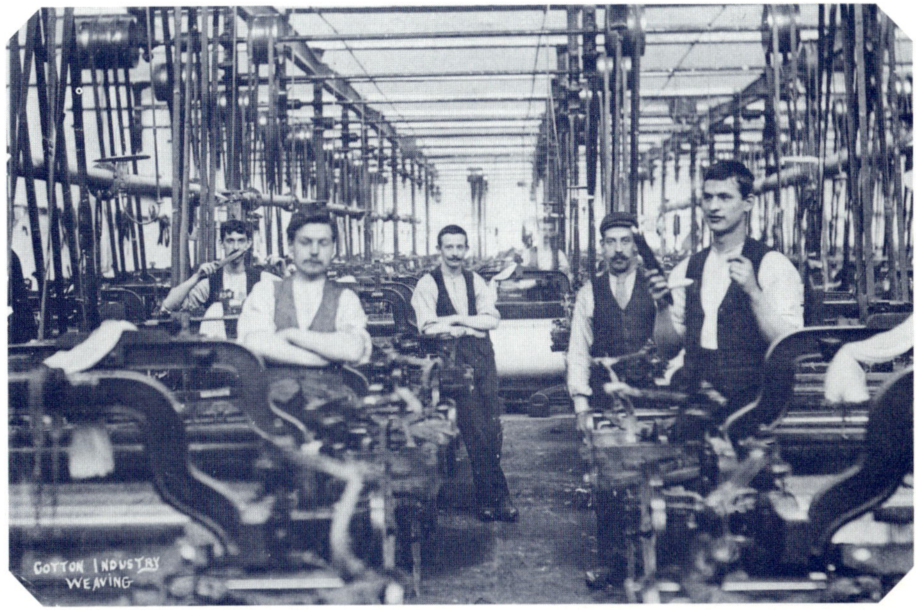


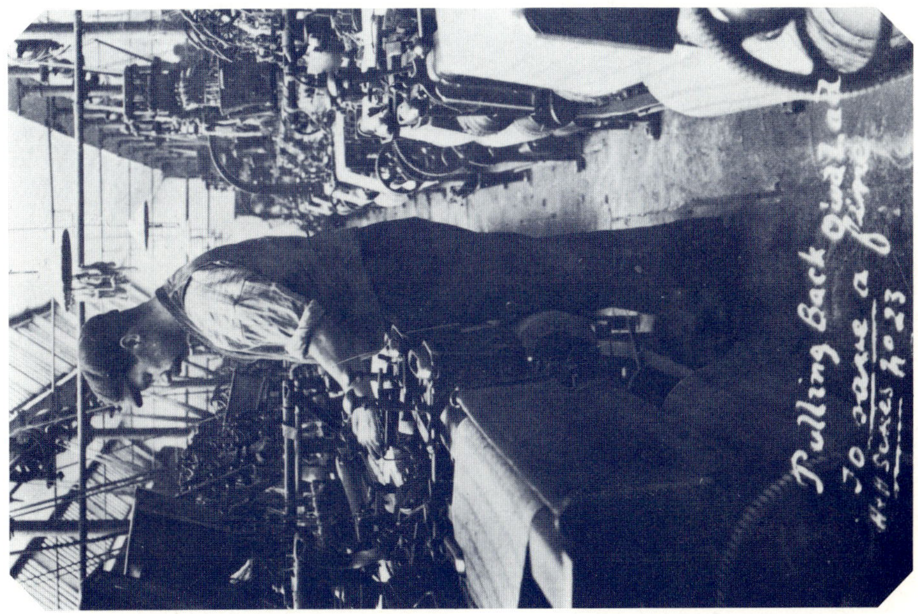

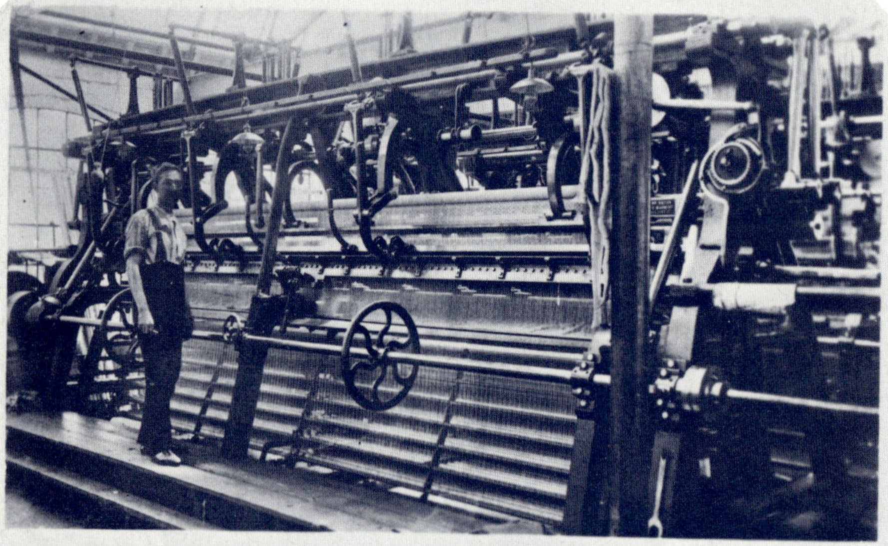

S 9406. A MODERN LACE MACHINE, LONG EATON.

## 13. LACE MANUFACTURE

The hosiery and lace trade, concentrated in the east midlands, provided employment for more than 90,000 people early in the century, most of them women. Both trades were factory based but lace, catering for growing demand in fancy dresses and curtains, was growing the more rapidly. Nottingham developed as the lace trade's commercial centre; surrounding towns like Long Eaton supplied it with manufacture. The number of lace workers doubled between 1890 and 1907 and much investment was made in new machinery to satisfy a growing export market. Here we see a skilled worker standing proudly before a new lace machine. Domestic lace-making, previously so common in much of southern England, has been eclipsed.

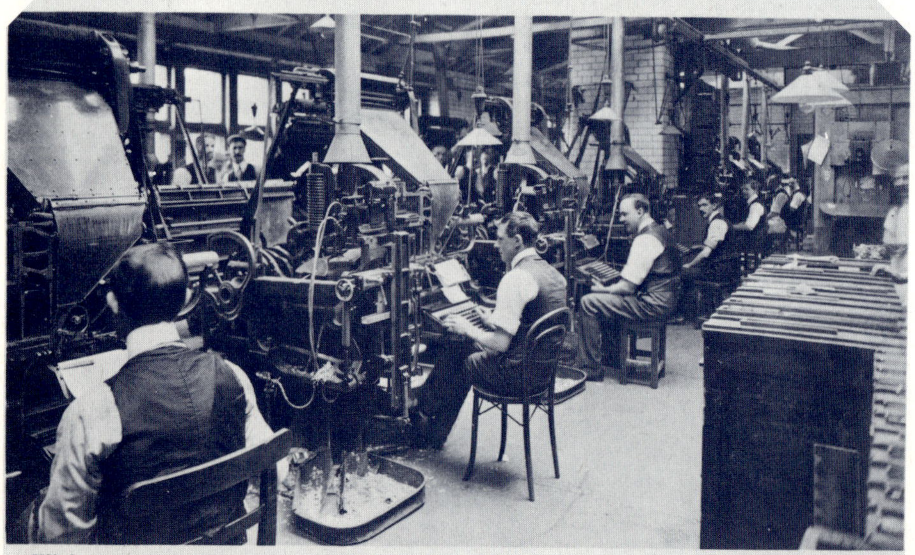

7521–2 A SECTION OF THE LINOTYPES.
EVENING NEWS CELEBRATION WEEK, 10,000th NUMBER, NOV. 21st, 1913.

## 14. PRINTING

Printers have always been at or near the top of the wages league. The combination of dexterity and literacy was much prized, particularly in the fiercely competitive world of newspapers, and brought premium rates. It was also generally true that printers, about 40 per cent of them unionized in the Typographical Association in 1911, were able to use new technology to screw even higher wages from their employers. London printers are seen here operating the new Linotype machines on a successful evening paper in 1913. These men would be earning more than £3 for a 50-hour week, while few hand compositors would make more than £2. This machine had come to Britain from the United States in 1889 and its use before 1914 was almost exclusively confined to the newspaper industry. It enabled larger journals to be produced more economically and was a vital weapon in the circulation war.

15 and 16. STRIKES

1911 and 1912 were years of massive industrial unrest as workers sought higher pay and better conditions during a period of rising prices. 872 strikes took place in 1911, causing the loss of 10 million working days – the worst year for strikes since 1889. In 1912 it was even worse, culminating in a miners' strike with the loss of almost 41 million days. These cards concern the short but dramatic railway workers' strike on 18–19 August 1911. Winston Churchill, then the Liberal Home Secretary, was in no mood to be conciliatory; he rarely was. He had warned his colleagues in July of 'the disquieting condition of the industrial world and the almost daily outbreaks of strikes . . . accompanied by a passing tendency to resort to violence.' This strike was met by the declaration of a state of emergency and troops were despatched to ensure the movement of essential supplies and to guard railway property. Card No. 15 shows Cameron Highlanders guarding locomotive sheds. Clashes between troops and strikes did take place and two people were killed when troops opened fire at Llanelli. Card No. 16 shows holiday-makers and day-trippers stranded at Blackpool Central station at the height of the season.

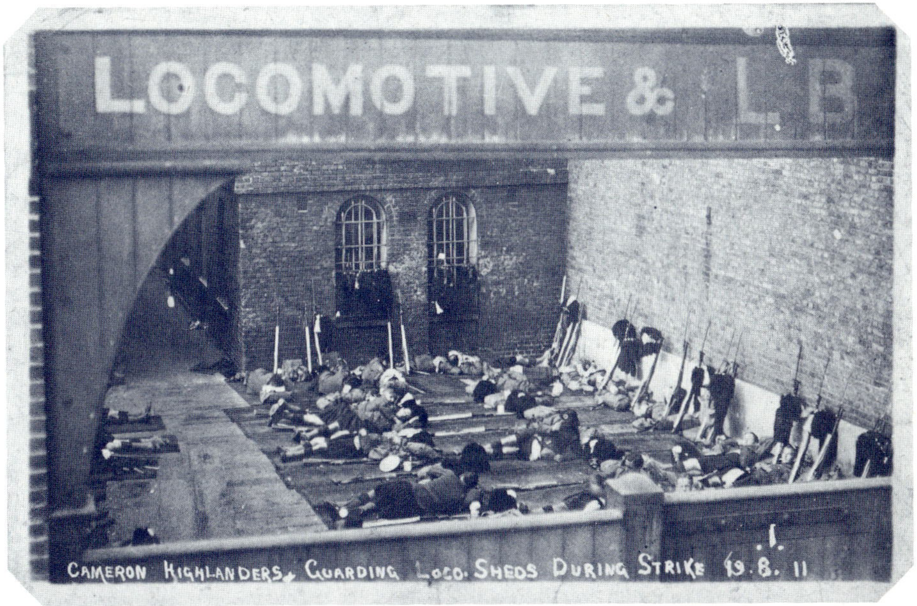


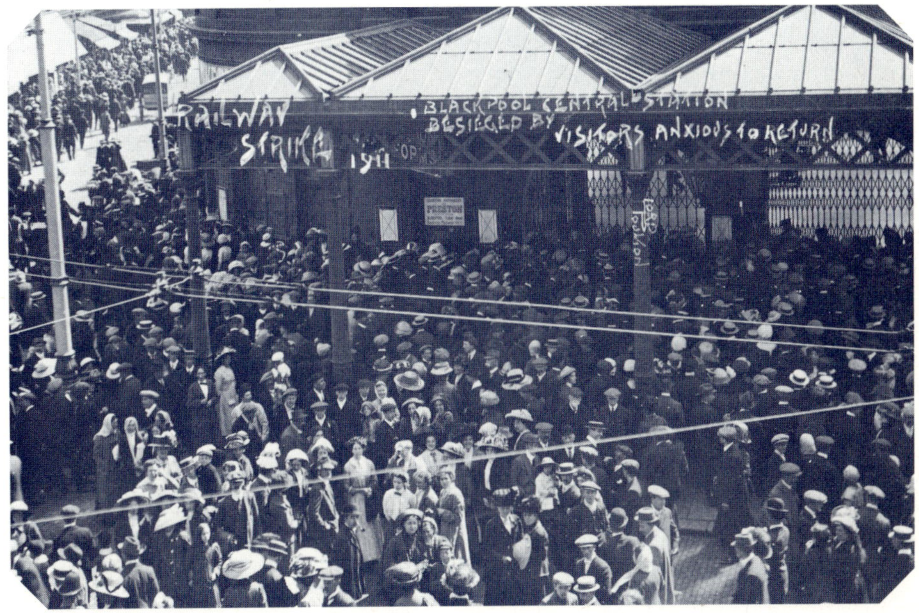

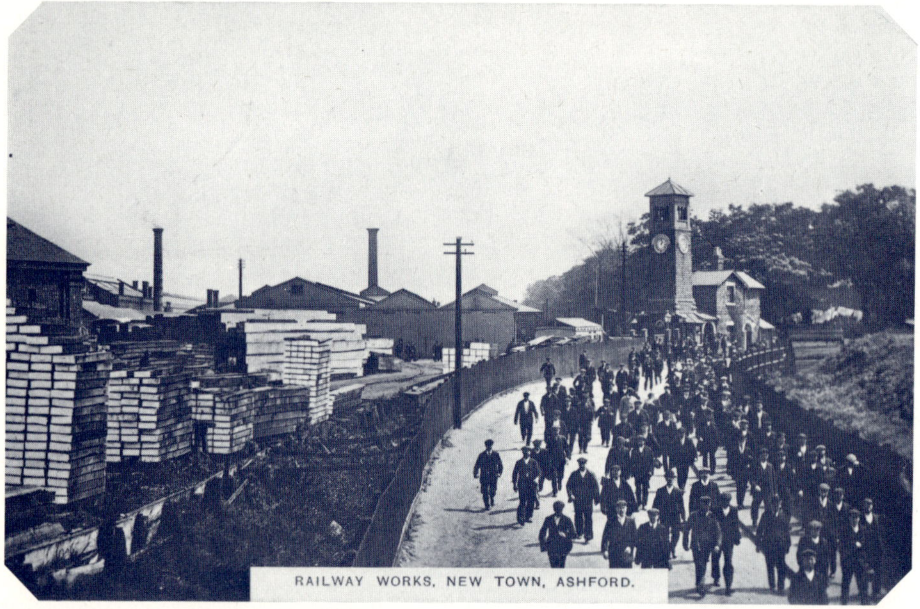


17. RAILWAY WORKS

The decision of the South Eastern Railway Company to build their locomotive and carriage works at Ashford in 1846 precipitated the building of a Victorian new town. Ashford's population doubled to 7,000 between 1847 and 1861. At first the works and associated housing estate, planned round a village green and including a public baths, was physically separate from the old town but soon was incorporated in it. It provided work for previously under-employed rural labourers and also drew skilled engineers from London and further north. By the Edwardian age Ashford's population comfortably exceeded 13,000 and its railway works gave employment to 2,000 after expansion of the engineering and carriage works in 1894. The Company, mindful of the needs of improving artisans, built a Mechanics' Institute equipped with 2,500 books; classes in machine construction, arithmetic, French and the new shorthand were also introduced. Interestingly, the card's message was in French and concerned purely domestic matters. There is no clue as to the writer.

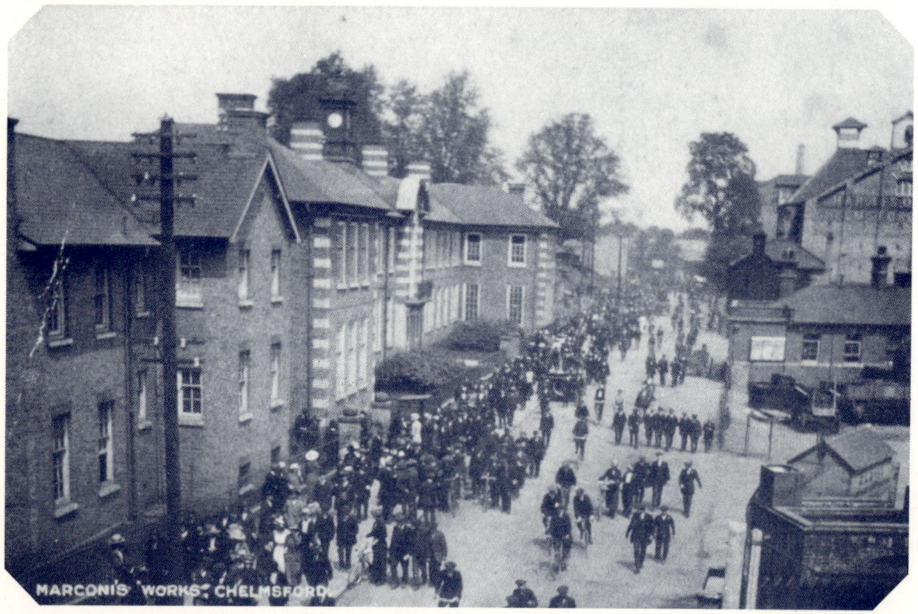


18. COMMUNICATIONS

Communications is an excellent example of vigorous, new light industry which would shift the economic balance of power from north to south in the inter-war period when the traditional heavy industries were hit by recession. Marconi of Chelmsford, still one of the largest employers in Essex's county town, was founded in 1899 as the Wireless, Telegraph and Signals Company and moved to these premises in New St in 1912. This card shows the new buildings, whose exterior is little altered today, soon after completion. It was the first purpose-built radio factory in the world and took only 17 weeks to complete. Marconi was receiving enormous publicity, firstly by the wireless telegraphy which was used to trap the murderous Dr Crippen in 1911 and then in an unsavoury financial scandal of 1913 which touched Lloyd George without breaking him. The workers on their way home here were not by any means all Marconi workers. Many would have been employed at Hoffman's ball-bearing factory and at the flour mill opposite.

19. BISCUIT FACTORY

Biscuits were a convenience food which grew greatly in popularity as living standards rose. In 1860 the business partnership begun by the Quakers Thomas Huntley and George Palmer was the biggest biscuit firm in England with 500 employees and producing 3,200 tons of biscuits a year. In 1914 they employed over 5,000 and produced almost 24,000 tons of biscuits. The range of their lines was world famous and their decorated biscuit tins by special appointment to much of the royalty of Europe were a characteristic feature of Christmas gift-buying. Employees were given regular 'treats' and outings; in July 1919 they were given an extra week's wages to celebrate the signing of the Peace of Versailles. Reading was decidedly a 'biscuit town'. During the inter-war period, biscuit sales continued to soar though Huntley and Palmers were becoming steadily less dominant. Its share of overseas trade slumped and Peak Frean was consolidating its technical lead. Output of Huntley and Palmers biscuits slumped by almost a half between 1917 and 1930 and though it still traded at a profit this too had been dramatically reduced.

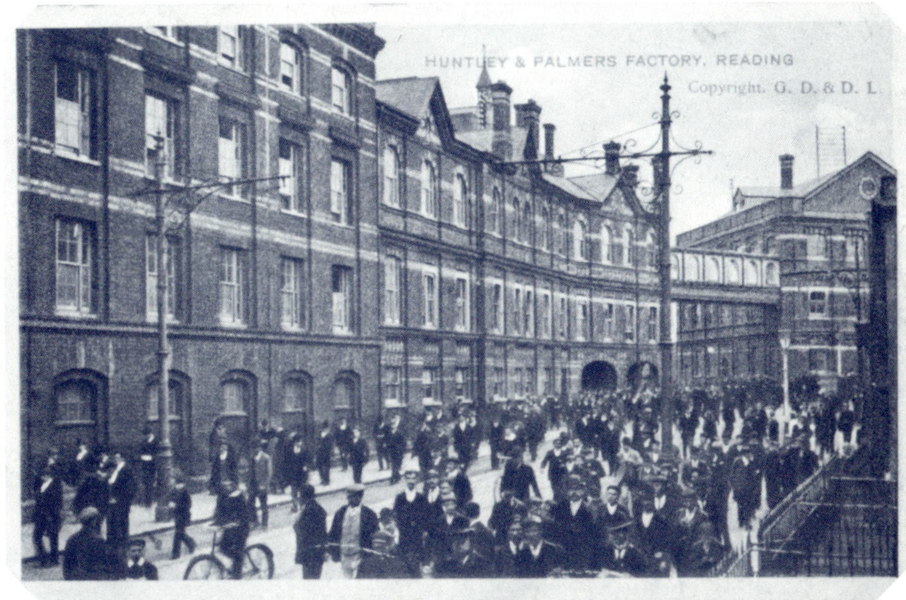


20. POTTERY

Most of Britain's commercial pottery in 1900 came from the 'Five Towns' of North Staffordshire (more accurately six: Tunstall, Burslem, Hanley, Stoke, Fenton and Longton) incorporated within the borough of Stoke-on-Trent. Much of the impetus had been provided by Josiah Wedgwood's famous Etruria works which pioneered mass production of high quality pottery. Of Stoke's 215,000 population in 1901 it has been estimated that about 46,000 were pottery workers, 21,000 of them women. Until the 1860s children were commonly used in the factories as 'mould runners', running around and even between factories putting newly made pots near a stove to harden and running back with empty moulds. Pictures of the characteristic bottle kilns, nearly all demolished in the last thirty years, abound but here is a rare interior shot. The saggers – one is on one of the men's head – were the large, rough vessels of fireproof baked clay in which all the crockery was placed when taken to the ovens for firing. Potters were subject to occupational disease which came only slowly under the control of the inspectors. The use of lead in glazing caused brain damage, manifested in high rates of epilepsy and blindness. Clay dust in the lungs also caused much damage. Silicosis was known locally as 'potter's rot'.

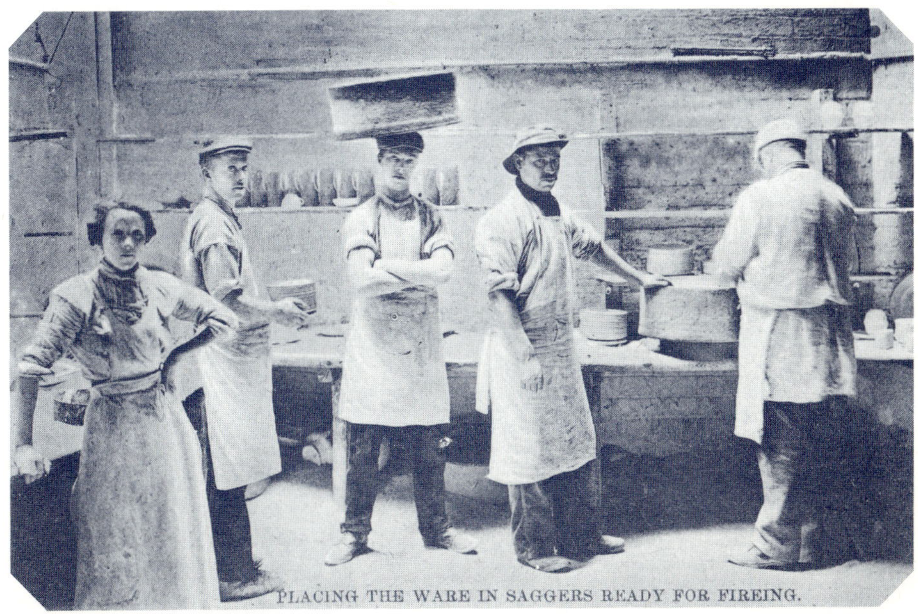

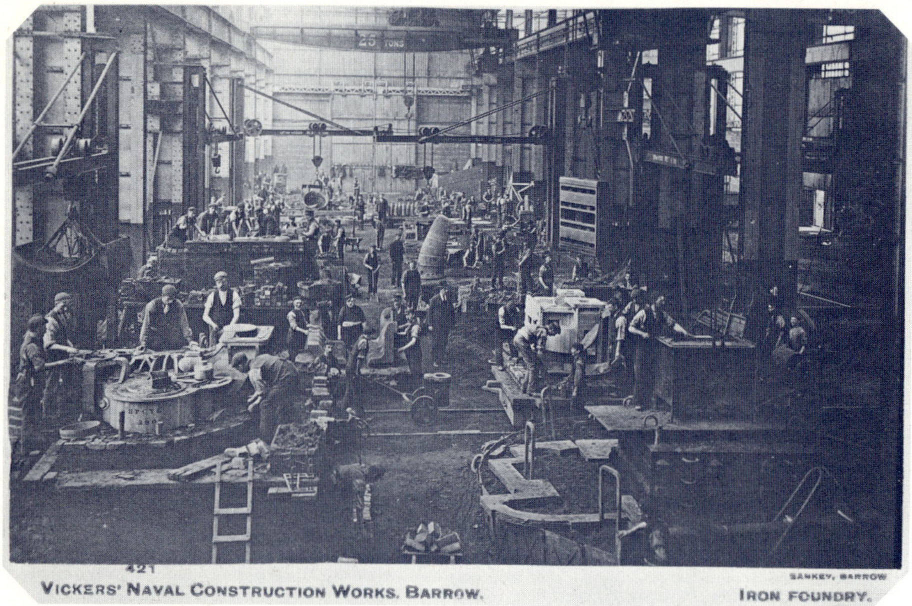


21. WAR WORK (i) NAVAL CONSTRUCTION

War preparations gave a great boost to engineering and shipbuilding firms like Vickers and Armstrong. Vickers built warships both for the British government and for foreign powers like Brazil. Vickers was also the main company involved in submarine development. Vickers machine guns were vital weapons in Flanders. The company had large plant in Sheffield, Birmingham, Crayford and Dartford, but major naval expansion naturally took place at Barrow after Vickers acquired the Naval Construction and Armaments Company in 1897. In the years before the first war Vickers expanded its workforce from 5,000 to 10,000 as it exploited to the full its ability to supply ships equipped with guns and all machinery.

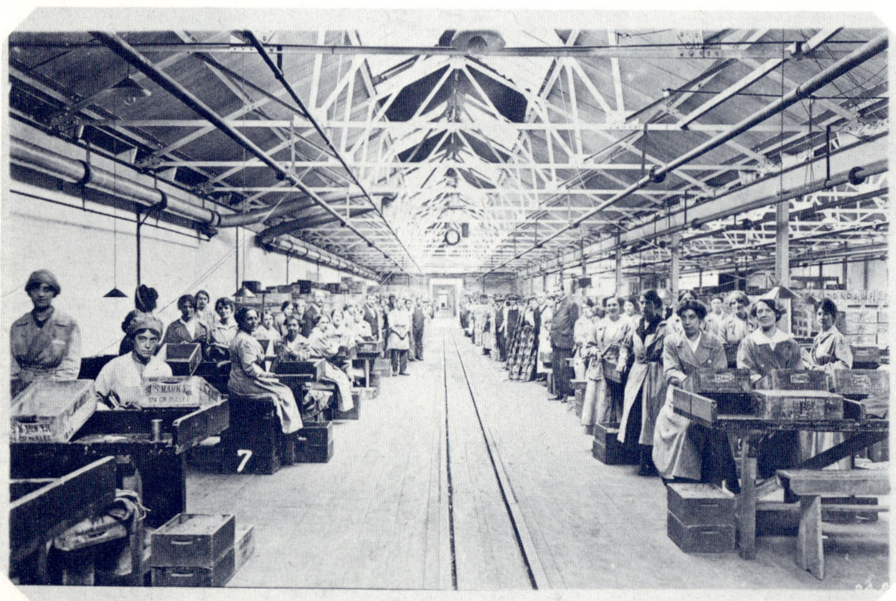

22. WAR WORK (ii) MUNITIONS

Particularly after conscription of men into the services in 1916 the need for women to plug the gaps in the national economy became paramount. The number of women in employment increased from just over 2 million to almost 3 million during the war. Of these almost 1 million were employed in munitions factories. Women workers on piece rates in metals or chemicals factories organized by Lloyd George to aid the war effort could earn more than £2 a week, and some even £3 or £4, much to the envy and annoyance of women in more traditional occupations. Women making shells could earn more than twice as much as women making uniforms. Here we see women in an airy factory making bullets. Not all of the expansion of women's work was in munitions. Some women became bus drivers; far more became typists, clerical workers or teachers. The war undoubtedly educated a male-dominated society to accept women as colleagues in a wider range of occupations. The necessary corollary was the grant of the vote to women (though still only the over-30s) in 1918.

23. BELLMAKING
Bellmaking is a specialized branch of the iron trade. Numerous small firms operated but two suppliers of church bells dominated the trade, Taylors of Loughborough and the Whitechapel Bell Foundry in east London. The inscription on these bells (not visible to the naked eye) indicates that they were made by Mears and Stainbank, which was the name adopted by the Whitechapel Foundry, 32 & 35 Whitechapel Road from the 1870s to the 1960s. The foundry was established originally in 1570. Unfortunately, it is not possible to identify the church into which they are being placed.

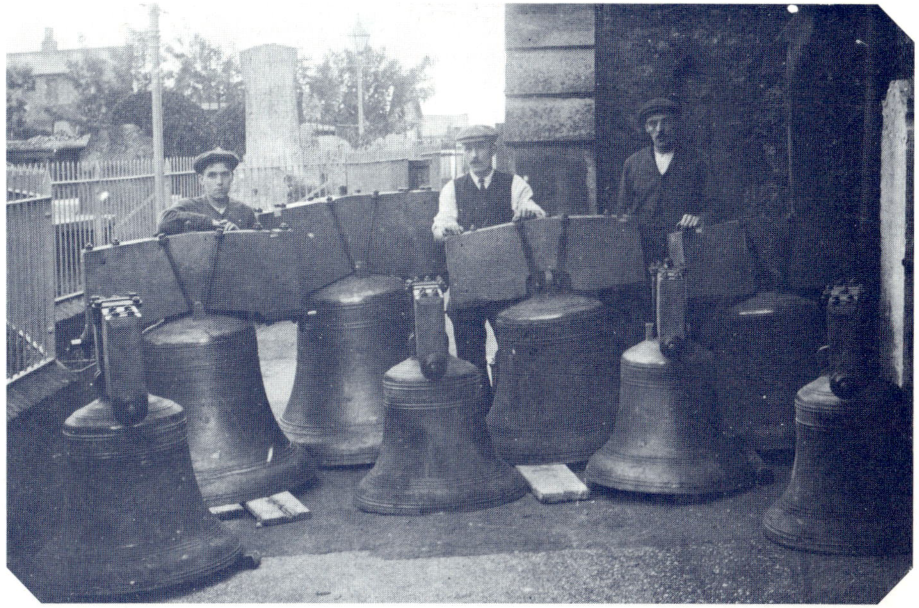

24. BREWING
Many trades retained ancient customs to celebrate festivals or important moments in a worker's career such as the ending of an apprenticeship. Here we see a coming-of-age ceremony at Burton-on-Trent early in the century. Burton was the pre-eminent provincial brewery town, famous for its 'pale ales' and bottled beers. Its brewers were in the forefront of that process of amalgamation and rationalization whereby the number of independent breweries was cut from 11,000 to 4,000 between 1880 and 1914. Little of this presumably worried the young man about to be put into one of his own barrels and rolled down the nearest hill.

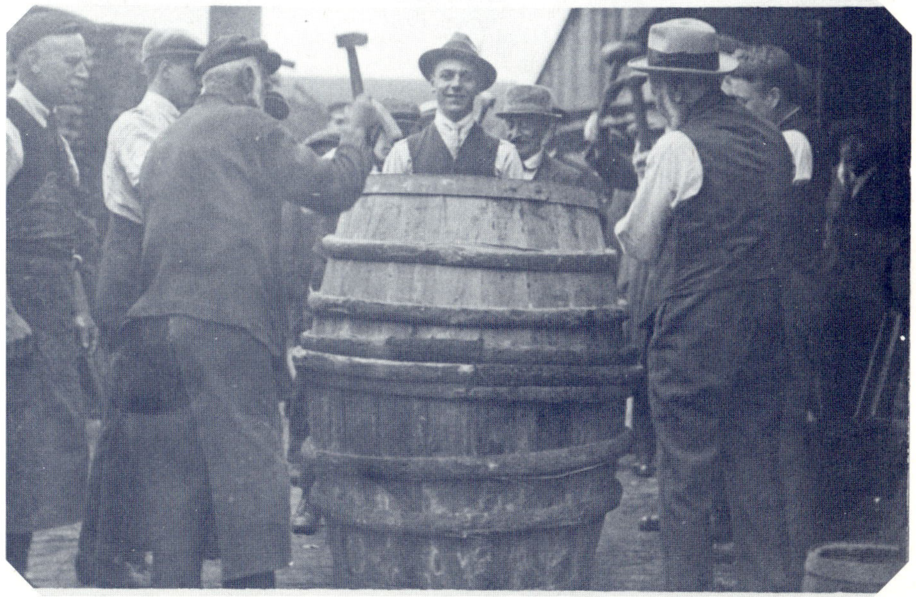

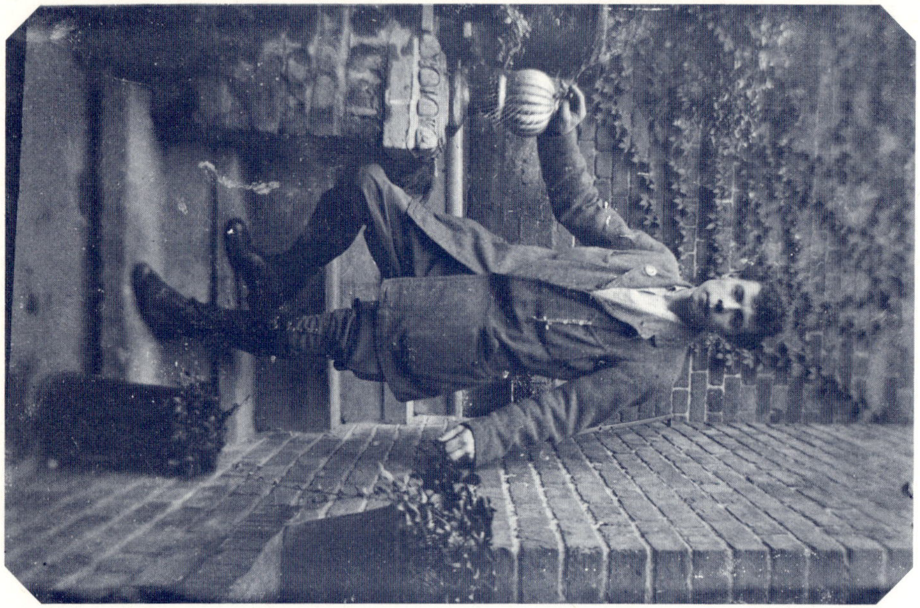

25. MALE DOMESTIC SERVANT

Far more opportunities existed for female domestic service than for male. Females outnumbered males by more than 20 to 1 in the 1880s. Upper middle-class families still had need of coachmen, gardeners and grooms, however, and before 1914 the new category of motor-car chauffeur had come into being. This young man is probably a groom. Grooms' tasks varied greatly. In the best-appointed households he would just tend the horses. Where fewer servants were employed he would also drive the mistress of the house, tend the pony and trap and, probably, also wait at table. A groom at the turn of the century would have to make do on about £30 a year plus meals and accommodation.

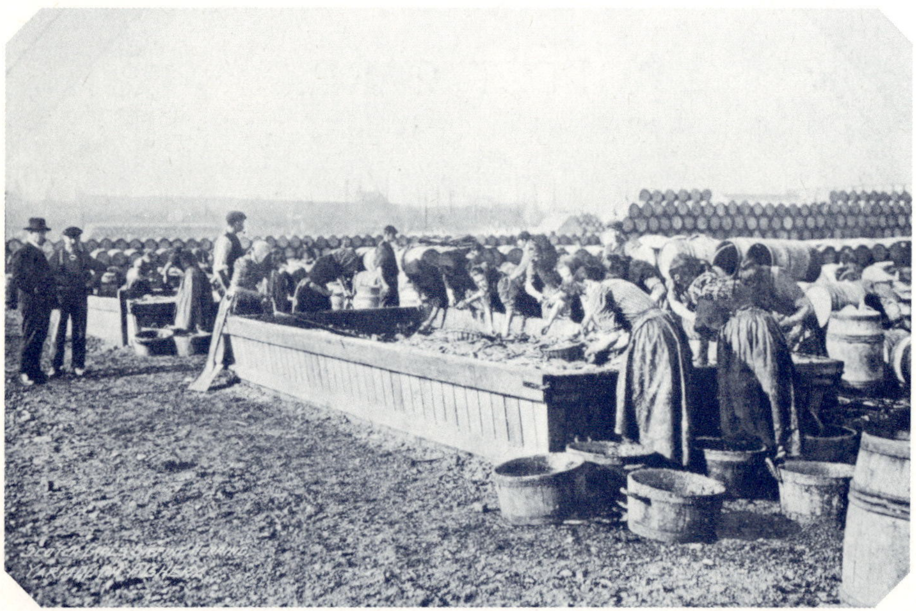

26. FISHING

Great Yarmouth was one of the country's leading herring ports. At the end of the nineteenth century roughly 20 per cent of all herring landed on British shores came through the port before being forwarded to all the large centres of population. Between August and December specialist Scottish fishergirls were employed on the wharf to fillet and cure the catch landed from more than 700 boats. Their speed and skill were legendary. Here we see them working on the fish wharf built in the 1860s to deal with the vastly expanded trade. The male onlookers are probably fish salesmen.

27. SEAWEED COLLECTION

Though some varieties can be used to make lava bread the primary use of seaweed was as a fertilizer. In this card men and women are collecting seaweed for manure on the beach at Flamborough and making use of donkeys to transport it up the chalk cliffs. Notice the men in fishermen's hats. Between 1890 and 1914 the local fishing trade was severely depressed by competition from steam trawlers which it could not match. Soup kitchens were even set up for distressed local fishermen. However humble, seaweed collection was one means of supplementing an inadequate income. Donkeys were important beasts of burden in Edwardian England and these were doubtless used to take the cod catch up the cliffs.

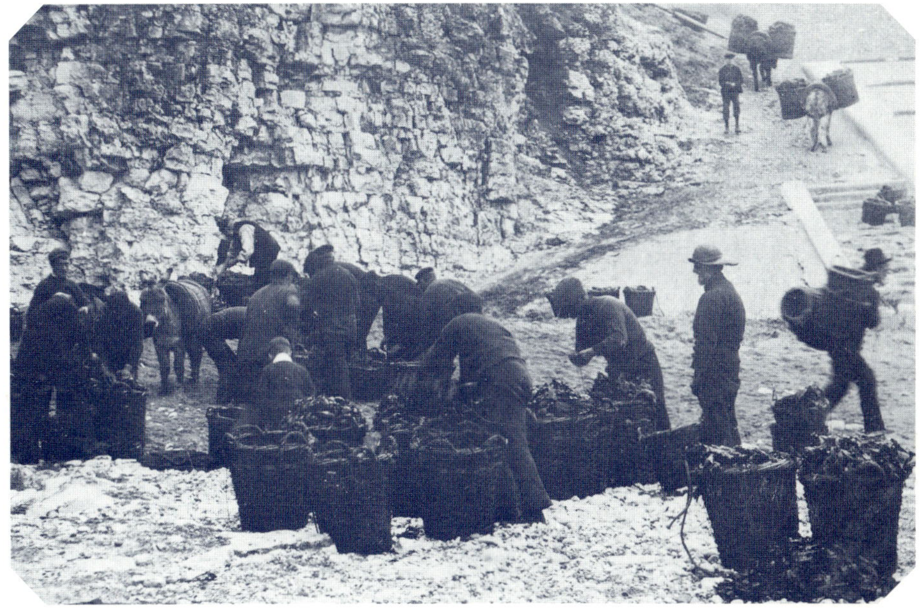

28. RURAL CRAFTS (i) BLACKSMITH

The blacksmith was the essential village craftsman while the horse remained the essential means of transport. Since all horse-owners brought their animals to him he became the repository of much local information. His forge offered the blacksmith many opportunities to diversify from the manufacture of horses' shoes to the making of various iron agricultural implements and also wheels if there was no wheelwright in the village. In this unidentified card the village blacksmith clearly employs sons or apprentices (there seems to be a family likeness). Blacksmith's shops often descended from father to son through several generations. A sharp drop in the number of working horses after 1900 put the blacksmith's trade in jeopardy from the tractor. Many smithies fell silent as that most secure of rural trades crumbled before the might of the internal combustion engine.

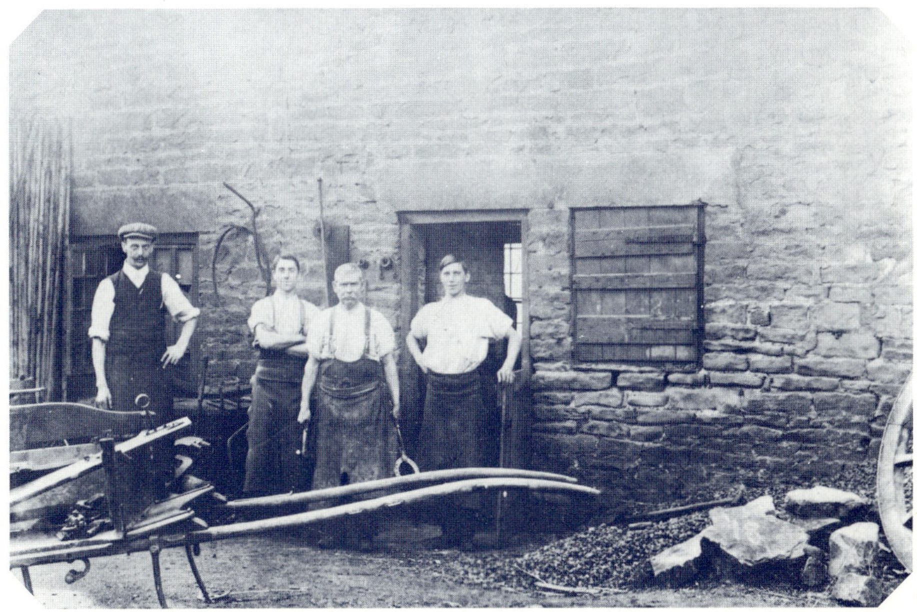

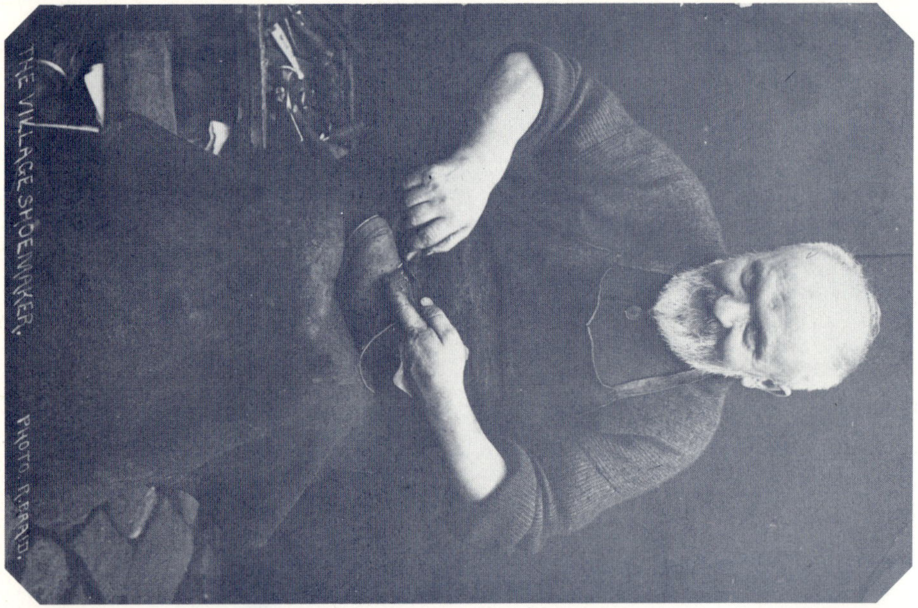


## 29. RURAL CRAFTS (ii) SHOEMAKER

Village shoemakers were beginning to be affected by the mechanization of the industry by 1900, but they had been important figures in rural society. They supplied ordinary villagers while the gentry would go to the market town or to London during the season for their more fashionable requirements. Possibly this induced in shoemakers a kind of resentful independence, for it is remarkable how often they were in the van of what radical politics or agitation the world of the village afforded. They tended to be anti-establishment and, because independent of the gentry, in no need of their largesse and unlikely to accord them deference. Anderson Graham's study of rural life in 1892 picked out the shoemaker as 'the most revolutionary spark in the village. . . . With both the parsons he is at feud, for lying beside his awls, his broad knives, his files, and his paste-pot, is a copy of *The Rights of Man* which is his Bible . . . neighbours whisper that he fears neither God, man, nor devil.'

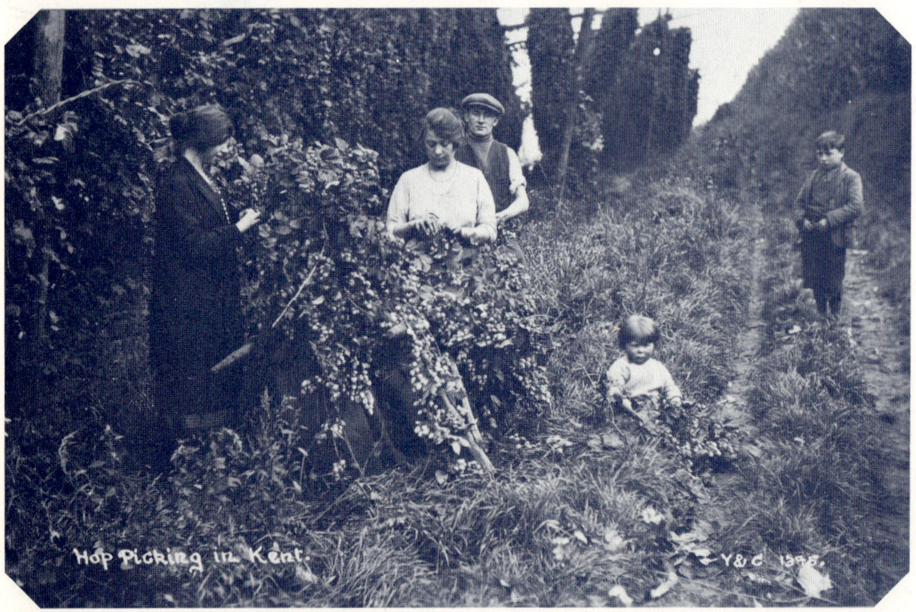


## 30. HOP PICKING

This is an idealized portrait of an occupation which was not so romantic as it sounds. Hop-picking attracted labourers' families supplementing insecure wages by a month's hard, physical labour in late August and September. Such seasonal work naturally attracted those from the great cities, particularly London, who did not have secure employment. Respectable commentators complained about the insanitary habits, squalor and profligacy the pickers brought into the Garden of England. Rider Haggard complained in 1902 that 'The adult pickers can scarcely any of them read, the young men being as ignorant as the old. . . . The majority, both of men and women, have no thought except for the public house and drink, and the girls are very wild.' It was a subject of adverse comment also that the hop-picking season took too many poor children away from the prying eyes of school attendance officers. As Haggard conceded, however, the annual sojurn in 'the blue sky of English summer' was a rare treat for those used to equally insanitary but much more crowded and oppressive conditions in east end slums. 'Hop and fruit picking is the annual holiday of tens of thousands . . . to them, indeed, what the autumn visit to sea or countryside is to other classes of town dwellers.'

# CHAPTER THREE | FOOD, SHOPS AND MARKETING

Almost four times as many people lived in Britain in 1900 as in 1800. 37 million mouths to feed as opposed to 10½ million represented a supreme challenge to British society and, more particularly, to food growers, importers, wholesalers and retailers. The challenge was met, if not effortlessly, then without undue strain, and it is arguably the biggest success story in British history. Not only was this vastly increased population fed; it enjoyed substantial rises in living standards after 1850 as the benefits of economic growth began to be enjoyed at last by a substantial majority of the workforce. This higher standard of living created yet larger demands for food, clothing and even luxuries which, again, wholesalers and retailers were able to meet. It was a truly stupendous achievement and one to which historians have paid too little attention.

Money wages doubled between 1850 and 1910, bringing obvious benefits to those workers, predominantly skilled, who were able to bargain with their employers for a larger slice of the growing industrial cake. A more important and more rapid development, however, was the 40 per cent fall in prices which took place between 1870 and 1895. Price falls in basic commodities benefit everyone but the poor are more substantially advantaged than the rich. The poor in an underdeveloped community spend nearly all their earnings on basic foodstuffs in the struggle to survive, probably on foods rich in carbohydrates for immediate energy but relatively low in protein and vitamins for balanced nourishment: more coarse bread than meat, far more potatoes than green vegetables and fruit. As real wages rise consumption patterns change. Not only is a smaller proportion of disposable income spent on low-grade foodstuffs but more is left for clothes and a few luxury items.

Britain experienced this transformation in stages between 1850 and 1940 but particularly during periods when prices fell. The only exception to this generalization, and it is an important one, concerns the unemployed. Prices fall generally during periods of economic depression; economic depression means higher unemployment; the unemployed and the underemployed do not share the privileges enjoyed by others. Between 1877 and 1887 the retail price of a typical workman's budget fell by 30 per cent. The reason is not far to seek. Far more food was imported during the last quarter of the nineteenth century than ever before. The American prairies, connected to the east coast by a developing railway system, provided enormous quantities of grain for Britain, disastrously undercutting the prices of the home producer. Refrigerated holds in the new steamships enabled the transport of beef from the Argentine, lamb from Australasia and pork from the United States. By 1914 British farmers supplied only half the home demand for meat. Similarly, steam trawlers and the use of ice enabled fish to be brought to ports like Fleetwood and Great Yarmouth and thence inland to the great industrial cities.

Caution has already been expressed about the extent to which all shared in the benefits of cheap food. The researches of Charles Booth and Seebohm Rowntree in the 1880s and 1890s revealed how meagre, stodgy, unappetizing and generally inadequate remained the diets of those on the margins of poverty. But for those earning, say, 25 shillings a week (£1.25) at the end of the nineteenth century meat and vegetables could be eaten daily with perhaps some breakfast-time bacon to supplement the diet. In working-class communities care was taken to ensure that the head of the household, on whose physical labour the wellbeing of the family in large part depended, 'ate his fill' to 'keep his strength up'; a utilitarian pecking order at table was commonplace. Women and children were more likely to be undernourished.

Bread remained the staple in the diet, of course, and at this time advances in technology provided a better loaf for the housewife to buy. Roller mills crushed the grain more effectively and even in the thousands of small bakeries which survived improvements were made in flour-sifting and dough-kneeding. Output and quality both improved and the range of grain-based foodstuffs was widened still more by the emergence of a mass-production biscuit industry. Huntley and Palmer of Reading, Peak Frean of Bermondsey and Carr of Carlisle offered hundreds of different lines for both the luxury and working-class markets. Co-operative stores alone sold 6 million lb of biscuits a year at the end of the century.

The most startling changes in nineteenth-century diet concerned the enormous growth in popularity of both tea and sugar. Only after 1850 did the 'cuppa', previously an upper-class luxury, become the national drink, a solace particularly of women whose menfolk sought escape from the bleakness of an industrial city in the public house. Just under 2 lb of tea per head per year was consumed in 1851; this had leaped to 6½ lb by 1911. The tea trade benefited from Gladstone's reductions in duty in the middle of the century. The resulting influx of Indian tea, which virtually displaced the China trade, permitted the new multiple stores, led by Lipton, to sell packaged tea at around 1*s* 6*d* (7½p) a pound from the late 1880s, undercutting by about 1*s* a pound traditional grocers who blended their own tea. The tea trade was in the forefront of commercial competition and some of the most adventurous competitors, like International Tea Stores, incorporated the word in their trade names in acknowledgement both of the speciality of their trade and its growing popularity.

The famous British sweet tooth, reflected also in jam and chocolate sales, was most notably exploited by the sugar refiners and traders. The same pattern of reduced duties, lower prices and increased consumption was observable, much West Indian sugar finding its way to the bottom of late-Victorian tea cups. Consumption increased from 13 lb a head a year in 1800 to 23 lb in 1850 and over 80 lb by 1900.

Not only were the British consuming more food; what they ate after 1870 or so was purer. Food adulteration was a major cause of illness in mid-Victorian Britain; the practice was harmful as well as fraudulent. Alum added to bread to whiten it, sulphuric acid to 'harden' new beer or iron sulphate to froth it, sand or China clay in tea, mineral dyes in sweets were all too common and the most common adulteration – dilution of beer or milk – was often by impure water anyway. Food legislation of 1872 and 1875, extended in 1899, brought the reports of public analysts before educated men and exposed adulteration officially. A few well-publicized cases brought rapid improvement and by 1914 minimum standards for the sale of spirits, milk, butter and margarine had been brought into effect. For the first time British consumers could be reasonably confident about the purity of the food and drink they bought.

The importance of alcoholic drink, especially beer, in late Victorian England is attested by the strength and determination of the temperance movement. Teetotallers regarded beer as the ultimate social and economic disaster, taking the head of the household away from the bosom of his family except when he returned to it to lay about wife and children in fits of inebriation. Drink deprived children of necessities; drink encouraged fecklessness and vicious habits; drink rendered the workman less efficient next morning; expenditure on drink was utter, woeful, waste. Non-beer drinkers might well share temperance reformers' distaste of this bulky and rebarbative beverage. In the 1870s more of the stuff was consumed than ever before or since. At its peak in 1876 more than 15 per cent of all consumer expenditure went on drink; the average per capita consumption was a staggering 34 gallons per head of the population, which probably meant almost 80 gallons for every adult male or 1¾ pints for every day of the year. Charles Booth estimated that many East-enders in London spent a quarter of their income on drink. Certainly the working classes committed themselves to greater proportionate expenditure on drink than their middle-class counterparts, and however sanctimonious some temperance criticism, it is futile to deny the deprivation this selfish male consumption engendered for wives and children.

Fortunately, the 1870s was a peak. By 1914 only 9 per cent of consumer expenditure was going on drink as the range of food and clothing options was widened by a retail revolution. Drink became less of a social problem and the wind, so to speak, was taken out of temperance sails. Improved living standards and increased leisure made the pub relatively less attractive to working-class men as the sole source of fun. Even at the height of its popularity, however, it was hardly the all-pervading source of iniquity characterized by the temperance reformers. Pubs provided the cheapest available source of heat, light and company in many a Victorian slum and most pubs were decently run. Nor should the nutritive value of beer to the working man be overlooked, though this was hardly an operative factor in taking him to the pub.

How did the retail trade cope with the expansion of consumption? During this period shops assumed a much more important role in working-class lives than hitherto. Before the industrial revolution fixed shop premises catered largely for middle-class and aristocratic clients. Also the production and retailing elements were much more closely integrated than became the case after 1850; shopkeepers tended to specialize in particular lines, having a knowledge of, and frequently investment in, production. Grocers would be primarily known for their tea, say, or their cheese, building up a reputable clientele through deep knowledge of that specialism.

This pattern was naturally adapted either to a small market town or to the fashionable areas of London where gentry and 'persons of quality' repaired during the season to sample the latest fashions or to stock up on blends of China tea for the winter. The needs of the lower orders were more basic. What they did not grow for themselves they bought at the local market, often haggling over the price, or from itinerant salesmen, peddlers or hawkers, many of whom offered cheap 'luxury' goods such as brightly coloured ribbons or buttons to provide that limited variety and individuality which brightened dull and monotonous lives. Few working-class wives were shoppers in the modern sense before the industrial revolution.

Markets remained important for working-class shoppers in the second half of the nineteenth century and, as consumer choice was widened by the availability of a larger range of mass-produced goods, they tended to become more specialized. Some towns, like Pontefract, sought release from the smells of rotting carcases in the open streets by building covered meat markets. Fish markets, as in Birmingham, became common but the old open market usually in the town centre continued to be a place of first resort for vegetables, cottons and a range of basic domestic requirements. The physical expansion of the larger towns made city-centre markets less convenient for day-to-day shopping at least until the development of adequate public transport and even then the poorer working-class families could rarely afford tram fares for shopping trips. Itinerant traders could fill some of the gaps by selling flowers, pots, cups and even glasses of beer around the streets. Street traders remain an important part of working-class purchasing patterns well into the twentieth century. But both they and the fixed central markets were losing ground to shops, and especially to the corner shop which became a focal point of many urban communities.

Corner shops were of necessity general stores stocking primarily non-perishable proprietary foodstuffs, confectionary, biscuits and a range of domestic necessities from cups to candles and boot laces to bromides. The advent of factory production of everyday commodities made it possible for families with no prior knowledge of the retail trade to set themselves up at little initial cost as shopkeepers. But corner shopkeepers in working-class areas needed to be acute businessmen, keen psychologists and prodigiously hard workers to survive. Serving communities which lived perilously close to the breadline and under it when depressions or strikes hit, they had to offer credit or lose vital trade, yet decisions on how much to allow and for how long had to be nicely calculated. Bankruptcy awaited both the unwary and the merely unlucky. Many suburban shopkeepers, like Robert Roberts's shrewd and determined mother in *The Classic Slum*, must regularly have taken decisions determining which families went hungry and which were trustworthy enough to be allowed a little more 'on the slate'.

It is difficult to document the rise of the corner shop and much more scholarly attention has been lavished on the multiple trading establishments. It needs to be remembered that as late as 1920 80 per cent of all retail sales were made in independent establishments (not all of them working-class corner shops, of course) and not in any of these larger and more ambitious enterprises. Working-class women shopped locally for a variety of reasons. It was convenient; many shops were open all hours; regular needs could be accommodated; local grocers might accede tactfully to delicate requests, such as the thin slicing of meat to make it 'go further' when money was short. Most of all, perhaps, the advance of credit to trusted customers eased the gap between pay days and enabled 'Sunday best' clothing to be redeemed from the pawnshop. Only the destitute or the feckless were refused modest credit by practical shopkeepers who were, after all, integral members of the community they served. With the emergence of other retailing outlets, moreover, credit and convenience were the small man's main hold on his trade as competition hotted up.

Though the importance of the local shop has been underplayed by most historians it cannot be denied that what Peter Mathias has called the 'Retailing Revolution' implied more exciting forms of selling. Increasingly severe competition for cash custom was experienced, especially in Scotland and the north of England, by the success of the Co-operative movement. The principle of profit sharing through the regular declaration of a dividend on purchases was one great attraction; the other was common ownership of the trading enterprise. Trading remained according to the tenets of the famous Rochdale 'pioneers' who established the first profit-sharing Co-op in 1844, but the scale expanded vastly at the end of the nineteenth century. Between 1881 and 1914 membership of Co-operative societies increased from 500,000 to more than 3 million. The basis of trading was food, but diversification into boots, shoes and drapery, amongst others, began. Profits were high and dividends of 4*s* – 5*s* in the pound (20–25p) were not uncommon, especially in the north. The establishment of the Co-operative Wholesale Society in 1863 enabled societies to rely increasingly on their own brands. The range of food goods available for sale was vastly increased.

Independent grocers hated the sales attraction of the 'divvi' almost as much as they were outraged by the co-operative principle against the sturdy precepts of individual self-reliance which their own ethos inculcated. The grocers launched vituperative attacks: Co-op service was inadequate; their wholesale products were inferior, despite vaunted claims to purity and no adulteration; their dividend was essentially fraudulent in that customers received back only a portion of what they had paid out over weeks and months in the form of higher prices. This counter-attack, if we may so term it, had little success. The onwards march of the Co-ops was not halted. But the independent grocer retained an important advantage in the battle for custom. He could use credit as a weapon to retain customers not absolutely confident of their unvarying ability to pay cash on the nail. Co-ops were primarily cash concerns, though some branch managers, against strict official policy, were persuaded of the value of limited credit to keep favoured and regular customers. Cash sales were not only a business principle for the Co-ops. They derived from a feeling, strong among members of the societies, that the only honourable course was 'pay as you go; if you can't pay, you don't go'. The links between northern nonconformist principle and co-operative practice were firm.

The other prong of the dual challenge to the independent shopkeepers was provided by the multiple stores. Although W. H. Smith and John Menzies had established profitable chains of station newspaper and bookstalls for a literate travelling public in the 1850s the real expansion of multiples came from the 1870s and concentrated on food. Among the pioneers were Lipton, Home and Colonial and Maypole. Thomas Lipton built up a flourishing business in Glasgow, then in Dundee in the 1870s by selling large quantities of imported meats, Irish beef and American hams, at prices 25–50 per cent lower than those in traditional shops. With butter, cheese and eggs these formed the basis of his early success. Not until 1889 did he diversify into the famous blends of tea which bore his name. These he sold for 1*s* 2*d*–1*s* 9*d* a pound when family grocers charged 3*s*–4*s* (15–20p). In 1889 he had more than 30 shops and employed over 1,000 people. Due to the phenomenal success of his teas he had no less than

242 branches 9 years later, 72 of them in London, to which he had now moved his head office.

The Maypole chain, by contrast, developed from an established middle-class base into the working-class market. Its specialism was dairy produce, butter, margarine and the new line, condensed milk. Its main period of expansion was the Edwardian age, a period of generally rising prices when the ability of the multiples to announce cost-cutting or cost-pegging promotions was especially attractive. Maypole bought in bulk a relatively small range of products of reliable quality. From the beginning the multiples aimed at consistent standards as well as lower prices; they undoubtedly helped to improve the overall quality of food available to working-class families. Home and Colonial, with a strong southern emphasis, began trading in 1885 and had opened over 500 branches by 1903. The firm specialized in creamery butter, cheese and tea.

The whole rationale of the multiple stores implied lower profit margins than those of the established grocers, but a much faster turnover. Widespread advertising was also important to bring the offers before public notice. Lower prices do not automatically attract customers to lines they have not previously considered buying. The most telling advertisements, which even the smaller grocers were forced to emulate, were town centre shop windows carefully decorated with a range of goods prominently, even vulgarly, priced. Additionally, the new shop chains were among the first to offer gimmicks – prizes, special offers, publicity stunts and the like. In this latter field Thomas Lipton, an enormous self-publicist, took a prominent part. He was said to spend £40,000 a year on advertising in the 1890s. He offered Queen Victoria a five-ton cheese to celebrate her golden jubilee in 1887 (an offer politely declined) and he distributed free jubilee gifts of bacon and eggs to the poor with maximum publicity. Advertising hoardings, space on buses and, at first gingerly, newspaper space were all exploited. The age of mass advertising had begun.

The spread of multiple stores in foods was particularly rapid. Jeffereys calculated that the 277 grocery and provisions multiples trading in 1880 had been expanded to 5,870 in 1910 and 7,880 by 1920. Meat and milk multiples, virtually unknown in 1880, had 3,828 and 324 stores respectively by 1910. Changes after this date were more in style and presentation than in kind. Food shops were by no means the only multiples, however. Factory developments in hosiery, knitwear, tailoring and shoes all invited retail competition in the High Streets. In the last decade of the nineteenth century stores such as J. Crook of Manchester, J. Hepworth of Leeds, Hope Bros. and G. A. Dunn of London expanded the number of their retail outlets to cater for an expanding working-class market in ready-made clothes and the ubiquitous hats and caps of the period. By 1900 Hepworths, with over a hundred branches, was the largest tailor in Britain.

Between 1900 and 1920 the more complicated but professionally more rewarding move towards mass orders for made-to-measure suits and jackets was made. Some famous names, like Montague Burton, had begun in ready-made clothing but concentrated more heavily between 1900 and 1920 on the 'bespoke' trade; others, like the County Tailoring Company of Leeds and London and Rego Clothiers were specialist bespoke firms. Edwardian shop frontages were plastered with Burtons or Rego price stickers boldly advertising the 20*s* or the 30*s* (£1–£1.50) suit. In an age which necessarily made a clear-cut distinction between working apparel and 'Sunday best' these developments were almost bound to succeed. The established middle-class market also found it worthwhile to adjust to some at least of the marketing innovations and promotions pioneered by Hepworths and Burtons. Austin Reed Ltd, while retaining a firm base in the quality trade reflected in a higher run of prices and better cuts of cloth, expanded the range of their activities and appealed to a wider market.

Before the 1870s boot and shoe shops were regionally based, but once factory production became feasible the cost-cutting and aggressive selling of the national chains moved into the trade. George Oliver, with branches in the midlands and south Wales, was among the early leaders, but his more famous competitors, Freeman Hardy & Willis and Stead & Simpson, were well established by 1900 with fully national retail chains emerging thereafter.

The British, urban Englishmen in particular, are a race of hypochondriacs. Every adult knew that Beecham's pills were worth 'a guinea a box' as the advertising slogan confidently but unspecifically put it. Anyone who scans the pages of local or national newspapers from almost their earliest days will be struck by the extraordinary amount of advertising space purchased by the makers of proprietary medicines. Only the prevailing targets of the advertisers change. Readers in the 1980s want to know how to cure acne, to alleviate 'pressure headaches', to ward off coronary disease by a diet rich in polyunsaturated fats or, merely, to acquire a quasi-Mediterranean tan. Their Edwardian forbears were more interested in lumbago, sciatica, gout, kidney complaints or how to cope with being 'run down'. The pharmaceutical companies profitably nourished the appetite for 'cures'. It is not surprising that so much advertising space should be lavished on medicines and placebos; profits, then as now, were among the highest in the retail trade. Where health is concerned the public is all too easily convinced that the dearer the medicine the more efficacious its properties.

Between 1865 and 1905 the number of licensed vendors of medicines increased from about 10,000 to over 40,000. The opportunities for an entrepreneur with a basic knowledge of 'remedies' and appropriate drive were immense. Such a man was Jesse Boot, son of a fervent Wesleyan Methodist shopkeeper selling 'vegetable remedies' in a little Nottingham shop. His father died young and Jesse took over the shop in Goosegate. By direct purchase from the manufacturers he was able to sell, as his shop window announced, 'Drugs and Proprietary Articles at Reduced Prices'. From the late 1870s people sought out Boot's shop to obtain drugs at prices cut on exactly the same principles as those employed by the great food chains: bulk purchase from carefully selected wholesalers, large turnover, lower profit per unit compensated by number of units sold. Until the 1890s Boot consolidated in the east midlands and south Yorkshire; thereafter expansion, both in the number of shops and the range of goods stocked, was phenomenal. In 1907 he was striking a recognizably modern note by advertising in the *Daily Mail* 'We have branches in all the principal towns and are the largest gift sellers in the country.' The combination of medicines, perfumes, stationery and gifts was proving exceptionally attractive.

No survey of changing shopping habits would be complete without mention of Marks & Spencer. Other multiple traders worked on the principle of a clearly marked list of prices undercutting the competition. Michael Marks's original concept was to have a fixed price for an enormous range of household goods, sold first from market stalls and, later, a bazaar. 'Don't ask the price; it's a penny', ran the slogan. Five 'penny bazaars' had been established in Leeds, Castleford, Wakefield, Warrington and Birkenhead, by 1890. In 1900 Marks & Spencer (the partnership began in 1894) owned 36 outlets, only 12 of which were shops, and the concern was spreading south. In 1903 a branch was opened under the railway arches in Brixton (south London). The sign outside read 'Original Penny Bazaar, Admission Free' and the location was characteristically resourceful. Until 1914, though some unsuccessful attempts were made to create 6*d* bazaars in larger branches, the penny bazaar policy held the field.

After 1918 Marks & Spencer concentrated on town-centre sites and on selling good-quality British textile goods bearing the distinctive 'St Michael' label. Competition was increasingly reckoned to come from the American Woolworth chain of High Street stores which had been successfully transplanted from the early years of the century and which also offered a wide range of fixed price lines. A new Marks and Spencer price limit of 5*s* (25p) was introduced in 1927, ushering in a period of further change in marketing. If Marks were consciously moving up-market from their bazaar origins they took many of their working-class customers with them. Middle-class shoppers were increasingly attracted to the lower prices and reliable quality of the better shops designed originally for their social inferiors, while the department stores began to find customers from the skilled workers in permanent employment. In shopping perhaps earlier than in any other aspect of life social distinctions were becoming blurred.

No change in middle-class shopping habits was more important than the emergence of the department store. Department stores expanded in London from the 1870s, often in shops previously specializing in drapery, linens and haberdashery such as Swan & Edgar or Marshall & Snelgrove. The aim was to delight the eye of fashionable ladies with an array of household furnishings, china, pictures and possibly good food and wine all collected under one roof; some even offered a banking service and sold London theatre tickets. Two of the best known, Harrods and Fortnum & Mason began life as high-class grocers. The latter, formed as long ago as 1707, did not emphasize other activities until the twentieth century; the former took the plunge rather earlier and became, along with William Whiteley, the 'Universal Provider' (see Caption 9), one of the biggest of all department stores by 1900.

Department stores were successfully designed to become places of fashionable resort, at particular times of the day the female equivalent almost of the London club. Regent St, Oxford St and Bond St in London's west end had been fashionable long before department stores, but two new areas further west now gained fashionable status. The development of Kensington and Knightsbridge was due in no small measure to the success of Derry & Thoms (a partnership begun in 1862), John Barker (founded 1870) and Seaman, Little & Co. (1870). A little to the north, Whiteley held court at Westbourne Grove, Bayswater, on the very edge of Notting Hill. Whiteley, who set up shop in 1863, rapidly pulled in competitors and emulators. By 1909 Sir Walter Besant could remark that the ladies of the area 'are not obliged to go to Regent Street and Bond Street for the newest fashions and the most costly materials, for they can find these things on the spot.'

It would be wrong to imply that London had a monopoly of department stores or even that their development began there (Caption 8). However, Kendal Milne of Manchester and Bainbridge of Newcastle drew new ideas and vigour from the London renaissance as did other, later, provincial stores such as Lewis's of Manchester, Sheffield and Birmingham, Fenwicks of Newcastle or Bobby's of Margate and Torquay. The opening of Gordon Selfridge's mammoth purpose-built new trading establishment in Oxford St in 1909 marked the apotheosis of the department store and confirmed London's supremacy. Specialist window dressers were employed here full time for the first time in Britain; their designs were brightly lit until midnight. Cosmetics and perfumes were put on open display for the first time – a daringly un-Victorian innovation. A new stage in luxurious marketing had begun.

Mention should be made finally of the impact of the retailing revolution on the catering trade. Middle-class Englishmen are still less knowledgeable about restaurant food then they might be, but in the Victorian period the disturbing comforts of adolescent single-sex fraternization acquired perforce at public school and continued in the unnatural womb of the London clubs acted against the development of restaurants in which ladies could eat without exciting scandal. The situation was slow to change. But from the late 1860s good restaurants, associated as often as not with theatres, like the Gaiety restaurant, were opened. Some cosmopolitan souls even braved foreign cuisine in Soho. By 1900 the erstwhile monopoly of good eating places exercised by the direfully insular London clubs had been broken. In the provinces, however, specialist restaurants were slower to emerge. Theatres and other places of entertainment, to which a good meal could be added to round off an evening, were themselves thinner on the ground; and a good many of the wealthy men, who were in any case less numerous than in London, regarded eating out as a peculiarly wasteful form of self-indulgence.

Lower down the social scale a need for mass catering developed, particularly after 1900 as the expansion of office and clerical jobs meant more demand for town-centre lunches. It was met first by the Lyons tea shops and corner houses. Joseph Lyons opened his first teashop in Piccadilly in 1894, yet only 8 years later 1,000 dining rooms and 800 refreshment rooms were in existence. The secret of success was much the same as with the multiple shops: reliability, value for money represented by economy rather than mere cheapness, high turnover and low unit profits. A further parallel was the close relationship between manufacturing and retail. Indeed, Lyons were soon making more from their proprietary cakes, bread and teas than from sales of meals and snacks. Nevertheless, the rise in standards both of cheap meals and of the service provided by Lyons waitresses – the Nippys – was decisive. As the magazine *The Empire* reflected in 1900: 'Lyons have deliberately killed the old fashioned chop-house keeper with his dirty kitchen, horse-box cubicles, cracked crockery, discoloured pewter cutlery, fuddled waiters and steep prices.' Between the wars the spate of Lyons emulators, Kardomah and the rest, ensured that the gains won by the first successful mass caterers should not be lost when Lyons diverted more of their resources into food manufacture and wholesaling. It would be pleasant to think that Lyons and Kardomah did not open a direct line in succession to the transatlantic vulgarity of Kwikbite, Wimpy Bar and Tennessee Pancake House in our own day; sadly it would not be entirely accurate.

The development of the British hotel trade, at least in its upper reaches, depended significantly on the railway companies. Most of the big hotels in the industrial cities, like the Midland in Manchester, the Queen's in Birmingham or the Royal Victoria in Sheffield, were erected by the owners of the competing lines. By the early twentieth century some railway hotels were offering standards of such luxury that it might have seemed that the companies, having been responsible for bringing the customer to the town, wished to ensure that he should have no excuse to leave his hotel and explore it.

London strove mightily after 1850 to catch up with other European and American capitals in the provision of appropriately commodious accommodation for the well-heeled traveller. Again, the railway companies took a major part. The Great Western, Great Northern and

Great Eastern, all on the sites of major London termini, catered for visiting businessmen both from the provinces and from abroad. Private hoteliers found the speculation profitable, particularly as foreign business and tourist trades developed and new standards of luxury were set by such establishments as the Grand, Metropole, Russell and Cecil. By 1888 one xenophobe had had enough. Charles Eyre Pascoe blamed the 'monster hotel' for stooping to tout for custom from 'the idlers of the globe. Americans, French, Germans, Indians, Colonials . . .'

By the first years of the twentieth century hotel promoters had acquired a pretty precise notion of the clientele they aimed to attract. Lyons, who built the Strand Palace Hotel in 1909, employed the agency Samson Clark and Company to plan their promotional literature. Clark reported:

*In preparing my suggestive* [*sic*] *scheme for advertising I have paid most attention to methods of reaching the provincial middle-class public. It is from them that you will doubtless obtain most of your support, and accordingly, I have allowed more for papers with large general circulations than restricted 'class' papers of the Times type.*

When the hotel opened its doors a single room with breakfast could be had for 5*s* 6*d* (27½p) and dinner cost between 2*s* 6*d* and 3*s* 6*d* (12½–17½p). At a rough calculation, therefore, dinner, bed and breakfast in a good quality (but not the most opulent) London hotel could be had in 1909 for about one-third of the average weekly wage at that time. Though the raw figures seem impossibly generous, the proportion is not significantly different in the early 1980s. By 1934 the price of a single room had risen to 9*s* 6*d* (47½p) with 1*s* (5p) slot meters in bedrooms, giving 6 hours' heating; *table d'hôte* supper, however, remained at 3*s* (15p).

That a good hotel could be built, designed to cater primarily for the provincial middle class, is indicative of rising general standards of prosperity. Food was now cheaper in real terms; the range of options open both to the working class above the poverty line and to the middle class had expanded remarkably since the mid-nineteenth century and a 'retailing revolution' had taken place to accommodate and to extend still further already rising expectations. Retailers played a full part in making Britain a more prosperous society able to enjoy the fruits of economic growth. Though millions remained desperately poor in 1930, as in 1914 or 1900, millions more were learning how to escape from that grinding poverty which suppresses choice and makes life nothing more than a constant struggle for survival. In these years Britain was beginning to emerge as a consumer society.

## FURTHER READING


Adburgham, A., *Shops and Shopping, 1800–1914* (London, 1964)

Alexander, D., *Retailing in England during the Industrial Revolution* (London, 1970)

Burnett, J., *Plenty and Want: A Social History of Diet in England from 1815 to the Present Day* (London, 1966)

Chapman, S., *Jesse Boot of Boots the Chemists* (London, 1974)

Davis, D., *A History of Shopping* (London, 1966)

Dyos H. & Wolff, M., *The Victorian City* (London, 2 vols, 1973)

Harrison, B., *Drink and the Victorians* (London, 1971)

Jeffereys, J., *Retail Trading in Britain, 1850–1950* (London, 1954)

Mathias, P., *Retailing Revolution* (London, 1967)

Oddy, D. & Miller, D., (eds.) *The Making of the Modern British Diet* (London, 1976)

Olsen, D., *The Growth of Victorian London* (London, 1976)

Rees, G., *St Michael: A History of Marks and Spencer* (London, 1969)

Roberts, R., *The Classic Slum* (Pelican edn., London, 1973)

1. OPEN MARKET, WOLVERHAMPTON

This card, dating from *c.*1905, shows the importance of markets in the centre of a large industrial town. This open-air market sold fresh fruit, vegetables and flowers. On the right of the picture stands the Retail Market Hall, built in 1853 at a cost of £30,000; it provided a light, airy location for the sale of meat, fresh fish, poultry, glass, cheap china and bric-a-brac. Just visible (extreme left) is a significant new development, the Wholesale Market in Wulfruna Street. This large and elaborate brick and terra-cotta building was opened in 1903, primarily to supply the surrounding area with imported goods, fruit and vegetables. Vendors and purchasers are easily distinguishable in this card and it is clear that the open market was a proper place for respectable ladies to shop. The imposing church in the background is St Peter's, Wolverhampton's parish church.

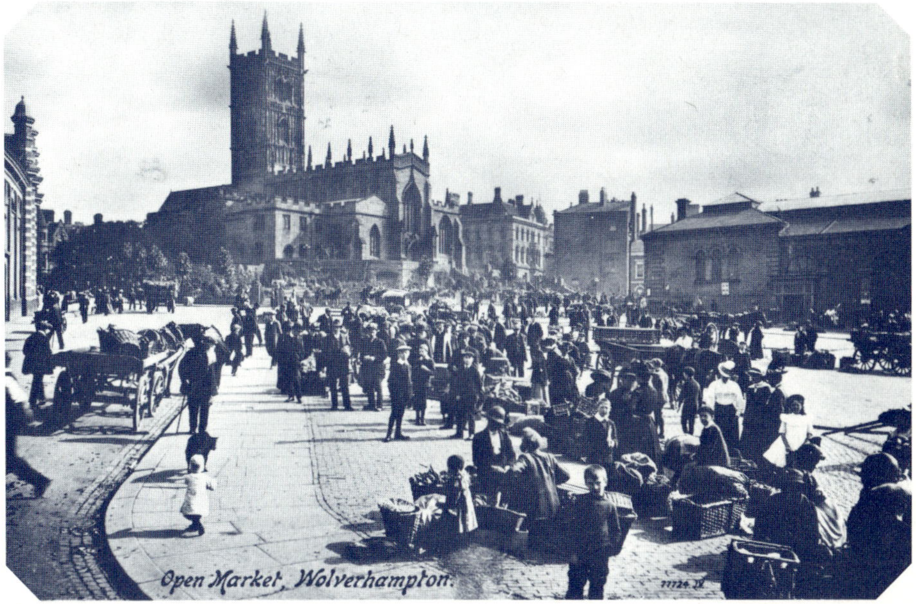


2. BIRMINGHAM MARKET HALL

A covered market, giving an impression of bustling activity. The Doric market hall, designed by Charles Edge and opened in 1835, was lit by gaslight and sold a wide range of provisions but specialized in flowers, fresh fruit and vegetables. Birmingham had a separate covered fish market. Bird's have established a monopoly of rafter space in this Edwardian card, advertizing their famous custard and blancmange powders and lemonade. Note the '1*d* Bazaar' on the right. This was in emulation of Michael Marks's brilliant idea to offer a range of goods at a fixed price. The combination of enormous variety (from cups to confectionery and haberdashery) and bargain prices proved irresistible and Marks's penny bazaars – the foundation of the Marks and Spencer stores – spawned many imitators. The hall was demolished during construction of Birmingham's inner ring road (Queensway) in the late 1960s.

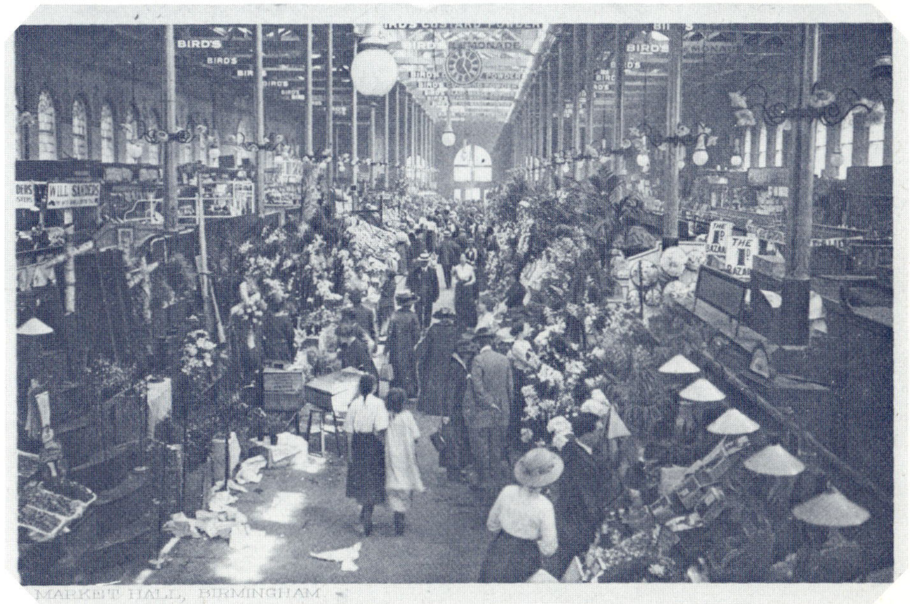

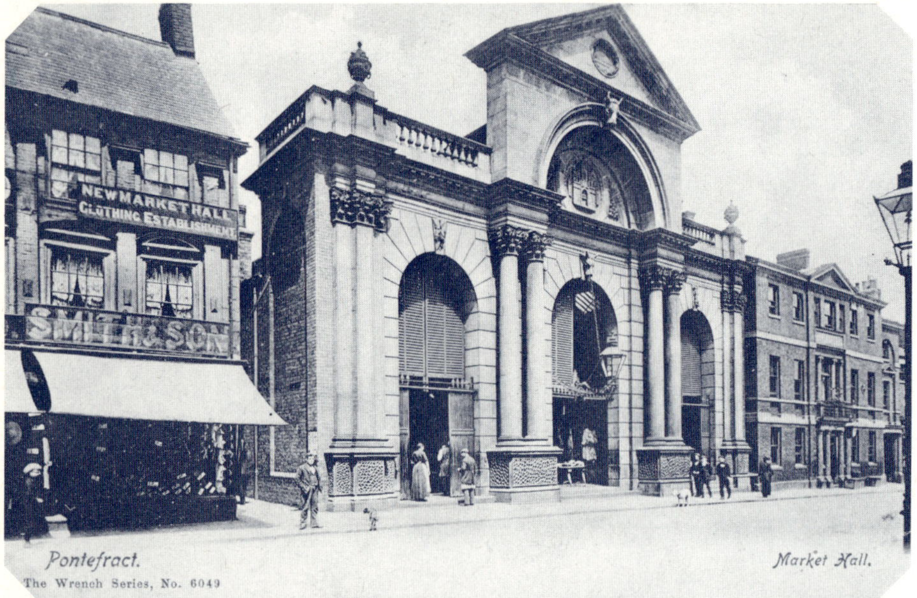


3. PONTEFRACT MARKET HALL

Pontefract was one of the west riding's leading market towns and a centre for the meat trade. This monument to commercial pride was built in 1859–60 to house butchers whose offal in the open markets around the old Shambles created health hazards. The facade, shown here, was designed and built by the Bath architect, James Wilson; it cost more than £5,000. The two bulls' heads (centre colonnade) are clear; less obvious are the small fowl on top of the arch to left and right of the central pillars. The town crest is carved between the two bulls' heads. Palmerston, then Prime Minister, opened the building with much pomp in 1860. Behind the facade, things did not go well. Butchers complained of excessive heat, dust and gloom in the 40 market stalls. Customers shopped in poor conditions and the heat only accelerated the process of decay; much meat all too obviously outstayed its welcome. The meat market was pulled down in 1957 and replaced by a more general modern trading area. Local pressure fortunately preserved this Cotswold stone facade, incongruous now in an otherwise unremarkable pedestrian precinct.

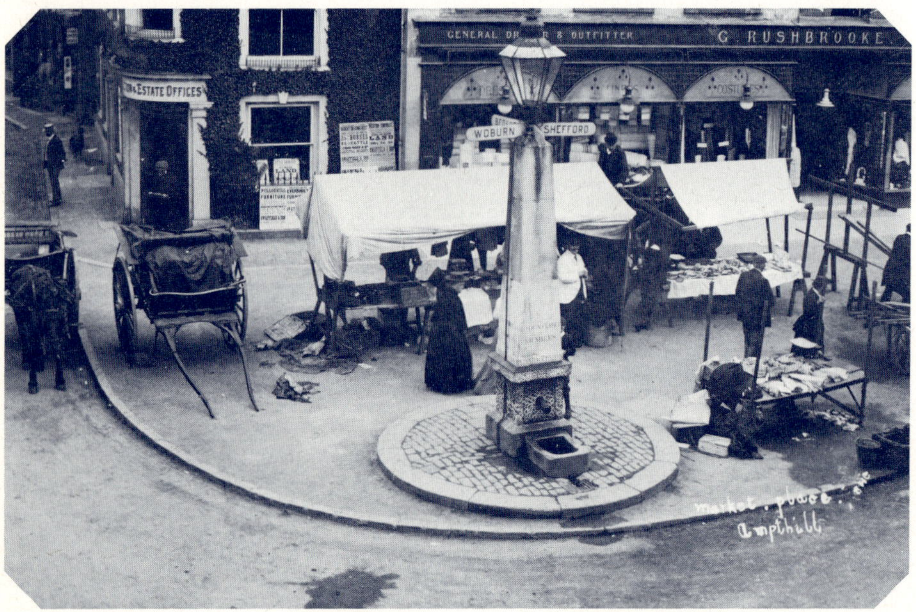


4. AMPTHILL MARKET

A small open market in a country town. Ampthill, eight miles south of Bedford, had a population of just over 2,100 in 1901, about the time this picture was taken. The lady in the foreground seems to be wearing a Bedfordshire straw hat, a product of one of the local industries which still survived. This market supplied only domestic necessities but a cattle market was held twice a year and an annual fair on Michaelmas Day. George Rushbrooke's shop, in the background, amounted to a department store. He advertised himself as 'draper, milliner, costumier, gents' outfitter, complete house furnisher, cycle dealer and warehouseman' and he had one other store in the town. The estate offices were the premises of Swaffield & Son, who also arranged insurance. The card offers a neat example of old and new trading juxtaposed in a rural area.

5–7. STREET TRADERS

Street trading remained a most important source for goods at least until the First World War. In general, street traders were of lower status and greater transience than shopkeepers, but a strict hierarchy existed. At one end regular traders with a vegetable or milk round, at the other casual itinerant hawkers selling wares of dubious origin at cheap prices in the slums. The casualty rate was high among traders, but the overheads were low and the opportunity to make a quick profit lured many into transient flirtations with a barrow and assorted trinkets. Hawkers were the Edwardian descendants of pedlars and the freedom, if uncertain rewards, of the life was valued. In respectable areas, forbidding iron notices brusquely announcing 'No Hawkers' were designed to distance the well-to-do from scruffy itinerants. Working people were happy to buy tin mugs (if they could not afford china), colanders and bowls from street traders and save on shop prices. Seafood was often hawked on carts. Card No. 5 shows Morecambe Bay shrimps on sale in the streets of Barrow in 1906. In Edwardian Birmingham regular sales of sprats were made by street dealers and enough bream could be bought to give a family of five a meal for 2½*d* (1p). In poorer quarters, milk could be bought in the streets by the cupful; ½*d* a cup was the regular pre-war price. Cards 6 & 7 show street traders operating in 'respectable' neighbourhoods. 'Guinea Pig Jack' presumably hoped to sell children's pets and he has an envious young onlooker. The young man with the horse is a flower seller. The possession of horse or, as here, donkey to pull one's cart was a symbol of superior trading status.

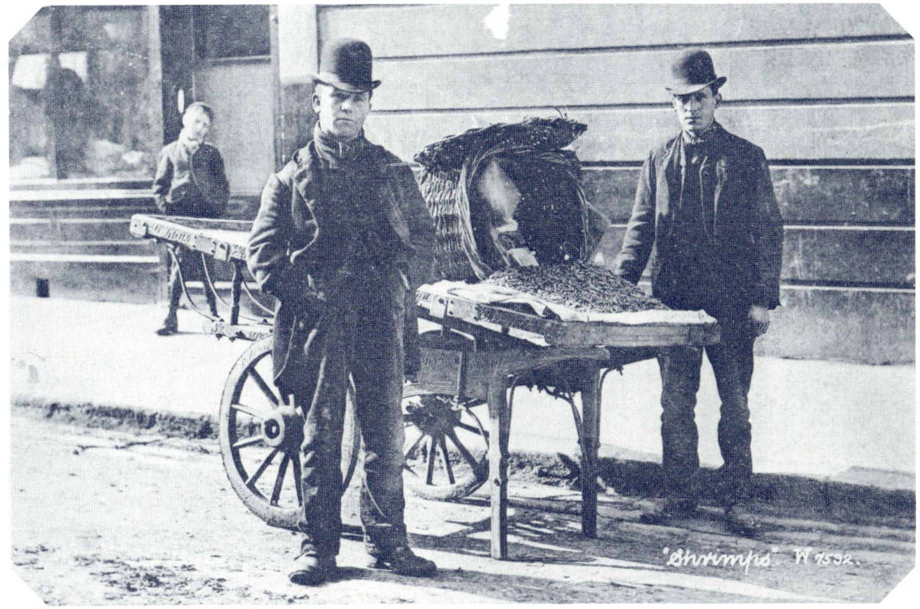


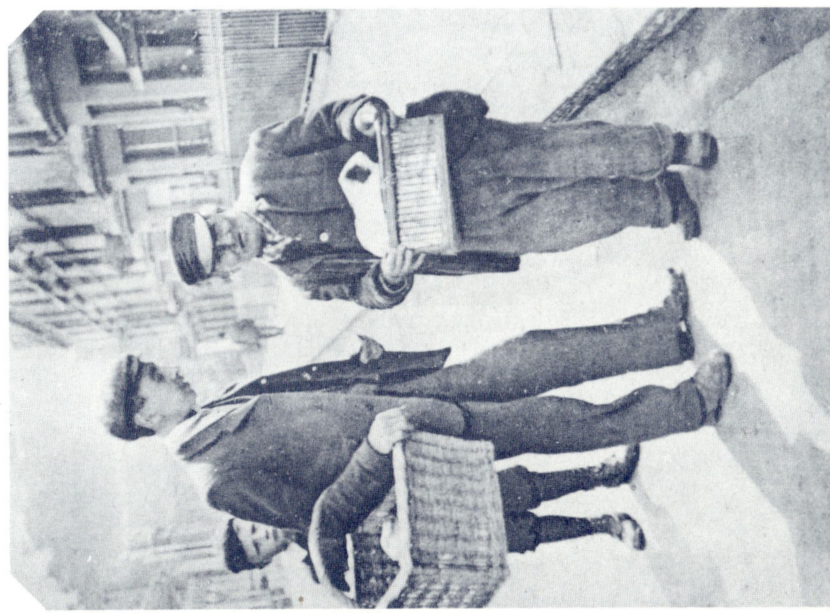

GUINEA PIG JACK

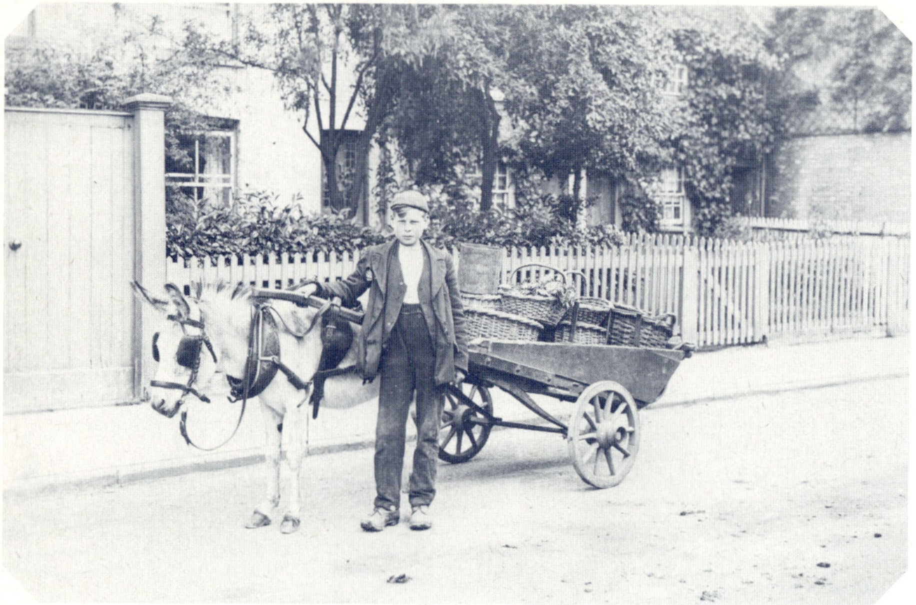

7. (See page 67)

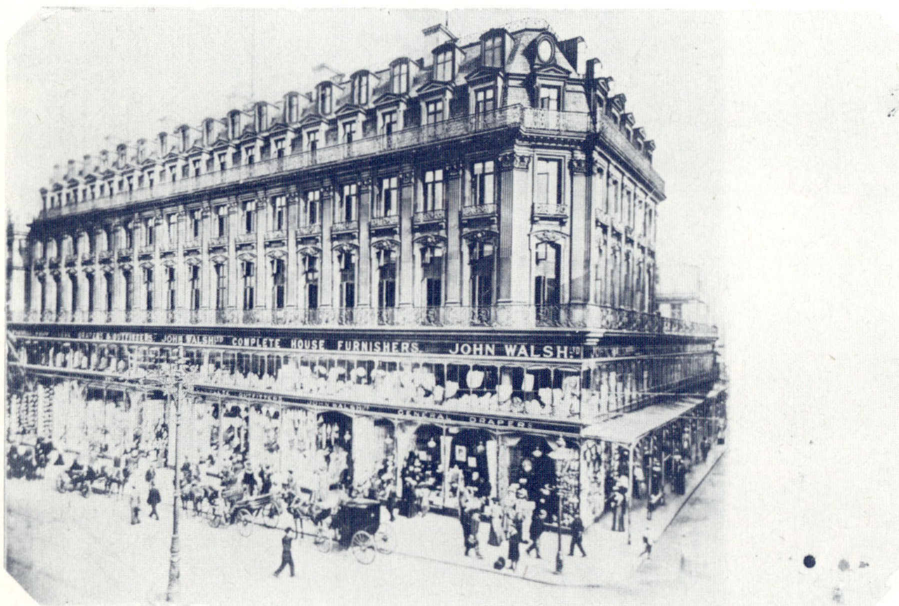


8. JOHN WALSH, DEPARTMENT STORE, MANCHESTER

Department stores offered an initially prosperous clientele the opportunity to shop in comfort and luxury for a wide range of goods, though the basis of all was clothing, haberdashery and millinery. Customers could browse, with no obligation to purchase, from department to department, picking up ideas for fashions and furnishings in the process. The emphasis was on presentation and style, attributes by no means a monopoly of fashionable London society. In many respects Kendal Milne & Faulkener of Manchester and Bainbridge of Newcastle anticipated Selfridges and Debenhams in London's West End. Both were trading as recognizable department stores as early as the 1830s. Though credit was offered to favoured regular customers, the main means of purchase in department stores was cash, since the stores prided themselves on a rapid turnover of good quality items at lower prices than those of fashionable milliners offering extended credit. Late afternoons became the fashionable time to shop at department stores and here we see ladies' carriages drawn up outside John Walsh Ltd, 'Drapers & Outfitters, the Complete House Furnishers' in Manchester in 1908.

## 9. WESTBOURNE GROVE, BAYSWATER

Westbourne Grove became a fashionable shopping centre in the late nineteenth century as middle-class dwellings were erected to the west of London. By 1887 *Modern London* called it 'the Bond Street of the West'. The most important influence on the street was undoubtedly William Whiteley, whose competitive north country business sense launched him from modest beginnings in haberdashery to the self-styled eminence of 'Universal Provider'. His store occupied Nos. 31–55 and here, in the lace department, he was murdered by a man alleged to be his unacknowledged, illegitimate son in 1907. Henry Dobb's drapers at 5–7 Westbourne Grove stood from the late nineteenth century until the early 1930s. He kept other drapery establishments in W2 at Queen's Road and Douglas Place. Next to Dobbs at No. 3 stood one of the famous Lyons tea shops. Interestingly, Bourne & Hollingsworth's first department store was opened in Westbourne Grove before they took the prudent decision to move to Oxford Street.

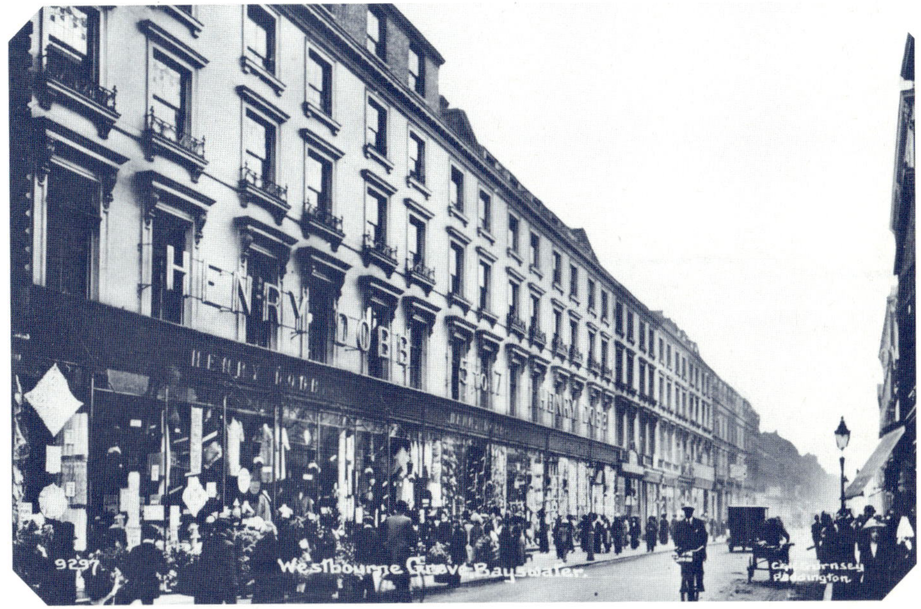


## 10. QUEEN STREET, BARNSLEY

This card, dating from 1914 or 1915, shows a typical town-centre combination of both multiple and individual stores. The Maypole store occupied its site from 1911 to 1929 but Hepworths (left) removed from rather cramped accommodation in 1916. The shop nearest camera next to Maypole was Jackson's the hatter and the prominent advertising display '3/9' was the price of a bowler. Ladies' and gents' boots also sold at the unvarying price of 10*s* 6*d* (52½p). Prominently displayed, permanent prices were an important element in shop design. Next to Jackson's stood Benjamin Gaunt, a prosperous local jeweller, whose shop stood on this site until 1929. It is now occupied by the Samuel jewellery chain. Queen St in the 1980s is a pedestrian precinct; all the buildings on the right have been demolished and the space is now filled by a featureless plate-glass Woolworth building.

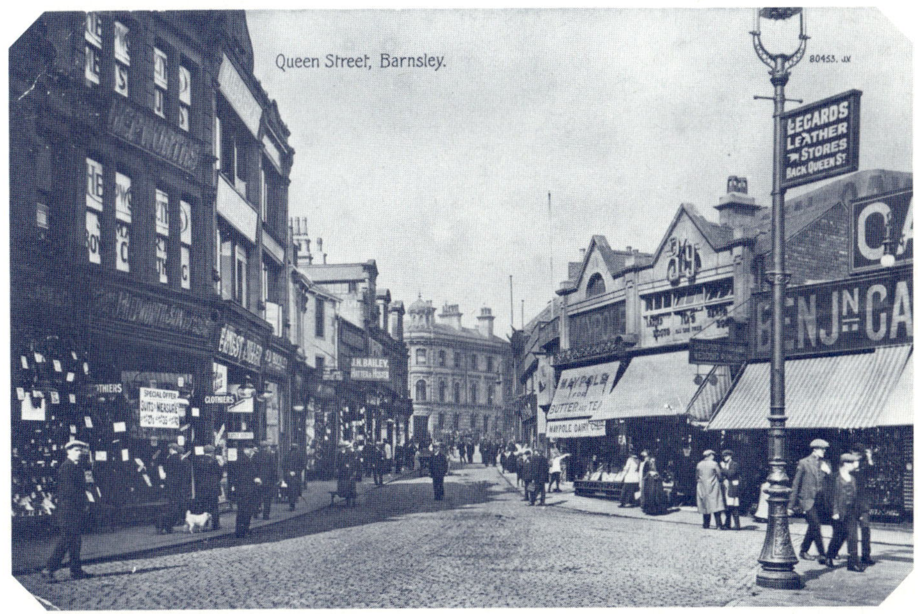

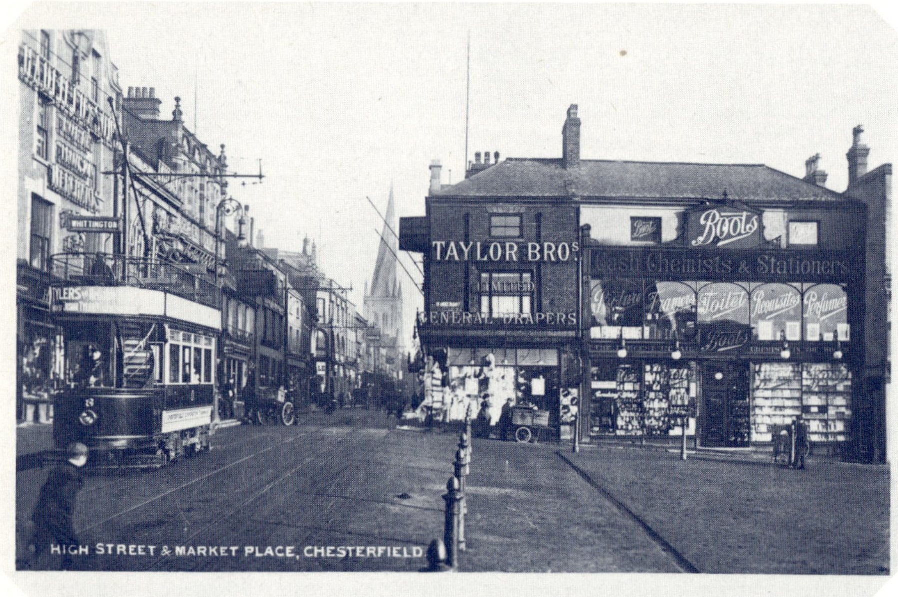


11. HIGH STREET AND MARKET PLACE, CHESTERFIELD
As in Barnsley the main shopping street, seen here *c.*1920, is a mixture of multiples and individual stores. Next to Taylor's general drapers on High St stands a 'Mourning Warehouse' and opposite it, with unintentional ghoulish irony, a photographic shop. The prominent position of Boots the Chemist is no accident for this is a Boots card, in its Pelham series of leading Boots stores. By 1920, over 600 branches were in existence, though its midland and northern origins were still reflected to some extent in their regional distribution. Boots early branched out from proprietary medicines into toilet requisites, perfumes, stationery and photography. By 1917 the company's manufacturing and retail work-force exceeded 12,000 and it advertised proudly on its shopfronts, as here, 'The Largest Retail Chemists in the World.' By poignant contrast a solitary knife and scissors grinder is at work outside the shop. In the background the famous crooked spire of Chesterfield's St Mary and All Saints Church is plainly visible.

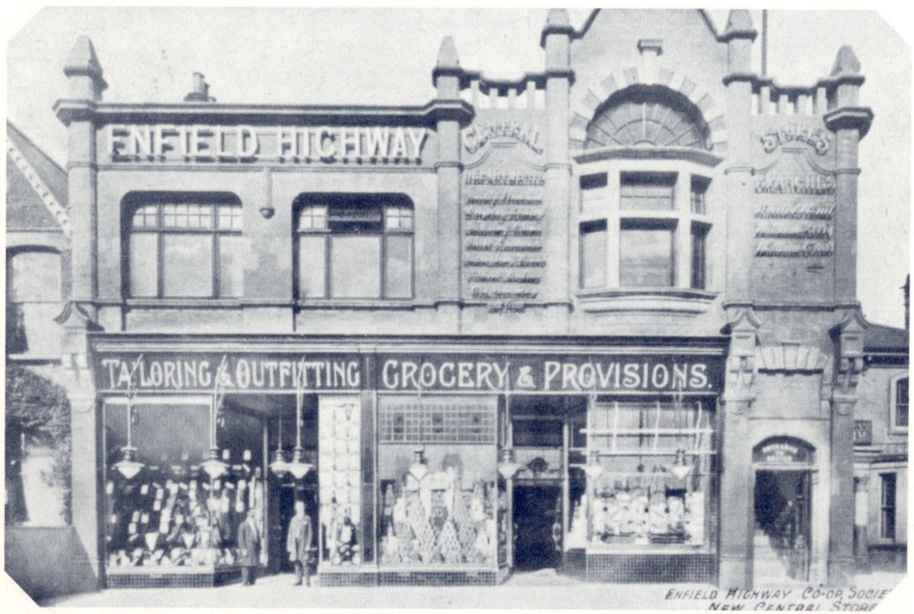


12. ENFIELD HIGHWAY CO-OPERATIVE STORES
'Co-ops' began in Lancashire but by the turn of the century they had penetrated the south, with particular success in London's ever expanding suburbs and surrounding towns. This store, away from the main shopping centre in Enfield town, served the outer fringes of suburbia. Note that the building on the extreme left remains a private house. This card illustrates both the range of goods on offer and also the Co-op's branch policy. This small society opened branches in Ponders End, Waltham Cross and Waltham Coney. The 'central' store here supplied 'general provisions, drapery, tailoring, china, glass, hardware, furnishing, boots, shoes, bakers, confectionery and coal.' Note the powerful overhanging lights to aid display. This Co-op also embarked on housing ventures; it built houses to the north of Enfield High Street in the 1930s.

13. DERBY CO-OPERATIVE SOCIETY
The development of the Co-operative Wholesale Society (CWS) was crucial to the success of the co-operative movement after the 1870s. Co-ops could concentrate heavily on 'own-brand' products of proven reliability and competitive price. This shop proudly announces that all goods on display are 'C.W.S. Productions'. It was well known in the grocery trade that 'own-brands' offered the best profit margins at prices attractive to the customer. In this tightly packed but well-organized window may be discerned jams, cocoa, biscuits, chocolate cream, table jellies, dried fruit and wines. The entire right-hand side of the display (as the viewer looks) is given over to varieties of blended tea. The shop assistants' neat, white apparel adds to the impression of reliability and service.

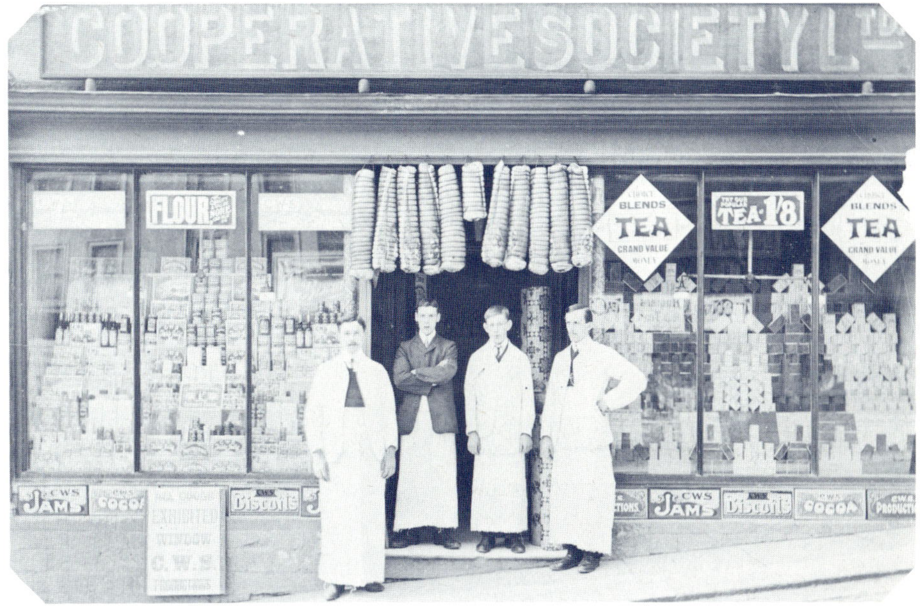


14. W. VASEY, GROCERY STORE, SCARBOROUGH
Vaseys was a well-known name in grocery in the town with three stores in the town and one just outside in the Edwardian period. This shop, 1 Ramshill Road on the corner of Albion Street, stands next to a sub-post office. It is in every way a superior establishment; the windows are large and carefully displayed with goods; separate low-hanging lights set off the display; the shop assistants are neatly attired. The *Practical Grocer* in 1906 emphasized the importance of smartness among shop assistants in the better class of shop 'well-groomed, with spotless collars and clean white aprons – and on the provision side with white jackets too – they are good-looking young fellows, whose speech and manner bespeak intelligence and education.' Note also the importance of a choice of blended teas and coffees to the superior grocer; many developed into general-provision merchants from an earlier base in tea or coffee specialisms. The premises remain a grocery store in 1980 and the original shop front is perfectly recognizable.

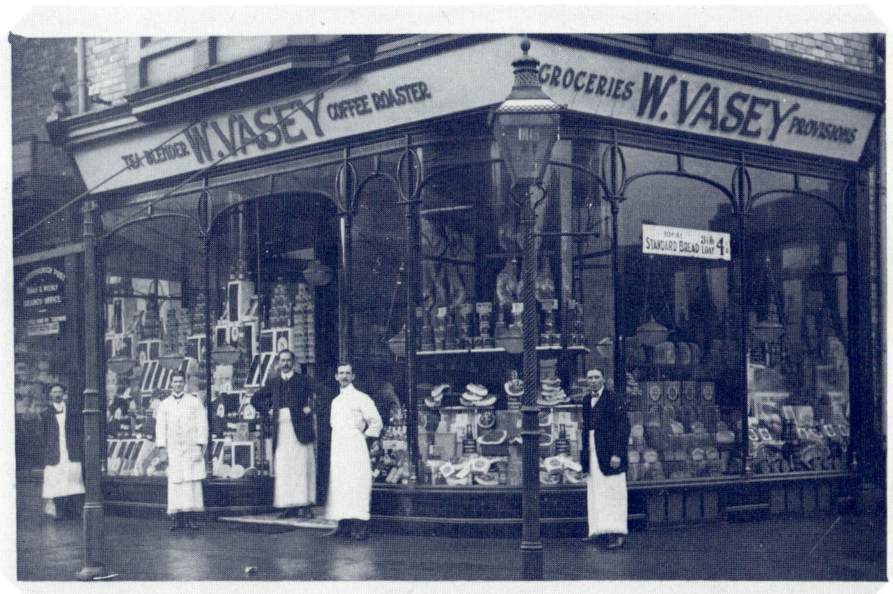

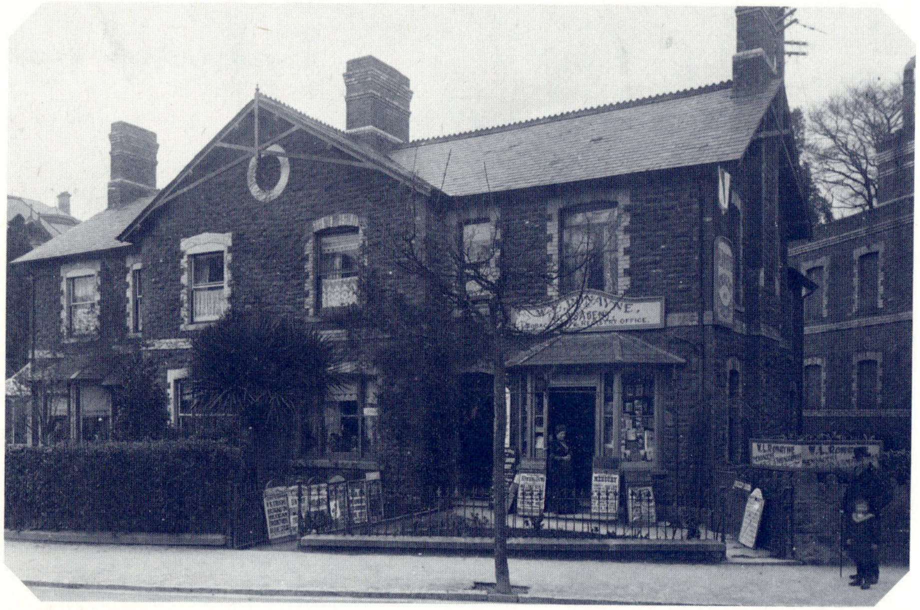

15. W. L. RONAYNE, NEWSAGENT, CHELSTON, TORQUAY
Though it looks older we can date this card from the United States/Mexico crisis to 1914–16. William Ronayne had been trading at 27 Walnut Road for a few years as a bookseller but converted his shop to a newsagents in 1914. Originally the house was a private dwelling, as is the other half of the property, and it is interesting to observe that by 1923 27 Walnut Road was again a private residence with Mr Ronayne no longer occupying it. By then W. H. Smith, at 15 Walnut Road, seem to have taken over the local newspaper trade. The papers advertised here are two south-west dailies, the *Western Morning News* and the *Western Daily Mercury* (nowadays incorporated with the *News*). National papers on sale included the *Daily News* and *Daily Express*.

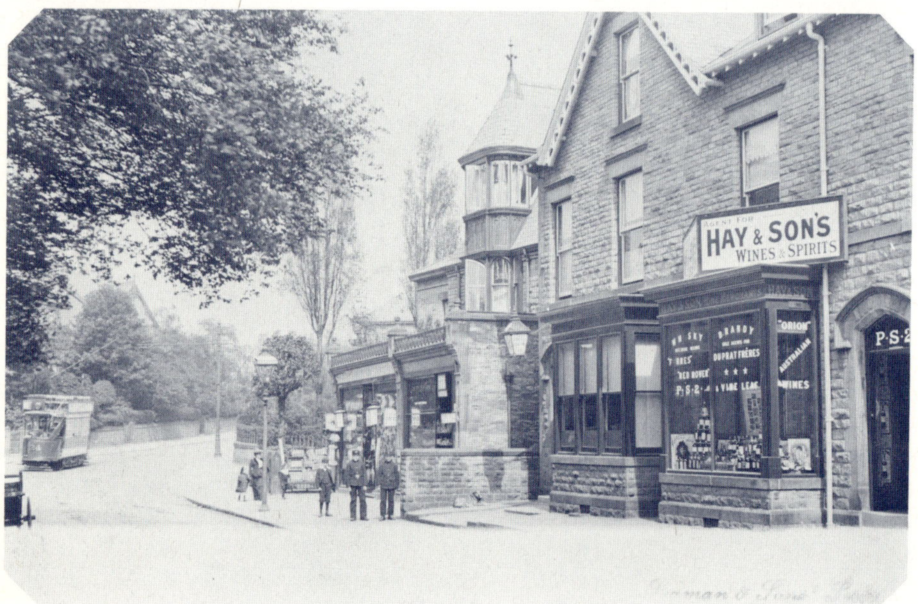


16. SHOPS IN SUBURBAN SHEFFIELD
This card splendidly illustrates the manner of shop development in the suburbs at the turn of the century. The picture was taken in 1903, the year that the well-known Sheffield wine merchants, Hay & Son, opened a branch on Nether Edge Road, two miles south-west of the city centre, taking over from a grocer. Hay's had had a wine shop in the centre of Sheffield since the 1850s but only began a 'branch' policy during the building boom of the 1890s. By 1906 they had 10 shops in Sheffield and Rotherham. Next to Hay's is Joseph Tomlinson, cab proprietor, and furthest from camera are the Nether Edge sub-post office (with smart telegraph boys posing outside) and Matthias Hubbard, Draper. Opposite the shops stood, and still stands, a bowling green. A tram (pictured here) terminated here and ran from the middle-class suburb to the city centre every 6 minutes. In 1980 off-licence (though under different management) and post office stand where they did.

17. MANOR PARK DAIRY, ESSEX

This quite beautiful card from the first decade of the century tells us much about commercial life in a then-prosperous outer suburb of London, near Romford and Ilford. The proprietor, George Gilbert, stands foresquare and solidly watch-chained in the doorway while his milk delivery man (a relative?) also exudes success with his gleaming churn and hand-painted cart. Gilbert owned another shop in Manor Park, a good guide to more than average prosperity. The regular delivery of 'pure rich milk' was not only a desirable service in pre-refrigerator times; it was that token of extra service which independent tradesmen used in their battle against the hated 'Co-ops' and their 'divvies'. Specially treated 'nursery milk' was almost certainly a factor in reducing the infant mortality rate after 1901. Station Road, on which this store stands, was a typical mixture of private dwellings and commercial premises. Gilbert's was next door to a baker, William Backer, and a 'costumier and furrier', Philip Barr. It stood only thirty yards from Manor Park's commuter station, ideally situated to attract passing trade. Note the neat, uncluttered window of the superior trading establishment; note, too, the absence of vulgar price lists. Nos. 32–8 Station Road are now knocked together and house a carpet and linoleum shop.

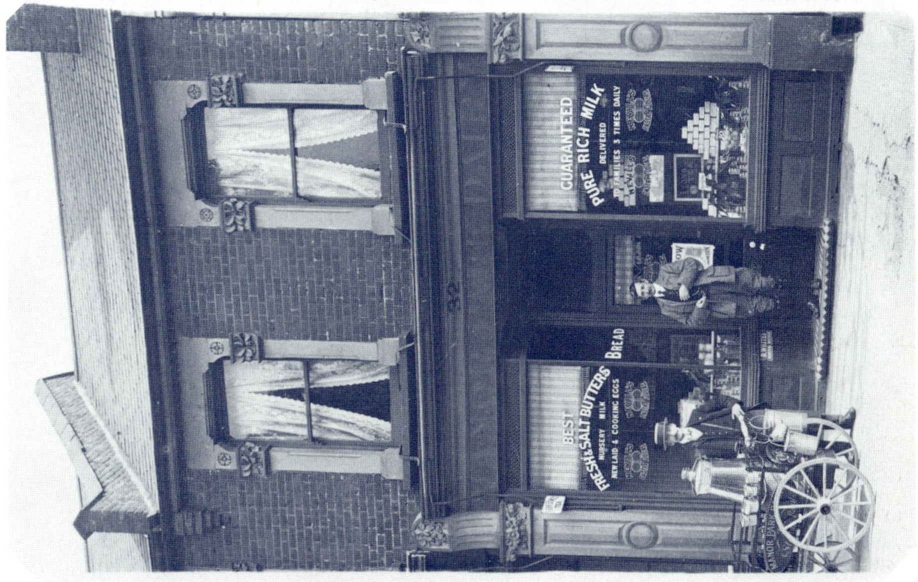


18. FRIED FISH SHOP, BARKING, ESSEX

This is a very rare card. Fried fish shops grew in popularity in the 1890s, though authentic 'fish-and-chip' shops were still much more common in the north than the south before 1914. Here we see the proprietor and his brother-in-law in front of their town-centre shop, 46 Broadway, just a few yards down the road from Barking's old, thatched town hall. It was one of 7 fried fish shops in Barking in 1908, a town then of some 22,000 people and still a port at which fish was landed. Most such shops sold both wet and fried fish. All the shops on the south side of Broadway together with the town hall, were demolished between 1926 and the 1950s, leaving St Margaret's parish church in solitary state amid a flush of unexpected greenery. The hoarding advertises variety at the nearby Borough Theatre, Stratford, (See Chapter 5 card 28). Halfway down the bill is Archie Pitt, then a minor comedian but subsequently to promote the early career of Gracie Fields, and, indeed, to marry her.

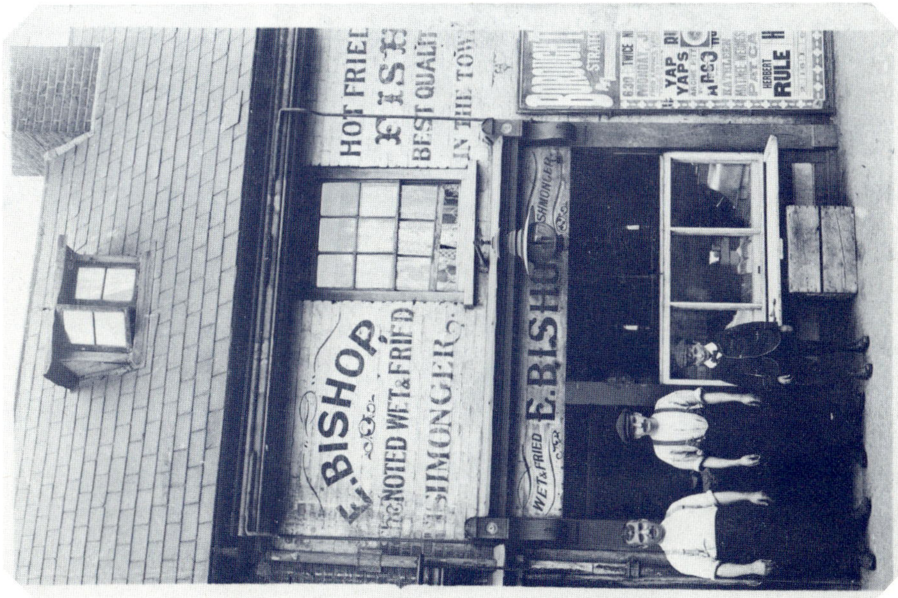

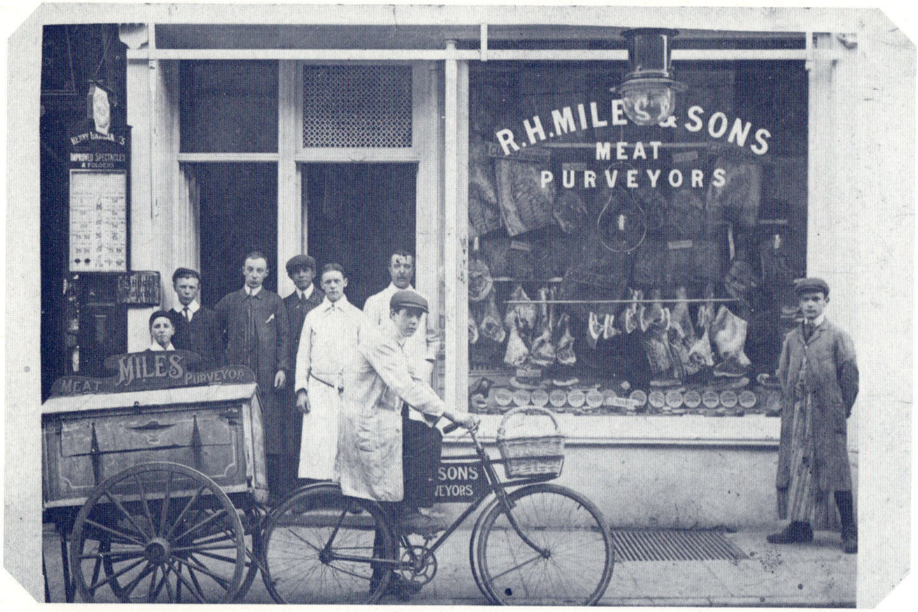


19. MEAT PURVEYORS, ABERDARE

Meat consumption was a sensitive indicator of living standards and the growth of specialist butchers' shops between 1880 and 1914 provides reliable evidence of improvement. Imported, refrigerated meats at lower prices changed the national pattern of meat consumption but the housewife continued to prefer freshly killed meat if she could afford it. For ease of curing and consequent longer keeping ham and bacon were preferred. Butchers' shops varied greatly in status from the high-class 'purveyor' of home-killed meat down to 'slink' butchers who traded in cheap meat, including that of animals who died of disease. Only the respectable trade was represented by a permanent shop equipped with delivery service as here. Mr R. H. Miles clearly has apprentices and runs a thoroughly reputable establishment, even though the absence of refrigerated counters and the propensity of glass to trap the sun makes the sight less appealing to modern eyes. The absence of prices again suggests quality trading. Curing and smoking on the premises enables the shopkeeper to give guarantees of quality to his customers.

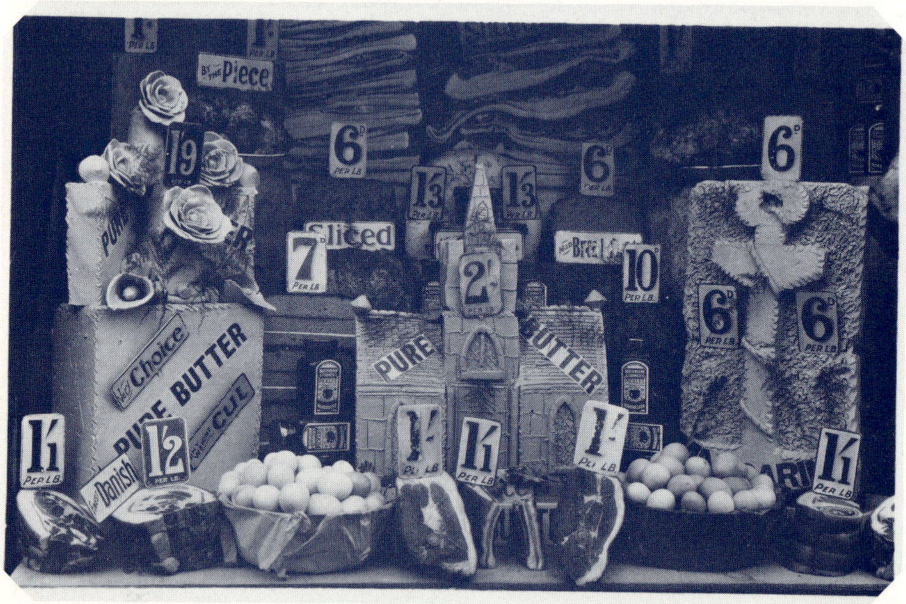


20. A GROCERY WINDOW DISPLAY

As competition became keener, grocers had to learn the arts of adornment to tempt their customers. The development of the 'prize window' was an extreme example of advertising blandishments. Grocers' exhibitions offered prizes for the most imaginative and alluring displays. As the *Practical Grocer* reminded the trade: 'A regular succession of attractive windows, of original and striking designs, will grow to be a subject of interest and remark with the public, an interest which the utmost should be done to sustain.' In this example local interest was doubtless sustained by enquiring how such florid and rococo designs in butter coped with the pitiless sun. Doubtless Houters Stores in Swadlincote High Street was the talk of the town.

21. ICE-CREAM PARLOUR

Ice-cream sellers, often of Italian origin, operated widely in Britain before the First World War. Many outraged strict Welsh sabbatarians by their practice of Sunday trading. Between the wars more British-owned shops began to operate ice-cream parlours. Mostly, as in this example from the Rhondda, they developed in already established retail outlets. This shop seems to have been a baker and confectioner first and to have added a cafe and ice-cream parlour later.

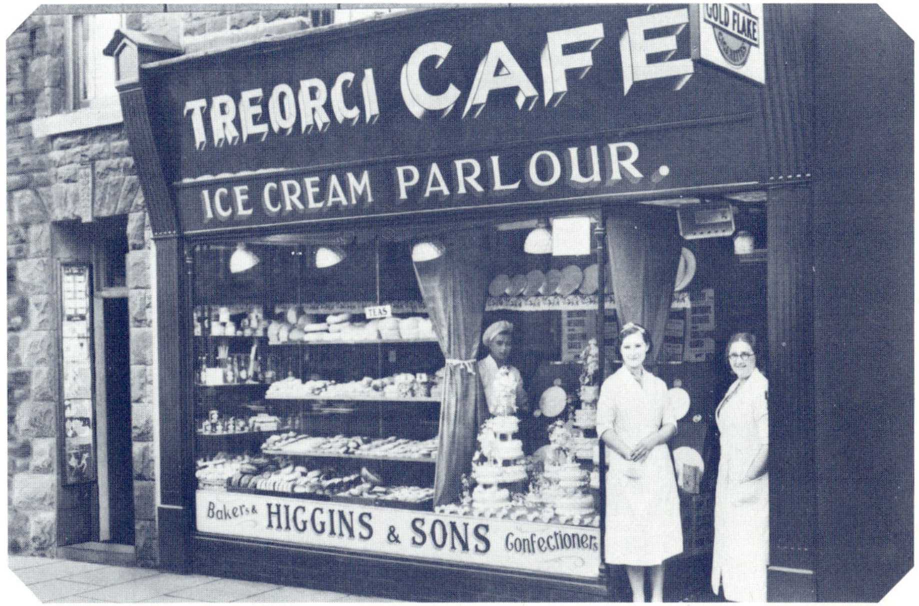


22. BUCKINGHAM'S BOOT SHOP, CHELMSFORD, ESSEX

Buckingham's occupied this site, 13 High St, from the mid-1880s to the mid-1920s. Boots and shoes were not only sold but made here. This card was sent by a serviceman to his sweetheart in Oxford in 1915. Note the shop's ability to meet a heavily increased demand for army boots during the war. Among the boots and shoes of every description the large mechanized manufacturers, Lotus and 'K' boots, were making a large contribution. This shop also sold Kiwi boot polish. Just three doors down, at Nos. 9–10, Freeman, Hardy & Willis had been established since 1890 and their competition eventually proved too much for the smaller concern. Freeman, Hardy & Willis still occupy the same site in 1980 that they have held for 90 years. Next door to Buckingham stood, and still stands, Herbert Chapman's jewellers' shop. In 1908 he was described as 'watch maker jeweller and optician' but the firm is now a specialist jeweller and watch dealer only.

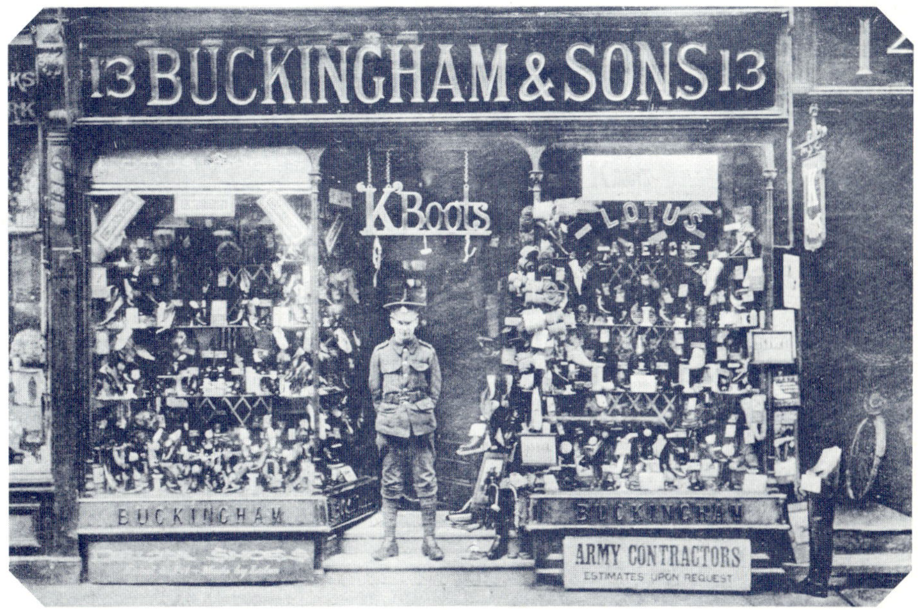

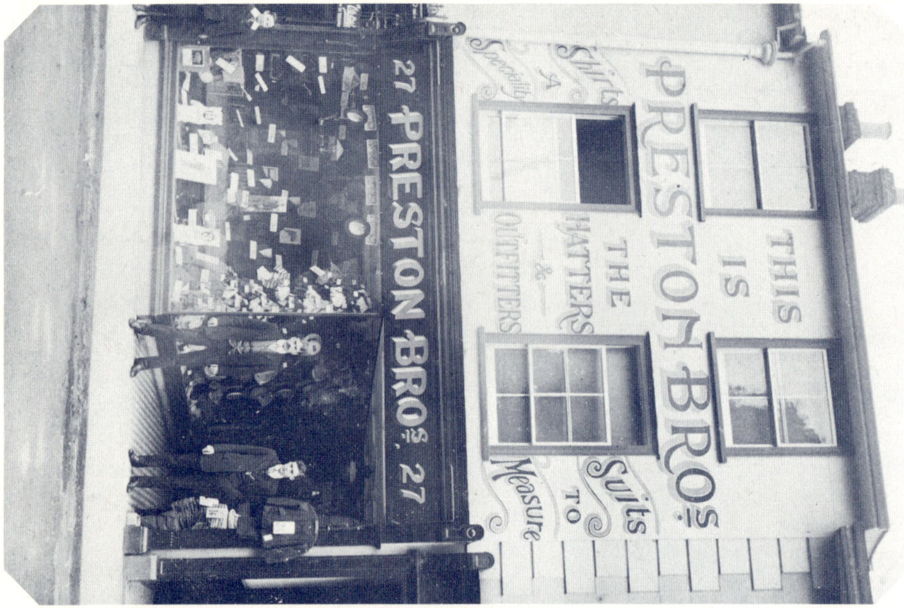


23. PRESTON BROS, HATTERS AND OUTFITTERS

The clothing trade expanded with rising living standards at the end of the nineteenth century. By 1914, respectable working men and their families would need 'Sunday best' even if, in hard times, they needed to get them back from the pawnshop on Saturday night. This clothing establishment caters for a middle-class market. It sold suits made to measure, probably on the premises. Good quality bowler hats and shirts were also prominently advertised. From the jacket with a price tag of 2*s* 11*d* (14½p) on the right of the picture it may be inferred that some ready-to-wear factory-produced clothing was also being sold. Between 1890 and 1914 factory clothing was extensively developed and multiple tailors like Hepworths of Leeds and Hope Bros of London provided a sharp challenge to the small stores. In clothes shops for working men it was usual to put a large stock on rails for the customer to sift through. Here the clothes are more discreetly arranged, and mostly behind glass.

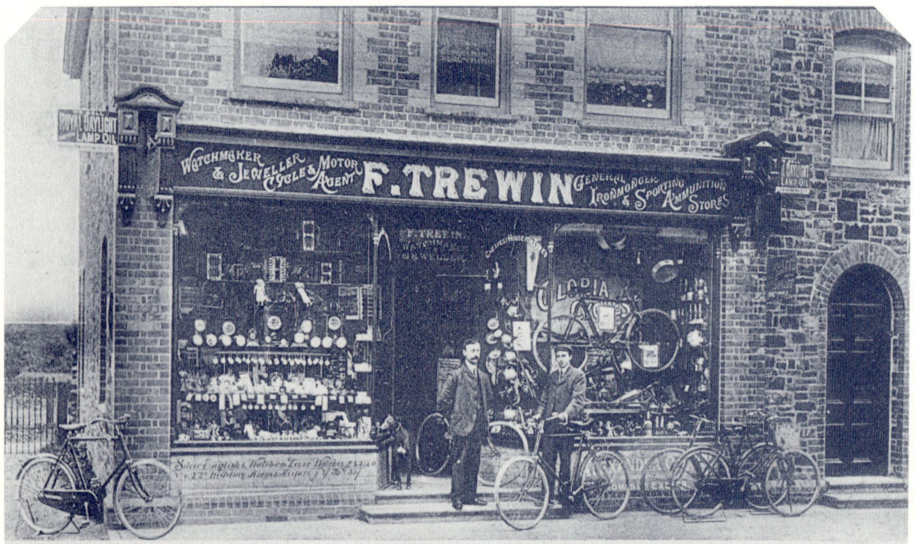


Frank Trewin, Jeweller, Ironmonger and Cycle Agent, Kilkhampton, Cornwall.

24. JEWELLER, IRONMONGER AND CYCLE AGENT, KILKHAMPTON

Kilkhampton is a small village on the River Tamar on the Devon–Cornwall border. It had a population of 832 in 1901. This card illustrates the rapid changes brought about by cycling (see Chapter 5). The Trewins were Kilkhampton's only non-agricultural traders in the Edwardian period. Frank Trewin, pictured here in the centre of his shop doorway, seems to have diversified into both cycles and watches from a basis in ironmongery. This is his advertising card, which listed 'jewellery, electro plate, cutlery, guns, cartridges, tinware, brushes, lamps, motor spirits, turpentine, "Alexandra & Royal Daylight Lamp Oils", Machine and Linseed Oils.' Silver watches were sold from 2 guineas (£2.10p) – a price constant enough in Edwardian England for him to have it etched in the shop front brickwork. Alfred and John Trewin were beer retailers and shoe makers; Annie Trewin was deputy registrar of births and deaths as was Joshua Trewin, the local shoe maker.

25. WATCH AND CLOCK SHOP, HAWES
Many small specialist shops like this, in a remote north Yorkshire town, survived before 1914. Clocks and watches were made, sold and repaired here by a local craftsman. The proprietor clearly lived above his shop. Note the small display window filled with pocket watches and chains. These were in great demand not only for display with 'Sunday best' clothing but also as an indication of the importance of correct time keeping in an increasingly busy 'time-oriented' society. The card dates from 1905.

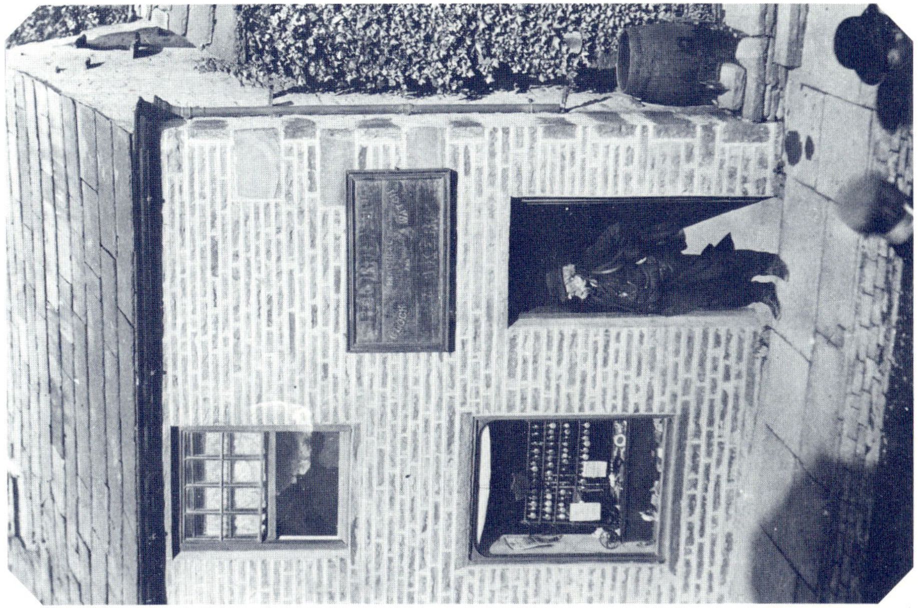

26. WINTER GARDENS, STRAND PALACE HOTEL, LONDON
The Strand Palace, opened in 1909, was a pioneering venture by Joseph Lyons and Company to bring high-quality accommodation and amenities within the range of the provincial middle classes on their visits to the capital for business or pleasure. As the first advertising bill stated: 'Every convenience, every luxury, everything that the most expensive Hotel can furnish – except the expensiveness – is here.' The ground-floor Winter Gardens, ornately designed in marble with stuccoed cherubs, had a large dome for its centrepiece. In the far corner, beyond the two marble arches (middle-left) a band entertained guests. Extensive redesigning of the ground floor took place between 1958 and 1968, during the course of which the dome was completely covered over. This magnificent room was destroyed as a unit to form part of the current Mask and Carvery bars.

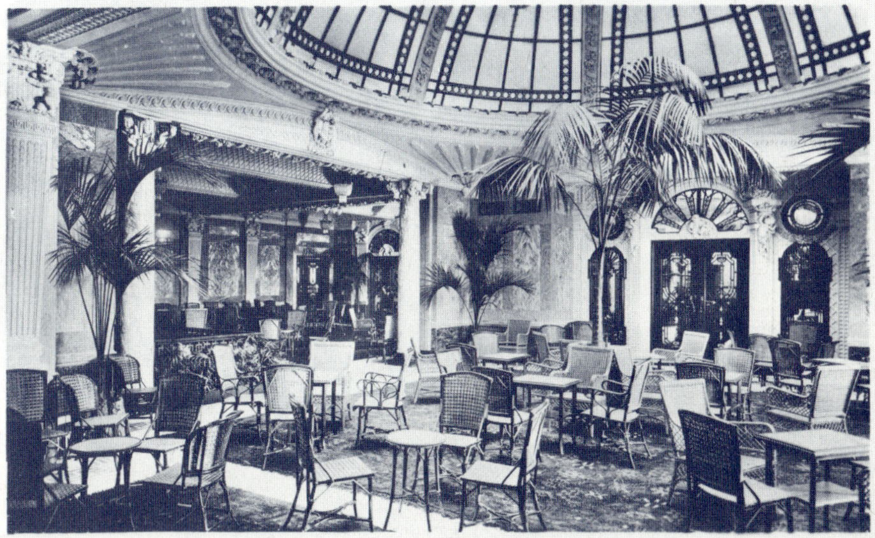

THE WINTER GARDEN. STRAND PALACE HOTEL

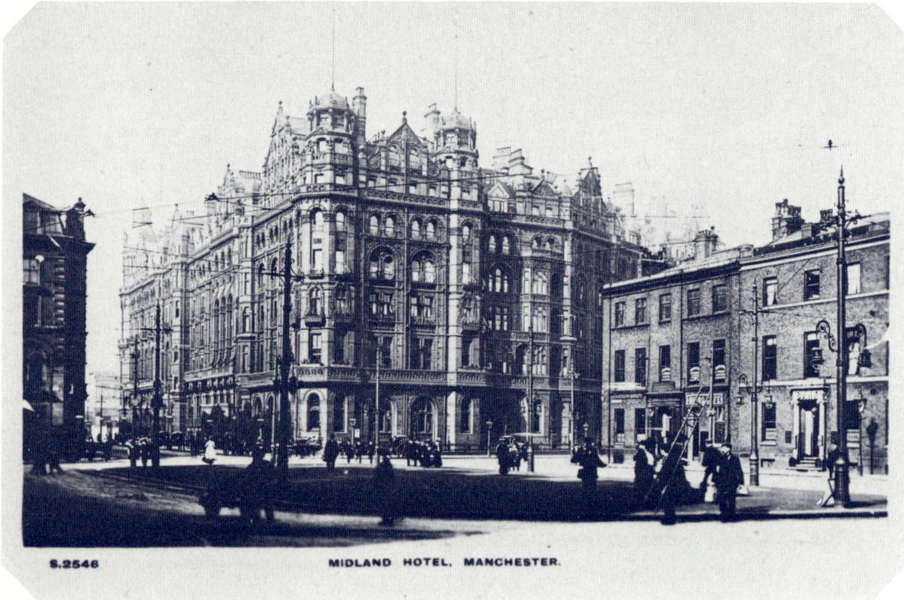


27. MIDLAND HOTEL, MANCHESTER

This hotel is a good example of a prestige establishment occupying a prime city-centre site, in this case overlooking Manchester's St Peter's Square. The hotel was built by the Midland Railway Company within a few yards of the now defunct Central Station. It stands, confident to the world, in brown vitrified terra cotta and was designed by the Derby architect Charles Trubshaw. Its lavish establishment included 600 rooms, 300 of them bedrooms. It boasted a concert hall seating 850 in the style of Louis XIV in white and gold with Cuban mahogany panelling, a French restaurant, a dining room. In the basement was a Turkish bath and on the roof a specialist garden. It opened in September 1903 and the *Manchester Guardian* proudly announced: 'A family here could shut themselves off from the world without; eat, drink, sleep, and be merry withal, and live as luxuriously as the millionaires of Park Lane.'

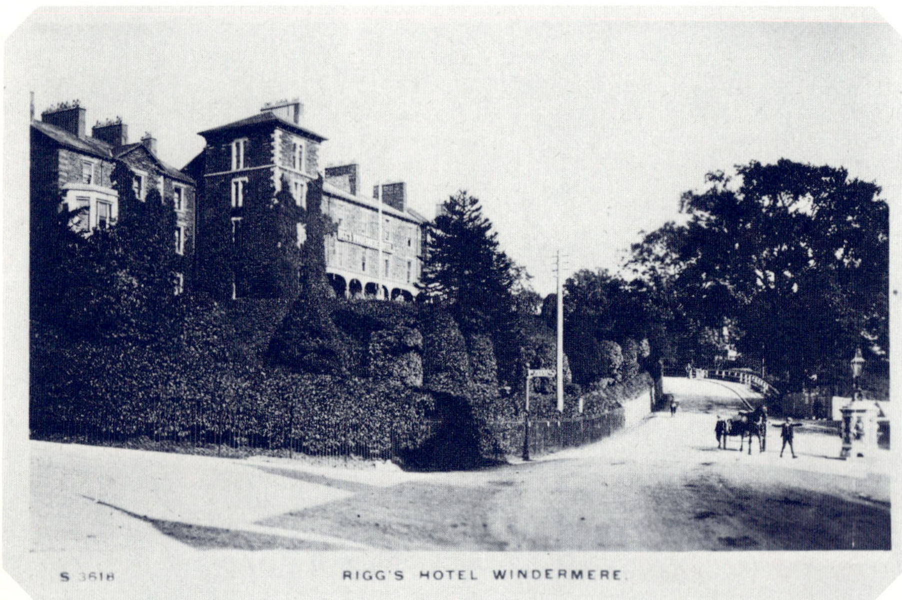


28. RIGG'S WINDERMERE HOTEL

The southern Lakeland area became popular with businessmen and gentlemen of leisure at the end of the nineteenth century. A commuter train ran direct from Windermere to Manchester to accommodate bankers and traders who set themselves up in large stone mansions at the lakeside or in the fells beyond. Hoteliers here were frequently men of property. The proprietor of this hotel, Thomas Rigg, was a Westmorland J.P. He held the coaching monopoly from the London and North Western Railway to convey visitors between Windermere station and Ambleside. His family's hotel interests were extensive. Another member of the family kept the luxurious Belsfield hotel in Windermere early in the twentieth century. Some idea of the hotel's clientele may be gauged by the fact that the writer of this card, sent in 1910, had travelled from Bury by motor car. Before 1914, cars were the luxury of the rich. He complained about seven stoppages *en route*. 'Perhaps our motor may not be ready to take us home tonight. No upset – only punctures.'

29. THRELFALL'S COMMERCIAL HOTEL, FLEETWOOD

A good example of a functional commercial hotel, well away from the luxury range, to accommodate travelling salesmen. Tourists were also welcome as the sign 'Good accommodation for cyclists' indicates. As so often in posed cards, the proprietor and his wife stand in the doorway. The ground floor of these premises also did duty as a corner shop with chocolate and confectionery on display in the window. The attached dining rooms offered square meals for fishermen on their return to the port.

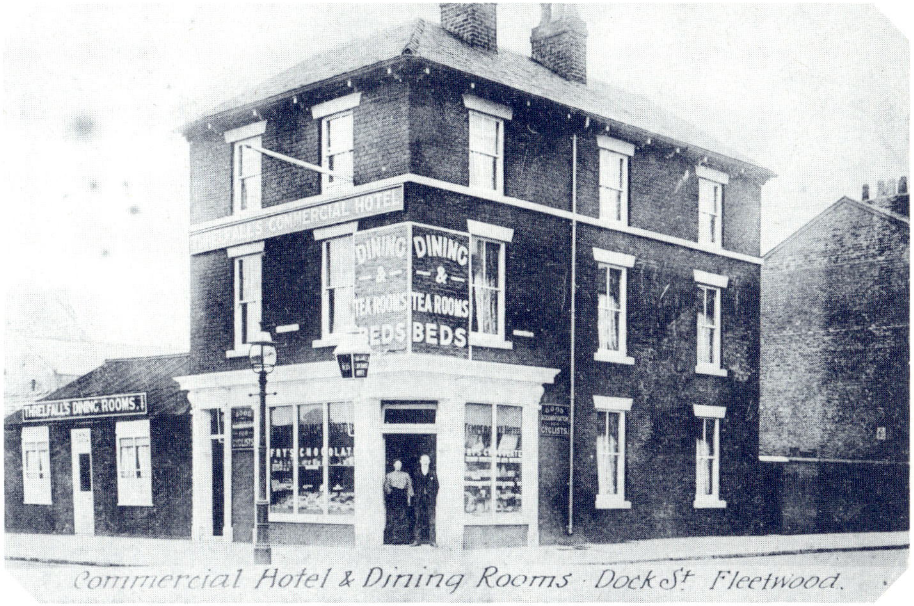

# CHAPTER FOUR | TRAVEL AND TRANSPORT

The golden age of the picture postcard saw the development of mass public transportation. In particular, it was the era of travel by rail. A comprehensive system of train and tram lines constituted the steel vertebrae of the country, facilitating that wholesale movement of people and goods which is a hallmark of the advanced industrial society.

There is no more potent or dramatic symbol of the industrial revolution than the railway. Although the precise nature of the economic change the railways wrought is still debated, their impact cannot be gainsaid. The Victorians equated the railways with progress and civilization. Their coming was hymned in art and literature on a scale of imagination and power which the steam train's unromantic successor, the motor car, wholly failed to inspire. The engravings of J. C. Bourne showing the building of the London to Birmingham railway or of Gustave Doré revealing the impact of the steam train on the capital, J. M. W. Turner's elemental 'Rain, Steam and Speed' and W. P. Frith's kaleidoscopic picture of Paddington 'The Railway Station' stand out from a wealth of railway-inspired art. The fire-breathing leviathans thundering through the landscape inspired poetry by such diverse writers as R. L. Stevenson, Thomas Hardy, Rudyard Kipling, G. K. Chesterton, Rupert Brooke, Siegfried Sassoon, W. H. Auden, Stephen Spender, T. S. Eliot and Sir John Betjeman. A whole new range of buildings and engineering works became part of the landscape – tunnels, viaducts, bridges and, most memorably perhaps, railway stations. In every major city, great echoing cathedrals of glass and iron arose, colonnaded, canopied, buttressed and turretted, living temples to the god steam. In an intoxicating cocktail of styles, architects like William Tite, John William Livock, Francis Thompson and David Mocatta created what became the familiar landmarks in the lives of several generations – scenes of arrivals and departures, reunions and separations, joy and tears. Everyone knows the fantastical splendours of that fairytale castle called St Pancras station and the lost magnificence of the Euston Arch, but at their shoulders stood other wonders – the medieval Gothic abbey that was Richmond station, the handsome Jacobean mansion that was Stamford East, the classical temple that was Birmingham Curzon St, and the elegant French Renaissance chateau of Southport Lord St. In their own humbler way the picture postcards were part of the visual celebration of every aspect of the world of steam.

The opening of the Liverpool and Manchester Railway in 1830 had decisively demonstrated the feasibility and the profitability of a railway passenger and freight service and had launched the heroic age of railway expansion. Visionary engineers and buccaneering entrepreneurs like Robert and George Stephenson, Joseph Locke, Thomas Brassey and Isambard Kingdom Brunel converted the dream of speed and steam into a reality and ended the equine domination of transport. With hordes of toiling navvies, they hewed the permanent way out of rock and clay, spanned valleys and glens with breathtaking viaducts, meshed the country in a network of iron rails that dramatically increased the pace of life and work.

By 1870 the heroic age of railway development was over. The network had been established. It stood at 13,500 miles of track and no major population centre was without its rail link. Thereafter it was a matter of filling in the gaps and by 1913 the route mileage stood at 20,281. By 1870 the hundreds of companies spawned by the successive speculative booms had been reduced by amalgamation and takeover so that 28 companies controlled 80 per cent of the track, with giants like the Great Western, the Great Eastern, the Midland and the London and North-Western dominant. By 1870 the railways were carrying 336.5 million passengers annually, a total that was to rise to 1,294.3 million by 1913.

After 1870, the railway companies concentrated on improving speed and facilities rather than carving out new routes. To improve passenger comfort, sleeping cars were introduced in 1874, dining cars in 1879, lavatories in 1880 and corridor trains in 1891. Gaslight appeared in 1876 and electric light in 1881, though the latter spread slowly. To reduce accidents automatic signalling was introduced in 1893, excessive working hours were reduced and improvements were made in track, rolling stock and suspension. The desire to increase speed was dramatized by the race to the North with the companies on the East and West coast routes vying to win the race from London to Aberdeen in ever shorter times.

Perhaps the most dramatic development came in the 1870s. In 1872 the Midland Railway announced its intention to admit third-class passengers to all its trains at a penny a mile fare and in 1874 to abolish second-class and reduce first-class fares to second-class rates. Other companies reluctantly followed, though it was not until 1910 that the GWR had phased out the last of its second-class carriages. This marked a major transformation in railway-company thinking. The railway companies had from the first encouraged the 'quality' and lavished their attention on the first-class passengers. When compelled by Gladstone's 1844 Act to introduce cheap workmen's trains every weekday, these 'parliamentary' trains became a byword for slowness, dirtiness and discomfort and were satirized by Gilbert and Sullivan's *Mikado*, in which the Mikado made malefactors travel on them as a punishment. But the Midland cannily saw the profit to be made by exploiting the potential mass market and led the way. The figures speak for themselves. In 1845, 40.51 per cent of all passengers carried were first class, 42.34 per cent second class and 17.15 per cent third. In 1875, 8.6 per cent of passengers carried were first class, 13.9 per cent second class and 77.5 per cent third. By 1922, 1.72 per cent were first, 0.37 per cent second and 97.91 per cent third. There was both an upsurge in traffic and a democratization of that traffic.

The most obvious effect of the railway was in linking the nation together. In 1842 the celebrated epigrammatist Sydney Smith declared of the railway 'Everything is new, everything is immediate – time, distance and delay are abolished'. The railways carried newspapers and the Royal Mail with undreamed of rapidity to the four corners of the kingdom, making news for the first time really current affairs. The railways spread the use of GMT or 'Railway Time' by adopting standardized timetables, and were instrumental in the diffusion of the electric telegraph. Speed and standardization went together, and fads, fashions and information became national phenomena.

The railways carried foodstuffs and raw materials, feed and fertilizers, facilitating the reduction in prices of essential goods and the creation of new centres of industry away from the traditional waterway routes. The Royal Commission on the Railways declared in 1867: 'The introduction of the railway system has entirely altered all the conditions of (goods) traffic, and has enabled industry and trade to spring up, which, without the railways, could have had no existence'.

But the railways did not just transport goods and businessmen to lubricate the wheels of commerce. They helped to reduce crime and disorder by permitting the movement of troops and police in large numbers. They advanced the growth of mass democracy by allowing the movement of politicians, speakers and ideas, permitting political parties and movements like temperance to be truly national. They facilitated the creation of organized sport on a national basis, by transporting football and cricket teams, even their supporters, to distant away fixtures and back.

Every centre of population, however small, wanted the railway. If the railway companies proved reluctant to provide branch lines to out of the way towns and villages, local businessmen often clubbed together to raise the money and build them themselves. These lines were invariably taken over by the big companies, merged into the network and became vital lifelines. The village station became the hub of the community, a centre for news, advice and gossip, the home of bookstall, telegraph office and often adjoining pub. The country railway never made a profit; it could not by its very nature. But it was a vital social service and remained so until the infamous Beeching axe substituted the crass motive of economic viability for that of communal need, ripped out the steel vertebrae of the nation and left whole areas more isolated than they had been since the eighteenth century.

Although the railway created some new towns (Crewe, Swindon, Wolverton) and effectively promoted the growth of some others (Cardiff, Barrow-in-Furness, Carnforth, Middlesbrough), its most dramatic effect was on existing cities. It literally transformed them. J. R. Kellett, tracing the effect of the railway on Manchester, Liverpool, Birmingham, Glasgow and London, writes of the Victorian city:

*it was the influence of the railways more than any other single agency which influenced the topography and character of its central and inner districts, the disposition of its dilapidated and waste areas, and of its suburbs, the direction and character of its growth: and which probably acted as the most potent new factor upon the urban land market in the 19th century.*

Large areas of slum housing in city centres were demolished to make way for central termini. In Birmingham for instance, 7 acres of slums were cleared to create New St station. But this had both positive and negative results. There was a 'knock-on' effect, as the displaced slum denizens moved into the next area of houses, with the inevitable consequence of overcrowding, social dislocation and health hazards. The new central stations inevitably provoked traffic congestion, as cabs and wagons fed passengers and goods into them. The stations attracted shops, hotels, pubs and lodging houses but they also facilitated the migration of industry and middle-class property-owners to the suburbs, leaving city-centre housing to decline both in value and in quality. So while on one side the coming of the railways destroyed some notorious slums, on the other side it created new ones by altering the social tone and function of central areas, and provided them with strict demarcation by the addition of sidings, viaducts, tracks, yards and bridges to the urban topography. Another entirely unforeseen effect has been isolated by Brian Harrison, who writes: 'The railway probably did more for temperance in the 19th century . . . than the temperance movement.' The speeding up of travel and the reduction of the number of stops reduced the need for accommodation en route, forcing many coaching inns out of business, and the railways brought in fresh milk from the countryside, the so-called 'railway milk', to replace the frequently contaminated urban milk and provide one of a range of alternative beverages.

Dr Thomas Arnold wrote of the train: 'I rejoice to see it, and think that feudality has gone forever. It is so great a blessing to think that any one evil is really extinct.' But it would be a mistake to think of the railways as egalitarian. What they symbolized essentially was the shift of power from the landed aristocracy to the middle class. The railways were their preserve – to facilitate their business, their leisure and their domestic arrangements. Indeed in encouraging the middle classes to move to the suburbs, the railways actually advanced the rigid stratification of society. Even if second class was eliminated, the railways still clung to a class structure of travel which eloquently testifies to the spirit of the age which effectively created the modern class system.

The working classes were not, by and large, users of trains. Indeed the railway companies resisted the idea of workmen's trains, for which from the middle of the nineteenth century on there was a vocal lobby. Charles Booth wrote in the 1890s: 'It is only the man whose position is assured who can treat railway and tram fares as a regular item of his daily budget.' The 1883 Cheap Trains act made general and compulsory concessionary fares for workers. But the LNWR and GWR were criticized for their poor provision of workmen's trains in 1892. The Select Committee on Workmen's trains was still recommending cheap trains for the workers in 1905. The railway companies resisted them, however, on both social and economic grounds. On the one hand, they did not want the workers swarming all over the country causing mayhem. They were only too aware of the complaints from some seaside resorts about the descent of the *hoi polloi* on them at bank holidays. They also feared that the workers, inclined to swearing, smelling, spitting and assorted vandalism, would deter better-class passengers. On the other hand, there was no profit in short journeys and irregular running of trains at peak times. There was also the fear that clerks and shop assistants, who could afford the more expensive fares, would use the cheap trains for preference.

An exception to this general attitude was the Great Eastern Railway who as the price for gaining parliamentary permission for the extension of Liverpool St station in 1872 introduced workmen's trains with twopenny return tickets for a journey of up to 10 miles. Under the stimulus of this concession, large working-class suburbs developed at Ilford, Leytonstone, Walthamstow and Tottenham. This led to the GER becoming known as 'the workmen's London railway'. But other London railways did provide workmen's trains, the London, Brighton and South Coast, the South Eastern, North London and the Metropolitan, so that by 1913 there were some 1,000 workmen's trains a day.

The railways did not take the lead in developing the suburbs, but their existence made suburban development a real possibility. Suburbs often developed before there was a rail link but the rail link almost invariably followed. Building companies often helped to pay for the building of a station to serve a new estate and around London, Birmingham, Manchester and Liverpool a ring of suburbs developed, where a self-contained middle-class life was lived, with the husband going to work and the wife going shopping in town by the regular suburban train. As they lost the inner city traffic to trams and buses, some of the London-based companies in particular saw the profit to be made from the new market and all of them followed the Great Northern Railway in issuing from 1906 onwards magazines eulogizing life in the suburbs. An official of the Great Western railway declared that the company's suburban passengers had produced 'a species of regular traffic which is of the utmost importance from the revenue standpoint'. 34 new stations appeared on suburban lines in London between 1900 and 1904. Perhaps the most famous of these suburban promotions was the Metropolitan Railway's Metroland, which lured London's managerial classes to the leafy delights of Pinner, Harrow, Rickmansworth and Chorleywood.

But just as the receipts of the railways rose in the Edwardian age, so too did their operating expenses. Railway workers, long overworked and underpaid, became unionized and militant. In 1911 there was a national Rail strike and in 1913 the NUR was created. Better pay and conditions for the workers, improvements in services and rolling stock ate into the profits of the companies. Although passenger figures were up, much of the increased traffic came from branch lines and suburban services which were expensive to maintain. The great period of expansion and profitability was coming to an end as was the peace of Europe. When war broke out in 1914, the railways were taken over by the government and contributed heroically to the war effort, carrying men and materials in vast numbers and quantities. By the end of the war the railways were exhausted, their rolling stock completely run down, their pre-eminence doomed by the irresistible advance of the internal combustion engine. The value of co-ordinated central control had been demonstrated by the war and to meet the challenges of the postwar world, the companies were formed into 4 major groupings – the LMS, LNER, SR and GWR – in 1921. But the railways were tied to Britain's declining traditional heavy industries, were hard hit by the postwar economic decline and depression, and could not compete in flexibility or convenience with the fast-developing road transport.

The internal combustion engine also signalled the end of the other rail-borne form of transport – the tram. In a very real sense it complemented the railway service by providing a form of inter-urban transportation for the people. It was, in Richard Hoggart's words, 'the gondola of the working classes'. The tram enjoyed a far shorter period of eminence than the train. It was developed in the United States and on the Continent and made its first appearance in Britain in 1860 when an American, the appropriately named George Francis Train, set up the Birkenhead Street Railway Company and inaugurated the first passenger tramway in England. He extended his operations to London, Darlington and the Potteries but experienced such difficulty and opposition that in 1862 he left England in frustration.

Interest in his system revived in the late 1860s; in 1869 Liverpool and in 1870 London introduced horse-drawn trams. Their success demonstrated the viability of the system, which had been criticized on the grounds that it would obstruct other traffic and would destroy the road surface. Tramway systems spread rapidly. Manchester, for instance, eventually had a fleet of 953 tramcars.

Although there were experiments with steam trams, the great breakthrough which was to make the tram a cheap and speedy means of transport for the masses was electrification. Blackpool introduced in 1885 the first electric street tramway and other towns followed suit. The two great developments of the Edwardian era were electrification and municipalization, when private tramway companies were acquired and run by local corporations. Trams now provided a very real alternative to urban railway lines and some rail services were superseded by them. The Nottingham Suburban Railway, for instance, opened in 1889, closed in 1916, put out of business by the trams. By 1900, there were 1,000 miles of street tramways in Britain and the peak year for the tramways was 1919–20 when they carried 4,800 million passengers. Thereafter they began to decline. Route mileage fell from 2,624 miles in 1924 to 1,861 miles in 1933. In the 1920s particularly trams began to give way to buses, though in some places there was a half-way house in that curious hybrid, the trolley bus, half-bus half-tram, introduced into Leeds and Bradford in 1911. In the 1920s Wolverhampton became internationally famous for its trolley bus system. The tram disappeared first in the smaller towns, like Hartlepool, Keighley, Jarrow, Lancaster, Lincoln, Hastings and Burton-on-Trent from the 1920s onwards. The big cities kept faith with it until after the Second World War and it was not until the 1950s that the last trams ran in Birmingham, Liverpool, Edinburgh and Leeds. Glasgow, the last big city to maintain a regular tram service, continued until 1962. Now only Blackpool retains trams, largely as a tourist curiosity.

Robert Roberts writes in his study of slum life in Edwardian Salford: 'Except for the war itself, this revolutionary new form of transport contributed more than anything else to breaking down that ingrained parochialism which had beset millions in the industrial slums of pre-1914 England.' The electric tram was half as dear and twice as fast as the horse-drawn tram and it widened both the horizons and the expectations of the working classes. It took them to work and to play, to football matches and the shops, to parks and to libraries, to schools and to colleges, where before they had gone, if at all, on foot. Like the train, therefore, it contributed its part to the decline of drunkenness as it made easily accessible for the first time a variety and geographical spread of alternative leisure activities to the local pub. Publication in 1907 of a booklet entitled *Tramway Trips and Rambles*, listing 23 London suburban tram routes and 40 walks between tramways, indicates their increasing use to gain access to fresh air and green fields. In 1911, when the national rail strike stranded many people in Blackpool, some adventurous souls in fact took the tram, walking from the end of one system to the beginning of the next, until they reached home, eloquent testimony to the pervasiveness of this form of transportation.

Although the development of railways had ended the predominance of the horse as a means of transportation, equestrian travel had by no means been eliminated. Hackney carriages operated within towns and cities, short haul deliveries were done by horse and cart and the remoter areas of Britain like the Lake District, the West Country and the north of Scotland retained coach networks linked to the railways. The ubiquitous presence of the horse in cities led to the roadway being described colloquially as the 'horse road' until after the Second World War.

An important addition to horse-drawn transport was the omnibus, developed in France to provide for intra-urban transport and introduced in London by George Shillibeer in 1829. The combination of scheduled operation, low fares and punctuality ensured the success of the idea and by 1830 there were 39 omnibuses running in London. Other big cities followed London's example and the need for mass urban transportation revealed by the Great Exhibition of 1851 provided a boost to the service. But a falling off in traffic after the exhibition closed and the effects of cut-throat competition by a multiplicity of rival concerns led in 1855 to the formation of a combine which eventually became known as the London General Omnibus Company. It merged several existing firms, bought out others and by the end of 1856 controlled 600 of the 810 London omnibuses. This process of combination set the pattern for omnibus operation nationwide.

The London omnibus, despite the advantage of access to the city centre which was denied to trams, faced formidable competition both from the tram and from the underground railway, both of which were electrified by the 1890s. The omnibus's answer was at hand – the motor bus. Significantly, while Britain invented the railways, the symbol of the nineteenth century, the motor car, the symbol of the twentieth century, resulted from experiments in France, Germany and the United States. Just as Britain's economy was being overtaken by other countries, so too were British inventions being superseded by those of her commercial and industrial rivals. The development of the internal combustion engine, petrol and the motor car was associated with such names as Daimler, Benz, Renault, Peugeot and Diesel, soon to become household words. The first motor car, a Benz, was imported into Britain in 1894 and with it the motor car lobby was born. By 1896 its pressure had resulted in the passing of the Locomotives on Highways Act, which removed many of the restrictions on road transport imposed by the notorious 'Red Flag Act' of 1878 and which raised the speed limit to 14 mph. There was an immediate move to motorize the omnibus and the first motor bus service was inaugurated in Edinburgh in 1898, only to close down in 1901. London's first motor bus service began in 1899; it closed in 1900. Technical teething troubles, the opposition of rival interests and continuing legal restrictions made the early life of the motor bus difficult, but an order of 1904 under an Act of 1903 raised the maximum weight of heavy vehicles to 5 tons and their maximum speed, if equipped with rubber tyres, to 12 mph. This, coupled with technical improvements, promoted the 1905 'bus boom'. Horse buses gave way to motor buses and by 1910 for the first time the motor bus outnumbered the horse bus in London. In 1914 the last London horse bus was withdrawn.

Outside London, the motor bus was making its presence felt. Eastbourne was the first local authority to introduce it in 1903. Birmingham followed in 1913 and Liverpool in 1911. Ironically, the railway companies were among the foremost pioneers of motor bus operation, particularly the Great Western and the North Eastern Railways, who used them to link isolated communities to the rail network. By 1906 the GWR owned 80 buses.

In the provinces, the bus companies rapidly worked out a *modus vivendi*, dividing up the country into non-competing operating territories, approved, enforced and protected by the provincial Omnibus Owners Association founded in 1913. The war brought a temporary halt to bus development. Many buses were requisitioned and in 1917 fuel rationing was introduced. But after the war, there was further dramatic expansion. Many new rural services were introduced. Long-distance express coach services began, sometimes following the routes of the old mail coaches displaced by the steam train, 128 regular coach services by 1930, a very real rival to the railways. Local authorities began to undertake bus operation, particularly as many of the smaller authorities phased out their trams. In 1914 there were 18 local authorities operating bus services; by 1929 it was 90.

The motor bus, however, still operated for the most part under regulations and by-laws designed for horse-drawn vehicles and the passing of the Road Traffic Act in 1930 set the seal on the arrival of the motor bus as a permanent and increasingly dominant part of the transport scene. The road service licence for public buses and coaches, special tests for their drivers and new speed limits provided a new and enduring framework for their operation. The tram was ultimately doomed to make way for the bus since the latter was far more flexible in its operational ability.

It was this flexibility which was to be the lasting contribution of the bus to Britain's development. As John Hibbs has written:

*The spread of towns that took place in the Thirties could hardly have occurred at such a low density of population if the electric tram had remained the prevailing form of transportation, for tramways need a concentrated population to justify the heavy capital outlay involved in their establishment. Even the trolleybus has this drawback, and only the flexible motor bus could ever have served the housing estates that have been built around the fringes of our cities.*

The other product of the internal combustion engine of course was the motor car, and in the long run this was to prove even more significant in transforming the face of this country and the way of life of its people. The importation of the first car led inevitably to the growth of British motor car manufacturers, with the names of Herbert Austin and William Morris pre-eminent. The motor car became the status symbol of the rich and by 1914 a third of a million cars were riding the roads of Britain. The First World War gave a powerful stimulus to the motorized vehicle with its use of armoured cars, tanks and motor cycles. British manufacturers in postwar years adopted the mass-production techniques pioneered in the United States by Henry Ford and with prices falling and hire purchase and credit facilities widely available the motor car now came within the range of the middle class. The car became a status symbol for the middle class in the inter-war years and was to become one for the working classes in the 1950s. Between 1919 and 1939 the number of motor vehicles on British roads increased ten fold. British car production rose from 71,000 in 1923 to 182,000 in 1929 to 390,000 in 1937. Although the motor car remained way beyond the range of the working classes, the internal combustion engine altered their transport habits too; gradually the bus rather than the tram took them to work or recreation and the express motor coach or heavy charabanc rivalled the excursion train to take them to the seaside.

The 1914–18 war provided the watershed. The railways entered their long decline, hit by the loss of middle-class passengers to the motor car, freight to the goods lorry and working-class passengers to the charabanc. The tram entered its shorter decline, culminating in its total disappearance from the life of the city. The age of the automobile was at hand. The motorists' pressure groups, the AA and the RAC, wantonly opposed every attempt to preserve life, as the death toll on the roads rose from 373 killed in 1909 to 6,138 killed in 1928. Speed limits, driving tests, pedestrian crossings, compulsory insurance and the publication of accident figures were all seen as diabolical bids to restrict the freedom of the motorist, but all were eventually introduced. The road lobbies began the movement to cover the countryside in layers of concrete, to drive out new roads in all directions and to promote that ugly ribbon development that was the feature of Priestley's third England. What Winston Churchill by a deliberate slip of the tongue was to call 'the infernal combustion engine' gave mobility and freedom to the well off at the cost of the carnage, congestion and pollution that was to become a feature of twentieth-century Britain.

## FURTHER READING


Bagwell, P. S., *The Transport Revolution since 1770* (London, 1974)

Betjeman, J, 'Metroland', *The Best of Betjeman*, ed. John Guest (London, 1978)

Betjeman, J. and Gay, J., *London's Historic Railway Stations* (London, 1972)

Biddle, G., *Victorian Stations* (Newton Abbot, 1973)

Delgado, A., *The Annual Outing and Other Excursions* (London, 1977)

Dyos, H. J. and Aldcroft, D. H., *British Transport* (London, 1974)

Ellis, C. H., *The Trains We Loved* (London, 1947)

Ellis, C. H., *Railway Art* (London, 1977)

Hibbs, J., *History of British Bus Services* (London, 1968)

Joy, D., *Railways in the North* (Clapham, 1975)

Kellett, J. R., *The Impact of Railways on Victorian Cities* (London, 1969)

Klapper, C., *The Golden Age of Tramways* (Newton Abbot, 1974)

Klapper, C., *The Golden Age of Buses* (London, 1978)

Lee, C. E., *Passenger Class Distinctions* (London, 1943)

Morgan, B., *The Railway Lover's Companion* (London, 1963)

Morgan, B., *Railways – Civil Engineering* (London, 1973)

Nock, O. S., *Scottish Railways* (London, 1950)

Perkin, H. J., *The Age of the Railway* (Newton Abbot, 1971)

Perkin, H. J., *The Age of the Automobile* (London, 1976)

Richards, J., 'The Rape of the Railways', *Lancaster Comment*, **69** (October 1976) pp. 4–6

Roberts, R., *The Classic Slum* (Manchester, 1971)

Robbins, M., *The Railway Age* (London, 1962)

Rolt, L.T.C., *Red for Danger* (London, 1955)

Silvester, R. J., *Official Railway Postcards of the British Isles I; LNWR* (Chippenham, 1978)

Simmons, J., *The Railways of Britain* (London, 1961)

Thomas, D. St J., *The Country Railway* (Newton Abbot, 1976)

Thompson, F. M. L., *Victorian England – the Horsedrawn Society* (Bedford College, London 1970)

1. THE EUSTON ARCH

Few would argue with the proposition that the twin symbols of the heroic age of the railways were the Euston Arch and the St Pancras Hotel, testimony not only to the ferocious rivalry of their parent companies (the London and North-Western and the Midland) but to the rivalry of architectural styles in the creation of railway buildings. Just as all roads led to Rome, so all railways led to London, which boasted in its centre no less than 16 major stations. Euston Station, opened in 1838, was the London terminus of the London and North-Western Railway. It was built in the classical style and its arch, the veritable gateway to London, was designed by Philip Hardwick. In an act of official vandalism still so monstrous as to defy the imagination, the arch was demolished in 1967 by British Railways to make way for an office block. At the same time, the historic station was razed, and replaced by a new station, designed to resemble an airport. This postcard, issued in 1905 by the LNWR, conveys something of the awe which must have accompanied arrivals at and departures from this station in its heyday.

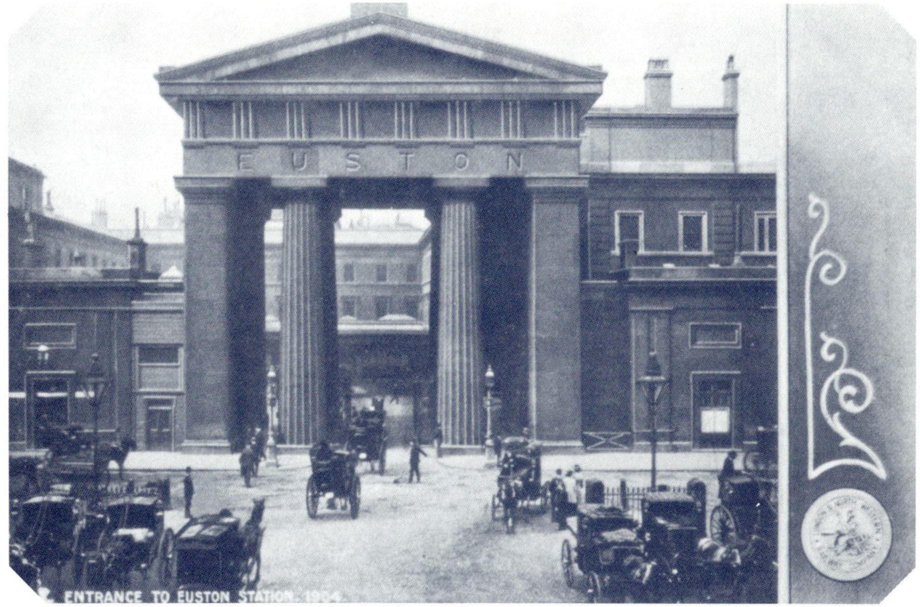


2. THE ST PANCRAS HOTEL

Happily still standing, St Pancras Station was the London terminus of the Midland Railway and is one of the architectural wonders of Victorian England. The Midland, based on Derby, reached London in 1868 and initially used Kings Cross Station by arrangement with the Great Northern. But it soon had its own terminal, next door to Kings Cross, with a trainshed, designed by William Barlow, which boasted the largest station roof without internal supports in the world, and Sir Gilbert Scott's hotel, a masterpiece of what Sir John Betjeman has called 'exuberant Gothic'. The trainshed was completed in 1868, the hotel in 1873. This card, sent in the early years of George V's reign, was from a father to his young son in Glasgow and bears a veritable Scotsman's lament: 'This is the station where I landed at and it cost me two shillings and a halfpenny for a cup of tea and a piece of ham and one egg.' Plus ça change!

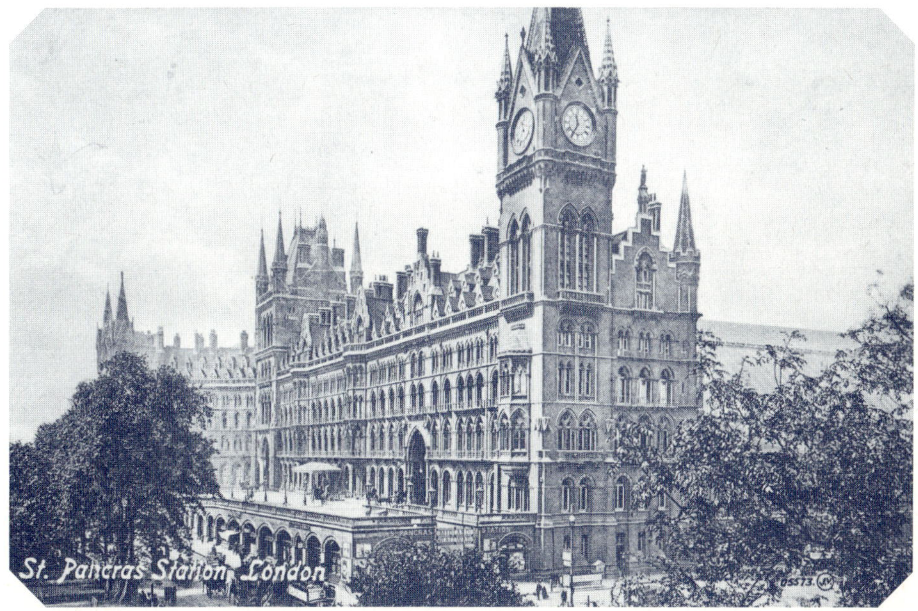

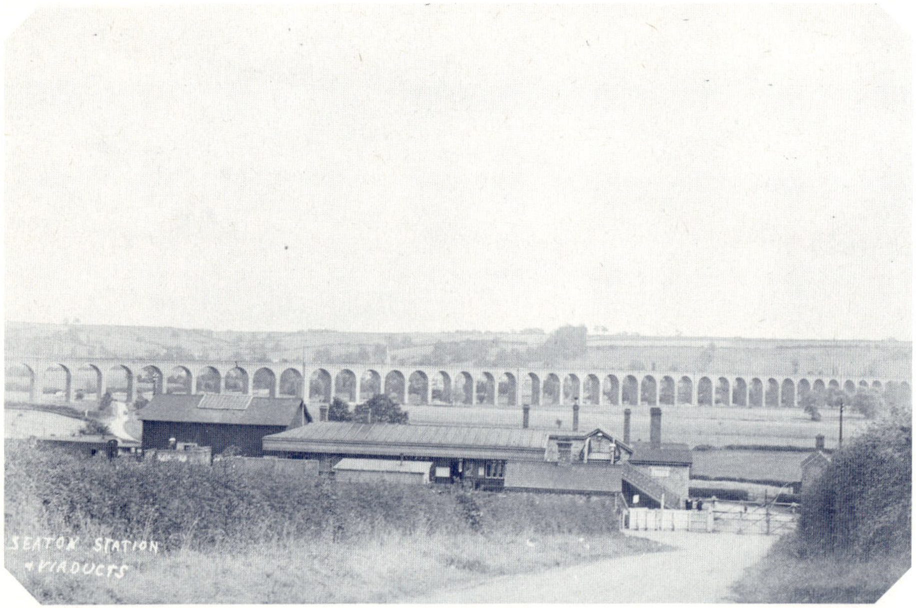


### 3. THE HARRINGWORTH VIADUCT

A whole new range of engineering works – viaducts, embankments, tunnels and bridges – became part of the landscape during the railway age. The Harringworth viaduct, seen here, spanning the Welland valley, was part of the Midland Railway's Nottingham to Glendon line, opened in 1879 to join the main Leicester–St Pancras line and provide a more direct route from Nottingham to London. It was closed in 1966. The viaduct was 1,275 yd long and comprised 82 arches. Seaton station, in the foreground, was on the LNWR line from Market Harborough to Luffenham, opened in 1851. It was extended to Peterborough via Wansford in 1879 and became an important through line from Rugby to Peterborough. It too closed in 1966. The card, sent in 1911 by 'R' from Harringworth to a young lady in Leicester, says cryptically: 'I tremble when I imagine what you are thinking of me. I think I must put it down to the hot weather this time.' Whatever can he be referring to?

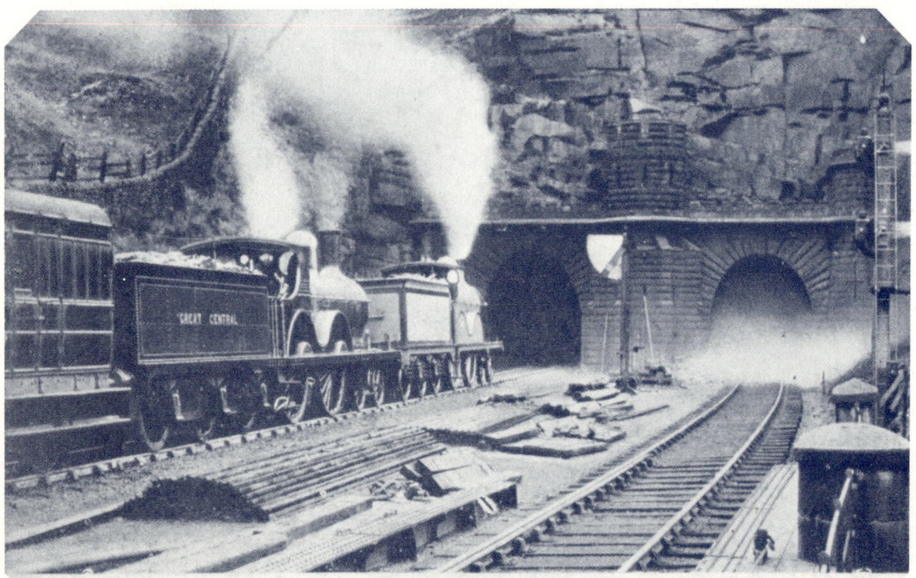


ODHEAD TUNNEL, GREAT CENTRAL RAILWAY. *By The Locomotive Publishing Company, Ltd., London, E.C.*

### 4. WOODHEAD TUNNEL

The world's first real mountain railway tunnel, the Woodhead Tunnel, was built by the great engineer Joseph Locke to provide a trans-Pennine route for the Sheffield, Ashton-under-Lyne and Manchester Railway (later the Great Central). It was the longest tunnel yet built at 3 miles long and 600 ft below the surface. The first bore was completed in 1845. The tunnel was in operation until after the Second World War, when it was replaced by a new tunnel 30 yd to the south of the old one. Here a double-headed Great Central train heads full tilt for the battlemented tunnel in the Edwardian age.

5. STEAM OVER SHAP

If for nothing else the LNWR would have earned its title 'the Premier Line' for operating one of the most breath-taking routes in Britain – the Lancaster to Carlisle line, engineered by Joseph Locke up the Lune gorge and across the Lakeland fells. Completed in 1844, it included a climb of 4 miles up a gradient of 1 in 75 over Shap Fell. It was over this route that the LNWR conducted its race for the North against its East coast rivals. This card, issued in 1904, depicts an LNWR 2–4–0 engine hauling the Aberdeen Express. The route remains an astonishing engineering achievement and one of the most fulfilling railway routes to travel.

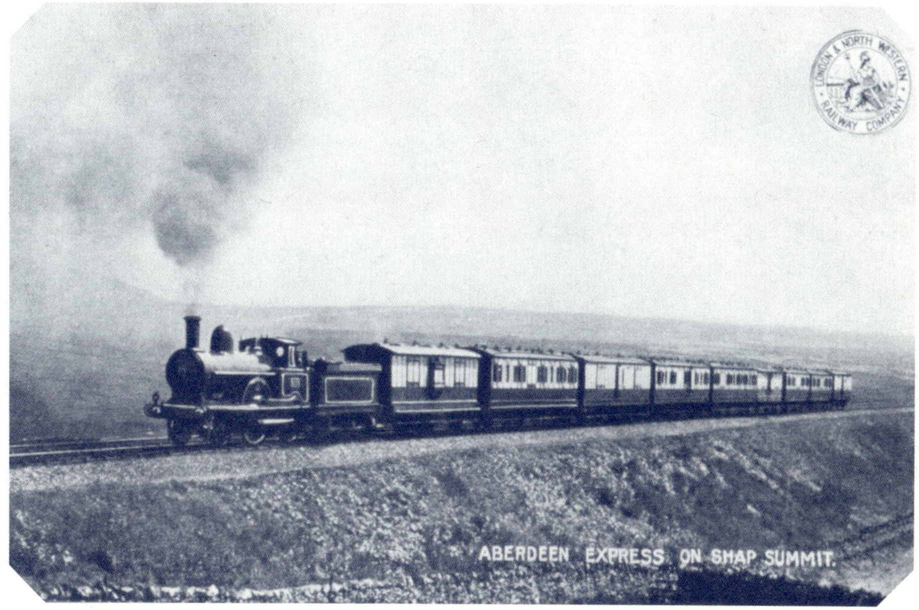


6. OFF FOR THE HOLIDAYS

The arrival of the railways transformed the lives of middle and working classes alike by making possible holidays of all kinds – a week by the seaside, a day trip to the capital, a weekend in the country, with beneficial results for health, work and education. *Knights Excursion Guide* (1851) declared: 'Railways have opened our island to the pleasure tourist; and the work of civilization which they are thus accomplishing is not amongst the least remarkable of their consequences.' *The Cornhill Magazine* (1867) noted: 'The typical John Bull is fast becoming a legendary personage: his vegetative life and stationary habits and local prejudices are all disappearing beneath the stimulating influence of the railway, the telegraph and the great cities'. This charming card shows an Edwardian holiday train drawn up at a remote country station on the London, Brighton and South Coast Railway. There seems to be an altercation going on on the platform, attracting the attention of the engine driver and the local bobby. The presence of the LBSCR engine *Buller* helps in dating the card to between 1902, when divided-back postcards were introduced, and 1905 when *Buller* lost its name.

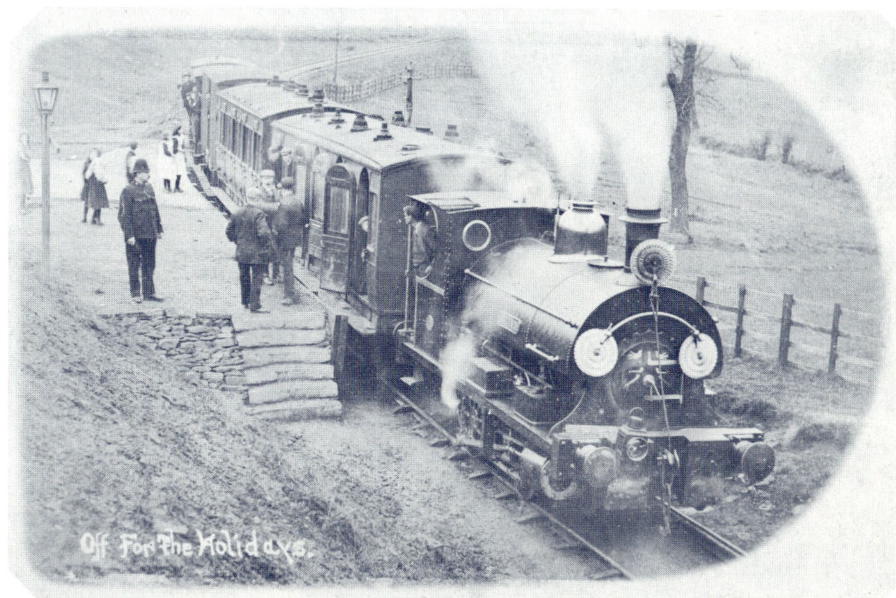

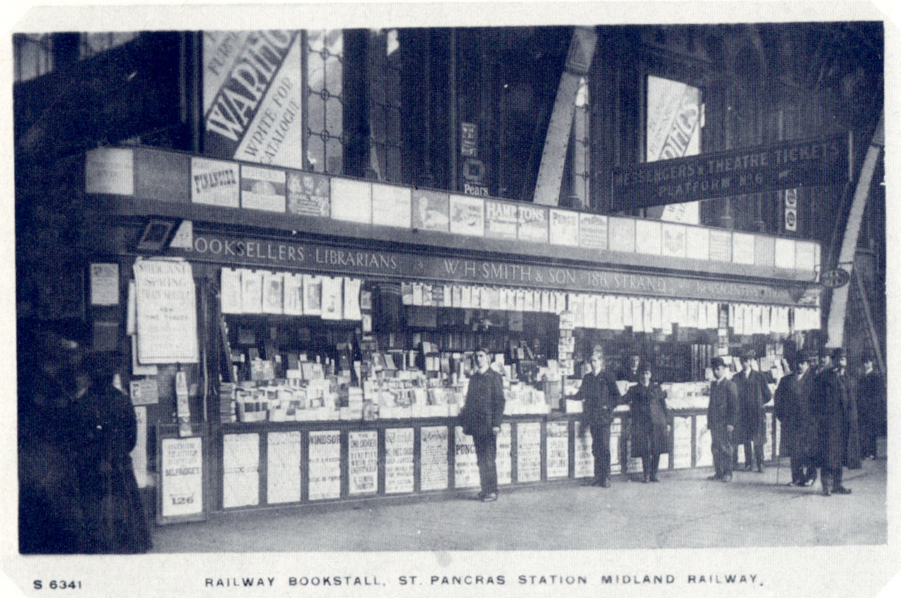


## 7. BOOKSTALLS

W. H. Smith's railway bookstall was an essential concomitant of most large railway stations, rural and urban. This card shows the bookstall at St Pancras station, being patronized by a group of respectable-looking middle-class gentlemen. The middle-class tone is supported by the hoardings which along with *Punch* and *Tatler* advertise *The World* with an article on 'Stage Morals and Stage Marriages' and a 'Spy' cartoon, *The Throne* with its special Japanese supplement, *The Automobile-Owner* testimony to the latest 'in' thing, and Selfridges offering their ostrich feather ruffles. Note also the sign indicating 'Messages and Theatre Tickets'. But it was not just the middle classes who patronized the bookstall. Robert Roberts, writing of the addiction of working-class youngsters in Edwardian Salford to the stories of Frank Richards, observes: 'I knew boys so avid for current numbers of the *Magnet* and *Gem* that they would trek on a weekday to the city railway station to catch the bulk arrival from London and buy first copies from the bookstall.'

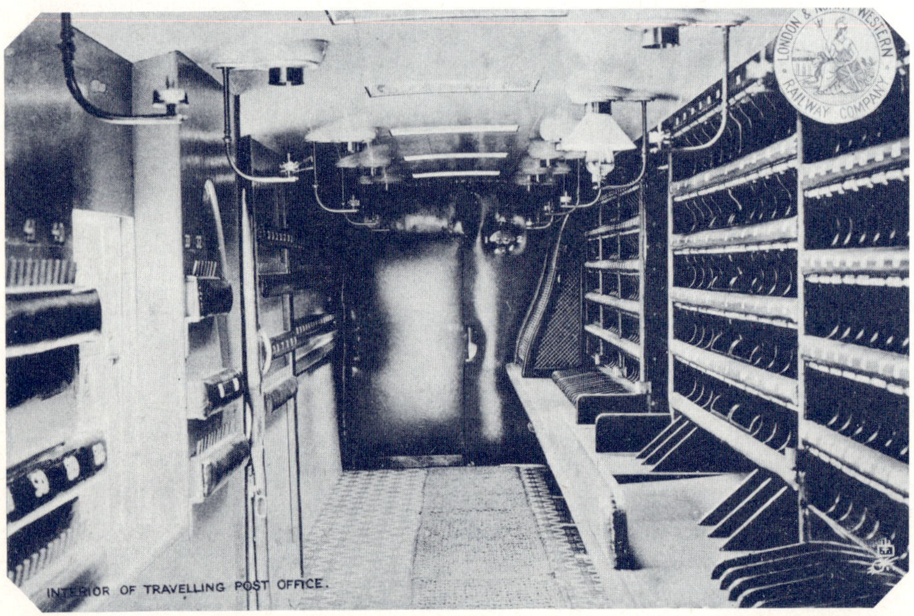


## 8. ROYAL MAIL

The Post Office started using the railways at once (1830) and the Mail Coach Office finally closed in 1854, acknowledging that link between the Royal Mail and the railways that has existed ever since. Here in an LNWR official card of 1904 is the interior of the travelling post office, where letters were sorted en route to their destinations. Several of the cards featured in this section are from the LNWR official series, remarkable for its clarity and breadth of subject, covering as it does every conceivable aspect of railway working. Most of the major railway companies issued their own cards, often depicting the scenic beauties of their routes and serving therefore not only as souvenirs but also as advertisements for the service. According to Reginald Silvester, the earliest official railway cards date from 1896. The LNWR series spanned the years 1904 to 1914, being discontinued on the outbreak of war. It sold an estimated 12 million cards during the decade.

9. SIGNALLING

The period of railway consolidation 1870–1914 was marked by steady advances in the improvement of track, signalling, engine and rolling-stock design. Here is the LNWR's most celebrated set of signals, its gantry signals at Rugby, photographed in 1906. On the back of the card is the slogan: 'The London and North-Western Railway is noted for Punctuality, Speed, Smooth Riding, Dustless Tracks, Safety and Comfort, and is the oldest Established Firm in the Railway Passenger Business.' Besides selling the railway, it is seen also to boost the virtues of the railway postcard, proclaiming: 'Buy the L and NW. series of Pictorial Postcards. 2d. per set of six different cards. Over 5½ millions sold.'

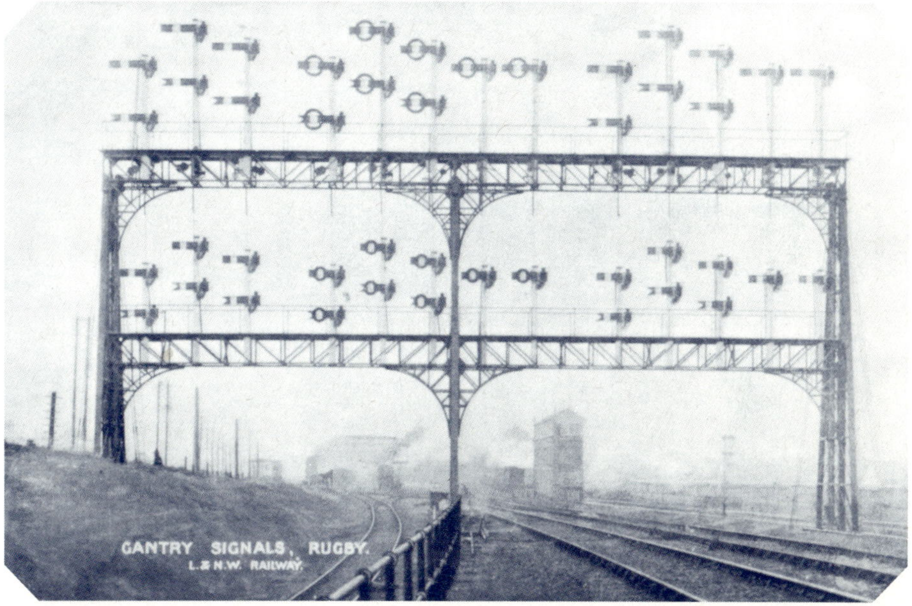


10. DINING CARS (i) LNWR

The London and North-Western introduced dining cars in 1889. This card depicts the luxurious dining car on the *American Special*, an express train introduced in 1906. The service is described on the back of the card: '*America via Liverpool*. Finest trains and boats in the world. The L and NW Railway Co. runs special non-stop trains from London (Euston) to the Riverside Station, Liverpool, in connection with the sailing of the Atlantic Liners. Similar arrangements apply in the reverse direction.'

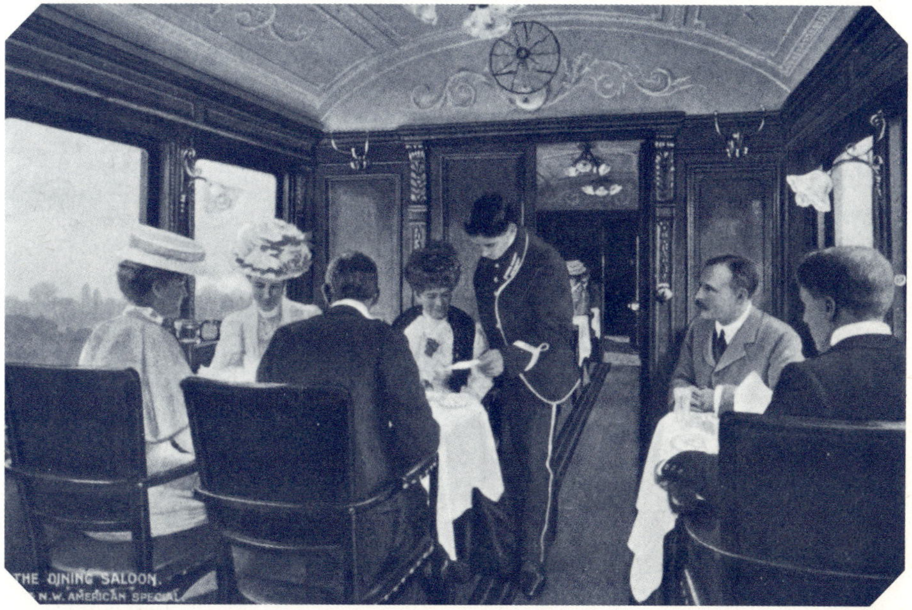

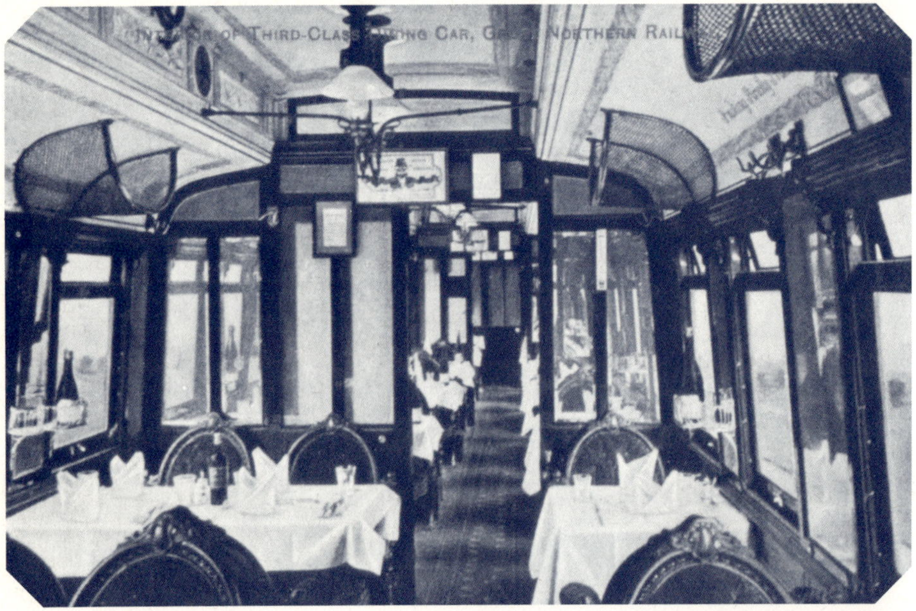

11. DINING CAR (ii) GNR

In its struggle with the Midland Railway to attract passengers by provision of better and better facilities, the Great Northern was the first company to introduce dining cars, on their London–Leeds route in 1879. In 1893 it introduced third-class dining facilities as part of the battle between the East and West coast routes to Scotland. This third-class dining car, complete with plush seats, wine racks and mirrors, is surprisingly opulent and far removed from the dusty compartments, hard wooden seats and total absence of lavatory and refreshment facilities which third-class passengers had once had to put up with.

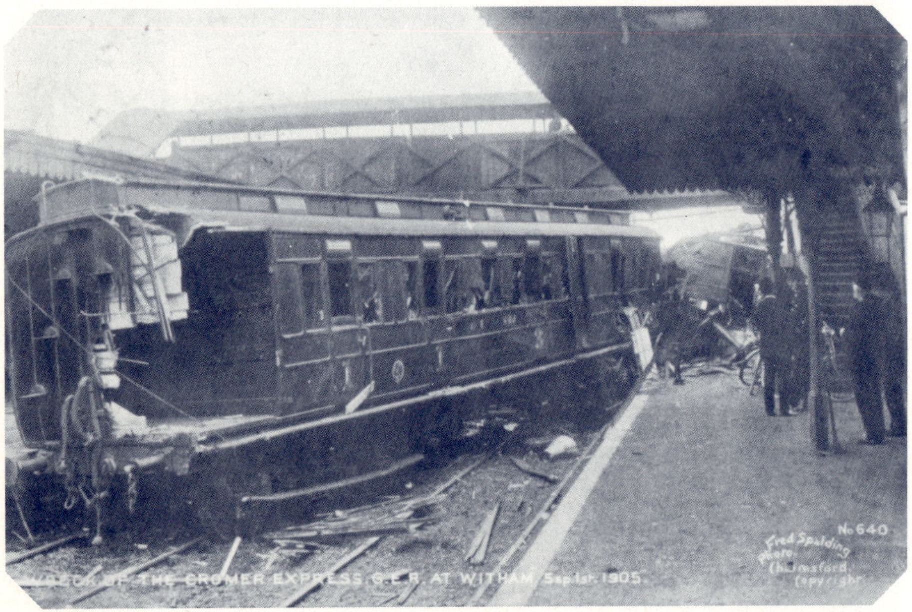


12. SPEED

Greater and greater speeds involved some danger to life and limb. On 1 September 1905 the Great Eastern Express from London Liverpool St to Cromer, travelling at 70 mph through Witham station, crashed spectacularly, the entire 14 carriages of the train being derailed. One of the carriages demolished the porters' room, killing a porter. Another carriage was smashed to pieces, killing all 8 occupants. The cause of the accident was later attributed to loose rail fastenings on the track. This card is a product of local enterprise, with Chelmsford photographer Fred Spalding racing to the scene, snapping the debris and rapidly producing a card. This particular card was sent on 2 October 1905, to Okehampton.

## 13. YORK STATION STAFF

The railways were one of the biggest employers of labour in the country and one of the most demanding. By the 1870s accidents caused by overwork were provoking a public outcry and in 1871 the Amalgamated Society of Railway Servants (ASRS), the parent of the modern NUR, was founded to defend the interests of the workers. It went on to play a major role in the creation of the Labour Party. But the battle for union recognition and improved conditions for the men was long and hard. The North Eastern Railway after a strike and arbitrated settlement in 1890 was one of the first railway companies to recognize and deal with the unions. Here some of the staff of York Station are gathered to be photographed in 1909, variations in uniform proclaiming their different functions and hierarchical status. York was the headquarters of the North Eastern Railway and behind the staff can be seen the majestic roof of the station, completed in 1877 by Thomas Prosser. It remains one of the grandest and most impressive stations in the kingdom.

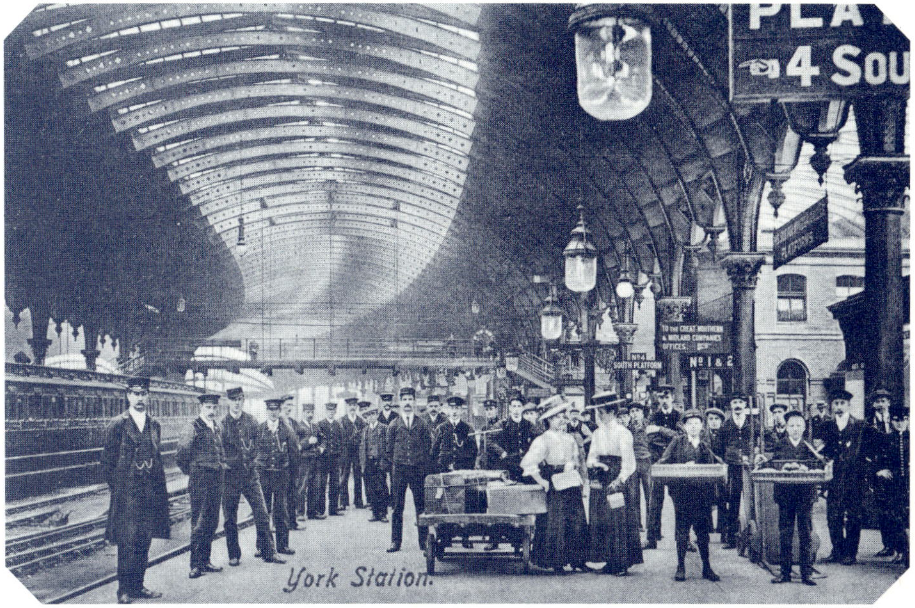


## 14. THE COUNTRY STATION

The country station was a vital element in the lives of the inhabitants of rural Britain. As David St John Thomas writes in his evocative memoir of the country railway: 'In most areas for at least two full generations all important comings and goings were by train . . . the pair of rails disappearing over the horizon stood for progress, disaster, the major changes in life: the route to Covent Garden and Ypres, the way one's fiance paid his first visit to one's parents, one's children returned for deathbed leavetaking, the way summer visitors, touring theatricals, cattle buyers, inspectors, came.' This delightful country station is Wellington College Station, on the South Eastern and Chatham line from Reading to Ash. It served, as the name indicates, Wellington College, opened in 1856 as a memorial to the recently deceased Iron Duke. The boys wore German-style cadet uniforms, designed by Prince Albert. But they were rapidly replaced after the Prime Minister, the Earl of Derby, arrived at the station en route for the school and handed his ticket to the Head Boy under the impression that he was an official of the railway company.

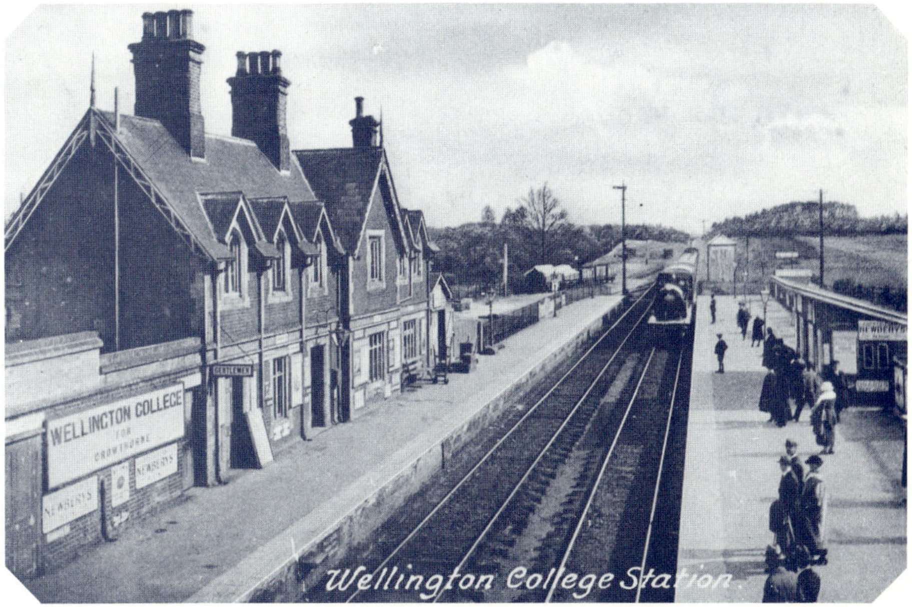

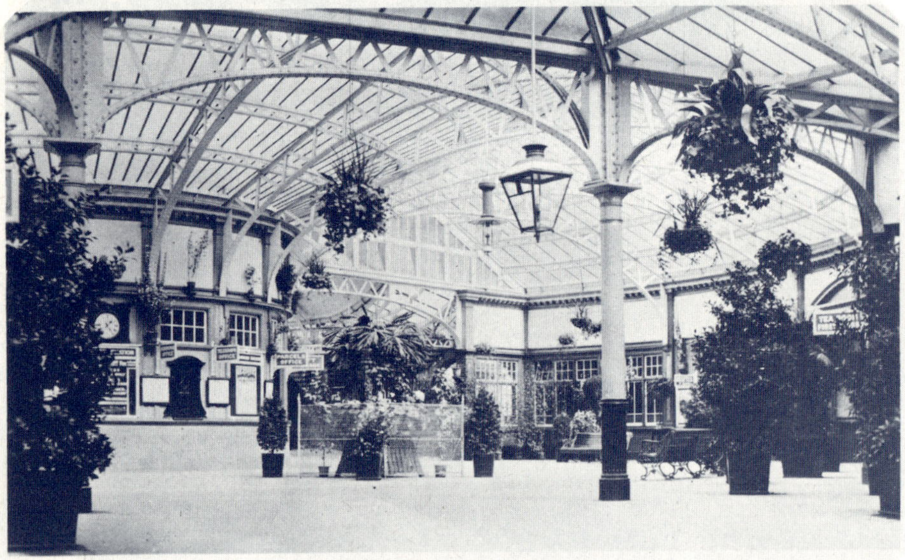

WEMYSS BAY STATION.

## 15. WEMYSS BAY STATION

Wemyss Bay station on the Clyde, the Caledonian Railway's terminal for steamer sailings to Rothesay and the Isles, remains much the same today as when this photograph was taken in the Edwardian era. It is a sort of grand Edwardian summer house, from which to step, clad in blazer and flannels, for a bracing trip down the Clyde. O. S. Nock in *Scottish Railways* calls the station 'a credit to Scotland'. The line was originally opened in 1865, linking Port Glasgow and Wemyss Bay, and was built by a local consortium, the Greenock and Wemyss Bay Railway Company. But it was operated by the Caledonian Railway in return for 45 per cent of the profits and they eventually took it over completely in 1893.

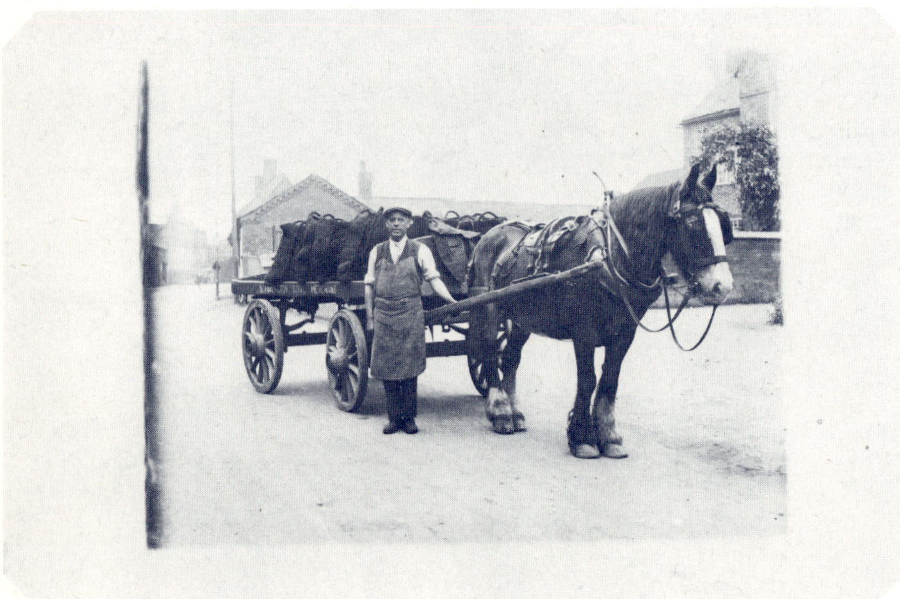

## 16. THE COAL MAN

Although its pre-eminence had been usurped by the railways, the horse remained ubiquitous as a form of transport both for people and goods. Coal men, milk men, brewers' draymen all delivered by horse. The first trams and omnibuses were pulled by horses. The railways themselves were served by cabs and delivery carts in abundance. It has been estimated that in the late Victorian period 1 horse for every 10 people was needed to keep society going. The smell of drying horse-dung perfumed the streets of the big cities in the summer. There was a good deal of ill-treatment of horses, provoking the foundation of the RSPCA in 1824 and the publication of Anna Sewell's propagandist *Black Beauty* in 1877. As late as the 1920s the cry 'There's a horse down' would bring children scampering from their courts and entries in working-class areas to see the horse thrashing between the shafts, one of the vivid sights of that eternal playground, the street. Here, a coal man stands proudly beside his horse and cart.

## 17. THE PONY AND TRAP

Here a respectable middle-class couple and their straw-boatered son pose in their pony and trap. The poster on the wall behind them, for the Halifax Hippodrome, indicates that they are in Yorkshire. Possession of one's own horse-drawn transportation was a mark of social status and in the Victorian age ownership of private carriages spread from the upper classes right through the middle classes, giving rise to the term 'the carriage trade' to denote the well-off. But as F. M. L. Thompson points out in *Victorian England: the Horsedrawn Society* this had far-reaching implications. A horse ate at least 6 tons of food a year, the product of 4 or 5 acres of land, and in 1902, the peak year of the horse population, there were some 3½ million horses in Britain. Privately owned horses and carriages required stabling, coachmen, grooms, creating the need for a large labour force. Another by-product was an estimated 10 million tons of horse droppings a year, providing work for an army of crossing sweepers and a permanent hygiene headache.

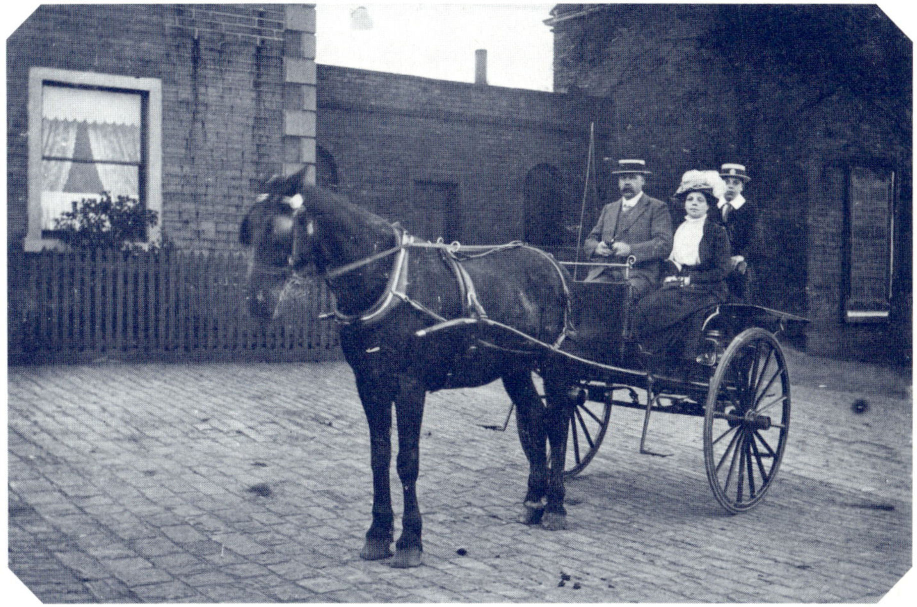

## 18. THE HORSE-DRAWN TRAM

The tramway was an application of the railway principle to the city street. The first horse-drawn trams came into operation in 1860 and many towns and cities adopted them to provide intra-urban transportation. The Morecambe Tramways Company began operations in 1887. It was taken over by the corporation in 1908 and remained in operation until 1926, the last horse-drawn trams in England. This card was sent from Morecambe to Middleton near Leeds in 1915.

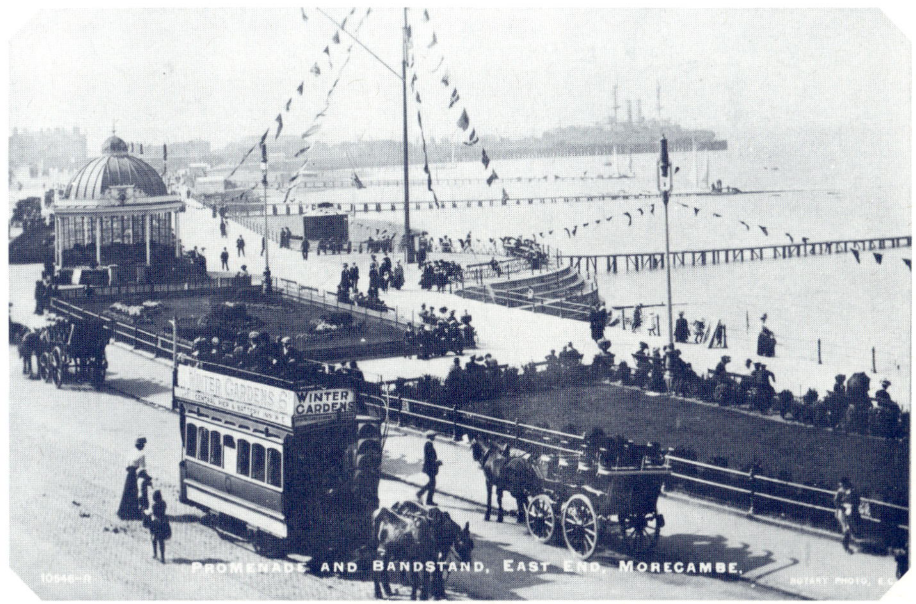

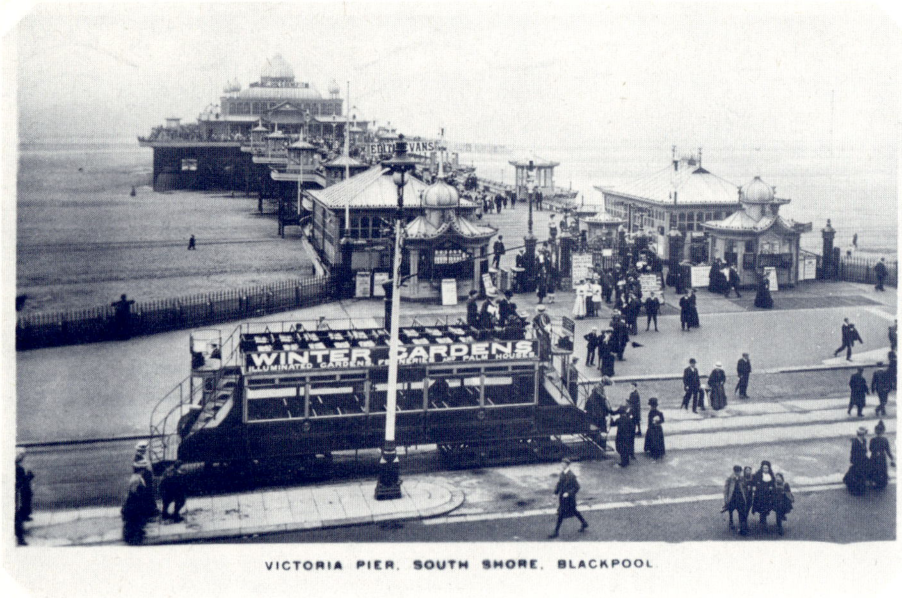


19. BLACKPOOL TRAMS

The electric tram inspired a similar romanticism to the stream train. The Irish poet 'AE' called electric trams 'those highbuilt glittering galleons of the streets' and Ford Madox Ford talked of 'the great rectangular blaze', calling them 'romantic and a little wonderful'. Blackpool was the first town to introduce the electric tram (1885) and it remains the only town to retain them today. Seaside towns were in the forefront of tramway electrification, finding them a valuable extra attraction for holiday-makers. This card was sent in 1917 from Blackpool to Doncaster and shows a tram passing the Victoria Pier and advertising the *Winter Gardens*, like its horse-drawn Morecambe counterpart in the previous card.

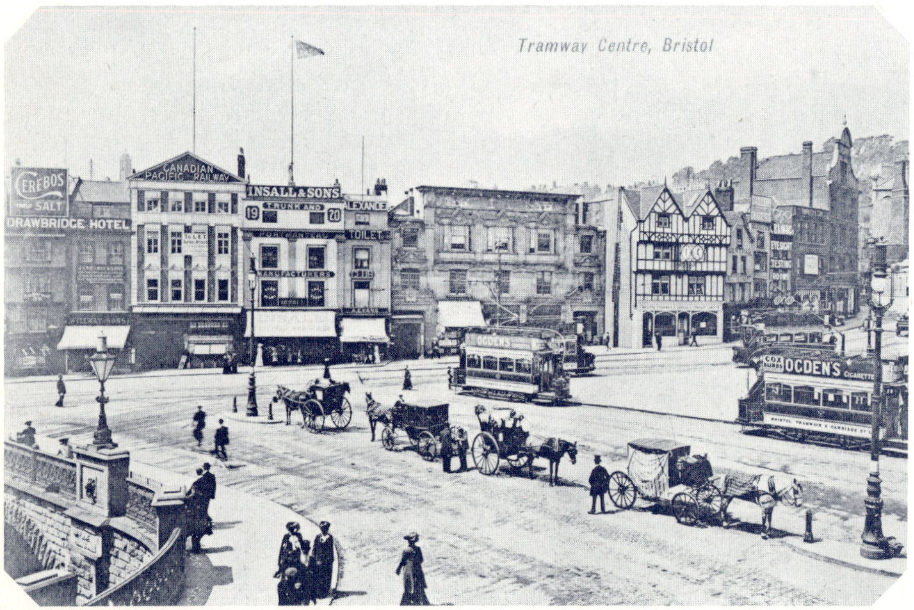


20. BRISTOL TRAMS

Bristol had one of the largest tramway systems in the West Country. The first tram line was opened by Bristol Tramways Company in 1875 and 'Tramways Centre' was in use by December of that year. The Bristol Tramways Co. merged with the local cab company, Bristol Carriage Co., in 1887 and there was a big expansion of tram lines. By 1900 all horse lines had been electrified. Eventually there were 31 route miles, operated in the early 1920s by a maximum number of 237 tramcars. The trams were replaced by buses in 1941. This card, showing both trams and cabs at 'Tramways Centre', was never sent but the photograph dates from between 1902 and 1914.

21. LEEDS TRAMS

In 1891 Leeds became the first city to introduce the overhead electrical trolley wire. Initially it completely disrupted the Leeds telephone service, whose lines were not insulated. This card, sent in 1903, shows trams in Briggate. Trams survived in Leeds until 1959 when they were replaced by the motor bus. The top of the tram was a favourite place for courting, and formed the basis of a song 'Riding on top of a car', recorded in 1905 by George Lashwood:

*Then we go, go, go for a ride on the car, car, car,*
*For we know how cosy the top of the tramcars are,*
*And the seats are so small and there's not much to pay,*
*You can sit close together and spoon all the way,*
*Many a miss will be mrs. some day*
*Through riding on top of the car.*

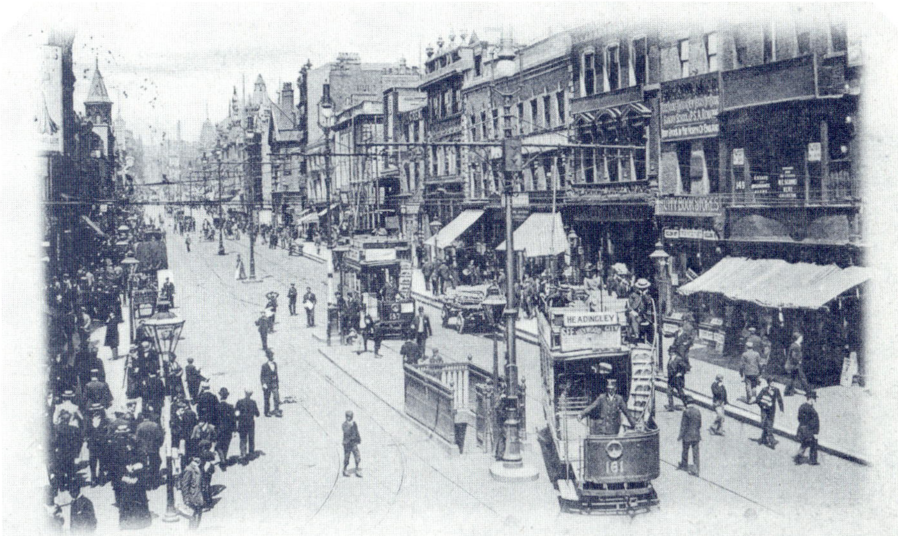

The Briggate, Leeds RELIABLE SERIES.

22. LIVERPOOL TRAMS

Liverpool was a pioneer in tramways, one of the earliest to introduce a system (1869) and one of the last to give it up (1957). Liverpool Tramways Company opened its first line on 1 November 1869. It merged with the rival horse bus company in 1876 to avoid destructive competition and in 1897 the corporation took them over. The system stood then at 75 track miles with 267 trams and 100 buses. Between 1898 and 1902 the system was electrified. This card, sent in 1904, must have been taken soon after the completion of electrification. It shows three trams, the one on the extreme right moving too fast for the camera to catch it. A line of cabs waits for the customers disgorged by the trams.

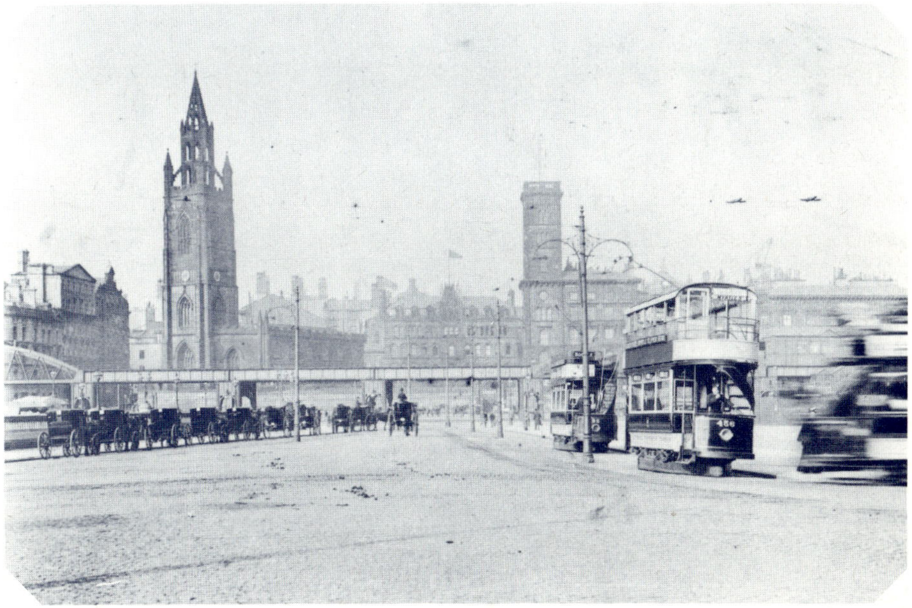

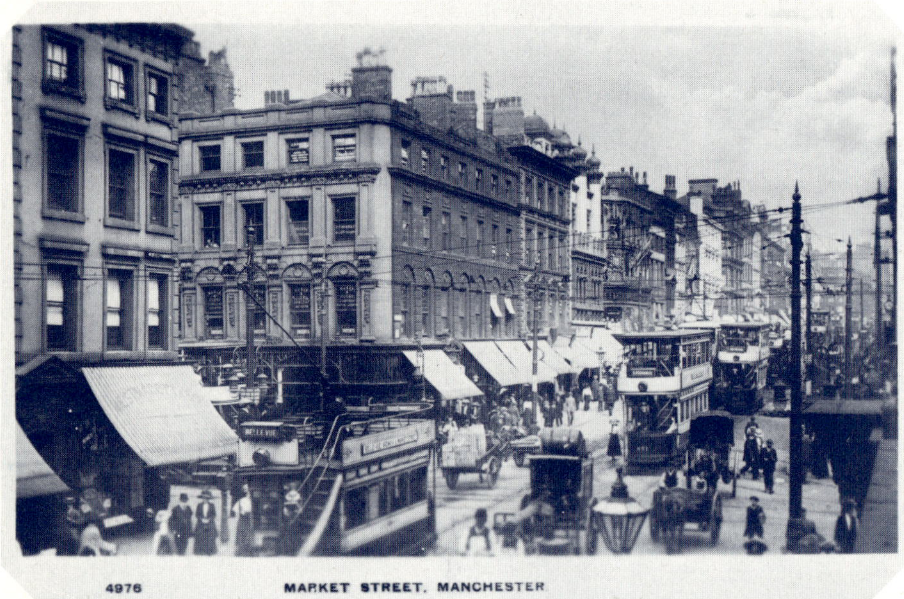


23. MANCHESTER TRAMS
Manchester was another city which put great faith in the tramcar. Its horse trams began running in 1877 and were electrified in 1901–03. By 1929 the fleet totalled 953 cars and there were 292 track miles. In 1924, they carried 295 million passengers. The trams went in 1949 to be replaced by motor buses and trolley buses. This card, sent in 1919, shows tram traffic in Market St and shows the continuing importance too of horse-drawn traffic. The card, postmarked Bristol and bearing an Indian 1 anna stamp with the head of the King-Emperor George V, bears an intriguingly cryptic message: 'Dear Mother, just a line to let you know I am alright and well. I left hospital in Manchester mid-day yesterday. I am at Bristol now but leaving at 8 a.m. for Salisbury I may be home Saturday'. It was sent to a Mrs Hackett at Bearwood near Birmingham, but is unsigned. The date, the stamp and the hospital reference suggest a recently discharged wounded soldier who had served until lately in India. But why is the card unsigned, why is he returning to Birmingham via Bristol and Salisbury and what is it all about? John Buchan would have had a field day with this.

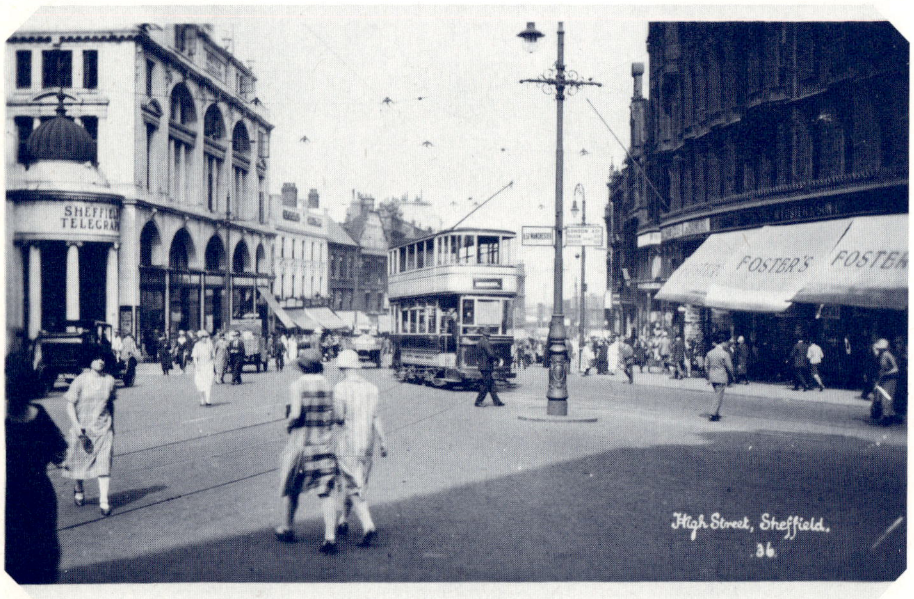


24. SHEFFIELD TRAMS
High Street, Sheffield, in the 1920s with a tram car and several motor vehicles; it presents a distinct contrast to Market St, Manchester, in 1919. Sheffield first had horse-drawn trams in 1873; electrified trams took over in 1899 and survived until 1960. As a pointer to the future, note the classification and numbering of roads as indicated by the road signs. The Ministry of Transport issued a road classification in 1921. Of some 150,000 miles of roads in England and Wales only 11.5 per cent was classified as Grade I ('A' roads) and a further 7 per cent as Grade II ('B' roads). Standardizing of road and traffic signs did not begin until the 1930s.

25. THE MOTOR BUS

The first motor bus service began in Edinburgh in 1898 and the idea rapidly caught on. Here is an early motor omnibus leaving Herne Bay for Canterbury, a journey of some seven miles, in 1905. It was made by Thornycroft and Co. of Chiswick, one of the pioneer British bus-building firms. It has attracted a crowd of interested onlookers, several of whom have moved as the picture was being taken.

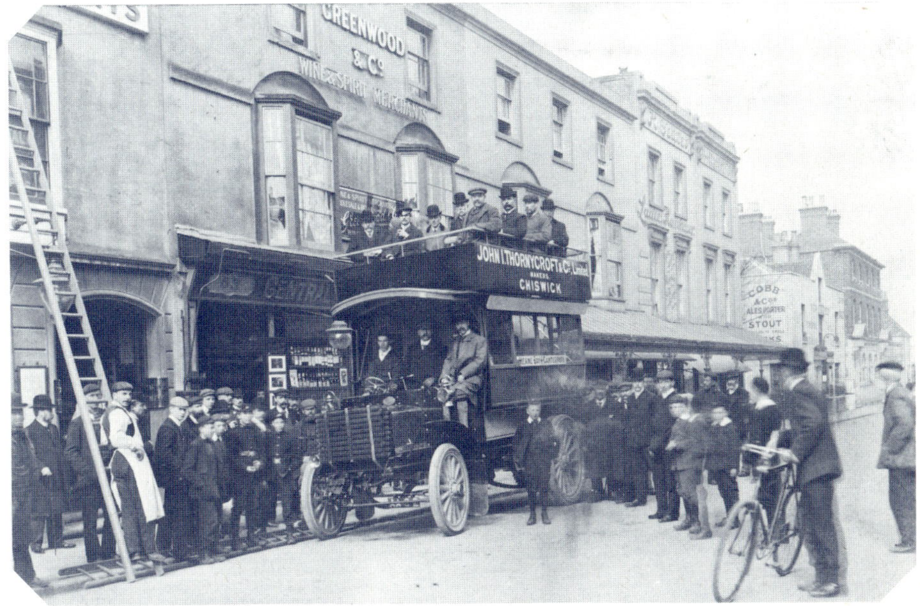


26. THE RAILWAY BUS

The railway companies were among the pioneers of motorbus operation, using their buses to link rural areas to the railway network. By 1905, the Great Western Company had 72 buses. The London and North-Western introduced their first motor buses in 1906 and this card, issued in the same year, shows one such linking Holywell in North Wales to the nearby station on the main Chester–Holyhead line. Gradient and width of road alike are proving a test for the primitive transmission system on the bus.

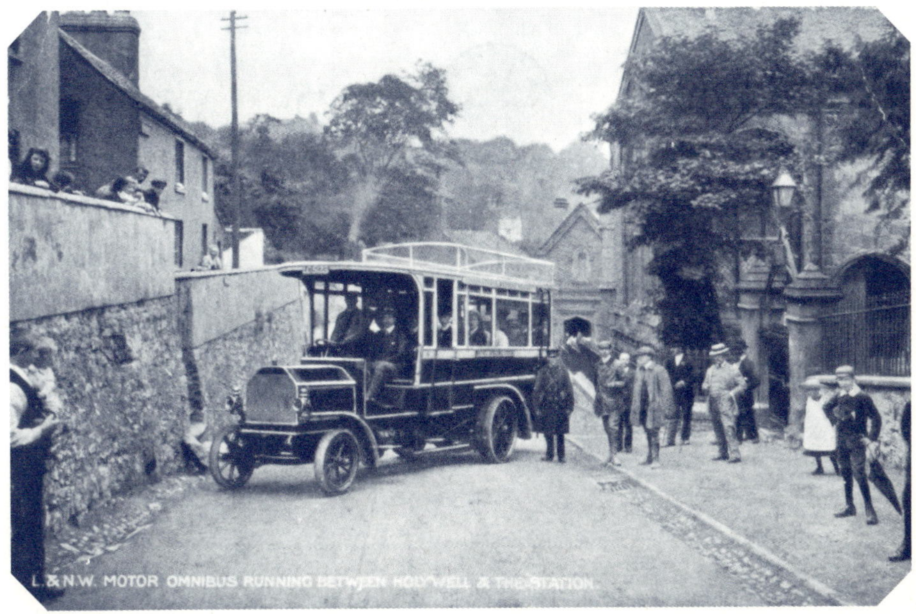

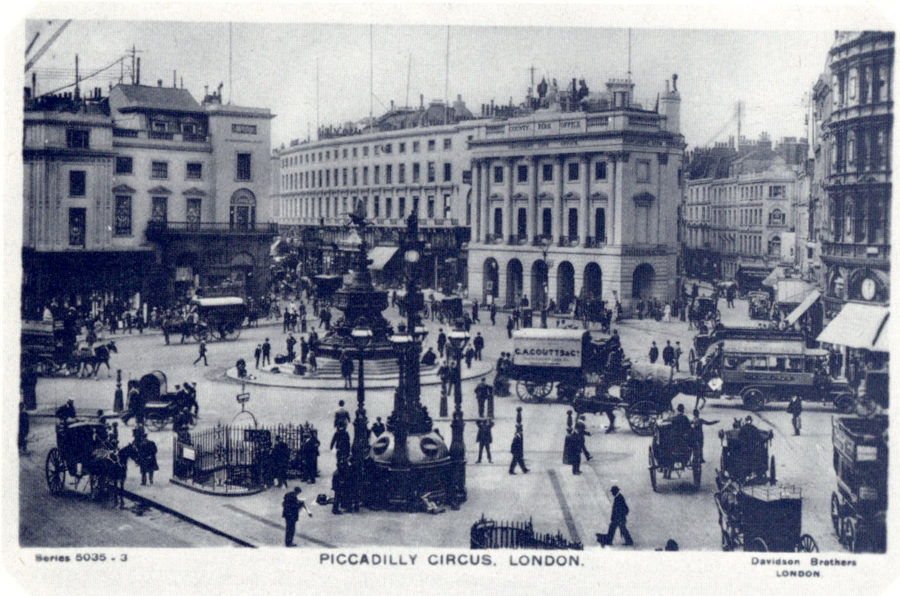


27. LONDON TRAFFIC (i) PICCADILLY CIRCUS

This busy scene shows the traffic in Piccadilly Circus in 1906, the date being deducible from the advertisement on the motor bus 'Union Jack' (centre right) for the musical comedy *The Dairy Maids*, put on at the Apollo Theatre by Robert Courtneidge in 1906. The card was sent to Bordeaux by a French visitor to London. On the extreme left is a horse bus; the last London horse bus was withdrawn in 1914. 'Union Jack', one of the London Road Car Company's fleet of motor buses, was so named to stress that it had none of the French connections of the rival London General Omnibus Company. There is much horse-drawn traffic but also a parked motor car (top right), the shape of things to come.

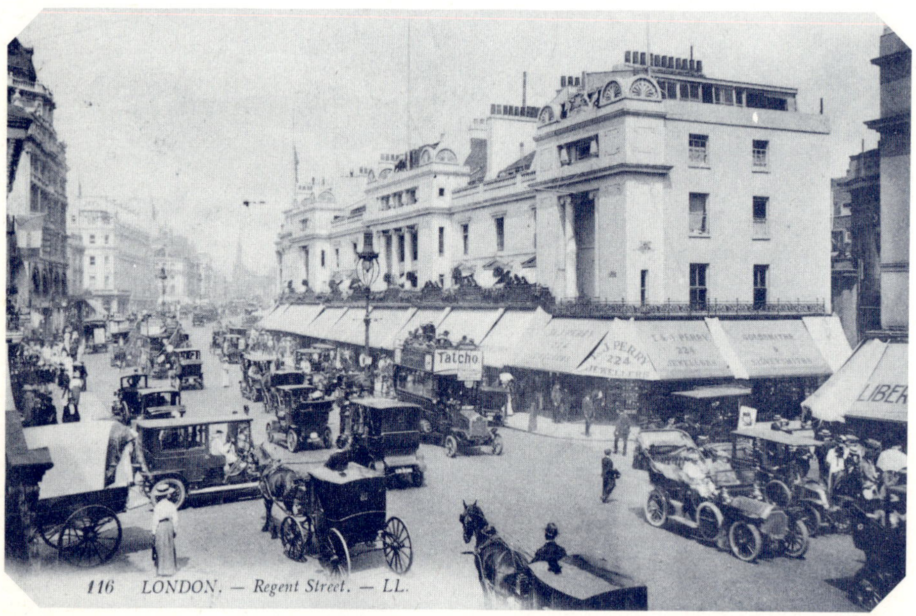


28. LONDON TRAFFIC (ii) REGENT ST

The rapidity with which the horse bus and the horse-drawn cab were replaced by the motor bus and the motor car is demonstrated by this card sent in 1912. It provides a potent contrast with the previous card. Some horse-drawn vehicles may be seen but the motor car, at this time still the plaything of the rich, is already dominant. 1910 was the first year in which there were more motor buses than horse buses in London and by 1915 the horse bus had vanished completely.

## 29. LONDON TRAFFIC (iii) THE BANK OF ENGLAND AND THE ROYAL EXCHANGE

Another card from around the same period shows the same situation obtaining in the heart of London's financial quarter. Note the use of routes showing intermediate destinations on the motor buses, a practice retained over the years. Note also the extreme longevity of the route numbers. Route No. 6 still terminates at Kensal Rise and few alterations have been made to the route west of the famous No. 11.

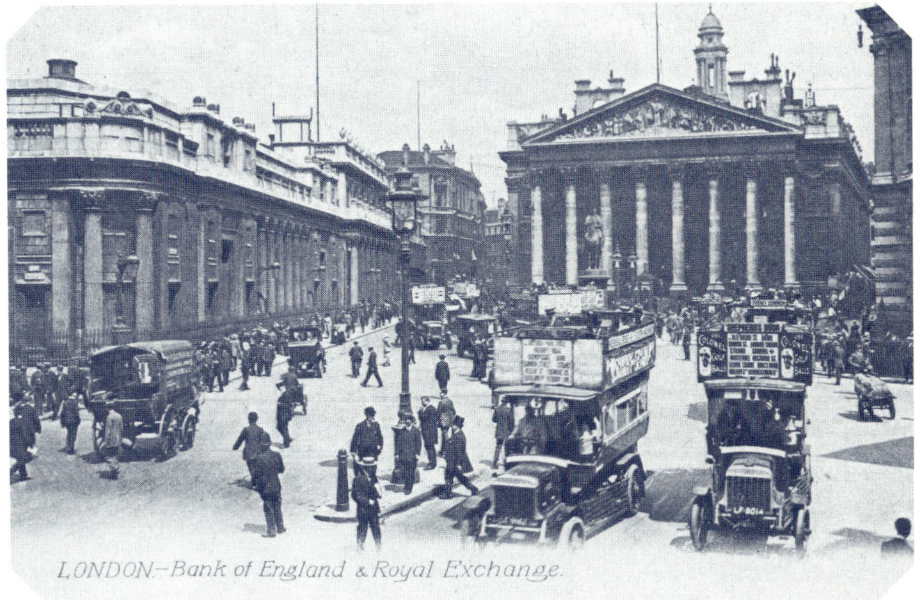


## 30. THE MOTOR CAR

The pride of car ownership is written all over this photograph, taken in July 1911 at Odsal near Bradford. It is a pride that was to percolate downwards from the upper class before the Great War to the middle class in the inter-war years to the working class in the 1950s and 1960s. It signals the beginning of the assault on public transport by the well-off, self-centred car owners, who resent paying for a socially necessary service which they themselves rarely use. Even in the midst of the energy crisis of the 1970s and 1980s this assault shows no sign of diminishing.

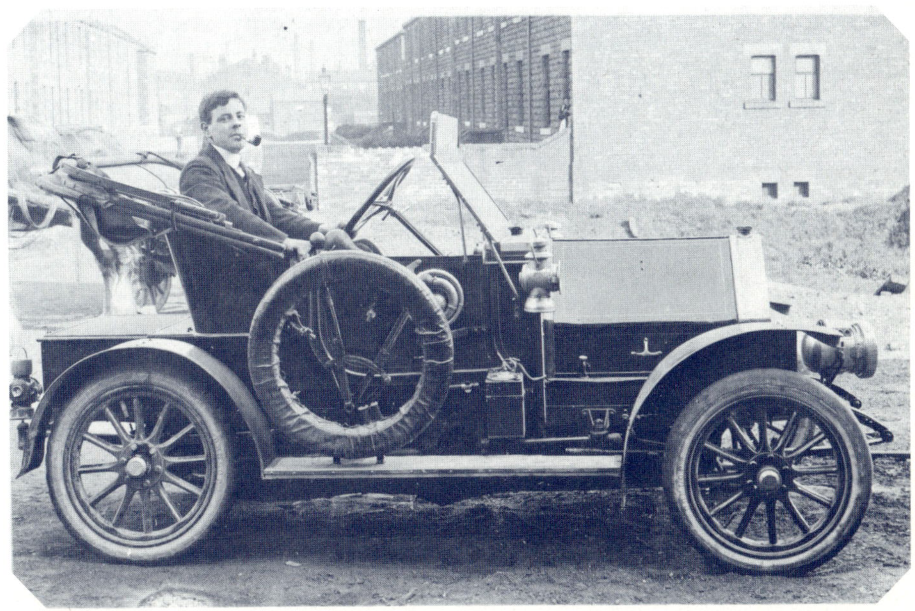

# CHAPTER FIVE | LEISURE AND RECREATION

The last three decades of the nineteenth century saw the creation of the mass entertainment industry. It was made possible by revolutionary technological developments, improvements in transport and perhaps most important – a dramatic increase in the amount of spare time and spare cash available to the working classes. It was a complete reversal of the situation which had obtained in the first half of the century. The twin processes of industrialization and urbanization had all but extinguished traditional leisure patterns. Open spaces, which provided sporting and feasting venues, were built over; street entertainments were suppressed by the newly established police force and the revolution-conscious authorities; spare time was ruthlessly absorbed into the working week by industrialists anxious to make a maximum return on their investments.

There was some alleviation, however. The practice of taking off Monday, known ironically as 'St Monday', was common in many industries and reluctantly tolerated by employers. In various parts of the North and Midlands traditional pre-industrial holidays – 'the Wakes' – survived and remained occasions for fairs, excursions and jollification. But by the middle of the century, prompted by the first of a stream of exposés of the conditions of working-class life, pressure began to grow for more leisure time for the masses. Evangelical and moralistic objections that leisure was mere frivolity while work ennobled and the employers' concern at losing valuable production time were met by the argument, increasingly supported by medical opinion, that rest and distraction were necessary to renew the workers' strength and commitment, hence the increasing use of the term 'recreation'. So first came Saturday half-holidays, then early closing days for offices and shops, the 1871 Bank Holiday Act and the trend towards company holidays first without and later with pay. This growth in leisure time was accompanied by a general improvement in living standards, as prices fell from the 1870s. More people had more time and money to spend on pleasure, though no less than a third of the population remained in poverty as turn-of-the-century social surveys revealed.

As the working classes found themselves with more and more spare time, so did the middle classes become increasingly concerned about how they would spend it. Various movements grew up concerned to direct the working classes into improving pursuits – what came to be called 'rational recreation'. This involved, first of all, an assault on all those working-class sports and pastimes that were regarded as brutal, degrading and provoking of crime, drunkenness and violence. Bear and bull baiting, cock fighting and public executions were banned; prize fighting and ratting were harassed by the authorities. But the principal haunt of the working classes remained the pub and the major problem of working-class life, as discerned by the improvers, was drunkenness.

The rise of a class society in Victorian England was reflected in leisure-time pursuits. The pub became unmistakably and inescapably plebeian. As Brian Harrison has pointed out, by the 1850s no respectable Englishman entered an ordinary public house. It simply was not done, whether because it offended the newly dominant middle-class canons of privacy and propriety or because it transcended principles of abstinence adopted by nonconformists. For the working classes drinking was the universal leisure pursuit. Drink was refresher and anaesthetic, consolation and escape. Alcoholic drinks were inevitable, since neither milk nor water were safe to drink and alternative beverages like tea and coffee were not initially as accessible as beer. However, besides drink the pub in the 1820s also provided heat, light, food, newspapers, lodgings, a meeting place for all kinds of society and political groups, an organizational centre for sports, gambling, savings clubs, excursions, a stage for theatricals and entertainers, a haunt for prostitutes, even 'an embryonic labour exchange'. Although the pub shed some of these functions as the century wore on, it remained a primary social focus.

It was this central institution of working-class life that the temperance movement in all its manifestations set out to undermine. The movement began life in 1828 and remained a vital force in British society throughout the century. It was not just a middle-class attempt to impose its values on the working class, for like many of the evangelical churches, some of its most prominent supporters came from the 'labour aristocracy', skilled working men and artisans with an improving ethic as a means to self-fulfilment.

The temperance movement, however, did not just aim to stop drinking, it was really, as Brian Harrison points out, 'an argument about how leisure should be spent'. The provision of counter-attractions was one of its themes and along with attacks on the secondary functions of the pub (attempts to rescind music licenses, restrict opening hours, exclude children, stamp out animal contests and gambling), the temperance movement built halls to provide alternative meeting places, staged concerts, lectures, galas and organized cheap excursions. Nevertheless, *per capita* consumption of alcohol continued to rise until the 1870s and when thereafter, it began to fall, it did so for reasons not directly linked to the temperance movement. Non-alcoholic beverages were becoming increasingly available and attractive, with improvements in municipal water supplies, deliveries of fresh milk by the railways, the development of fruit cordials, and the rising popularity of tea, coffee and cocoa, increasingly adopted by the working classes as an integral part of their diet. The growth of eating houses as non-alcoholic alternatives to the pub can be measured from County Durham, where in 1841 there were only 2 coffee and eating houses; by 1881, there were 104. Two of the major influences fostering drunkenness were also under attack in the 1870s: bad housing and the lack of alternative leisure areas to the pub. The beginning of slum clearance and the encouragement of the middle-class concept of 'home life' attacked the pub from one direction and the rise of alternative leisure pursuits attacked it from the other. Sport, music, the music hall and the popular theatre, the provision of municipal museums, parks, libraries, art galleries, coupled with the rise of the electric tram providing cheap and accessible transport, all challenged the hitherto unchallenged leisure eminence of the pub. Subsequently the cinema's rise constituted another assault and Seebohm Rowntree correlated the decline in drunkenness cases in York with the rise in cinema attendance. After the Great War, the position stabilized. The pub remained an important leisure centre in working-class life, though shorn of some of its auxiliary functions, but drunkenness ceased to be a major social problem and the much-touted spectre of a drink-crazed mob emerging from the lower-depths to butcher their betters was finally laid to rest.

In the early part of the nineteenth century, the principal alternative to the pub as a social centre was the church or chapel. But like pub-going, church-going was essentially class-based. The Industrial Revolution, in promoting the transformation of Britain from a primarily rural to a primarily urban nation, in causing the wholesale disruption of patterns of life and leisure and major shifts and transfers of population, also contributed perhaps more than anything else to the secularization of the new society. As a clergyman remarked in 1896: 'It is not that the church of God has lost the great towns; it has never had them.' Probably less than a quarter of the urban working classes went to church. Indeed the powers that be were deeply shocked to learn from the 1851 religious census that of a population of 18 million souls only some 7 million regularly attended church. The Church of England, with its Tory and Establishment associations, lost ground dramatically in the early nineteenth century and became in the towns just a church for the upper and upper middle classes. It was the nonconformist churches who possessed the religious dynamic, were animated by missionary zeal and preached the ethic which became the ethic of the Victorian middle class (thrift, work, self-help, individualism) and drew into their ranks the lower middle class and the labour aristocracy. There was thus a fundamental disjunction between church and chapel perhaps not so much on class lines, as between tendencies to deference and independence. The position changed somewhat in the second half of the nineteenth century as Anglicanism revived, with internal reorganization, the recruitment of better clergy and the adoption of a missionary strategy, and nonconformity lost its impetus, as it became itself institutionalized, exclusivist and somewhat complacent. There were still, however, the revivalist crusades of Moody and Sankey, the foundation of the Salvation Army by General William Booth and the creation of missions and settlements in poorer areas where pious and principled middle-class social workers could put the Christian teachings into practical effect. But Christianity as a whole, whether it be of the church or chapel variety was being undermined as part of a longer-term trend between 1860 and 1914 by other major social developments: the crisis of faith which accompanied the publication of the theories of Darwin and Freud, the growth of materialism which accompanied rising living standards and rising expectations, and the growth of alternative creeds, in particular socialism and trades unionism, which sometimes went hand in hand with religion but increasingly did not. Nevertheless, the churches continued to play an important social role, quite apart from catering to the spiritual needs of their congregations. They organized concerts, excursions, lectures and sports clubs, provided meeting places and companionship for those not drawn to the beery camaraderie of the pub. More significantly, even if the working classes did not go to church as a rule, they, like the middle classes, often sent their children to Sunday School, if for no other reason than to get them out of the house. In the second half of the nineteenth century the Sunday School continued to play an important role in promoting literacy and basic education, as well as providing for children a recreational alternative to the street, with trips, festivals, parades, choirs and prize-givings. Church-going, however, continued to decline in the aftermath of the First World War and the rather sober and improving attractions of church social life were swamped by the palaces of pleasure provided by the new entertainment industries: music halls, cinemas, the palais-de-danse. It is somehow symbolic that many a narrow, tin-roofed, backstreet chapel became converted into a primitive cinema as the craze for moving pictures seized the nation.

It was middle-class improvers rather than the middle classes as a whole who sought to introduce for the working classes 'rational recreation'. For the middle classes were concerned about having their own leisure pursuits swamped by an influx of the masses, as happened for instance at the seaside. In the big industrial cities civic elites, animated by religious beliefs, philanthropic ideas, social responsibility, civic pride or a mixture of all four, set about providing parks, gymnasia, art galleries, museums, libraries and swimming baths and encouraging the masses to use them. They initiated evening classes, industrial exhibitions and adult schools, a byproduct of Sunday schools, to supplement and extend the rudimentary education of the masses. It was felt that by so doing they would promote social harmony, and cultural consensus. But their schemes were doomed by the technological advances which made possible vast entertainment industries which they could not control and by the actions of the working classes themselves. At least in part they were able to subvert such attempts to direct their leisure.

Peter Bailey has demonstrated convincingly the ways in which the working classes successfully resisted attempts to channel their interests in 'approved directions'. For instance the working-men's clubs movement, founded in 1862, began as a middle-class bid to introduce the workers to temperance and intellectual pursuits. By the 1880s, they had been taken over by the working classes and had abandoned their temperance and intellectual connotations. By the last three decades of the nineteenth century, the economic pre-conditions were there for the development of the mass entertainment industry – a large and concentrated urban population, the increase in real income and in spare time, cheap and improving urban transportation by train and tram, cheap and mass-produced printing of newspapers, advertising and sheet music. With these ingredients, sport, music and theatre were all transformed into mass leisure pursuits. Then in the 1890s a clutch of new inventions – wireless, gramophone and cinema – heralded the birth of new and exciting leisure pursuits. The mass entertainment industry was animated not by the desire to improve but to entertain. 'Rational recreation' was doomed, but ironically its aim – the reduction of drunkenness and drinking – was achieved. Symptomatic perhaps of the replacement of education by entertainment is the conversion in 1864 of the Panopticon of Science and Art in Leicester Square into the Alhambra Music Hall.

The 1860s saw the rise of the 'New Athleticism', the organization and codification of sports and games with the clear aims of promoting physical fitness, moulding character, instilling self-discipline and bridging class differences. Its progress can perhaps best be charted in football. Pre-industrial football had been violent and disorganized and had declined with the rise of the cities, the disappearance of open spaces and the clamping down on disorder. It survived in the public schools, however, and became one of the instruments by which Dr Thomas Arnold and his disciples sought to transform the public schools from hotbeds of drunkenness, violence and indiscipline into the seedbeds of a new Imperial ruling class of Christian gentlemen. The rules of football were codified and the concepts of 'playing the game', 'being a good loser', teamwork, manliness and modesty were developed from it.

The railway network enabled school teams to travel to play each other and the passion for the game survived schooldays to prompt the formation of teams by public school old boys. In 1863 the Football Association was founded by several London and suburban clubs to provide a national framework for the game, though the public schools themselves remained aloof from this development. In 1872 the F. A. Challenge Cup was introduced to encourage competition among the growing number of football teams. It created an immediate focus of interest and further stimulation for the development of the game. There was now a two-way process in operation: a spontaneous upsurge of interest among the working classes for a game which was cheap, simple, energetic and competitive and a deliberate propagation of it by public-school educated or influenced teachers, clergymen, social workers and industrialists. Many of the most celebrated British football clubs originated thus: from church teams (Aston Villa, Bolton, Everton, Wolves), from school teams (Blackburn Rovers, Leicester City, QPR), from working men's teams (Manchester United, Arsenal, West Ham). Public interest grew, facilitated by mass literacy, the development of sports pages in the local newspapers and the accessibility of cheap transport. Whereas the first F. A. Cup final attracted 2,000 spectators in 1872, that of 1900 attracted 69,000 and the 1913 final 120,000.

The public school elite gradually lost control of the sport which was rapidly democratized to become 'the people's game'. Its original organizers set their face against professionalism and commercialization. But the rising popularity of the game with the masses necessitated it. The members of working-class football teams needed travelling expenses and when their football became their work, they needed paying. After a fierce and prolonged debate, the payment of wages was legalized in 1885 and professionalism arrived. Symbolically in 1883 the working-class Blackburn Olympic beat Lord Kinnaird's Old Etonians in the F. A. Cup final, ending ten years of public school victories. Commercial entrepreneurs entered the field, football teams became limited companies, new stadia were built, ancillary trades developed, the game became big business. The public school amateurs retreated from the field, many of them turning to rugby, which had developed from the 1820s. But English rugby experienced its own crisis and split in 1895 with Rugby League, northern, professional and working-class, parting company with Rugby Union, which was predominantly southern, amateur and middle-class.

In 1888 the Football League was established to organize a regular programme of fixtures, a national league and eventually separate divisions. It was dominated by Northern and Midland clubs. By 1914, of the 40 clubs in the two divisions, only 6 were from the South and West. Amateur football flourished also with some 12,000 clubs registered with the F. A. in 1910. Although football was suspended during the First World War it resumed thereafter with even greater vigour. A third division was formed in 1921, the first Wembley Cup final was played in 1923 and football became an integral part of everyday life, with the introduction of football pools and the chance to get rich quick, the growth of cigarette cards, magazines and comics generating a lore and mythology of the game and the focussing on local teams of tribal loyalties and atavistic emotions.

Public school influence was also apparent in the development of other sports and a similar, though less extreme, pattern is detectable: a growth in popularity, national competitions, a split between amateurs and professionals – gentlemen and players – and the ending of social exclusivity. In 1873 the County Cricket Championship was set up and in 1877 the Wimbledon Tennis Championship. The Amateur Athletic Club, which had banned 'mechanics, artisans and labourers', was replaced in 1880 by the Amateur Athletic Association which welcomed them.

Technological developments made possible two sports which became great rages, particularly with the middle classes: the invention of ball-bearings facilitated roller-skating, a craze ('Rinkomania') in the 1870s and again later in the 1900s; the invention of the pneumatic tyre made cycling available, and cycling with its fresh-air appeal became enormously popular in the 1890s, the more so since women, excluded from many sports, could participate fully. By 1887 the sports editor of the *British Argus* could write: 'Legitimate sport or exercise for the grave and gay, for the young and old, for the rich and poor, for the male and female, is the great order of the day.'

E. D. Mackerness has written: 'it would be impossible to exaggerate the variety and profusion of English musical life from say 1897 to 1914.' These decades did indeed see the culmination of a movement which had been growing throughout the nineteenth century – the tradition of music-making by and for the masses. Music was everywhere – in the home, in church, in schools, in the streets even; Gilbert and Sullivan operas at the Savoy, Sir Henry Wood's Promenade Concerts at the Queen's Hall, music festivals in Birmingham, Leeds, Sheffield, Brighton, Norwich etc., symphony orchestras in most big cities (even Bournemouth had one), travelling opera companies, choral societies, brass band, schools of music springing up in the wake of the Royal College of Music (1883), musical comedies in the theatres, massive sales of sheet music and pianofortes for home music-making, German bands and Italian organ grinders in the streets, nigger minstrels on the sand.

A rigid division between high- and low-brow, which infuses present-day musical snobbery, had not yet arrived. Sir Edward Elgar, Britain's greatest composer and the leading light of the English Musical Renaissance which produced Parry, Stanford, Bantock, Sullivan, and later Holst, Vaughan Williams, Bax and Boughton, wrote symphonies and oratorios, brass band music, marches, salon pieces and popular anthems, while Sir Arthur Sullivan ranged from *H. M. S. Pinafore* and *The Gondoliers* to the grand opera *Ivanhoe* and from the Irish Symphony and the incidental music to *The Tempest* to the tearjerking ballad 'The Lost Chord' and the rousing hymn 'Onward, Christian Soldiers'.

The origins of the musical explosion lay in the need for people to make their own entertainment in the new urban society, in the emphasis on singing in the Nonconformist churches, in the desire of enlightened employers and middle-class improvers to provide alternative entertainments to the pub, and in the growing belief that music-making was character forming. Music was believed 'to wean the mind from vicious and sensual indulgences; and if properly directed, it has a tendency to incline the heart to kindly feelings and just and generous emotions.'

When Queen Victoria came to the throne, music was non-existent in English schools; by 1870 it was an integral part of the curriculum. Singing was given a great boost by the development and popularization of the Tonic Sol-Fa system of 'sight-reading' music, which brought music-making within virtually everyone's capability. Perhaps the two most characteristic products of Victorian popular music-making were the brass band and the choral society, which flourished particularly in the North and Midlands. It was surely of them that Elgar was thinking when he said: 'The true musical centre of England is not to be sought in London but much further North.' Many Northern choral societies were old-established (Bradford 1821, Huddersfield 1836, Warrington 1834), but many more were added as the century progressed, formed by churches, commercial and industrial companies and private groups. Oratorios were their particular delight; Handel's *Messiah* and Mendelssohn's *Elijah* easily eclipsed all other contenders to popular pre-eminence.

The development of choral competitions in the 1880s, yet another phenomenon facilitated by the railways, gave that extra edge of pride and excitement to music-making. It did the same for brass bands. By the 1890s there were no less than 222 brass-band competitions. Almost every institution of working-class life produced brass bands, factories, churches, trades unions, political organizations, temperance groups. Technical innovation in instrument making and mass production of both instruments and music hastened the rise of a pastime, which fostered comradeship, discipline, pleasure and excitement. Many factory owners and company bosses saw the brass band as valuable enough to give the bands subsidies and time off to rehearse and compete and bands like Black

Dyke Mills were to earn international reputations. By 1889, an estimated 40,000 brass bands were in existence. They inspired publication of their own magazines like *British Bandsman* and stimulated ancillary trades like the manufacture of uniforms. They achieved the stamp of musical respectability since composers like Elgar, Bantock and Holst composed pieces specially for them.

There was music too in the home. From 1850 onwards the pianoforte was commonplace, even in many artisan homes. By 1910, there were 2 million pianos in Britain and by 1911 some 47,000 piano teachers. A piano became a mark of respectability, piano-playing a valued escape for the women of the house and the musical evening a regular and popular feature of domestic social life. Firms like Boosey and Chappell poured forth cheap sheet music for home performance and the latter part of the nineteenth century became the heyday of the popular ballad. The very names of these still half-remembered songs conjure up the flavour of those evenings long ago when the visitor was greeted by the cry 'Have you brought your music?', and robust voices would render 'I'll Sing Thee Songs of Araby', 'I Dreamed that I Dwelled in Marble Halls', 'Where My Caravan Has Rested' and 'Come into the garden, Maud'.

Music and the stage met and mingled in the music halls, which grew out of the variety saloons and song and supper rooms of the early nineteenth century to become one of the principal sources of working-class entertainment in the second half of the Victorian era. The first purpose-built music hall, the Oxford in Oxford St, was opened in 1861 and others followed rapidly. By 1878 there were 347 licensed music halls in London alone. They were shunned by the middle classes, who saw them as excuses for drunkenness, nudity and raw sexuality, both on and off the stage. But the people flocked to them, creating several generations of star performers, who in their much-loved and oft-repeated songs expressed their fears and hopes, preoccupations and life-styles. Florrie Forde, Dan Leno, Little Tich, Gus Elen, Harry Champion, the list is almost endless and endlessly evocative of the music hall atmosphere that Kipling described as 'the smoke, the roar and the good fellowship of relaxed humanity'. Perhaps the best loved was Marie Lloyd, past whose grave 100,000 people reverently filed when she died in 1922.

The reformers launched a succession of attacks on them, aiming to eliminate the rowdiness and lubricity of both songs and audiences. Reform did come in the 1880s and 1890s but at the behest of music hall proprietors and theatrical entrepreneurs, anxious to broaden their appeal and make yet more money up-market. So they remodelled their buildings, banned drink from the auditoria, dispensed with the chairman, the fast-talking master of the revels, cleaned up the lyrics of the songs and kept out the obviously rougher elements. In the process, they created a bastard form of music hall called 'variety' which the people continued to flock to, joined now by the middle-class and upper-class audience. Its respectability was clinched by the staging of the first Royal Command Variety performance in 1912.

Working-class and middle-class audiences also enjoyed legitimate theatre. The removal of the monopoly of drama from the patent theatres in 1843 which had liberated the music hall likewise liberated the stage play and signalled a great upsurge of drama. For the quality, theatre-going was a great social event, with full evening dress, carriages at eleven and the chance to see the great actor-managers at the height of their powers. Sir Henry Irving was the first actor to receive the accolade but he was followed by other giants: Sir Herbert Beerbohm Tree, Sir Johnstone Forbes-Robertson, Sir John Martin-Harvey. The West End stage glittered with the plays of Wilde and Shaw, Pinero and Henry Arthur Jones, and there was always Shakespeare, staged in the greatest pomp and splendour. If you were in a mood for escapist relaxation, there were frothy musical comedies at the Gaiety Theatre, notable chiefly for the Gaiety Girls, several of whom married into the peerage.

But the nineteenth century was the era pre-eminently of the melodrama, highly coloured sensational tales which appealed equally to the patrons of the Britannia, Hoxton or the Theatre Royal, Drury Lane. M. F. K. Fraser, in his history of Birmingham's Alexandra Theatre, describes these plays:

*Patrons . . . liked their fare hot, strong and richly coloured. A highly moral tone was of course expected. Virtue must always triumph, the gallantry of the True British Gentleman (or an Honest British Tar) always win the day; but these ends had to be achieved the hard way, through blood and toil and tears and calumny and misunderstanding. Grey hairs must be brought in sorrow to the very verge of the grave; decrepit old mothers must be turned out by stony-hearted Sir Jaspers to beg their bread from door to door; heroines pure as driven snow must perish to slow music in an atmosphere laden with pathos . . . Always acceptable were plays about the Upper Crust, about Ruritanian monarchs and plotters, about queen mothers and mother-*

*superiors, about lords and ladies, frail, fickle and gay, about generals and admirals and flag lieutenants (whatever they may have been), about all the gallant, wicked, fantastic denizens of that tuppence coloured State, the kingdom of Melodrama.*

Even the poorest areas of the cities had their local 'Blood Tub' where down-at-heel third-rate travelling companies enthralled the populace with their renditions of such old war-horses as 'London After Dark', 'Drink', 'The Bells' or 'Pure As Driven Snow'.

Virtually all these areas of entertainment were to enjoy their last great heyday in the Edwardian era, a period which saw the development of those new inventions which were to signal the eclipse of live entertainment – the cinema, the wireless and the gramophone. Music hall, melodrama, live music-making all went into sharp decline, as the new media of mass entertainment found their feet and began to grow. The cinema was the first. Moving pictures had been a novelty in the last years of the nineteenth century, included on music hall bills and at fairgrounds. But the Edwardian era saw the arrival of small purpose-built cinemas (the first in Colne in 1908) and the First World War set the seal on its acceptance as a popular entertainment medium. Three and a half million people a day were 'going to the pictures' by 1917. The trend continued in the 1920s. The fare the public were offered was little different to that in the old stage melodramas but it was no longer bounded by the sides of a stage and enacted before painted backdrops. The whole world now passed before their eager eyes. The silent cinema gave the public new idols: Valentino, Garbo, Doug Fairbanks and Mary Pickford, Tom Mix. By 1926 some 3,000 cinemas were in operation with more opening all the time, some of them converted theatres, others converted music halls, still more converted chapels. By the same date, less than 100 music halls still survived in operation. By the 1930s, the cinema became, in A. J. P. Taylor's words, 'the essential social habit of the age'.

At home, sheet music sales plummeted and the pianoforte began to gather dust. First the gramophone enabled people to hear the voices of their favourites in ballad, opera and music hall song without having to leave the front parlour. Then came the wireless. In 1923 the British Broadcasting Company was founded and by 1925 2 million licence holders were eagerly 'listening in'. In the spirit of the nineteenth century advocates of 'rational recreation', the Director-General of the BBC, Sir John Reith, popularly known as 'The Czar of Savoy Hill', believed that the duty of the wireless was to educate and improve and he pressed ahead with schools broadcasts, discussions and lectures, classical music and classic serials. But newspaper surveys revealed that these were very largely ignored by the mass of listeners who switched on for dance band music, variety shows, the news and the football results.

Although stage plays, football matches and that new phenomenon, the palais-de-danse, still offered successful live, spontaneous entertainment, the 1920s saw the completion of a revolutionary transformation of leisure. Passive spectating replaced active participation; staying at home replaced going out. All was in readiness for the advent of the 'telly age'.

FURTHER READING


Bailey, P., *Leisure and Class in Victorian England* (London, 1978)

Beaver, P., *The Spice of Life: Pleasures of the Victorian Age* (London, 1979)

Booth, M., *English Melodrama* (London, 1965)

Briggs, A., *Mass Entertainment: the Origins of a Modern Industry* (Adelaide, 1960)

Cheshire, D. F., *Music Hall in Britain* (London, 1974)

Delgado, A., *Victorian Entertainment* (Newton Abbot, 1971)

Dobbs, B., *Edwardians at Play 1890–1914* (London, 1973)

Fraser, M. F. K., *Alexandra Theatre* (Birmingham, 1947)

Gilbert, A. D., *Religion and Society in Industrial England* (London, 1976)

Harris, H. A., *Sport in Britain: its origins and development* (London, 1975)

Harrison, B., *Drink and the Victorians* (London, 1971)

Inglis, K. S., *Churches and the Working Classes in Victorian England* (London, 1963)

Lowerson, J. and Myerscough, J., *Time to Spare in Victorian England* (Hassocks, 1977)

Mackerness, E., *A Social History of English Music* (London, 1964)

Mander, R. and Mitchenson, J., *British Music Hall* (London, 1974)

McLeod, H., *Class and Religion in the Late Victorian City* (London, 1974)

Meller, H. E., *Leisure and the Changing City* (London, 1976)

Morris, P., *Aston Villa – The First 100 Years* (Birmingham, 1974)

Pearsall, R., *Victorian Popular Music* (Newton Abbot, 1973)

Pearsall, R., *Edwardian Popular Music* (Newton Abbot, 1975)

Pearsall, R., *Popular Music of the Twenties* (Newton Abbot, 1976)

Phillips, J. and P., *Victorians at Home and Away* (London, 1978)

Roberts, R., *The Classic Slum* (Manchester, 1971)

Rubinstein, D., 'Cycling in the 1890s', *Victorian Studies,* **21** (1977–78) pp. 47–71
Stevenson, J., *Social Conditions in Britain Between the Wars* (London, 1977)
Walvin, J., *The People's Game* (London, 1975)
Walvin, J., *Leisure and Society 1830–1950* (London, 1978)

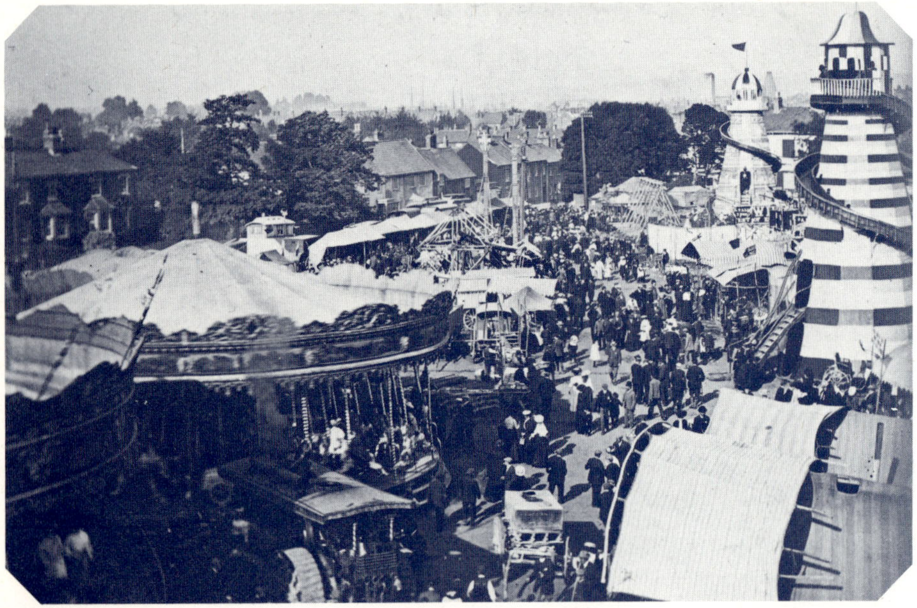

1. THE FUN OF THE FAIR

Although popular leisure patterns were changed dramatically with the coming of industrialization and urbanization, some pre-industrial entertainments survived. Despite being regarded by the authorities as a cause of violence, crime and general disorder, fairs continued to bring colour, novelty and excitement into the drab lives of the urban proletariat. They had begun as commercial gatherings for the selling of livestock and trade goods but turned into social occasions as they attracted entertainers of all sorts. Fairground amusements were revolutionized in the 1860s with the application of steam power and again in the 1880s with the introduction of electricity. It was from this decade that the still familiar amusements (roundabouts, big wheel, switchback railway) dated. This card, which from the masts in the distance and the divided back is from an Edwardian seaport, shows the full range of fairground attractions and includes both steam and electrically powered machines.

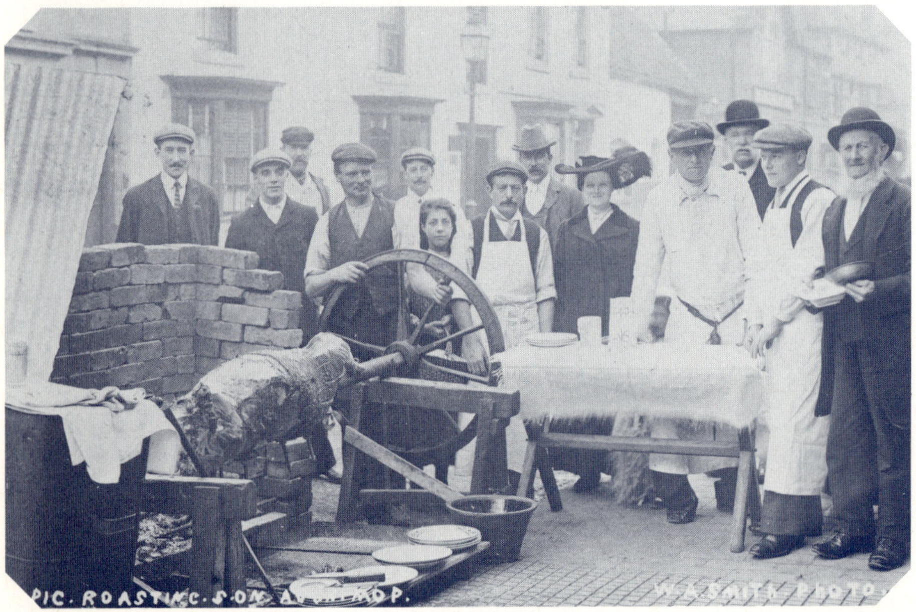


2. PIG-ROASTING IN WARWICKSHIRE

There was a great interest in history, folklore and archaeology in the Victorian age, particularly in an idealized medieval 'Merrie England'. It inspired many of the mainstream cultural developments of the nineteenth century, such as Gothic architecture, Pre-Raphaelite painting, the historical novel and the folksong revival. It also found expression in the deliberate revival of antique customs and practices, such as this open-air pig roasting. The card is dated 1906 and was sent to Haslemere, from Henley-in-Arden. It is another example of local photographic enterprise, in this case that of W. A. Smith, who took this unusual occurrence and turned it quickly into a postcard.

3. FLOWER SHOW

There was a definite class division in the spending of leisure time; the rich followed a strictly ritualized regime of pleasure, dividing their time between town house, country house and continental retreat and punctuating their year with regular functions: Henley, Ascot, Goodwood, grouse-shooting, the theatre, the London season. In the country, they would preside in paternalist squirearchical fashion over the village's annual social functions: harvest festival, the pageant, the flower show. In this card, which eloquently summarizes the social order of Britain on the eve of the Great War, Lady Watney distributes prizes at the flower show in the Oxfordshire village of Charlbury. With her on the platform is the vicar, straw-boatered and gazing reflectively heaven-ward. The children, in their Sunday best, seem rather more interested in the camera than in Lady Watney: their betters on the platform maintain a studied indifference. Lady Margaret Watney, third daughter of the 5th Earl of Portsmouth, was the wife of the local lord of the manor, Vernon Watney Esq. *Whittakers Peerage, Baronetage, Knightage and Companionage* (1911) gives his residences as: 'Cornbury Park, Charlbury; Fannich, Lochluichart, Ross-shire; 11, Berkeley Square, W'.

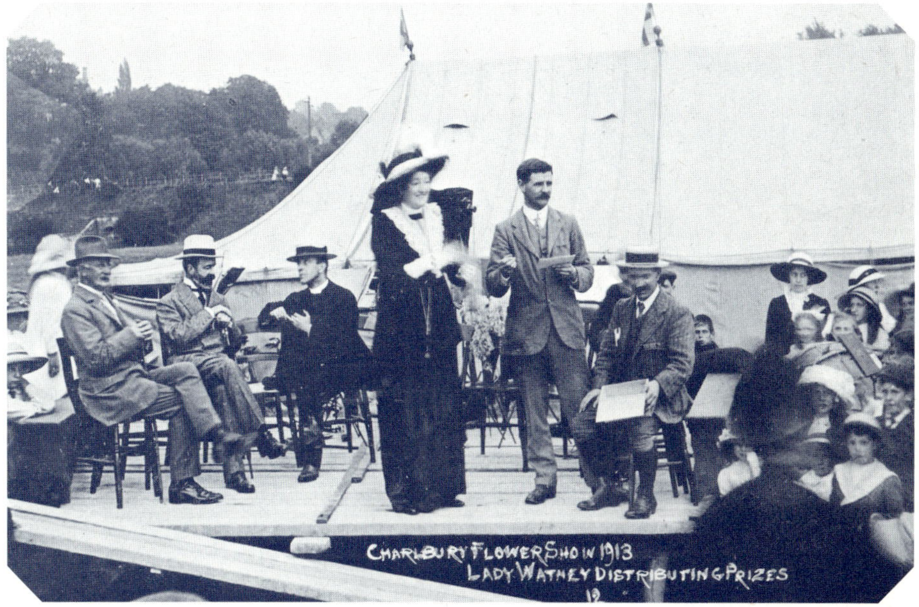


4. THE HUNT

The irony of the class division of leisure is encapsulated in the fact that while they busied themselves about their hunting, shooting and fishing, the powers that be set about systematically suppressing what they considered the brutal and brutalizing sports of the working classes, many of which involved cruelty to animals. Thus bear baiting and bull baiting were declared illegal in 1835, cock fighting in 1849; bare-knuckle prize fighting was harassed by the authorities and declined in the 1860s particularly after the introduction of the Marquess of Queensberry's Rules in 1866. Public executions, a regular source of excitement and fun, were ended in 1868. Ratting continued for longer, enjoying the patronage and support of army officers and wealthy gamesters, but by the end of the century had virtually disappeared. This hunt is setting out from The Saracen's Head at Great Dunmow. The hotel still survives.

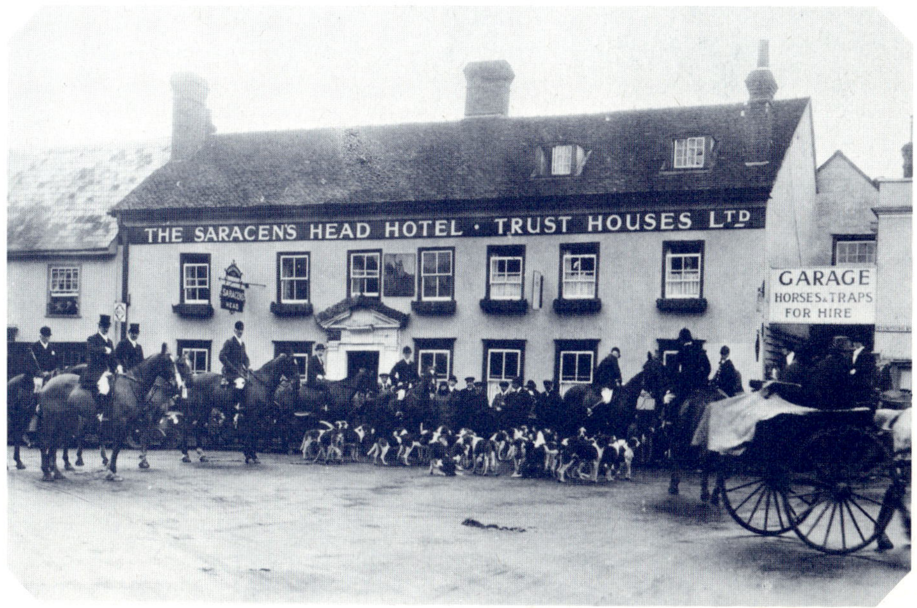

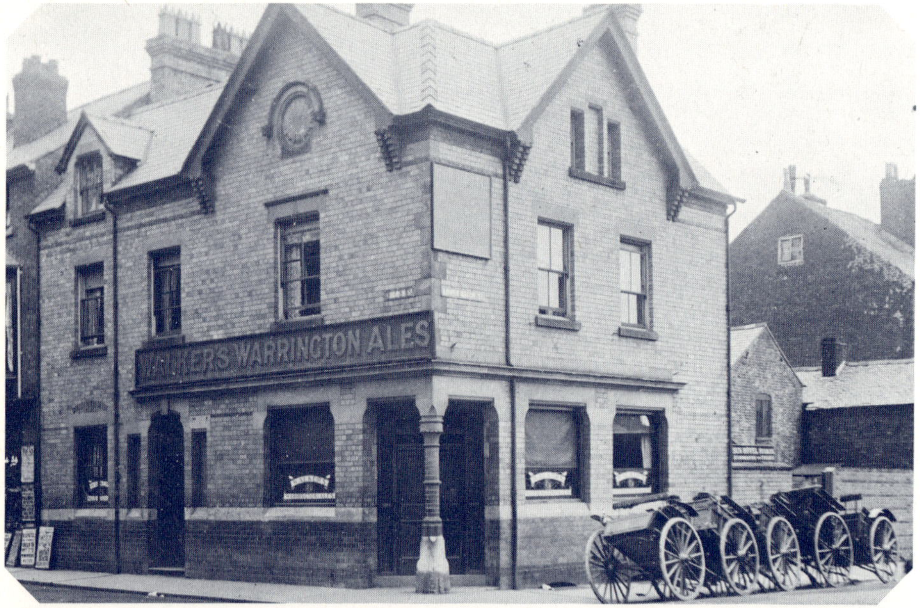


5. THE PUB (i)

Temperance campaigner John Burns described the public house as 'the antechamber to the workhouse, the chapel of ease to the asylum, the recruiting station for the hospital, the rendezvous of the gambler, the gathering ground for the jail' and it was the prime object of reform for moral improvers. But for the working classes, oppressed by bad housing and the lack of accessible alternative sources of relaxation, it was a vital social centre. The Sun Hotel, Warrington, depicted here, was built in 1876. It was clearly a superior class of pub, offering as it did stabling and accommodation for cyclists.

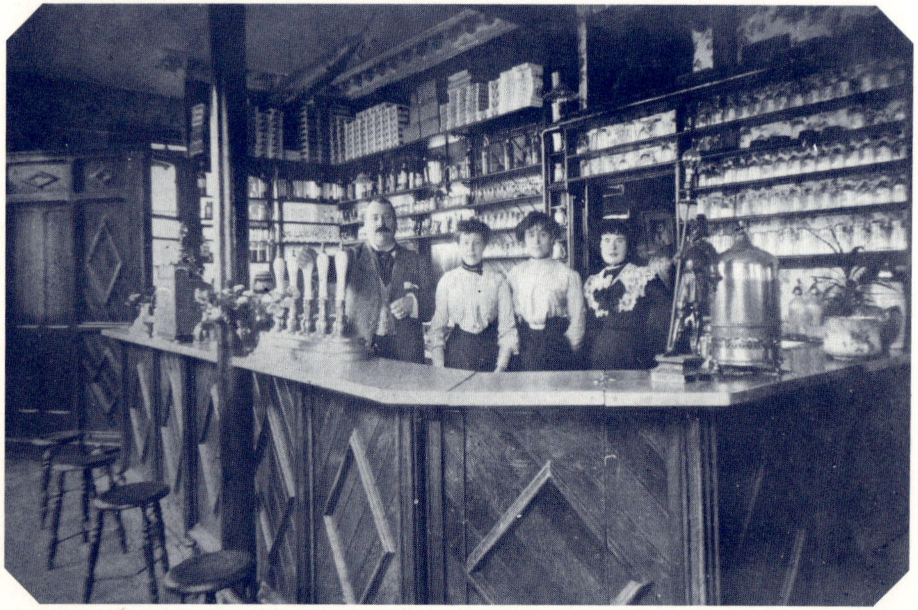

6. THE PUB (ii)

A rare card of a public house interior in Edwardian days. In 1908 there were 100,000 pubs in England and Wales and the handsome fixtures and fittings of this one show what a powerful attraction it must have been to the inhabitants of cramped and ill-lit slum housing. Behind the bar is the prosperous and substantial figure of the landlord with his staff. The landlord of the local was an important figure in working-class society. In *The Classic Slum*, Robert Roberts writes of him:

*After the squalor from which so many men came there dwelt within a tavern all one could crave for – warmth, bright lights, music, song, comradeship, the smiling condescension of the landlady, large and bosomy, for ever sexually unattainable, true, but one could dream, and her husband (the favoured called him by his first name), a man of the world dispensing wit and wisdom – and Tory politics too of course; publicans were Tories almost to a man and the party's self-appointed agents.*

7. THE PUB (iii)

The ubiquity of the pub in matters social, recreational, organizational and functional was increasingly challenged from the 1870s onwards. Temperance halls, church halls, schools and public buildings were opened up to provide meeting places for clubs and societies. The Post Office Savings Bank, opened in 1861, provided an alternative to pub-based saving clubs. The building of public lavatories meant that there was no need to visit the pub to relieve one's bladder. Working men's clubs, coffee houses and eating houses were opened as non-alcoholic alternative venues for food, drink and companionship. Most significantly, Church and temperance groups became active in providing counter-attractions in the form of concerts, lectures, outings and cheap excursions. It is significant that Thomas Cook, the pioneer of railway excursions, was a strong temperance supporter. Nevertheless many outings continued to end up at a pub and here a group of working men in their Sunday best, some with medals and button-holes and clearly part of an official formal outing, relax outside a charming country pub. Among them a local rustic sucks reflectively on his clay pipe. Unusually a woman is part of the group, perched uneasily on a chair arm. The pub was so exclusively a masculine preserve that she is likely to be the landlady of the inn.

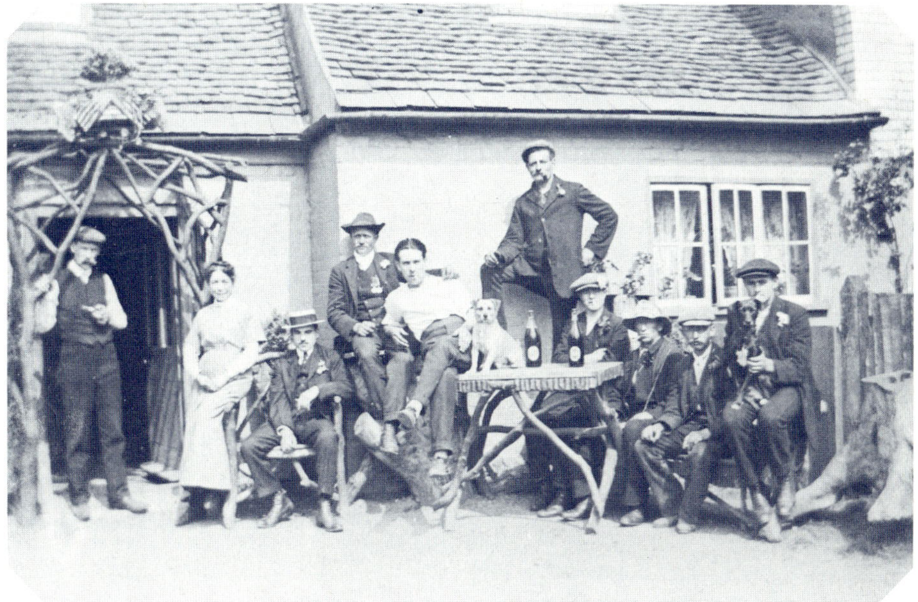

8. PUB SPORTS

One of the continuing attractions of the pub was sport. There was a long-standing association between sport and drink. Many retired prizefighters and retired professional footballers became pub landlords. Pubs became meeting places for sports teams of various sorts and the venues for sports particularly associated with the pub: ratting and, in more civilized days, darts, dominoes, skittles and bowls. Bowls was a long-established sport. But it was not until the mid-nineteenth century that it was organized and codified. Rules for bowls were first drawn up in Scotland by W. W. Mitchell in 1849. In England the game developed more haphazardly, but after 1850 there was a gradual move towards the adoption of the Mitchell Code. Local and regional associations were formed, beginning with the Northumberland and Durham Association in 1882. As in Rugby, there was a regional division, with bowls played on level greens in the south and crown greens in the north of England. Bowls became so popular in pubs that by the end of the nineteenth century many breweries, particularly in the Midlands, equipped new pubs with adjacent bowling greens.

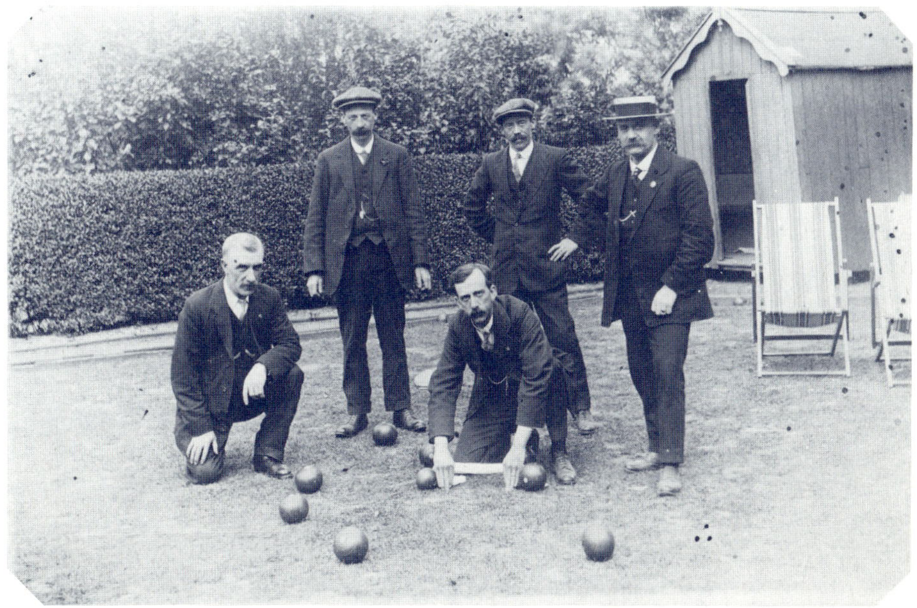

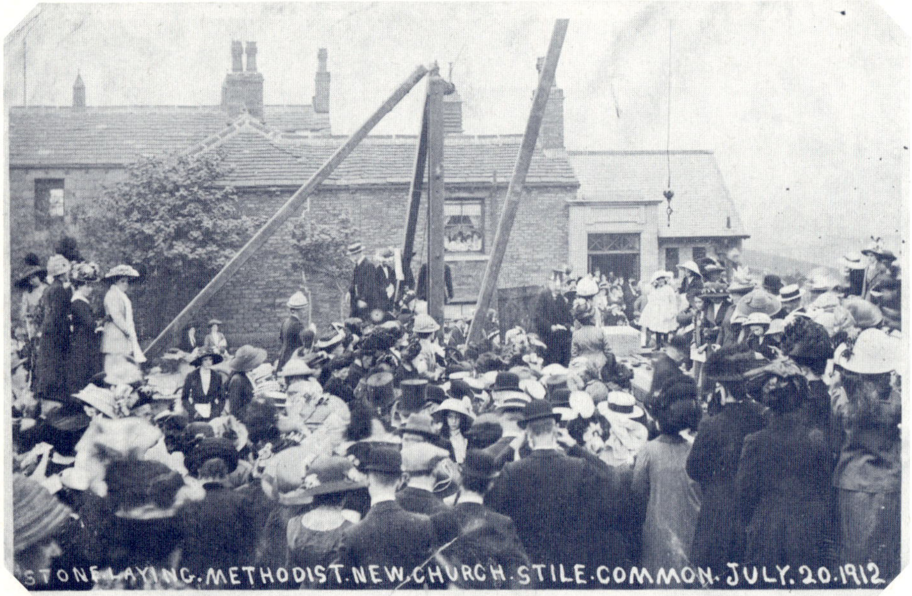


## 9. CHAPEL

The major alternative social centre to the pub in the early nineteenth century was the chapel. Nonconformity, with its missionary zeal, involvement of the laity, stress on sobriety, thrift and hard work appealed strongly to artisans, lower middle classes and skilled workers. It grew dramatically in the early years of the Industrial Revolution, became prominent in liberal and democratic movements and in temperance organizations. By the middle of the century it was becoming institutionalized and the growth of chapel building symbolized the achievement of permanence, consolidation and a degree of social and religious exclusivity. By 1914, membership of the Methodist Church had begun to decline. Nevertheless chapel building continued. This card shows the laying of the foundation stone of the new Stile Common United Methodist church at Primrose Hill, Huddersfield, on 20 July 1912. The church seated 350 people and the project cost £3,000, including converting the existing chapel into a school. The West Riding of Yorkshire was strong in Nonconformity and its association with politics can be seen in the fact that the church is being built next to the Liberal Hall. The top-hatted dignitary laying the foundation stone is Sir William Rayner, prominent Methodist, wealthy local wool merchant and 'one of the great pillars of Huddersfield liberalism'. He had been knighted only the previous month.

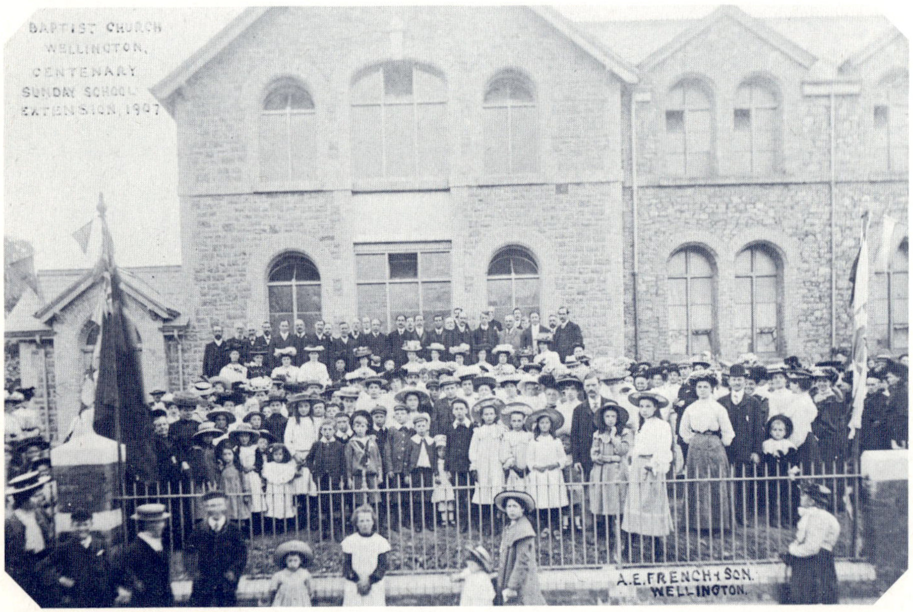


## 10. THE SUNDAY SCHOOL

A by-product of the Evangelical Revival of the 1780s was the Sunday School movement, which for 4 to 6 hours every Sunday provided reading, writing, moral and religious instruction to children and young persons. It has been estimated that the majority of working-class children attended Sunday school, even if their parents never set foot in a church. In many, it instilled a basic literacy and in some a desire for 'respectability' and self-improvement, stimulated by prize-givings and competitions. Colour and excitement was provided by choral concerts, street processions and trips. Initially the Sunday Schools were non-denominational, but by the mid-nineteenth century, the Nonconformist Churches moved to transform them into what one Congregationalist clergyman called 'the most fruitful nurseries of our churches and the finest bulwark of our Protestant communities and Sabbatic enjoyments'. There is no evidence that this made any real addition to church membership. However, Sunday School enrolments tended to increase temporarily whenever a treat was announced. Its real importance was as a source of reading and writing skills and leisure opportunities for children. Here the children of the Wellington Baptist Church Sunday School are assembled in 1907 for the church's centenary celebrations.

11–12. PROCESSIONS
'A good deal of what passes for religion nowadays' complained Bishop Fraser in 1875, 'seems fond of parading behind bands and flags, through the streets, but is seldom found in a place of worship.' In the first half of the nineteenth century Sunday School, religious and temperance groups in the north of England increasingly took over the traditional Whit walks and used them as occasions to witness to their faith. But by the later years of the century they were becoming more social and ceremonial occasions rather than spiritual. Parades and processions of all sorts were in any case by now familiar elements of street culture and provided much appreciated interludes of colour, movement and music in the pattern of city life. Here are two good examples of the Whit Walk procession in the north-west. The first (11) shows the All Saints Church, Higher Walton, contingent, complete with Union Jack, Church Banner and Brass band, heading for Preston. It is interesting to note that the smartly dressed members of the procession are being watched by a distinctly working class group, including apron-clad women and a burly, cigarette smoking workman in working clothes. The card was posted in Preston and sent to Higher Walton, clearly as a souvenir of the occasion. It is dated 20 July 1905. The second card (12), undated but depicting a Whit walk in Edwardian Chorley, shows the strong element of patriotism these processions also contained. The three splendid little chaps in the foreground carry Union Jacks and wear the sailor suits which were *de rigueur* for middle-class children in the late Victorian and Edwardian period. How many of them, I wonder, wore the King's uniform in reality in the Great War and how many survived to tell of it?

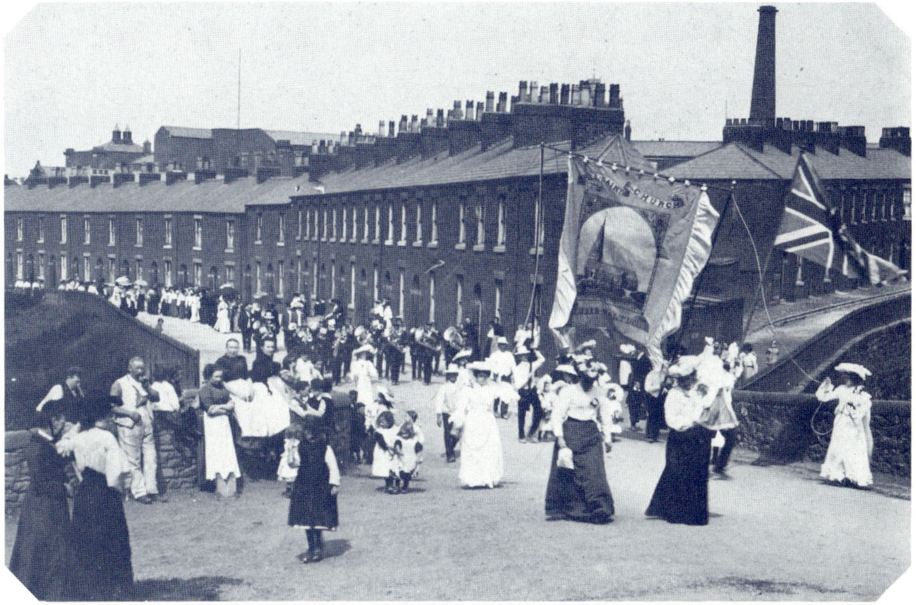

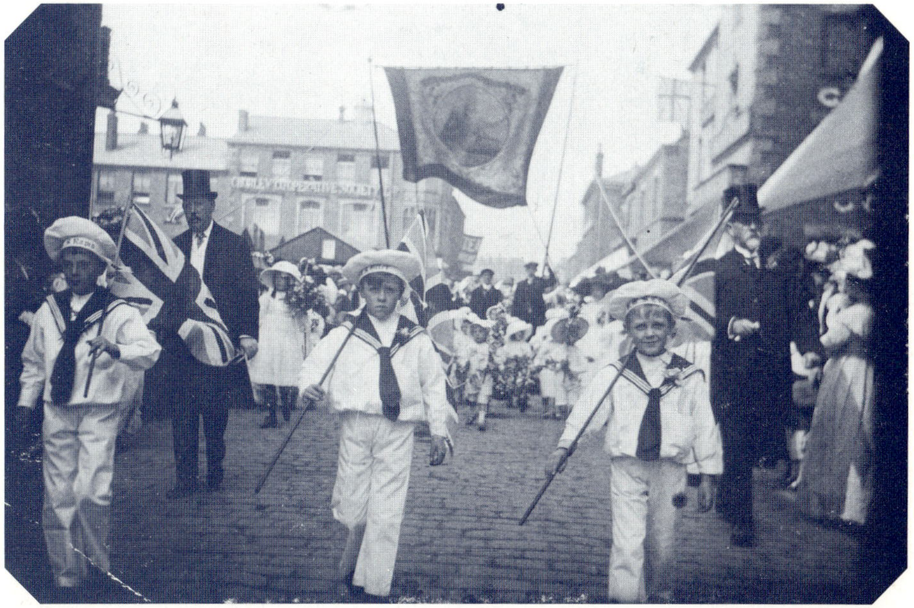

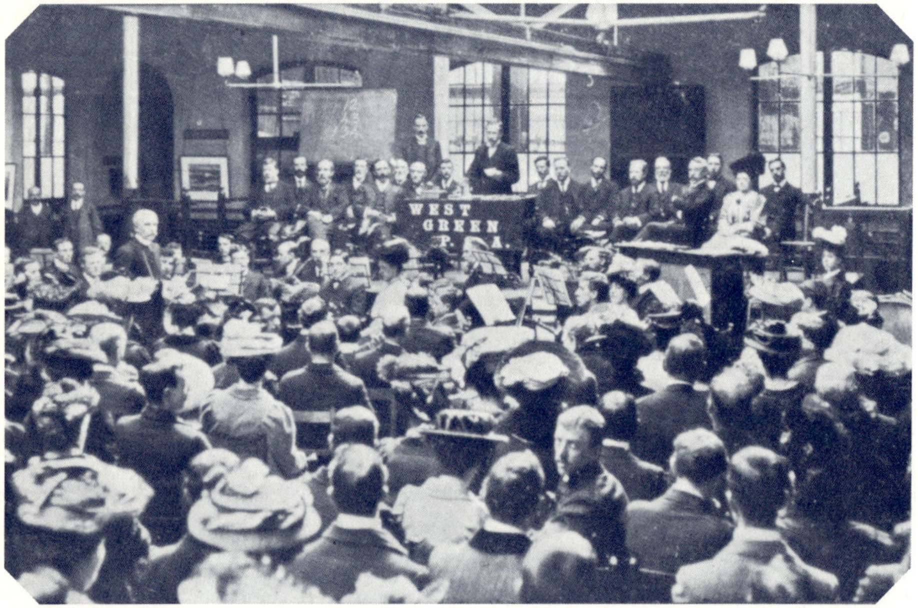


13. PLEASANT SUNDAY AFTERNOONS

The success of the Sunday Schools in bringing in working-class children for religious instruction led Nonconformist churches to try to apply the same principles to adults. Pleasant Sunday Afternoons (P. S. A.s) were invented in 1875 by John Blackham in West Bromwich. They spread rapidly through the Midlands to Yorkshire, Tyneside, Manchester and London. The organization was modelled on that of the adult bible classes and involved a nominal weekly payment and the election of a management committee. The motto of the P. S. A. was 'Brief, Bright and Brotherly' and a typical programme would include a Bible reading, a hymn, a prayer and uplifting songs. This picture of West Green P. S. A. shows that they even boasted on this occasion a small orchestra. The hymn numbers are chalked on a blackboard.

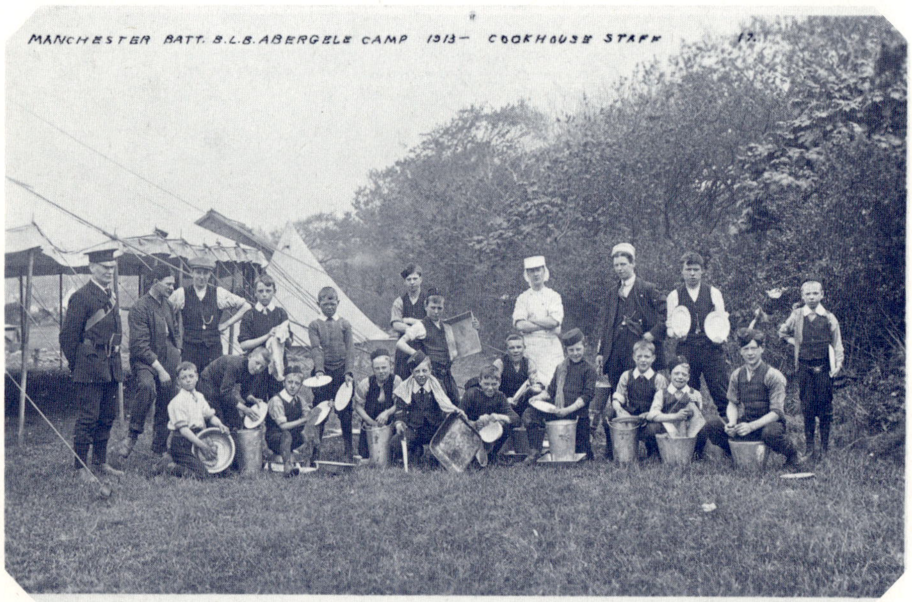


14. BOYS' BRIGADE

Several organizations aimed to instill in the young both religious principle and military discipline, and these included the Boys' Brigade, the Church Lads' Brigade and the Boy Scouts. The aim of the Boys' Brigade was 'the advancement of Christ's Kingdom amongst boys and the promotion of habits of obedience, reverence, discipline, self-respect and all that tends towards true Christian manliness.' Its programme involved sports, drill and summer camps. This card, taken by a Colwyn Bay photographer, shows the Manchester Battalion of the Boys' Life Brigade Summer Camp at Abergele in 1913. This cheerful group of lads in their cadet-style uniforms seem to be enjoying cookhouse fatigues; more likely it is being photographed that has produced the grins.

## 15. PARKS

Many of the recreational opportunities provided in the big cities in the second half of the nineteenth century were the result of the new doctrine of 'civic pride', preached and practised most notably by Joseph Chamberlain in Birmingham and widely imitated elsewhere. T. C. Horsfall, President of the Manchester Citizens Association and pioneer town planner and social reformer, declared: 'The town of the future – I trust the near future – must by means of its schools, its museums, its playgrounds, parks and gymnasia, its baths, its wide tree-planted streets, and the belt of unspoiled countryside which must surround it, bring all inhabitants in some degree under the *best* influence of all regions and all stages of civilization.' Parks were a high priority, as vital sources of fresh air and exercise, the 'lungs of the city'. They were created both by civic action and private philanthropic benefaction. The Whitworth Park, Manchester, is named after the engineer and philanthropist Sir Joseph Whitworth, who bequeathed large amounts of money for the provision of amenities for the city. The Whitworth trustees purchased and laid out the park and handed it over to the corporation in 1904. The Whitworth Gallery is situated in the park. The card was sent from Manchester to Penzance in July 1912.

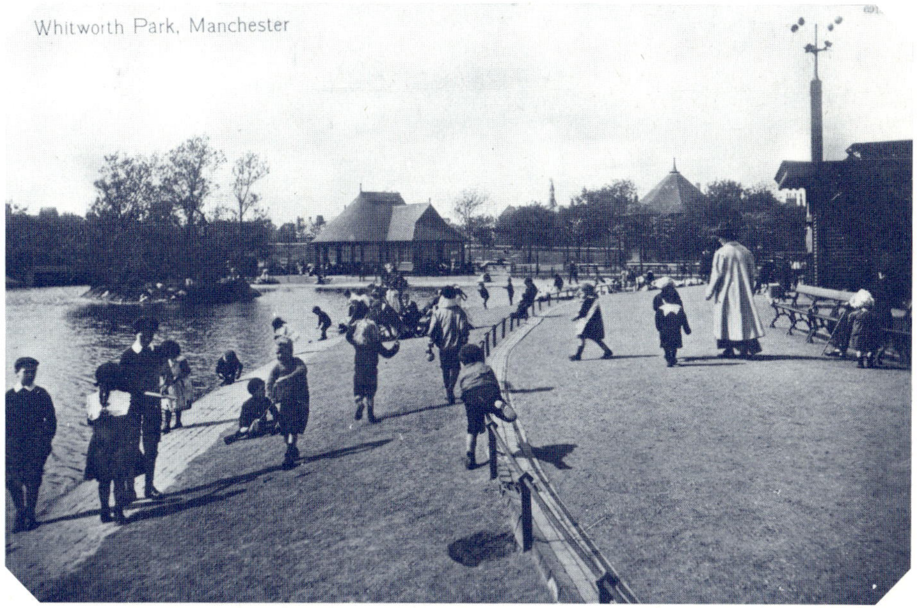


## 16. LIBRARIES

The 1850 and 1855 Library Acts authorized local authorities to institute free public libraries and impose a penny rate to pay for them. Libraries were seen as 'citadels of culture', vital strongholds in the campaign to promote literacy and civilized values among the populace. Manchester was the first big town to take advantage of the Library Act and its Free Library was established in 1852, in the Old Hall of Science at Campfield, near Deansgate. It was vacated in 1877 when it became unsafe and moved to the old Town Hall in King St, pictured here. The King St site was sold in 1911, so the Reference Library was housed in various temporary locations until 1934 when it moved to its present site in St Peter's Square. The card was sent from Manchester to Prestwich in 1905.

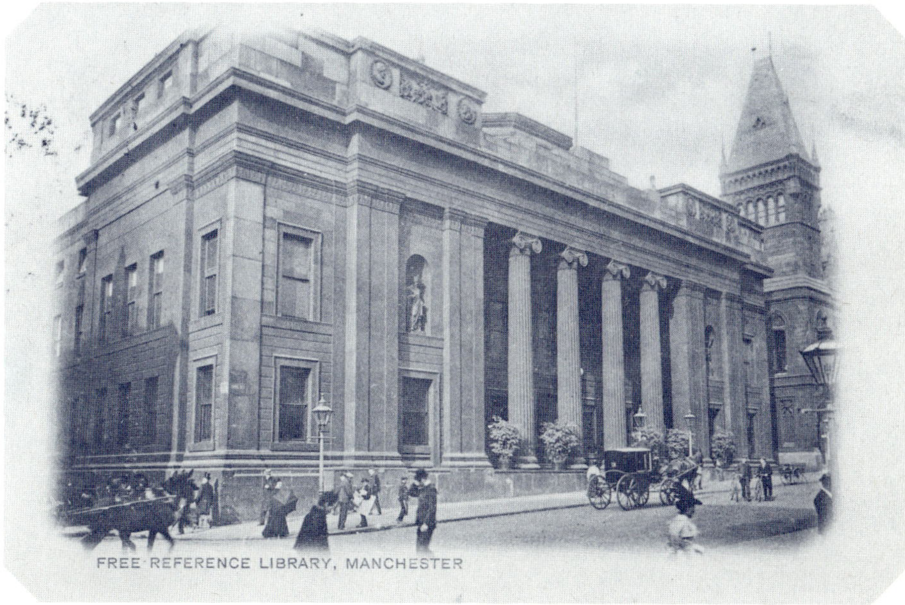

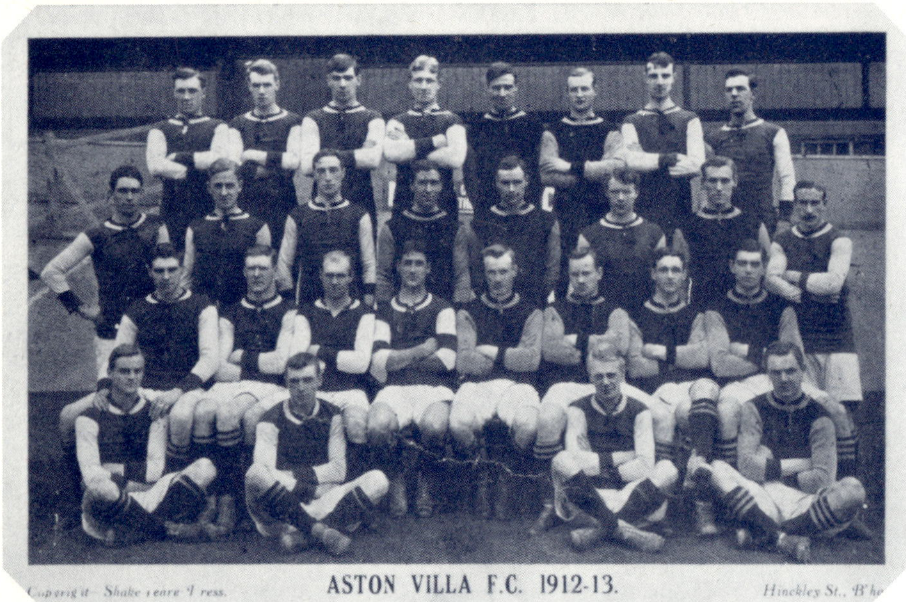


17. FOOTBALL (i)

The decades following the 1860s saw the rise in organized sport. Under the stimulus of Oxbridge and the public schools, national sporting associations for various sports were created and rules drawn up. Football was preached and spread by enthusiastic ex-public schoolboys in the church, teaching and social work and was just as enthusiastically taken up by the masses. Indeed the masses took it over and it became rapidly commercialized, professionalized and democratized. In 1888 the Football League was set up by 12 clubs from the North and Midlands. One of them, Birmingham's principal club, Aston Villa, became the most celebrated team in Britain before the First World War. Beginning as a Methodist chapel team in 1874, they went on to win the Division One championship in 1894, 1896, 1899, 1900 and 1910 and the F. A. Cup in 1887, 1895, 1905, and 1913. In 1897, they won the coveted league and cup 'double'. The almost mystical bond between the club and its supporters, forged in those golden days of matchless victory, still holds today as the club, restored to the First Division after years in the doldrums, strives to equal its feats of yore.

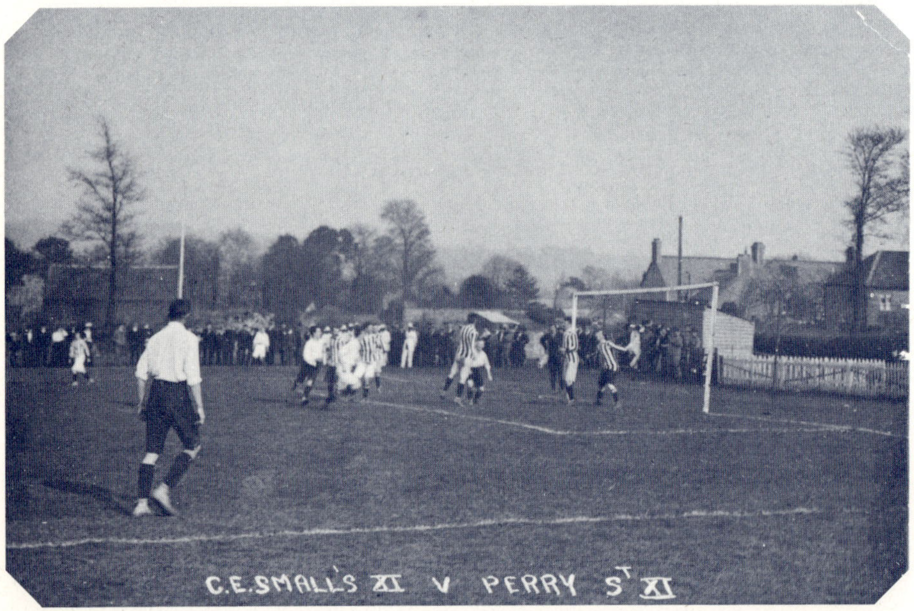


18. FOOTBALL (ii)

Standards of skill and organization in amateur football were raised by attempted emulation of professionals. Factories, youth clubs, churches and schools continued to turn out teams who played regularly in a variety of local leagues. In 1892 the F. A. Amateur Cup was instituted and by 1910, some 12,000 amateur clubs were registered with the F. A. Many of them were working-class teams but echoes of the old public school influence survived. Perhaps the most celebrated amateur side was the Corinthians, a largely Oxbridge team of dedicated amateurs, who survived until 1939, turning up to matches in top hats and playing in the F. A. Cup in the 1920s. In 1925 they achieved a famous victory over Blackburn Rovers. The term 'soccer' still widely applied to football is pre-First World War Oxford undergraduate slang, the product of an affectation of shortening words and adding 'er' to the end, thus breakfast became 'brekker' and rugby 'rugger'. Here we see two amateur West Country teams in action. The photographer was a local man with offices in Taunton, Bridgwater, Burnham, Wellington and Chard Lynton.

## 19. ATHLETICS

Modern British athletics began at Oxford in the 1850s. By 1864 Oxford and Cambridge were competing against each other in the sport. University graduates spread the idea and in 1866 the Amateur Athletic Club was set up to govern and organize the sport. But it was too socially exclusive to survive and the pressure for democratization led in 1880 to the foundation of the Amateur Athletic Association, which allowed the participation of working-class athletes. By 1886, it had 154 different clubs affiliated to it. Like other sports, running was thought to be good not only for good health but good character. J. H. Hardwick's *Distance and Country Running* (1912) urged the cultivation of the following qualities to achieve success: 'a genial disposition, unflinching courage and confidence . . . a watchful ear for the pistol crack and a smart, timely, graceful dash off the mark'. The card shows the runners in the Hastings Marathon (1908) assiduously cultivating these qualities.

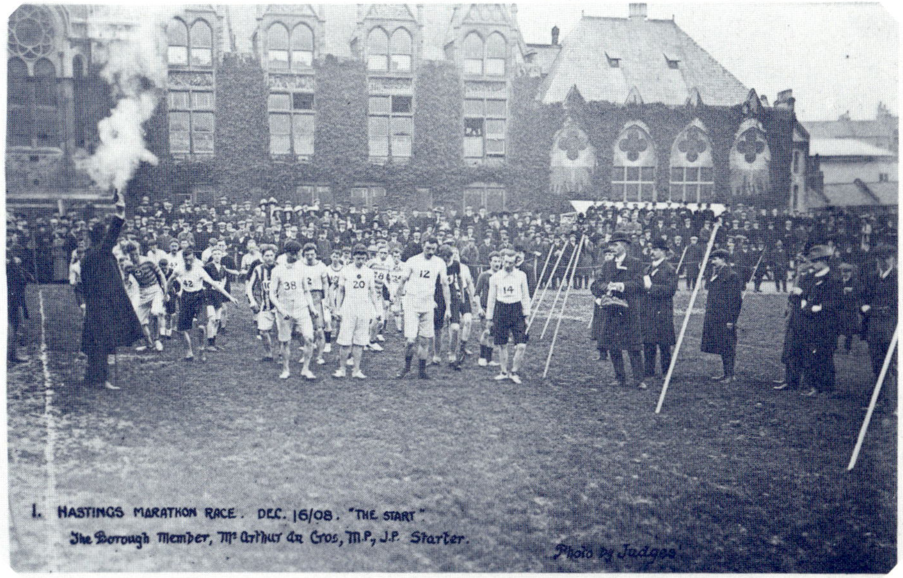


## 20. SWIMMING

Like athletics, swimming was promoted in the second half of the nineteenth century as a means of building up the physical strength of the population as well as providing them with a healthy distraction from the pub and its associated insalubrious pastimes. The Baths and Washhouses Act of 1846 had encouraged local authorities to provide these amenities, as an alternative to swimming and bathing in polluted rivers. Swimming baths became an integral part of the amenity programme inspired by the 'Civic Gospel'. Such baths were used by the schools for the provision of swimming classes. The Amateur Swimming Association was formed in 1869 to encourage the sport and help provide facilities and instructors. Competition became an important element in the sport, as the proud display of medals and trophies in this card of Huddersfield boy swimming champions indicates.

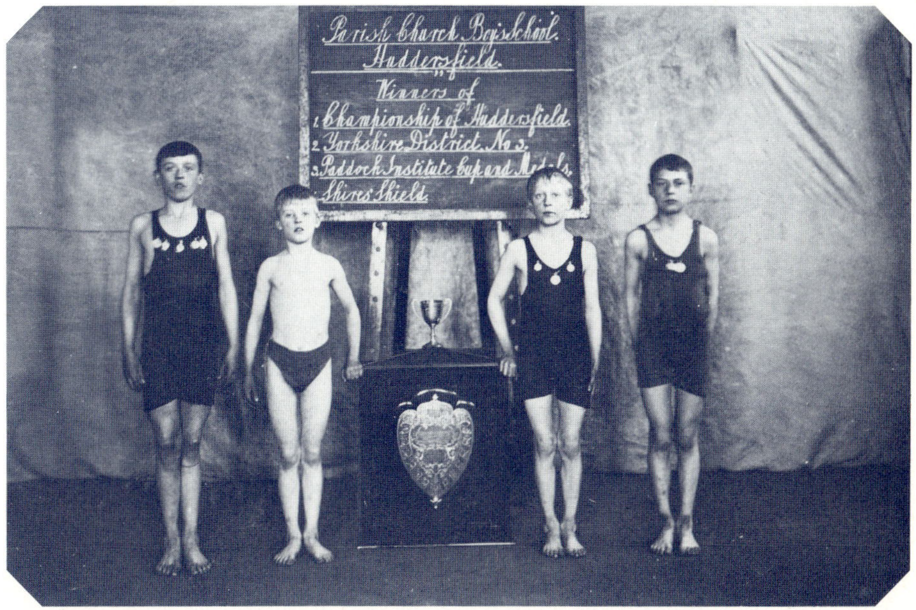

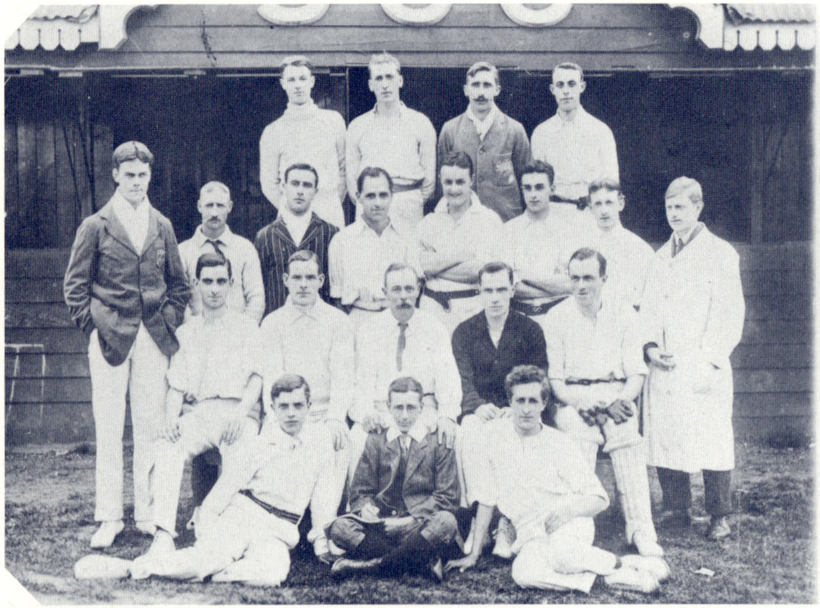

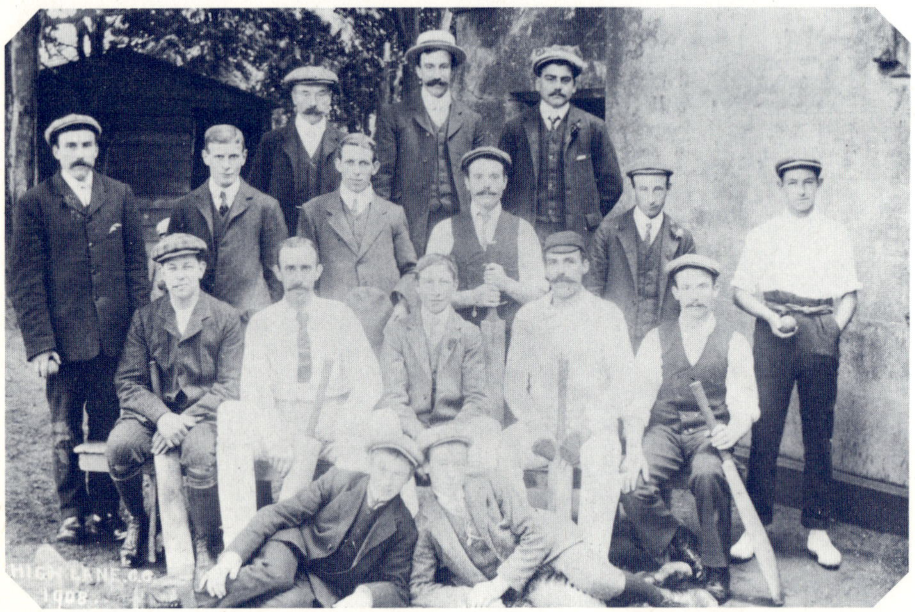


21–2. CRICKET

Cricket was also promoted as character forming. H. B. Philpot, an early historian of the London School Board, said that for children of all classes, cricket encouraged 'unselfish pluck, determination, self-control and public spirit.' It was indeed played by children and by men of all classes and it would perhaps be true to say that the real distinction was not between classes but between amateur and professional, gentleman and player. 'Please God no professional shall ever captain England', declared Lord Hawke, captain of Yorkshire from 1883 to 1910 and later President of the MCC. Cricket became *the* English summer game, its winter counterpart being football. Indeed many famous football teams including Derby County, Sheffield United and Preston North End developed out of cricket clubs looking for a way of profitably spending their winters in sport. These cards show two very different cricketing sides in the Edwardian period. The first (21), undated but taken by a Coventry photographer, shows a clearly middle-class side, complete with blazers and immaculate whites, several of their members looking like recent graduates from the 5th form at St Dominic's. Note the scorer in spectacles: just as enthusiastic but doubtless less competent than his fellows. The second (22), High Lane Cricket Club near Bromyard, Worcestershire, in 1908, with its majority of cloth caps, seems to be drawn primarily from skilled working men and the lower middle class. The contrast in type and appearance is striking, but note the classic Edwardian and Victorian sporting pose of the two seated gentlemen in front.

23. CYCLING (i)

The bicycle, or velocipede as it was initially called, was introduced into Britain in the 1860s and became a craze in the 1890s following the invention of the pneumatic tyre. Many celebrities took up bicycling, such as A. J. Balfour, H. G. Wells and Conan Doyle. The 1901 census revealed that the number of cyclemakers had increased by 173 per cent in 10 years. Fresh air, personal mobility and access to the countryside constituted its appeal, and soon cycling clubs were springing up all over the country in the wake of the Cyclists Touring Club, founded in 1878. The rise in membership of the Cyclists Touring Club from 142 in 1878 to 20,000 in 1885 to 60,000 in 1899 reflects the increasing enthusiasm for the bicycle. This card shows a cycling rendezvous at the Robin Hood Inn, Loughton, Essex, on the edge of Epping Forest.

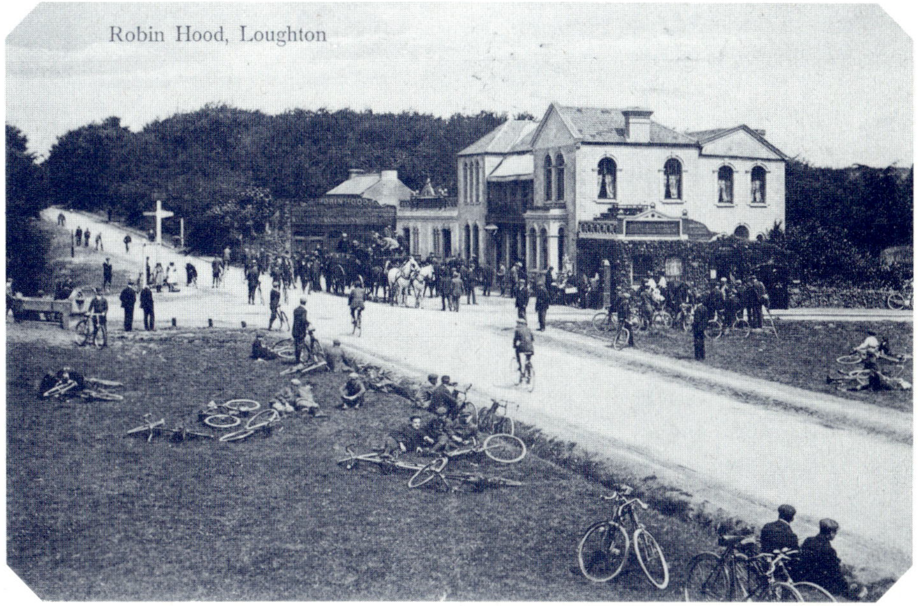


24. CYCLING (ii)

Cycling, like tennis and archery, was one of those sports enthusiastically taken up by women. There was considerable resistance to women participating in sport, an attitude typified by this comment from *Badminton Magazine* in 1900:

*For women . . . beauty of face and form is one of the chief essentials, but unlimited indulgence in violent outdoor sports, cricket, bicycling, beagling, otter-hunting, paper-chasing and – most odious of all games for a woman – hockey, cannot but have an unwomanly effect on a young girl's mind, no less than her appearance . . . Let young girls ride, skate, dance and play lawn tennis and other games in moderation but let them leave field sports and rough outdoor pastimes to those for whom they are naturally intended – men.*

For many middle-class women, cycling became a mark of emancipation, and there were those, like the formidable lady pictured here, who used their cycles not just for exercise and leisure but to get to work.

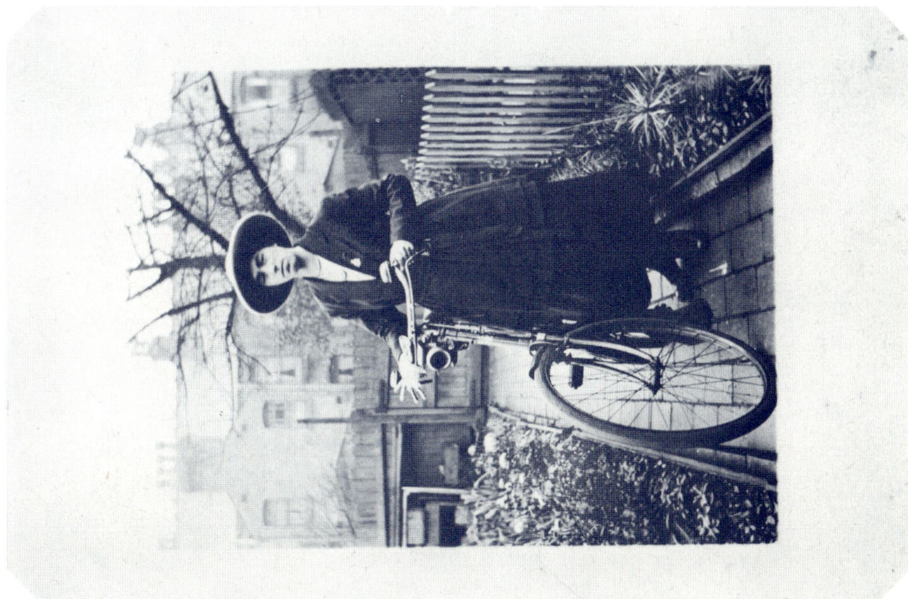

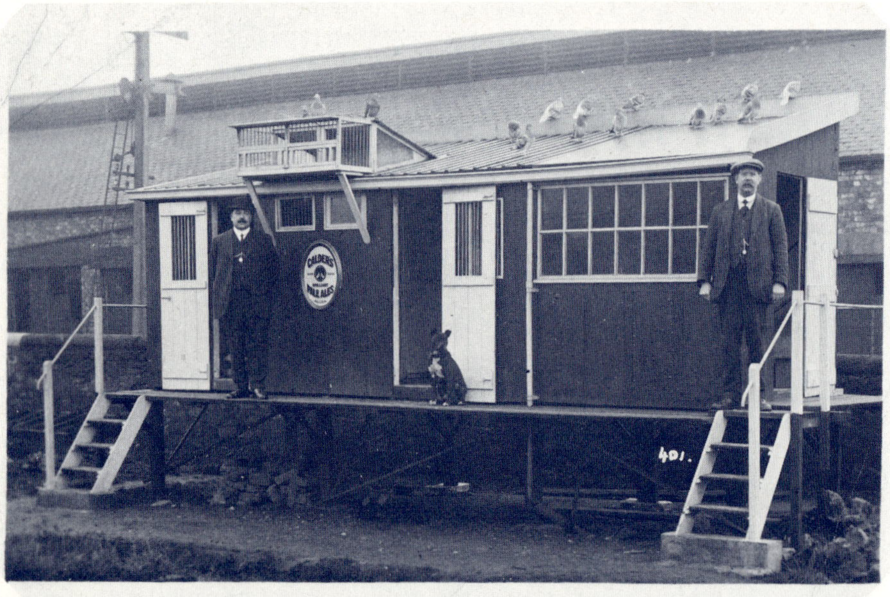


25. PIGEON RACING

Although the more brutal animal sports like ratting and cock fighting were suppressed, gentler pastimes like whippet-racing, fishing and pigeon breeding survived among the working classes. Pigeons were bred to be raced and there were two distinct forms of pigeon racing: short distance which, like the old violent animal sports, was linked to gambling and the pub, and long distance, which was organized on a national competition level and was highly respectable. Initially pigeons were bred and trained for the speedy transmission of information – hot news to the newspapers, military intelligence to the government, company and share information to the stock exchange. But the introduction of the electric telegraph obviated the need for pigeon post and pigeon racing became exclusively a sport. Interestingly pigeon racing was linked to specific trades – weavers, dockers, printers and miners. The smart pigeon loft in this postcard was, judging by the advertisement for Calder's Ales of Alloa, in the Clackmannanshire mining and brewing town. The two substantial and prosperous-looking gentlemen posing with the loft look to be rather more than ordinary pigeon-fancying working men – perhaps competition officials or, if the advertisement is anything to go by, publicans.

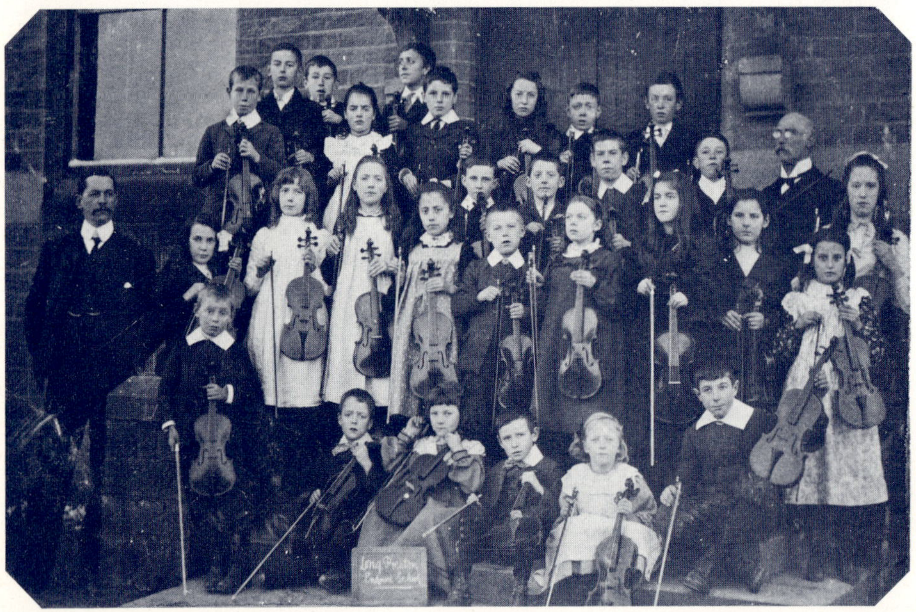


26. MUSIC-MAKING

By 1872 music featured in the curriculum in most schools. Private music-making was one of the major leisure activities, whether it was piano-playing, choral singing or brass-banding. Even a small town like Long Preston in Yorkshire was apparently able to muster 29 young violinists. Late nineteenth-century Britain was, it seems, able to anticipate the celebrated Japanese violin teacher Dr Suzuki's method of instructing young children in string playing, though many of these youngsters could have had extreme difficulty in playing the full-size violins they held.

## 27. BRASS BANDS

The brass band was one of the most distinctive products of Victorian musical culture. Smartly uniformed and playing martial airs, they were a familiar part of everyday life. We have already seen a brass band participating in the Preston Whit Walks. They were used also to provide entertainment in the public parks. In 1908 alone Manchester staged 500 band concerts and this card shows a huge crowd enjoying the doubtless patriotic music being played in Barrow Park, Barrow-in-Furness, in 1917. Brass bands became an integral part of seaside resort life too; and in the 1,000 bands of the Salvation Army contributed to the reclamation of souls.

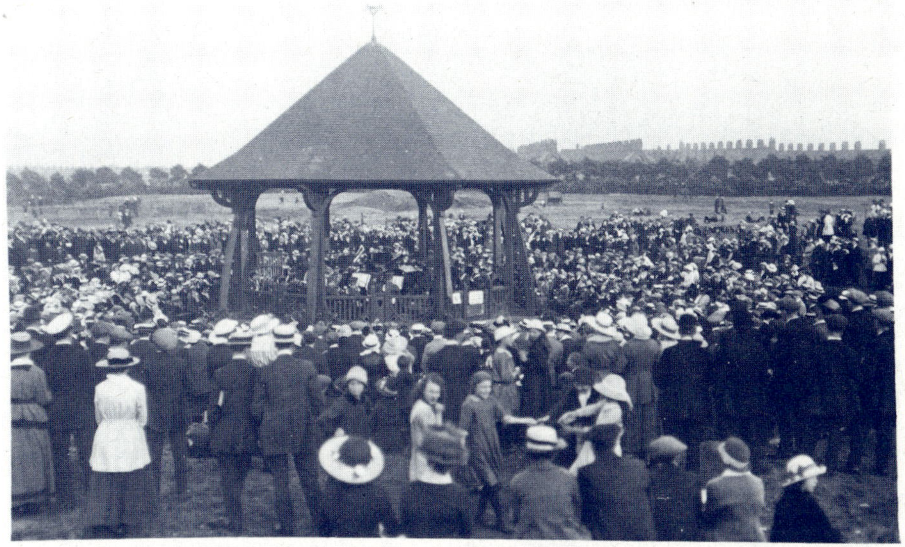

1 BAND CONCERTS IN BARROW PARK.

## 28. POPULAR THEATRE

M. F. K. Fraser, writing of popular melodrama in the 1900s, says: 'The fashion was all for titles with the word 'London' prominently featured, or the word 'woman' coupled preferably with some suggestion that her other name, Frailty, was involved in the argument.' The Borough Theatre, Stratford East, obligingly confirms this trend by advertising 'The Sins of London'. A. S. Jasper in *A Hoxton Childhood* recalled his trips to the 'Blood Tub' to see the melodrama:

*My sister Jo made life as happy as she could for my young sister Molly and myself. Sometimes on a Monday night she would come home from work and if she had a few coppers left over from the week-end she would say to Mum, 'Get yourself and the kids ready, we're going up the Brit'. This was the old Britannia Theatre in Hoxton, Jo loved the dramas that were performed there. If Mum could afford it we had a bag of peanuts or a ha'penny bag of sweets. We went in the 'gallery' for twopence – half-price for us kids. Among the dramas I remember was* The Face at the Window *– real horrible. Others were* Sweeney Todd, Maria Marten, Why Girls Leave Home. *Many times I have lain awake after going to the Brit, terrified to open my eyes for fear of seeing the murdered lying next to me.*

Both the Britannia and the Borough became cinemas as the craze for moving pictures caught on and both were eventually demolished.

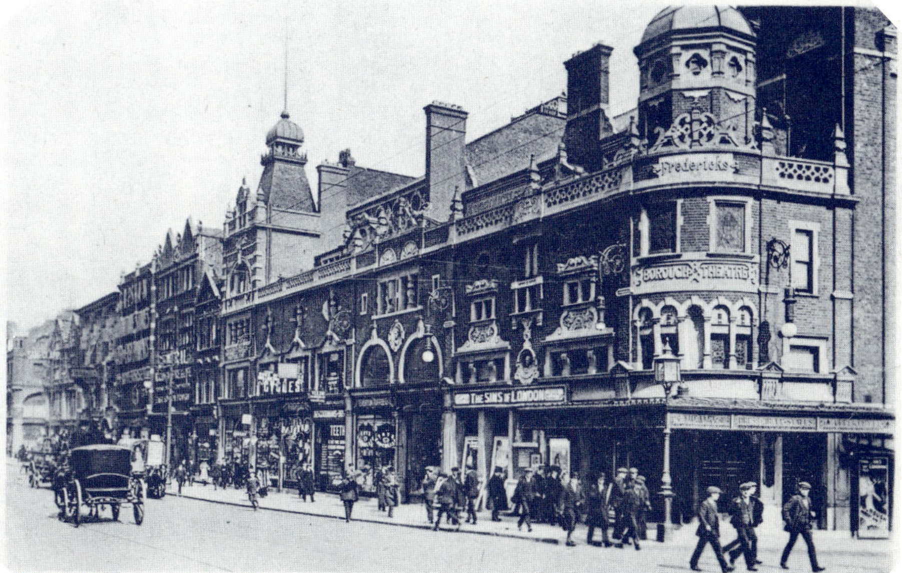


Borough Theatre, Stratford.

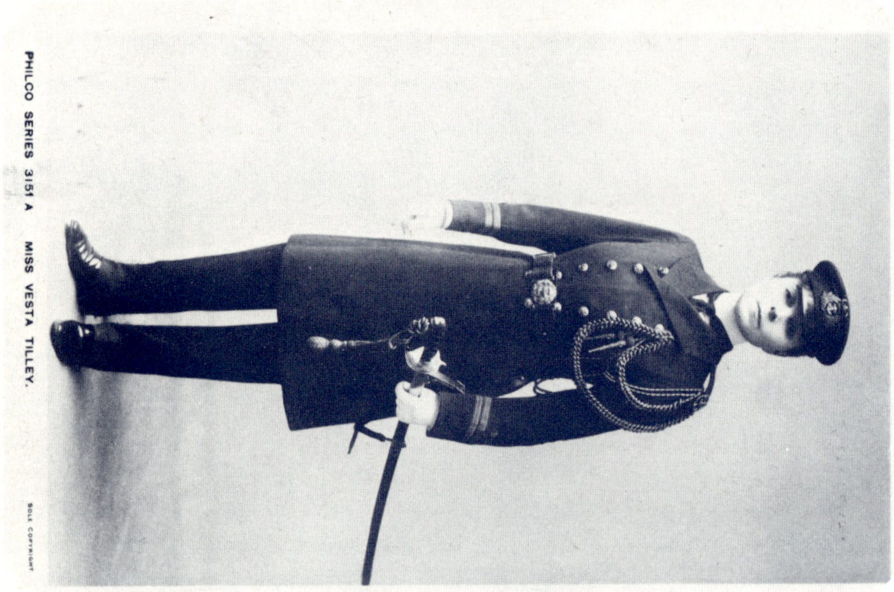


## 29. MUSIC HALL

Vesta Tilley (1864–1952) was one of the unchallenged idols of the halls. She has been called 'the greatest of the music hall male impersonators', a select breed which also included Ella Shields ('Burlington Bertie') and Hetty King ('All the Nice Girls Love a Sailor'). Vesta Tilley made her debut at the age of four and her first London appearance at ten. Her immaculate suits and costumes, meticulous observation of male mannerisms and a string of successful songs earned her a devoted following. During the First World War, when she sang patriotic, militaristic songs like 'The Army of Today's All Right', she became known as 'England's Greatest Recruiting Sergeant'. In 1890 she married theatre proprietor Walter de Frece and after he was knighted and elected to parliament in 1919, she retired from the stage to become Lady de Frece full-time.

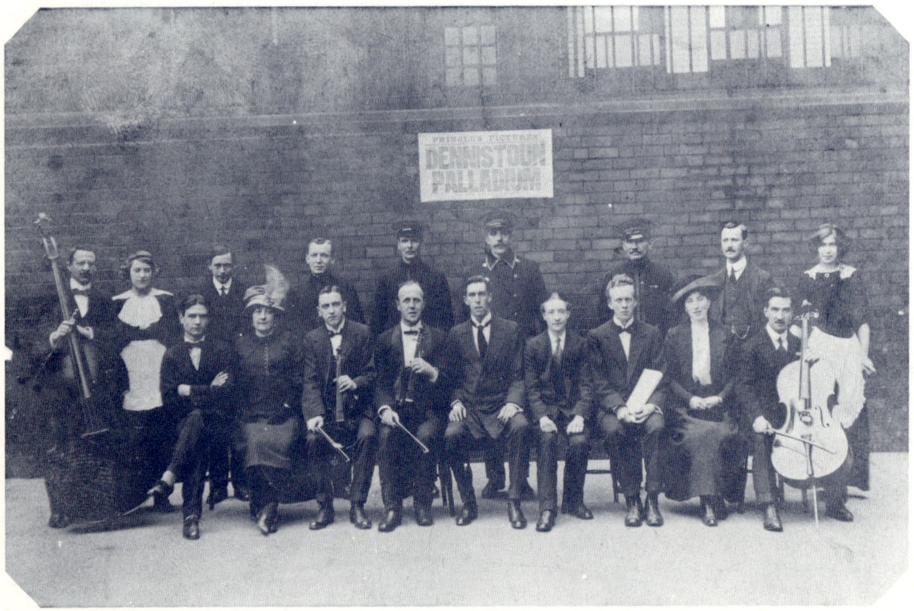


## 30. CINEMA

If ever there was a misnomer it was 'silent films', for all cinemas had musical accompaniment, whether from lone pianist or full orchestra. Indeed in 1929 it was estimated that between three-quarters and four-fifths of all professional musicians in Britain were employed in the cinema. An orchestral player could expect to earn £3–4 for a working day stretching from 3.00 p.m. to 10.30 p.m. By 1929 there were some 3,000 cinemas in operation in Britain, while the number of music halls had shrunk to less than 100. The musical repertoire for the films consisted of such old favourites as 'Hearts and Flowers' for pathos and 'William Tell Overture' for chases. But sometimes the music played could be embarrassingly inappropriate. One celebrated silent film pianist is still remembered for playing 'By the sea, by the sea, by the beautiful sea', during a tragic drowning sequence. This card shows the assembled staff of the Dennistoun Palladium in Glasgow, complete with four uniformed commissionaires and ten-piece orchestra. Virtually all the cinema musicians found themselves suddenly and dramatically out of work when talkies were introduced. Within a few years at the end of the 1920s their profession was virtually wiped out.

# CHAPTER SIX | BESIDE THE SEASIDE

The most frequently encountered vintage postcards are those depicting the many facets of that quintessentially British institution, the seaside holiday. Bathing machines and boarding houses, piers and promenades, shrimpstalls and sandcastles, brass bands and donkey rides, all were captured by the tireless seaside photographers whose views, mass-produced by the postcard companies, were sped by the mails to all corners of the kingdom, bearing on them unvarying litanies upon the weather, the accommodation and the amusements.

The heyday of the picture postcard coincided with a revolution in holidaymaking: the growth of the working-class holiday. The seaside holiday is a classic case of downward diffusion of tastes and habits from the wealthy, leisured elite to what Oliver Onions called 'the grey and unnumbered multitude'.

In the eighteenth century seaside holidays had largely been the preserve of the upper classes. It was an extension of the popular practice of 'taking the waters' at inland spas like Bath, Cheltenham and Tunbridge Wells. What had begun as a purely medical exercise in the seventeenth century was gradually transformed into a holiday for the well-to-do, with spas providing elegant leisure facilities.

By the mid-eighteenth century a new medical vogue had arisen: drinking and bathing in sea water allegedly helped to cure a wide variety of ailments from leprosy to arthritis. Of existing spas, only Scarborough was on the coast, and the valetudinarian rush to the sea turned various decayed ports and fishing villages on the South coast and the Thames estuary into maritime spas. Royal patronage of sea-bathing set the seal on its acceptance by fashionable society. George III descended from a bathing machine into the sea at Weymouth to the strains of 'God Save the King' from an attendant band. The patronage of the Prince Regent gave powerful impetus to the development of Brighton. In 1760 it was a tiny, sleepy fishing village. By 1800 its population numbered 7,000; by 1820,

24,000. Brighton's facilities – libraries, theatres, gaming and assembly rooms – mirrored those of the inland spas; the upper-class pleasure-seeking atmosphere was aptly characterized by *The Morning Post* as 'morning rides, champagne, dissipation, noise and nonsense.'

The seaside resorts were undergoing the first stages of the process that was to transform the seaside holiday from an exclusive recreation into a national institution. The Industrial Revolution gave birth to a larger, more prosperous middle class who were not slow to emulate their betters by travelling to the seaside to take the waters. In the last three decades of the nineteenth century the working classes followed suit, desirous of experiencing the benefits of sea air and sea water. They also sought amusement, relaxation from their work and a change of scene from the grim tenements and back-to-back houses in which they lived and the mills and factories where they toiled.

To bring the new holidaymakers to the sea, however, a transport revolution was necessary. Steam was the great liberator. From 1815 steamboats regularly plyed the Thames carrying holidaymakers to Gravesend and Margate, making those resorts so uncompromisingly 'common' that the 'better class of visitor' was driven elsewhere. By 1835, over 100,000 people a year visited Margate. The pattern was to be spectacularly reinforced with the coming of the railways. The railways carried middle-class visitors to the seaside in their thousands for a week's holiday and the urban proletariat on increasingly popular day-trips. The upper classes rapidly gave up the struggle to maintain social exclusivity in the seaside resorts and fled to the Scottish Highlands, to the Lakes and eventually to the Continent for long sojourns away from the prying eyes of their inferiors. By the 1860s the middle-class holidaymaker had taken over the resorts. The seaside holiday became a family affair under their patronage, something it had not been in the aristocratic heyday. The development precisely reflected the dominance of the family concept in Victorian society; for both middle and working classes, where the sexes tended to spend their leisure activities in strict segregation, it provided an outward and visible sign of family cohesiveness.

The railway companies failed initially to appreciate their potential for mass cheap travel and concentrated on catering for the better off. Only when enterprising individuals like Thomas Cook began chartering trains and organizing cheap day excursions did the working class seize the golden opportunity to get away. In Whit Week 1850 over 200,000 day trippers left Manchester for the countryside and the sea at a time when Manchester's population scarcely exceeded 300,000. Excursions developed rapidly during the 1850s; Sunday trips were particularly popular since for many people it was their only free day. The *Preston Chronicle* described excursions as early as 1844 as 'all the go and fashion'. Despite the fact that excursion trains were often extremely uncomfortable, slow and dirty, the volume of passenger traffic they conveyed eventually convinced the railway companies of the value of mass travel. In 1874 the Midland Railway abolished second class, provided third-class accommodation on all trains, reduced fares and improved facilities. Other companies followed suit and the rise of the working-class seaside holiday was now unstoppable.

The excursion phenomenon provoked a fierce battle which served to focus further attention on the seaside holiday. On one side were the sabbatarians who wanted no alternative to church attendance and therefore opposed Sunday travel vehemently and those influential groups in resorts who thought that Sunday excursionists lowered the tone. Day trippers were accused of filling resorts with 'drunken and disorderly persons who set aside all decency and whose conduct was an affront to public morals.' This conduct was alleged to include being drunk, violent, foul-mouthed and 'forward'. The trippers also tended to bring their own food and spend little money except on drink. On the other side were the anti-sabbatarians, an amalgam of various groups who advocated proper leisure facilities for the workers to provide them with health and welfare, who wanted an alternative to the pub (the only leisure activity for many) and who wanted 'rational recreation' to develop the culture and education of the ordinary man. They strenuously defended the seaside holiday and opportunities for cheap travel, and ultimately their view prevailed.

A railway link came to be essential for a seaside resort. The railway revived the flagging fortunes of Brighton. When the railway reached Torquay in 1848 a public holiday was declared. It was the opening of a direct rail link between Morecambe and the West Riding which created the strong tradition of Yorkshire holidays in that resort. The coming of the railways literally made possible isolated resorts like Rhyl and Skegness; conversely, the lack of a rail link retarded Eastbourne's development.

So just as the railways ferried the middle-class holidaymakers to the seaside in the 1850s and 1860s they also provided a means for the dramatic rise in working-class holidaymakers in the succeeding decades. The very existence of working-class seaside holidays testifies to increased leisure time compared with the early years of the century. In the first half of the nineteenth century most industrial workers had little leisure and few organized holidays. In general, they were grudged by employers desperate to retain their competitive edge and to maximize their return on investment in machinery. But in the second half of the century as a result of a combination of outside pressure (from unions, philanthropic groups and the prevalence of enlightened opinions about the value of rest and recreation) and of self-interest (a bid to legitimize absenteeism and increase productivity by creating a more contented and healthy workforce and, in some industries, to dispose of unavoidable slack periods) attitudes began to change. The 1833 Factory Act stipulated that workers under 18 years should enjoy eight annual half-holidays. The weekly half-holiday, usually Saturday afternoon, became universal. It was granted to textile workers in 1850 and thereafter demanded and obtained by other groups of workers, though some, in the north-east particularly, did not get it until almost the end of the century. The idea of an annual holiday for manual workers developed naturally from the half-holiday. Sir John Lubbock's Bank Holiday Act of 1871, which added the first Monday in August to the public holidays at Easter, Whitsun and Christmas, was evidence of the growing acceptance of the notion.

The traditional 'Wakes' holidays in the North, which had survived the coming of industrialization as occasions for fairs and merrymaking, were extended from one day to three and, by 1890, to a full week. A growing trend towards paid holidays developed in the 1880s. Many bank clerks had been granted one or two paid holidays as early as the late 1860s and in the 1880s they were conceded to some railway company employees, to drapery assistants and to various white-collar groups. Enlightened companies, such as Lever Brothers the soap manufacturers, gave paid holidays to all workers. But there was considerable opposition to the practice, even in some unions which regarded it as either demoralization or as a distraction from the important business of improving pay and conditions. Not until 1938 did holidays with pay become a statutory obligation.

Agricultural labourers, shop assistants and domestic servants did not enjoy even the limited holiday opportunities of the industrial proletariat. But between 1871 and 1900 there was still a great upsurge in holidaymaking, assisted by rising real wages, falling food prices and a gradual improvement in living conditions. Charles Booth in his survey of the London poor (1903) declared: 'Holidaymaking is spoken of as "one of the most remarkable changes in habit in the last 10 years" and the statement is applicable to all classes.'

A conflict of style between middle-class and working-class holidays remained and it determined the development of individual resorts, many of which had to make a crucial choice. The middle classes, descending on the resorts with their children and nannies, were concerned with matters of health (the air, the water) and of self-improvement. They supported lectures, concerts and libraries. In the mid-Victorian period there was a passion for collecting, identifying and preserving shells, seaweed and even pebbles. There was an earnestness, a propriety and a decorum about holidays which the better-off working-class holidaymakers from skilled and supervisory grades shared. It is small wonder that some of these worthies objected to the excursion trains disgorging 'the great unwashed' in search not of health and education but a 'good time': drinking, dancing, noise and bustle. In 1885 the *Blackpool Herald* wrote: 'Blackpool is becoming a place where the people expect to have a jolly care-for-nothing sort of scamper, rather than to avail themselves of the benefit of the breezes. . . . During the best months of the year the town is deluged by the lower classes, and it would be unreasonable to expect the higher grades of society to mix with them.' The triumph of this working-class ambience was in a sense the making of Blackpool.

In Lancashire and Yorkshire, the working-class seaside holiday, as opposed to the day trip, became common at least a generation before it developed elsewhere. By the 1870s skilled working men and their families were going to the seaside for a week. The number of visitors arriving at Blackpool stations in the season quadrupled between 1863 and 1873. There are several reasons for this. The survival and extension of Wakes holidays helped. So did a boom in textiles after the Cotton Famine which provided increased family income to which working wives and older children contributed. The strong tradition of saving with clubs and friendly societies was also an important factor, since 'saving up' for the holiday became an object of the thrift.

In large numbers and with increasing regularity these northern holidaymakers headed for Blackpool, since Blackpool welcomed them and offered a vast range of amenities, including three piers, the pleasure beach, the winter gardens and eventually the Tower. It welcomed them because the resistance to working-class visitors was defeated, thanks to the absence of a single dominant landowner concerned to preserve social exclusivity, and to the dominance of local government institutions by those who profited most from working-class holidaymakers. Fears that the better class of visitor would be driven away were never entirely realized since the North Shore remained select and refined; here all plans for fairgrounds, piers and amusement parks which had made the South Shore the Mecca for working-class trippers were successfully resisted.

The same conflict of interest presented itself elsewhere and resorts acquired a dominant social tone. This does not mean that the entire patronage of one area was exclusively by one class or another. Even Blackpool, working-class resort *par excellence*, had its areas of middle-class patronage and in Scarborough, Yorkshire's premier resort, middle and working classes rubbed shoulders. But a working-class influx often meant a middle-class exodus and the big, bustling, boisterous resorts often necessitated the growth of smaller, more select and sedate satellites. As high-class Lytham was to proletarian Blackpool, so Hove was to Brighton, Westcliff-on-Sea to Southend and Broadstairs to Margate. Others maintained exclusivity by designing their facilities to suit middle-class taste and making no concession to working-class visitors. Into this category fell Eastbourne, St Leonards, Bournemouth and Folkestone. Often, though not invariably, this was because a single landowner, such as the Duke of Devonshire in Eastbourne or Earl Delawarr in Bexhill, developed and dominated the town.

Whatever their social tone, the resorts boomed. The population of Brighton rose from 90,000 in 1871 to 107,000 in 1881 to 123,000 in 1901 to 131,000 in 1914. By 1901, 17 resorts had over 20,000 inhabitants. There were also important geographical changes. Until 1850 all the important resorts apart from Scarborough were in the south. By 1900, three of the top seven resorts were in the north. Railways and a growing working-class market had successively opened up the Isle of Man, North Wales, and the Lincolnshire coast to holidaymakers. Baedeker for 1890 observed that Douglas was 'practically one large playground for the operatives of Lancashire and Yorkshire; and their tastes have been so extensively catered for by the erection of dancing saloons and the like at every point of interest, as to seriously interfere with the enjoyment of the scenery for its own sake.'

It should be stressed, however, that holidays were by no means universal among the working classes. Excursions, organized by Sunday Schools, sporting clubs, street committees, chapels, temperance groups, Boy Scouts and so forth, were the most many people could hope for. The *New Survey of London Life and Labour* reckoned in 1934 that 'a large proportion, perhaps a majority, of London working class families are still unable to reach this very modest standard [a week's holiday] and have to be content with day outings on Bank holidays or Sundays.' Some could not afford even day trips. J. M. R's father, one of a Birmingham working-class family of six children, did not see the sea until he was 17 in 1928 and then only on a camping trip with the Boy Scouts to Paignton. The Workers Travel Association was founded in 1921 specifically to reduce the cost of working-class holidays. But trips organized by charitable institutions were still common in the inter-war years.

What were the attractions of the seaside? Pre-eminently, of course, the sea. Initially its attraction was to improve health. 'Taking the waters' meant literally that. Until the 1850s drinking sea water at regular intervals was an integral part of the cure, though enlightened physicians permitted it to be mixed with a little milk or port. When this practice declined, seabathing continued. The circumstances under which it was undertaken provide an interesting barometer of public morality. There was from the outset a distinction between the sexes. Men bathed naked; women in flimsy costumes. Both, but particularly women, utilized bathing machines, huts on wheels dragged into the waters, enabling the occupant to descend directly into the brine. They have been dated back to the 1730s and seem to have appeared first at Scarborough. Attendant 'dippers' were on hand in the eighteenth century to assist – or even force – the reluctant to take the plunge. Even the working classes were aware of the importance of seabathing and some had gone on foot to the coast before the railways came. Richard Ayton in 1813 found at Blackpool 'crowds of poor people from the manufacturing towns who have a high opinion of the efficacy of bathing, maintaining that in the months of August and September, there is physic in the sea.'

As the nineteenth century wore on, pressure grew for bathers to be decently clad. It was not just that one of the principal seaside entertainments was for the men to line up with telescopes on the prom feasting their eyes on female flesh as it tripped timorously through the waves. Nude bathing came to be seen as a major affront to prevailing public prudery. 'That almost heathen indecency', one commentator called it. Women began to wear ever more voluminous and all-encasing costumes complete with skirts, sleeves and caps aimed at concealing their contours; men too began to wear swimming costumes, though these served in many cases only to emphasize their outline. The new development did not please everyone. The celebrated diarist Rev Francis Kilvert recorded in 1874: 'At Shanklin one has to adopt the detestable custom of bathing in drawers. If ladies don't like to see men naked why don't they keep away from the sight.' But by the 1890s the swimming costume was universal. There was strictly segregated bathing too. The great relaxation began with the passing of the Victorian age. Bexhill permitted mixed bathing in 1901, the year of the old Queen's death, and it was one of the first resorts to do so. Bathing machines gradually disappeared. Complaints about their inconvenience had been voiced since the 1870s and paddling and beach tents began to take their place. During the interwar years both male and female swimming costumes became briefer and briefer. One of the unspoken but obvious attractions of the seaside, the semi-naked human body, was now accepted.

In the mid-nineteenth century a new medical fad, the sea air, was canvassed as being good for the pulmonary complaints that were the scourge of the Victorian cities. What was incorrectly known as 'the ozone' was breathed in lungfuls and resorts trumpeted the efficacy of their air with all varieties from 'balmy' to 'bracing'. In the twentieth century the sun became the major attraction both for its health-giving rays and for the attractive bronze tints it conferred. The call of the sun, of course, was ultimately to lead so many holidaymakers away from British shores to the fleshpots of the Costa Brava.

Given that the initial attraction of the seaside was sea and air the first amenities provided, the pier and the promenade, were designed to maximize their combined benefits. The promenade was the broad-paved road along the seafront which facilitated the health-giving stroll. 'Taking a turn along the prom' was initially a very formal occasion, a chance to see and be seen, a relic of spa elegance. But with the accretion of bandstands, seafood stalls, fortune tellers, deckchairs and covered seats from the 1870s onwards it became in many places less of a ritual than an obstacle course.

The focal point of the promenade was undoubtedly the pier. Seaside piers developed from the early nineteenth century when the best means of transport to the resorts was steamer. Piers were provided as landing stages, the first by Ryde in 1813–14. Brighton followed in 1822–23 and Margate in 1842. The function of the pier began to change in the 1840s and 1850s as more people started to use them to take the air, to see ships arrive and to look at the ocean. Wellington Pier, in Great Yarmouth, was opened in 1853 to cater for these needs; it was named in memory of the Iron Duke who had died in the previous year. Other piers followed. Southport Pier charged 6*d* for pure promenading and 1*s* for bath and sedan chairs.

With the upsurge in holidaymaking the function of the pier changed again. Simple promenading was no longer enough and more varied entertainments were offered. Bandstands, theatres, pavilions and refreshment rooms were added. Concerts, plays, even operas were performed in the pier-end theatres. The D'Oyly Carte Company, who had premiered *The Pirates of Penzance* at Paignton's Bijou Theatre in 1879, performed *H. M. S. Pinafore* on that resort's pier in 1880. The piers became cluttered with 'What the butler saw' machines (that surefire combination of sex and class), candy floss stalls, *camera obscura*, novelty emporiums selling rock and cheap bric-a-brac marked 'souvenir of Foaming-at-the-Mouth', men diving off the pier and so forth.

In the last third of the nineteenth century a pier-building mania gripped Britain. By the last third of the century, virtually every resort had a pier, some more than one. The pier appealed both to the showmanship and to the technological ingenuity of the Victorian builders and engineers. The most famous and most beautiful of piers was Brighton's Chain Pier, opened in 1823. Its superstructure was Oriental in design, part of the Regency vogue for things Eastern which had also produced the Brighton Pavilion. It set a trend followed by the majority of pier-builders who rivalled each other in producing floating Moorish palaces of pleasure, riots of domes, cupolas and minarets.

Pier-building activity was only a part of the massive growth in leisure and entertainment facilities in the last quarter of the nineteenth century, testifying to the need to appeal to a mass audience hungry for diversion and anxious to spend their money as if there were no tomorrow. Their facilities became one of the principal attractions of the resorts. Rhyl advertised its amenities in 1913 as 'Bathing, boating, fishing, croquet, bowls, tennis, golf, concert bands and theatrical performances, hippodrome entertainments (equestrian), cinematograph films, skating rink, water chute, miniature, scenic and figure-of-eight railways, coach and motor tours, steamboat excursions.' The seaside was always alive to the latest craze or sensation and was in the vanguard of the development of film shows, tram rides, skating rinks, balloon flights and electrically powered amusements like roller coasters and big wheels.

For the children there were the traditional and unvarying entertainments: Punch and Judy shows, donkey rides, buckets and spades. From an early date also music of every kind issued forth, creating an air of permanent carnival. More fastidious commentators like Charles Dickens complained bitterly about the unending cacaphony. On one Saturday in 1897 in Albert Road, Blackpool there were at the same time a string trio playing an Irish jig, two Italians with a piano-organ, a German band playing a polka and a blind accordionist. The brass band, that distinctive product of Victorian musical culture, was particularly associated with the seaside; smartly uniformed, it played selections from the light classics, Gilbert and Sullivan and military marches. Ornate bandstands were designed to accommodate them surrounded by deckchairs, those useful collapsible canvas seats, derived as their name suggests from the deck furniture of P. and O. liners. Turn-of-the-century Margate is credited with the first line of seafront deckchairs.

Nigger minstrels, popular from the 1840s, provided simple musical entertainments on the front until eclipsed in the 1890s by the Pierrots, introduced from France as a more gentle and refined musical 'turn' and rejoicing in such names as the Dinky-do's and the Fol-de-rols. In the last quarter of the century immense capital investment brought purpose-built pleasure domes. Theatres and music halls, ornamental gardens and dance palaces, indoor swimming baths, Winter Gardens, imitation Crystal Palaces housing concerts and flower shows, all appeared. Blackpool's celebrated Tower, opened in 1894, literally capped them all, to be disastrously emulated in Morecambe. Funfairs became an essential part of the seaside scene and in a brilliant idea to prolong the season into autumn the illuminations were introduced by Blackpool in 1912. All the machinery of fun and frolic necessitated more mundane but essential improvements such as improved sewerage systems, street lighting and public transport. For the masses, the seaside was a gaudy, glittering wonderland, the perfect setting for a week of abandon in which, as the popular song went, 'You can do a lot of things at the seaside that you can't do in town.'

Accommodation remained a black spot. The first holidaymakers found lodging in private houses. The growth of the resorts led to a rapid increase in lodging houses, frequently run by single women, widows or divorcees of middle age. From the very first there were complaints about cramped accommodation, overcharging, bad food and poor service. The popular image of the landlady was set early and sanctified by generations of cartoonists, caricaturists and comedians. The landlady became as much a staple of English humour as that other legendary harridan, the mother-in-law. In Blackpool the working-class dominance meant a higher proportion of lodging houses than in any other resort. When the Borough Surveyor wrote in 1893 that 'The great provision in most houses is bedrooms', the principle of 'packing them in' was already well established. In the nineteenth century the landlady provided apartments but guests brought in their food to be cooked by the landlady. She provided hot water for tea, and sometimes bread, milk and potatoes at extra charge; some even charged for the use of cruet. Fixed board and fixed all-inclusive menus became general between the wars and this period of 'rising standards and rising expectations', at least away from the depressed areas, saw reductions in overcrowding and offences against hygiene regulations. Improved facilities included wash basins instead of jugs, electric light and separate tables in the dining room.

Blackpool had three times as many lodging houses as Brighton, which had three times as many hotels as Blackpool. Hotel building began in the 1860s and the best resorts were soon able to boast a Metropole, a Grand or an Imperial complete with marble staircases, palm courts, wine cellars, terrace tea rooms, uniformed commissionaires, reading, smoking and billiard rooms in which the upper middle classes could live in the style to which they wished to become accustomed.

By the 1900s the pattern of the seaside holiday was established. The resorts were flourishing; the railway network was complete; holidays were accepted by employers and regarded by increasing numbers of workers as an integral part of the year. By 1930 the holiday industry was one of the biggest in the country. There were changes in the 1930s: the rise of motorized transport and in particular the charabanc to rival the railways, the development of holiday camps and the statutory enactment of holidays with pay. But the great challenge to the traditional seaside holiday came after the Second World War with the rise of foreign package holidays. The seaside holiday in Britain still survives, however, and the same motives draw its customers as drew their Victorian forefathers – the desire for a change, a rest and a good time. The resorts have adapted, of course. The steam trains and the steamboats have gone; the Punch and Judy shows are declining; the pierrots are a thing of the past; the piers succumb to age and the elements; holidays are staggered, with the old Bank Holiday exodus largely a memory. Postcards capture for us with a particular vividness and immediacy that lost atmosphere of mass holidaymaking in its formative period.

## FURTHER READING


Adamson, S. H., *Seaside Piers* (London, 1977)

Anderson, J. and Swinglehurst, E., *The Victorian and Edwardian Seaside* (London, 1978)

Bailey, F. A., *A history of Southport* (Southport, 1955)

Bridgeman, H. and Drury, E., *Beside the Seaside* (London, 1977)

Brunner, E., *Holiday making and the Holiday Trades* (Oxford, 1945)

Gilbert, E. W., *Brighton: Old Ocean's Bauble* (London, 1976)

Hern, A., *The Seaside Holiday* (London, 1967)

Lowerson, J. and Myerscough, J., *Time to Spare in Victorian England* (London, 1978)

Mellor, G. J., *Pom-poms and Ruffles* (Clapham, 1966)

Perkin, H. J., 'The Social Tone of Victorian Seaside Resorts in the North-West', *Northern History*, **2** (1975–76) pp. 180–94

Pimlott, J. A. R., *The Englishman's Holiday* (London, 1947)

Taylor, D. and Bush, D., *The Golden Age of British Hotels* (London, 1974)

Turner, B. and Palmer, S., *The Blackpool Story* (Blackpool, 1976)

Walton, J. K., 'Residential amenity, respectable morality and the rise of the entertainment industry: the case of Blackpool 1860–1914', *Literature and History*, **1** (1975) pp. 62–78

Walton, J. K., *The Blackpool Landlady* (Manchester, 1978)

Walvin, J., *Beside the Seaside* (London, 1978)

Walvin, J., *Leisure and Society 1830–1950* (London, 1978)

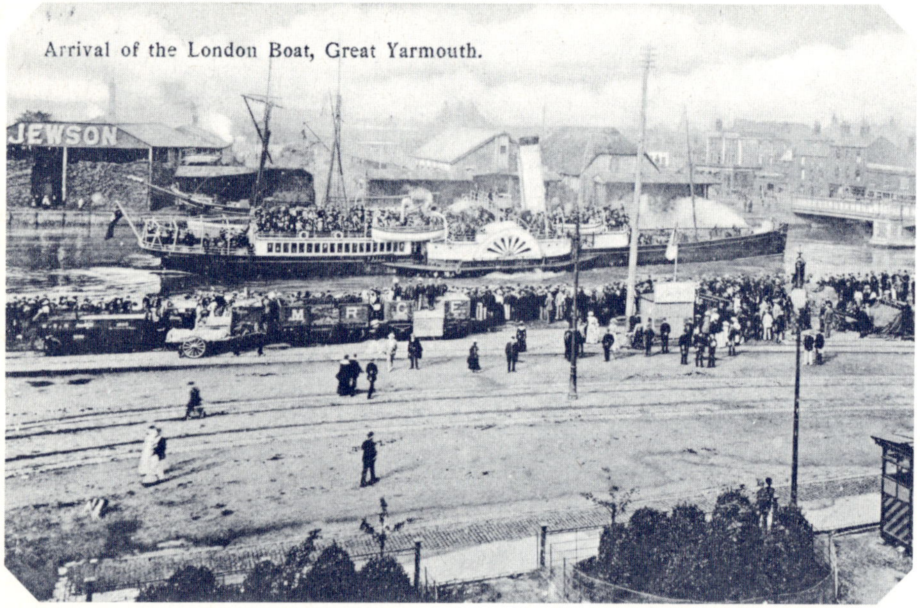


1. STEAMBOATS

The mass exodus from the cities to the seaside was made possible only by the coming of steam. Steamboats were first; from 1815 onwards they carried pleasure-seeking Londoners in their thousands down the Thames to Ramsgate, Margate and Gravesend, driving away 'the better class of visitor' in the process. The seaside piers, later centres for amusement and entertainment, were originally the landing stages for the steamers. Although they were superseded by steam trains as the primary means of transportation to the resorts, they survived as vehicles for pleasure trips and excursions. In this card, dated 1908, the London boat arrives at Great Yarmouth. Although primarily a port, Yarmouth became a popular seaside resort for day trippers and holidaymakers, particularly from the midlands. By 1897 there were some 430,000 visitors a year to the town. Only some 60,000 came by steamer; the vast majority by this time were transported by train.

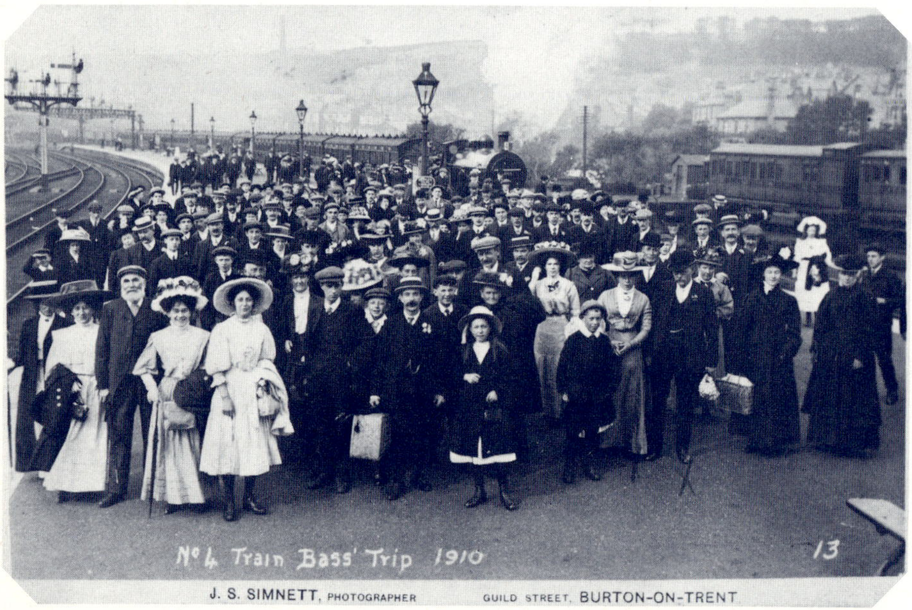


2. RAILWAYS

The coming of the railways provided the means for the working classes to make use of increased leisure opportunities and spending power by travelling to the seaside. Even in Edwardian times, however, many were still too poor to afford more than a day trip and even then only if arranged by a charitable organization. Many bodies organized day trips – Sunday Schools, sports clubs, street committees, chapels, temperance groups, Boy Scout troops, even factories and commercial firms. Here workers and their families from the Bass breweries in Burton prepare to embark on a day trip to Scarborough in 1910. This was the Number Four train of some 14 which Bass chartered that year. Note the Sunday best outfits. Crosses mark the couple who purchased the card as a reminder of their trip.

3. CHARABANCS

In the 1930s the charabanc began to rival the train as the primary means of conveyance to the seaside. But long before that, motorized sightseeing trips had become a feature of seaside life. The early charabanc, or 'chonkabonk' as it was colloquially known, was a large open car full of seats and it was in Edwardian times a popular way of exploring the hinterland. Here a loaded charabanc waits to depart from the Ormescliffe Boarding Establishment, Llandudno, in 1912.

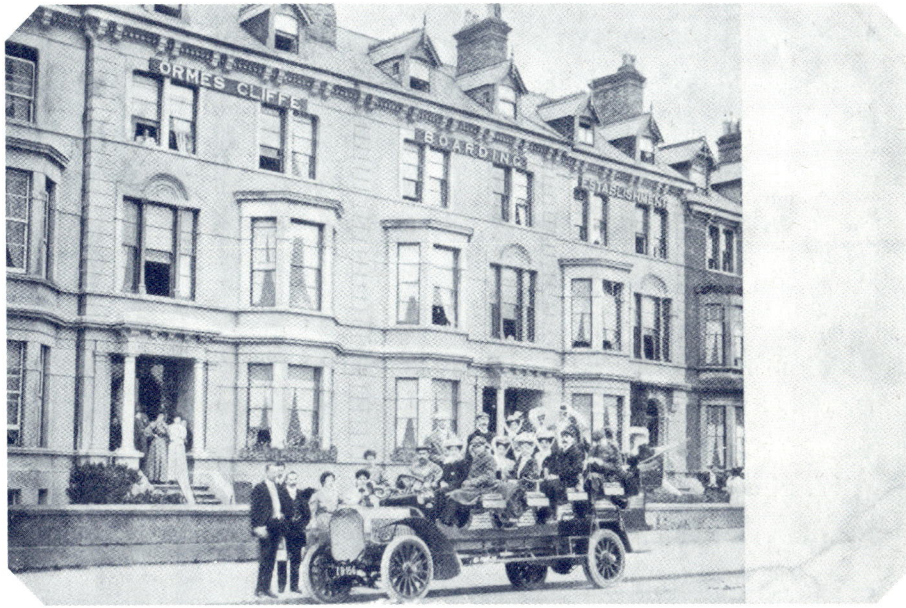


4. SEA-BATHING

From the mid-eighteenth century sea-bathing had been publicized as an efficacious treatment for a wide variety of complaints including 'ulcers, scabs, scaled hands, itching and leprosy, corns, tumours, pains of the limbs, hydrophobia, all inflammations, all catarrhal effects, nephritis, gonorrhoea, arthritis and many others.' 'Taking the waters' in the nineteenth century meant both bathing in and drinking it, though the latter practice died out in the second half of the century. Initially, men bathed naked and women in costumes, but by the 1890s costumes were universal and as all-enveloping as possible. After the Victorian age they diminished steadily in size. In this card an entire working-class family on a spree in 1912 immerse themselves; the ladies wear high neck-lines and bathing caps to preserve their modesty. The costumes were hired, as indicated by the shield with corporation initials on the costume of the young man on the right. The practice of hiring was common and corporation initials were a device to prevent theft. The card was posted in Canterbury and sent to Clapham Common.

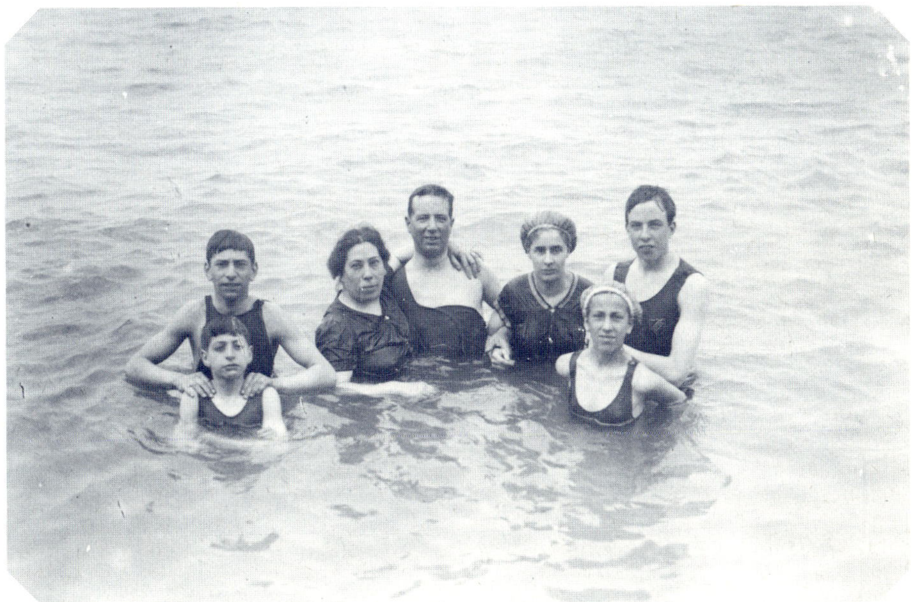

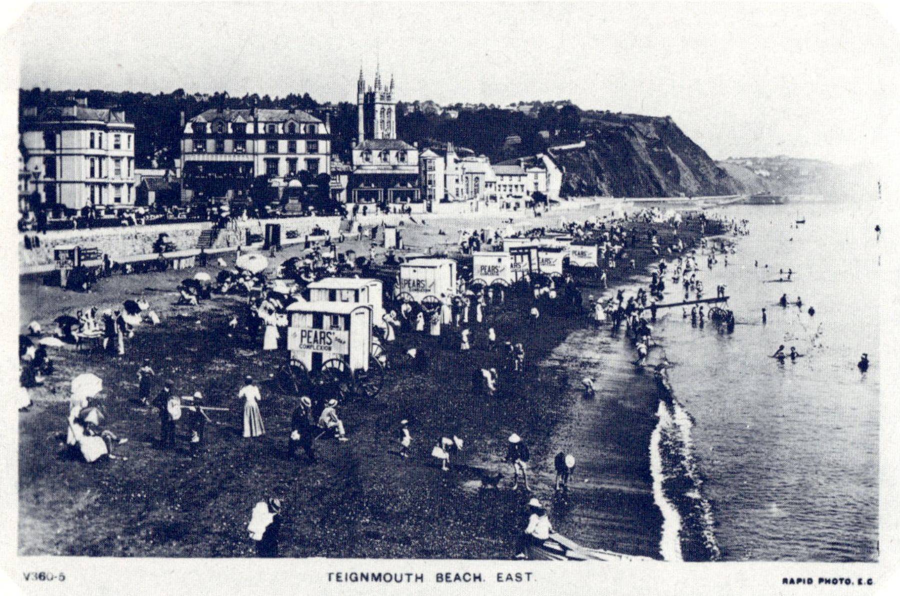


5. BATHING MACHINES

Bathing machines were a regular feature of seaside holidays in the nineteenth century. They date back at least to the 1730s. Bathers changed in them and then descended into the sea. Resorts vied to announce large numbers of such machines in their publicity. By the end of the century, however, they were being replaced by beach tents and paddling. Several beach tents can be seen on this card, which also indicates the value of the bathing machine for advertising. The card was sent from Teignmouth in 1910. Teignmouth emerged as a resort in the late nineteenth century as a result of the railway-stimulated discovery of Devon and Cornwall. Its lodging houses were described at this time as 'very numerous . . . comfortable . . . not for the most part pretentious.' The card was sent to the Central Hall, Birmingham, suggesting a Methodist outing, and declares appreciatively: 'We are just going to have some cream for tea. Cream with a big C.' Devonshire cream teas were already one of the county's distinctive attractions.

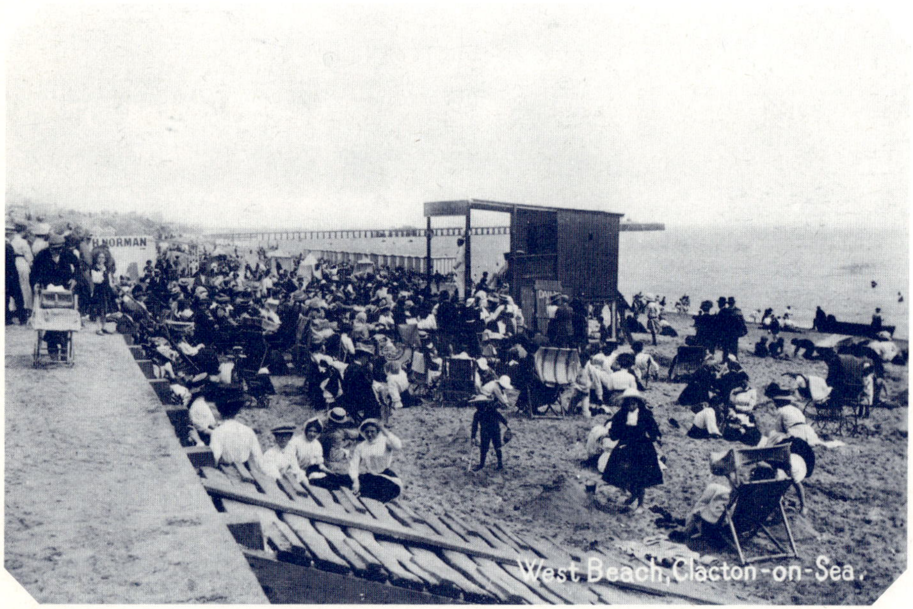


6. THE BEACH (i) CLACTON-ON-SEA

Like its neighbours, Walton-on-the-Naze and Southend, Clacton did not develop as an important resort until the 1890s, when working-class trippers began to arrive in large numbers by steamer and train. In 1876, accessible only by coach from the nearest station and with only two steamers a day, it was characterized as offering 'a select company and low prices'. By 1895 it boasted a pier pavilion and a new concrete esplanade and was being vigorously developed by the Clacton-on-Sea Land, Building and Investment Company. Here we see a packed West Beach in 1911. It is typical of beach scenes: a densely packed riot of deckchairs, perambulators, beach tents and bathing machines with the clear likelihood of a good audience for the concert party.

## 7. THE BEACH (ii) VENTNOR

Ventnor, Isle of Wight, was an up-market resort. The blazers, boaters, parasols and the 'Ladies Bathing Office' of this 1918 card evince a distinctly more middle-class ethos than do the denizens of Clacton beach. Ventnor remained very much a health resort, valued for the treatment of pulmonary complaints. Even so, Henry James complained in 1879 of 'a formed and finished watering place, it has been reduced to a due degree of cockneyfication.'

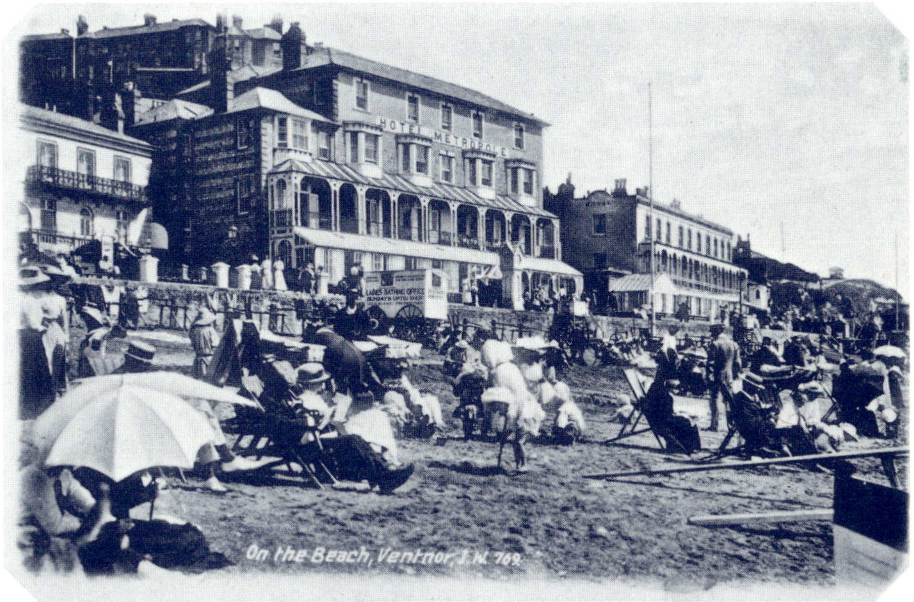


## 8. THE BEACH (iii) WESTON-SUPER-MARE

Weston-super-Mare developed as a resort for nearby Bristol and South Wales. But the excellent GWR connections between Bristol and Birmingham made it the supreme attraction for West Midlands industrial workers. From the late 1880s onwards Weston became increasingly concerned to control trippers, attracted also by the Bristol Channel Steamers. This card, sent from Weston to Cheltenham in 1913, was from one of those steamer-borne day-trippers. Note that one patriotic holidaymaker has erected a Union Jack next to his deckchair.

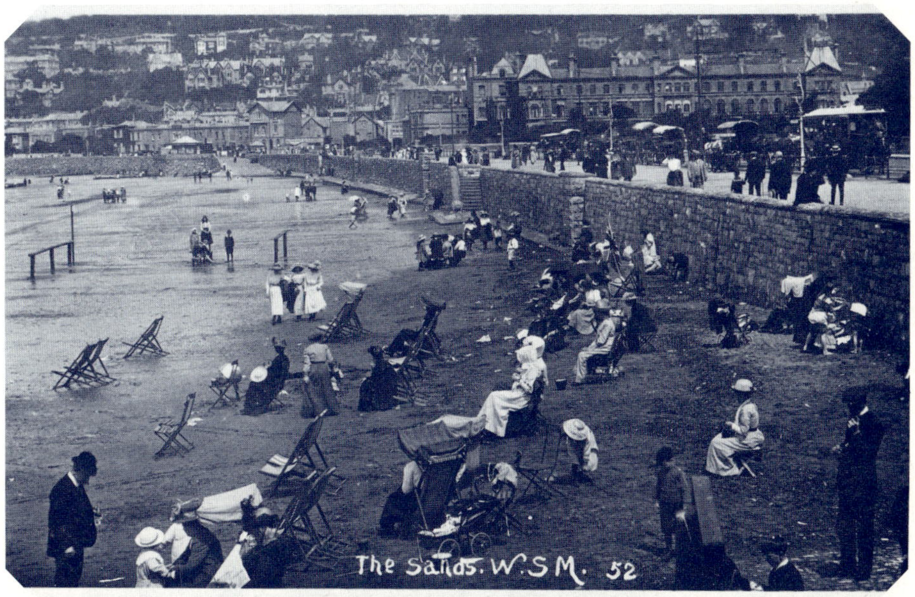

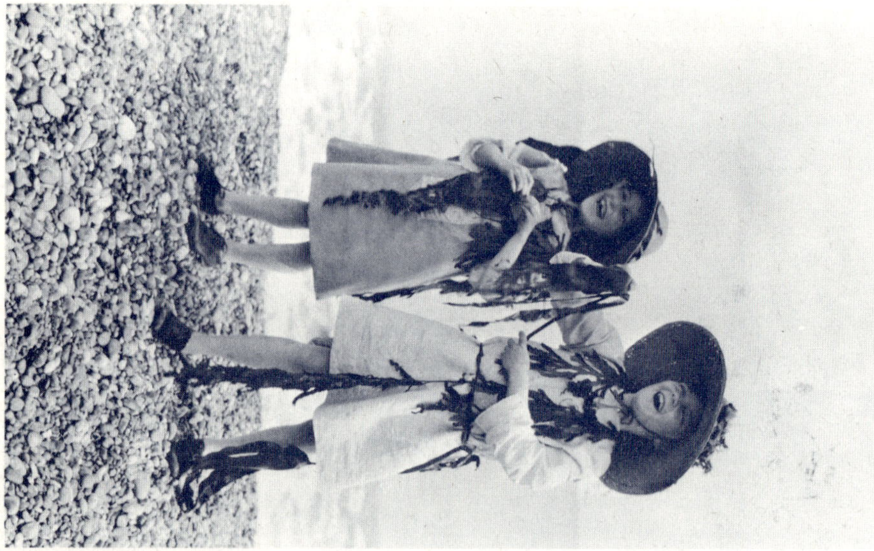

9. SEAWEED

The mid-Victorian middle class had a passion for improving themselves on holiday. Collecting, identifying and cataloguing shells, pebbles and seaweed was very popular. Philip Henry Gosse's works on marine biology were the Bibles of the craze. This passion did not survive the transformation of the seaside resorts into great pleasure grounds. But seaweed was still collected, partly because it was supposed to signal changes in the weather. These two middle-class girls seem particularly happy with the specimens on this card sent from Deal to Richmond, Surrey, in September 1912.

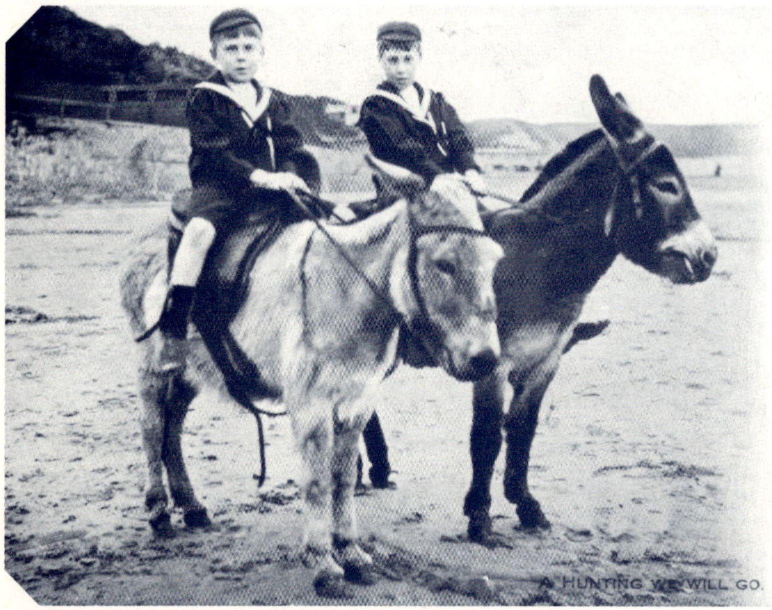


10. DONKEYS

The arrival of the middle classes in large numbers turned the seaside holiday into a family affair, something it had not been in the heyday of the aristocracy. For the children, the pleasures were unchanging and elemental: paddling, digging sandcastles and donkey rides. Here two young middle-class holidaymakers disport themselves in the sailor suits that were *de rigueur* in late Victorian and Edwardian England. Donkeys were ubiquitous. Their introduction to the seaside dates from the latter part of the eighteenth century. Introduced perhaps by the gypsies, they were initially utilized by ladies in rides along the beach and the cliffs. Miss Betsy Trotwood in Dickens' *David Copperfield* waged permanent war on the donkeys who passed her cliff-top cottage. One of the complaints levelled against working-class day trippers by those who wished to preserve resort exclusivity was that they were cruel to the donkeys.

11. GOAT CARTS

A refinement on the donkey ride was the goat cart, a feature of seaside resorts no more. This one is seen at Worthing in 1910 on a card sent to Datchet. Worthing, which grew rapidly in the late nineteenth century, remained a select and extremely fashionable resort, recommended for sufferers from chest ailments. It attracted the quality in Goodwood race week and boasted such unusual features as a choral society and subscription gardens.

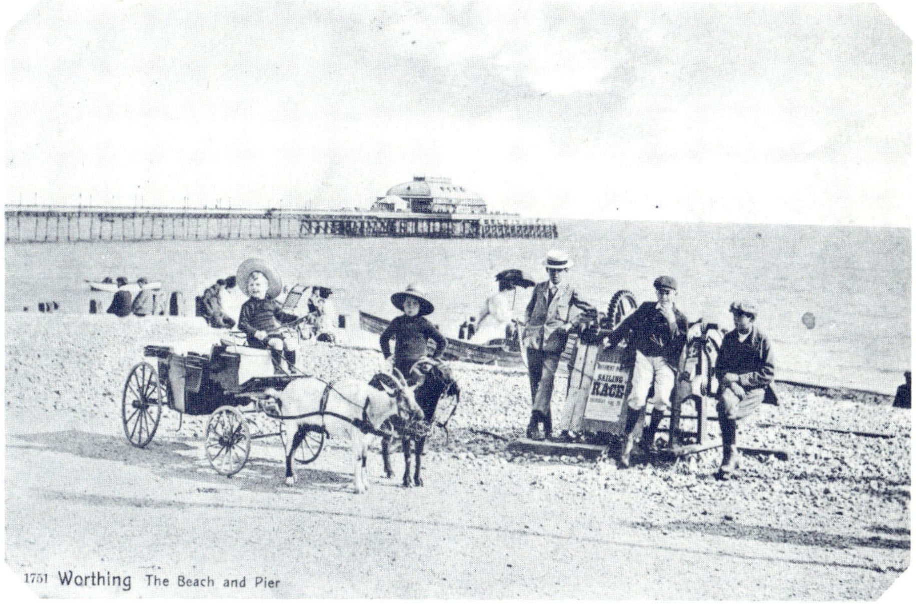


1751 Worthing The Beach and Pier

12. PUNCH AND JUDY

In the last quarter of the nineteenth century the facilities offered by Rhyl expanded dramatically until the visitor had an embarrassment of riches, from zoo to ballroom, from skating rink to Winter Gardens. Yet the traditional entertainments, like the promenade Punch and Judy show, continued to exert their timeless fascination.

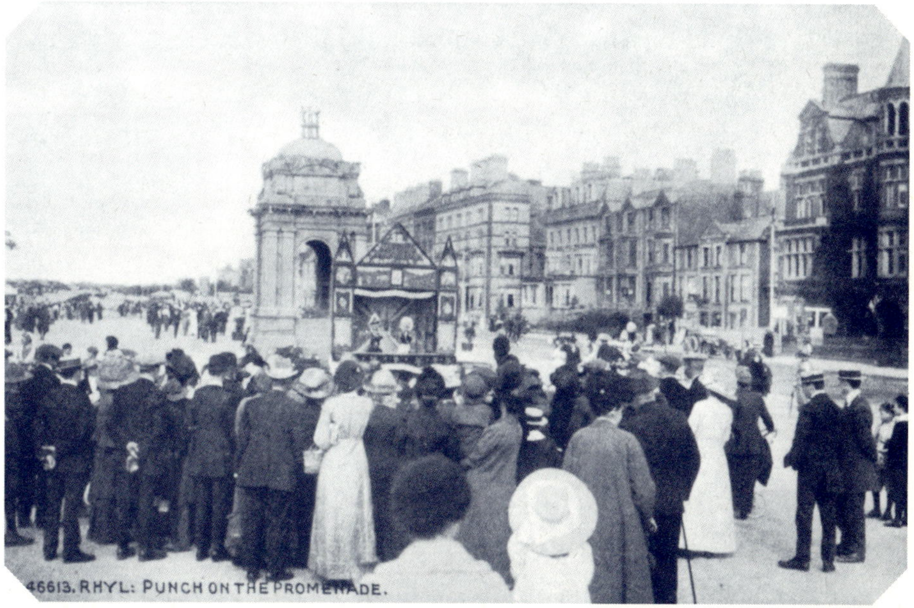

46613. RHYL: PUNCH ON THE PROMENADE.

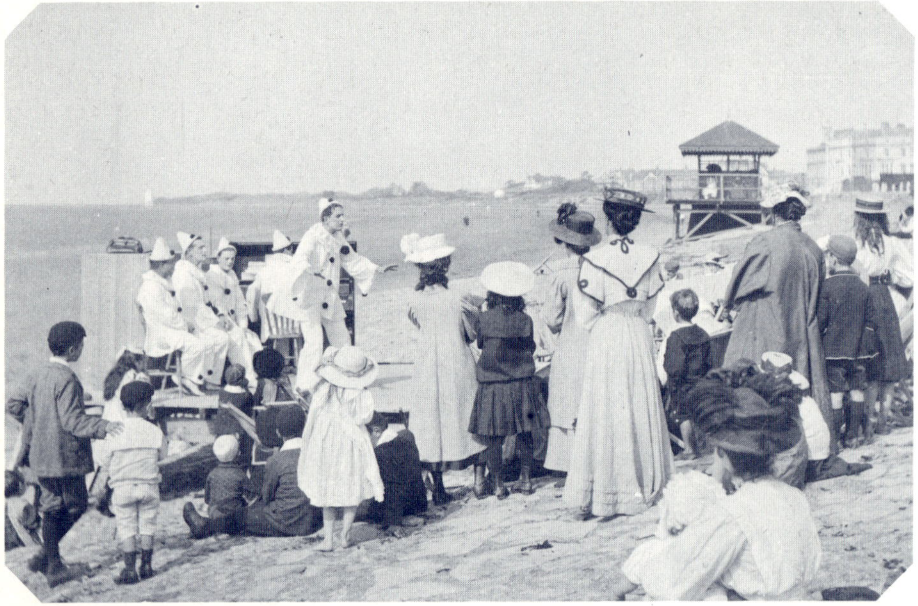

13. THE PIERROTS

From the 1840s to the 1890s the nigger minstrels were the pre-eminent beach entertainers. But in 1891 Clifford Essex introduced the pierrots from France to provide more refined seaside entertainment. These entertainers in their distinctive costumes rapidly became an integral part of the holiday scene. An Edwardian postcard of the Children's Corner at Filey records: 'This is where the Pierrotts (sic) have their stand. There is a very good group of Pierrotts at Filey and they get a good crowd round too. Filey is not a place with much indoor amusement, Mabel, but Filey Bay is very beautiful and the cliffs at each side of it are nice to walk on. When the tide is in the Pierrotts stand on the promenade.'

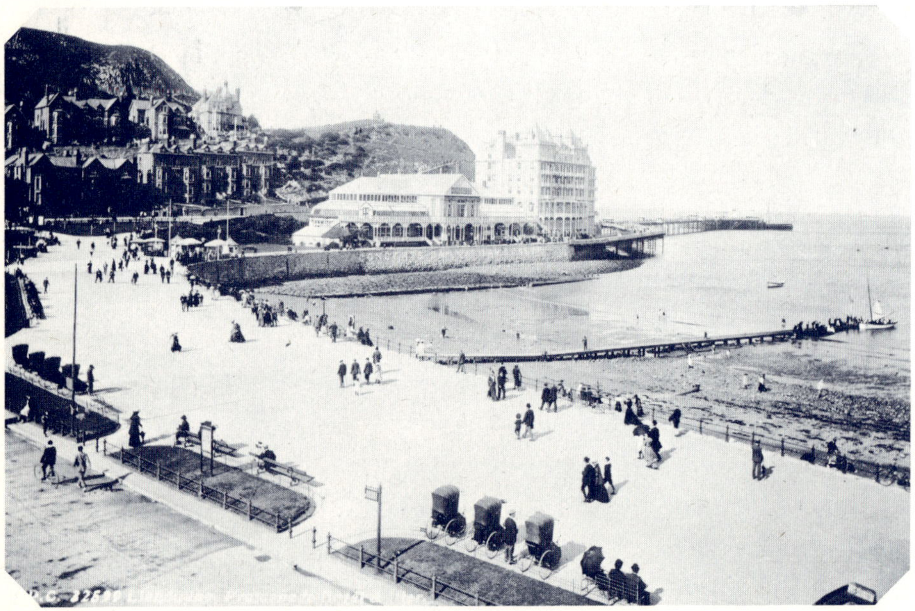

14. THE PROMENADE

The 'sea air' became the new medical fad from the mid-nineteenth century onwards and invalids were one constant group among the visitors to the resorts. The 'ozone' was widely canvassed by most resorts as health-giving and of special benefit in a wide range of chest ailments. Invalids seem generally to have accepted such claims. One such, Jim Summers, writing to his father from Blackpool in 1926, declared: 'It is very bracing here, I believe. I should get as strong as you say with a month or two of it . . . am having a very restful holiday, spending most of the time on the beach.' The promenade, a broad walk laid out along the seafront, was an ideal place to take the air. In Llandudno, seen here in 1909, bath chairs were for hire and the corporation announced: 'For the convenience of invalids and others who desire to regulate the amount of their daily exercise, the Promenade has been marked off into quarter mile distances.'

15. PIERS (i) BLACKPOOL, NORTH PIER

The promenade's focal point was the pier. By the 1920s some 90 piers existed in England; less than half survive today. Their complex structural engineering and fantastically elaborate superstructures have led latterly to their being recognized as prime examples of the Victorian and Edwardian builders' art. Their solidity is eloquently attested by the 15 unsuccessful attempts to blow up storm-damaged Margate Pier in 1979. The progressive decline and disappearance of so many piers is melancholy testimony to the philistinism of contempory society. Blackpool's North Pier, designed by Eugenius Birch, doyen of pier builders, was opened in 1863. The Indian Pavilion, modelled on the Temple of Binderabund, was added in 1877 and the theatre in 1903. The card, sent in August 1911 to Worksop, recalls: 'Gosh! it *is* windy today but quite warm. Hope H. R. H. will turn up, "Quaker Girl" is here this week – this is the last night, so shant be able to go. Cussed luck.' A royal visit for the opening of the Promenade extension was discussed in 1911 but in the event H. R. H. did not turn up.

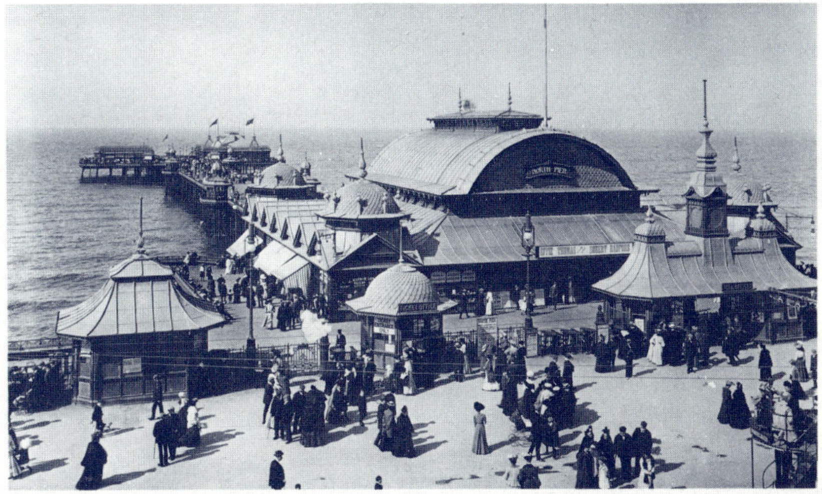

NORTH PIER, BLACKPOOL.

16. PIERS (ii) BRIGHTON PALACE

Brighton's Palace Pier, opened in 1899, was designed by R. St George Moore. It has been described as 'the grandest pier to be built.' The pier end theatre was opened in 1901 and the pavilion in 1910. The card, dated 1915, was sent by a man to his sweetheart in Blackpool. He was probably a soldier on leave, since he talks about 'a lot of our boys here.'

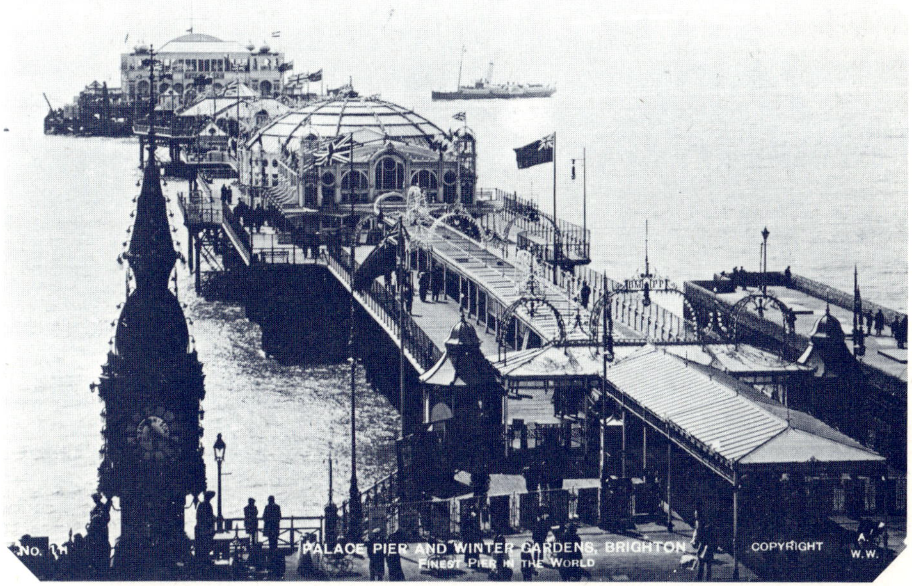

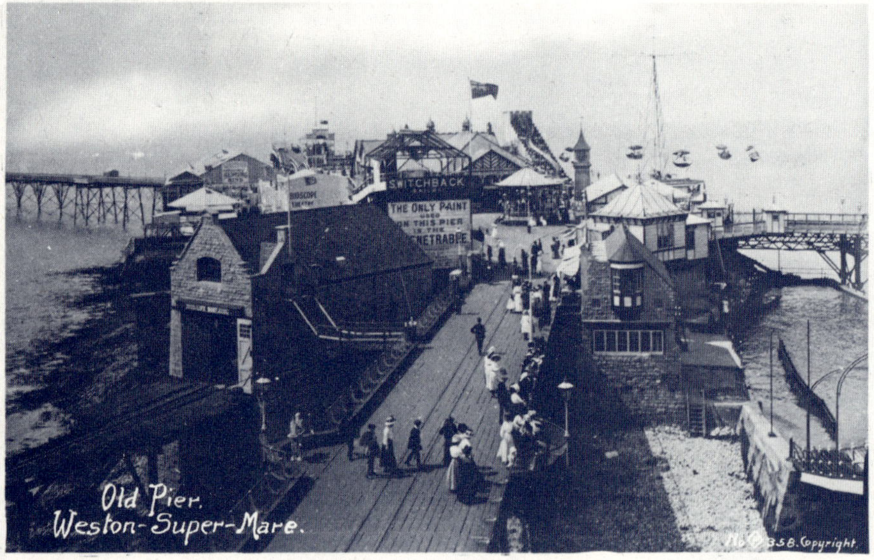


17. PIERS (iii) WESTON BIRNBECK
The Birnbeck or Old Pier at Weston-super-Mare, another Eugenius Birch creation, was opened in 1867. Unusually, it included an island, Birnbeck, which was levelled to provide a base for the entertainments developed in the 1860s. An opponent of the development wrote in 1896: 'In the first place it was a promenade pier where the residents and visitors used to assemble, it has now become more like a fair and a Punch and Judy show . . . a lot of cheap shows to suit the trippers.' This card, dated 1910, shows the variety of amusements: skating rink, film show, helter-skelter, switchback railway, merrygoround. They seemed to suit the trippers for the message on the back reads: 'Old Pier amusements – that's the place for a frolic.' Situated about a mile from central Weston, the Old Pier now shows clear signs of neglect and increasing decrepitude.

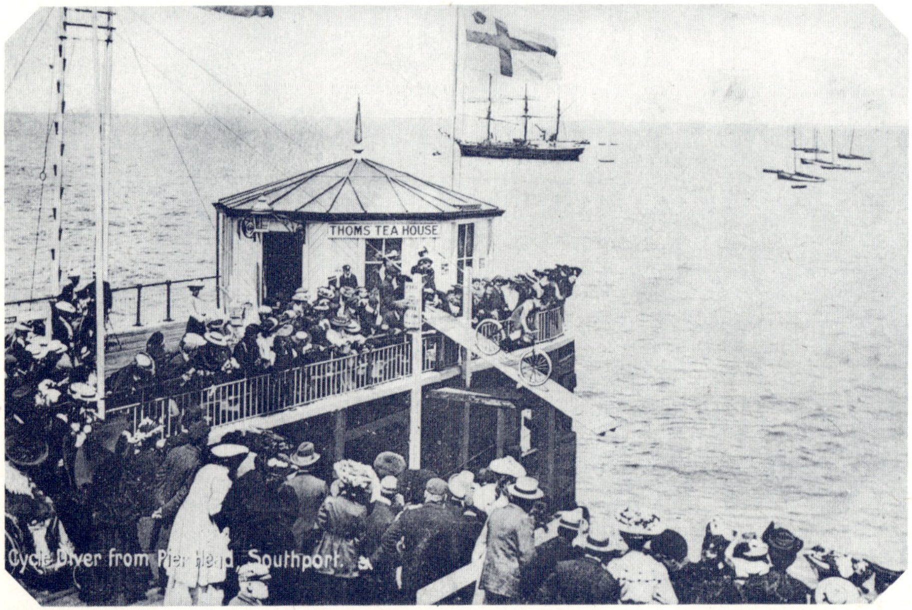


18. PIER DIVING
Among the regular attractions on piers was pier-diving by professionals, usually bearing the courtesy title of 'Professor'. Here, in a refinement, a bicycle is used. Southport Pier, the scene of this particular exploit, was opened in 1860, originally for promenading. It was twice extended.

19. SKATING
Roller-skating first became a craze in the 1870s and experienced a revival in the Edwardian period. Seaside resorts had to be alert to exploit each new fad in the battle for custom. Here we see open-air skating on Weymouth Pier.

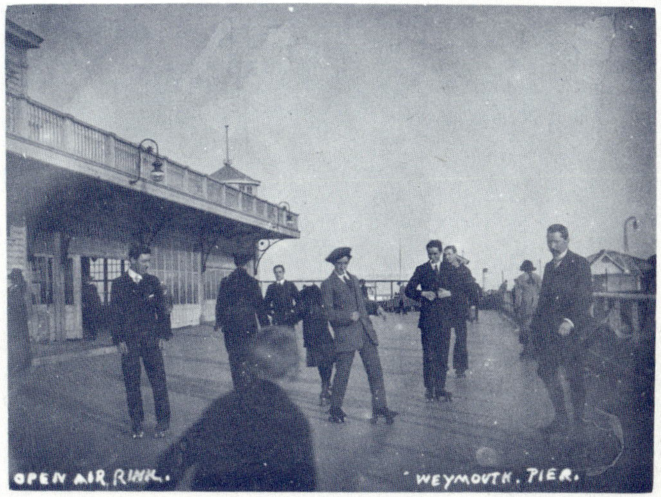


20. BRASS BANDS
Music was everywhere at the seaside. But perhaps nothing so typified seaside music as the brass band. 'I do like to stroll along the prom, prom, prom, where the brass band plays, tiddly-om-pom-pom' said the popular song, *I do like to be beside the seaside.* There were over 5,000 brass bands in England by 1900. This bandstand, at St Anne's-on-Sea, is characteristic of many such exquisitely wrought efforts. The card, written on 10 August 1908, was sent to 'My dearest Emily' and recalls a romantic tryst one Sunday evening near the bandstand.

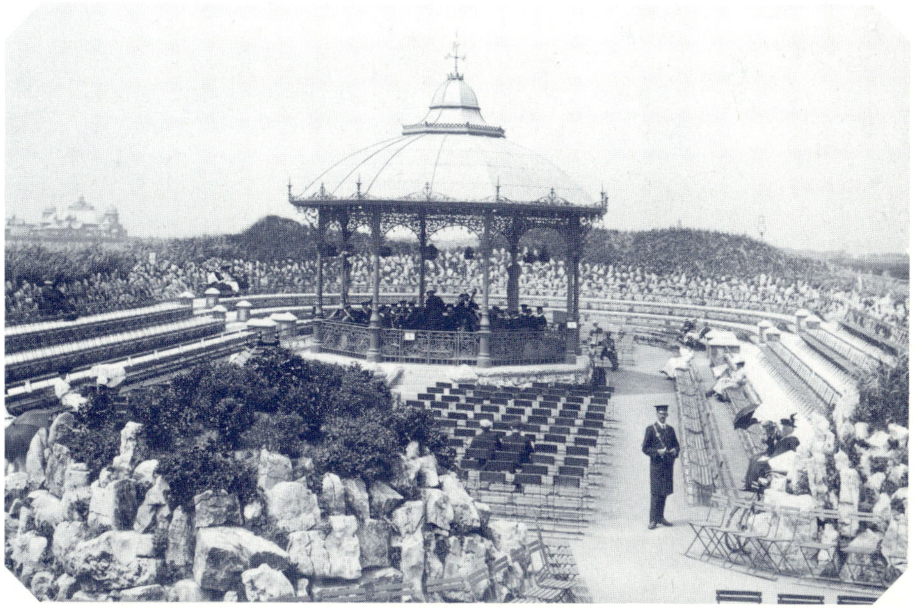

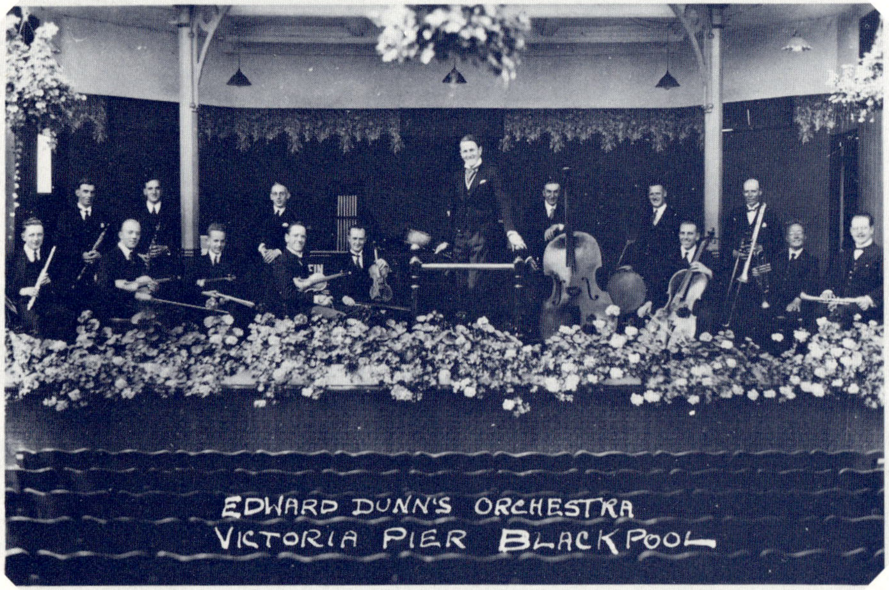


21. ORCHESTRAS

Besides brass bands there were orchestras which played popular classics, selections from musical comedies and ballads. Dancing was one of the popular attractions on the pier and many provided resident orchestras. Here is Edward Dunn's 14 piece orchestra at the Victoria Pier, Blackpool. The third and most recent of Blackpool's piers, it was opened in 1893 and boasted 36 shops and a bandstand. It changed its name to South Pier in 1930.

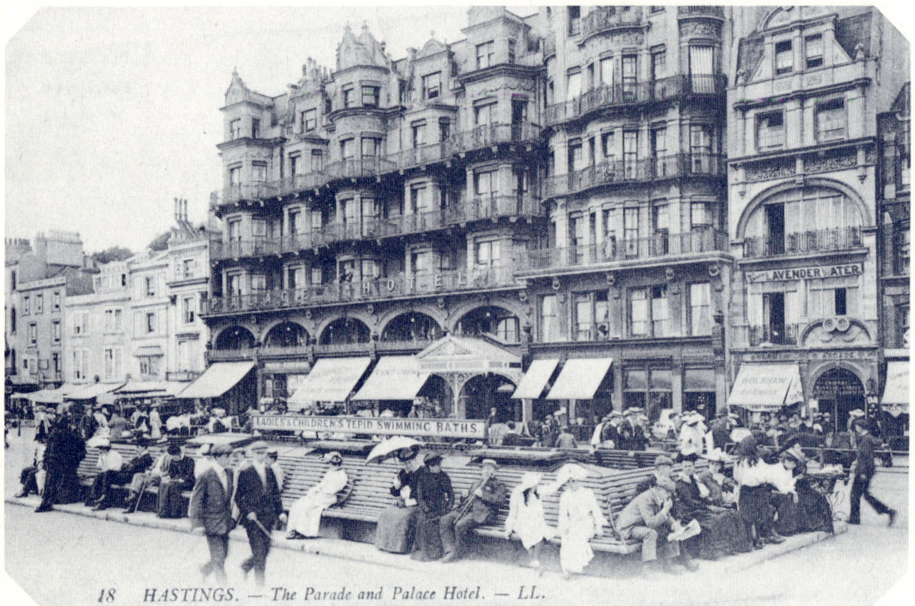


22. HOTELS

From the 1860s onwards hotels were catering for the 'better class of visitor.' The Palace Hotel, Hastings, was built between 1885 and 1887 by the Australian firm, Spiers and Pond. It still exists but no longer as an hotel. It is now a public house with private apartments above it known as Palace Chambers. Note the 'bicycle stable' in the arcade, a facility appreciated by the many cycling enthusiasts of the Edwardian age. The card, interestingly, was printed in France and preserves a distinctly French ambience.

## 23. BOARDING HOUSES

Working-class holidaymakers headed overwhelmingly for the boarding houses. Blackpool's Reads Road, pictured here in 1908, was at the centre of the town's boarding-house network. Its solidly respectable boarding establishments lay close to Central Station. They catered for the upper reaches of the working class and white- collar workers. The town also had its less salubrious quarters.

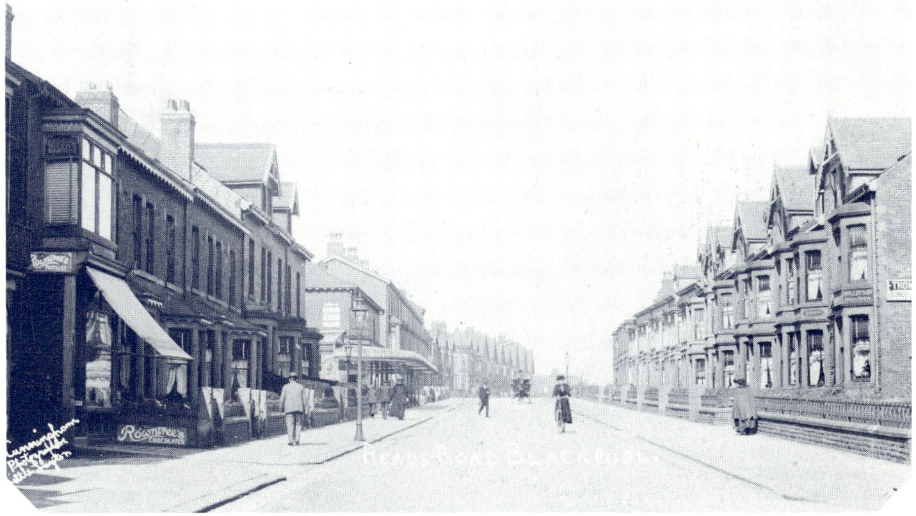


## 24. TENNIS

From the 1880s onwards sports facilities gained prominence at the seaside. Tennis was particularly popular since, unusually among the major sports, women could participate. Several women are playing on this card from St Anne's-on-Sea. The card, dated 1928 and sent to Barrow-in-Furness, says: 'We have been teaching father to play tennis, it has been ever such fun.'

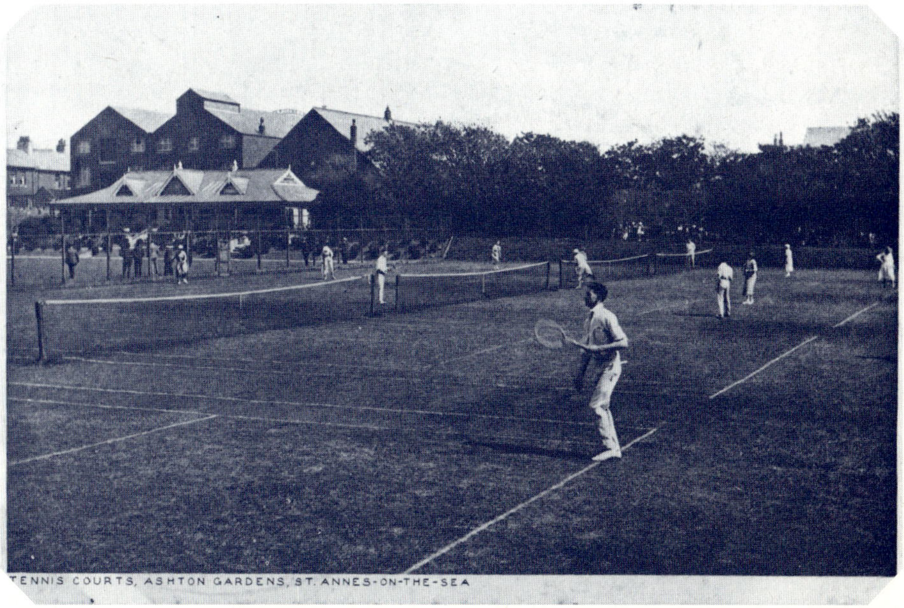

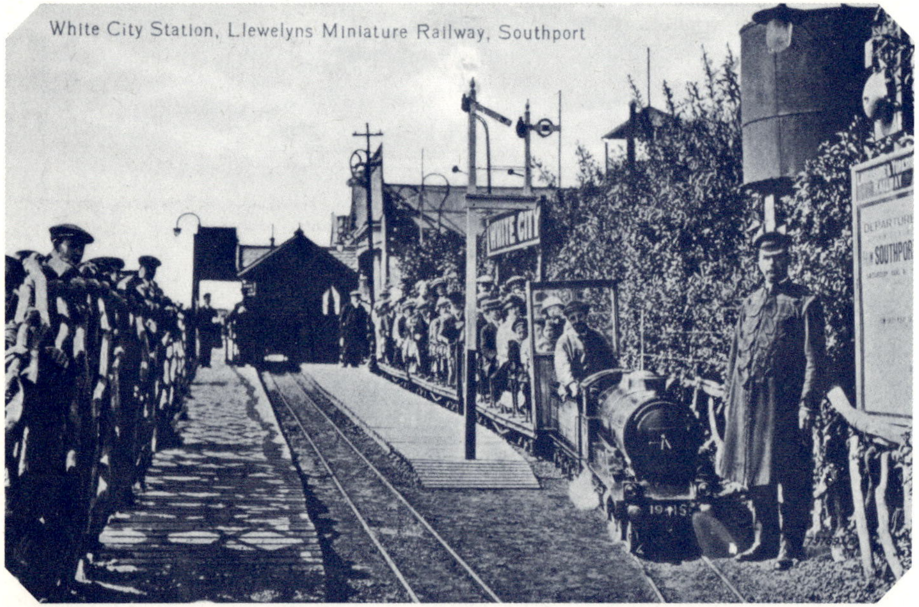


25. MINIATURE RAILWAY

The Southport miniature railway was opened in 1911 and run in its early days by Dr Ladmore, a local dentist. He was later joined in the enterprise by Mr Griffiths Vaughan Llewelyn, who operated it until the early 1930s when he went into liquidation. The card, produced by the Llewelyn Miniature Railway Company, was sent in 1918 from Southport to Buxton. It shows White City station on the fairground. Stephenson's *Guide to Southport* (1913) noted, 'Former visitors to Southport will remember the old Fair Ground which consisted of dilapidated wooden shanties, Aunt Sallies, coconut shies, and so forth. All this rubbish has been cleared away, and what is fittingly called "The White City" put in its place.' The Railway still runs from The White City's successor, Pleasureland, to Peter Pan's Pool.

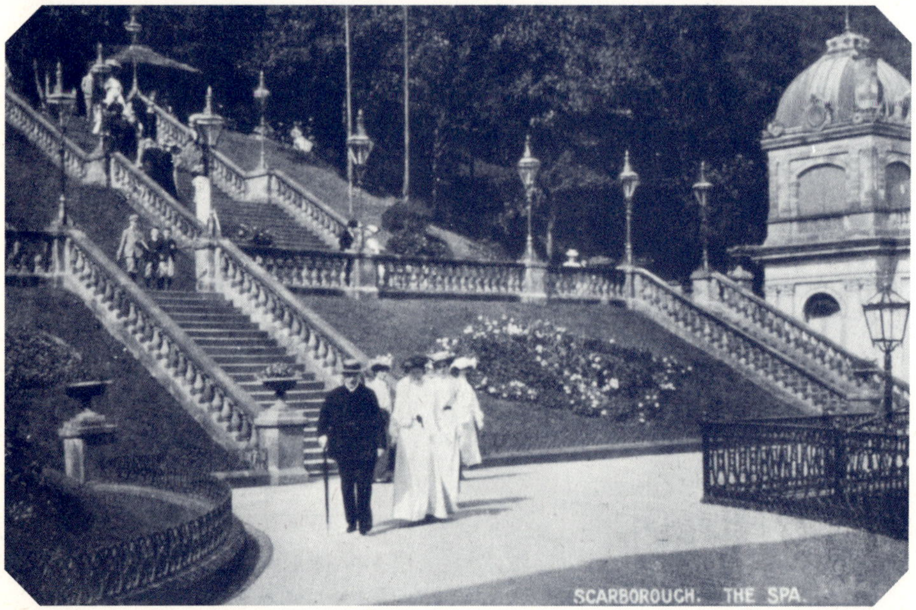


26. ORNAMENTAL GARDENS

In some places 'the quality' still rubbed shoulders with working-class visitors. One such place was Scarborough, 'the Brighton of the North'. Here the spacious gardens were a potent reminder of eighteenth-century spa days when specially appointed arbiters of elegance like Beau Nash prescribed a fixed, formal etiquette and sacrosanct social round to which fashionable spa visitors must adhere. Invalids enjoyed taking the air in these pleasant surroundings. Many resorts provided purpose-built invalid walks in their formal gardens.

27. WINTER GARDENS

In a bid to raise the social tone and provide for the better class of visitor Blackpool built the Winter Gardens at a cost of £100,000. It opened in 1878 and included the Floral Hall, the Indian Lounge, the Grand Pavilion and later the huge Empress Ballroom. For years a fierce rival of the Tower Company for the entertainment market, the Winter Gardens was taken over by that company in 1928. This card, sent to Keswick in 1911, was from another invalid: 'Pleased to say I have no pain whatever.'

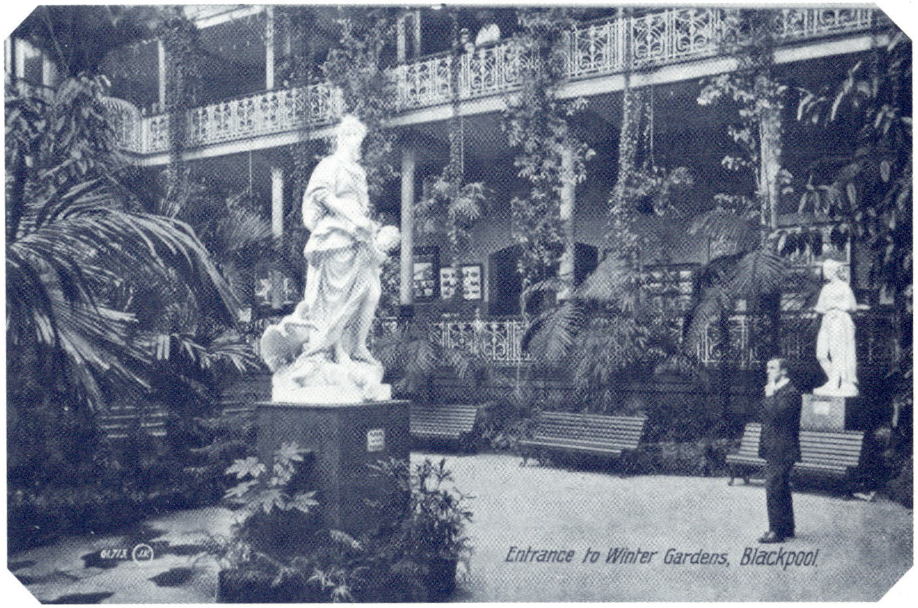
Entrance to Winter Gardens, Blackpool

28. SWIMMING BATHS

Blackpool continued to lead the way in the provision of new amenities. When he visited the resort in 1933 J. B. Priestley described it as 'the great roaring spangled beast.' The Open-Air baths on the South Shore were opened in June 1923 and still stand. The card, declaring 'Having a grand time', was sent to Oswestry in 1927. The baths featured in the 1934 Gracie Fields film, *Sing As We Go*, which was largely shot on location in Blackpool.

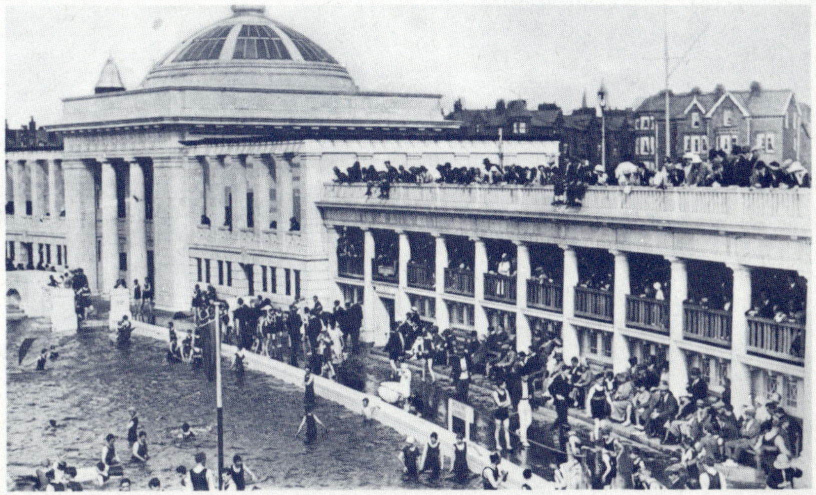
Open-Air Baths, South Shore, Blackpool. No. 106.

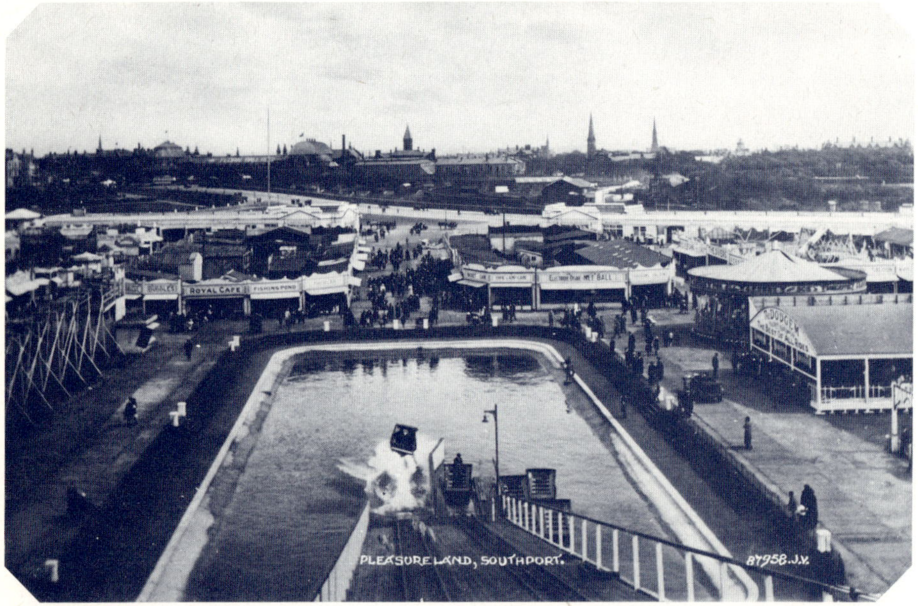


29. FAIRGROUNDS

Many resorts boasted fairgrounds which made use of the latest technology and gadgetry; their expanding range of delights included rollercoasters, roundabouts, switchback railways and big dippers. Blackpool's was known from 1905 as 'The Pleasure Beach'. Even select Southport down the coast had a fairground but, jealous of its reputation as the 'Montpelier of England', kept it within bounds near the pier. 'In the interests of a more restful Promenade environment', as the historian of Southport put it, 'the amusements were moved to the Pleasureland site in 1922.' This card shows Pleasureland in all its glory.

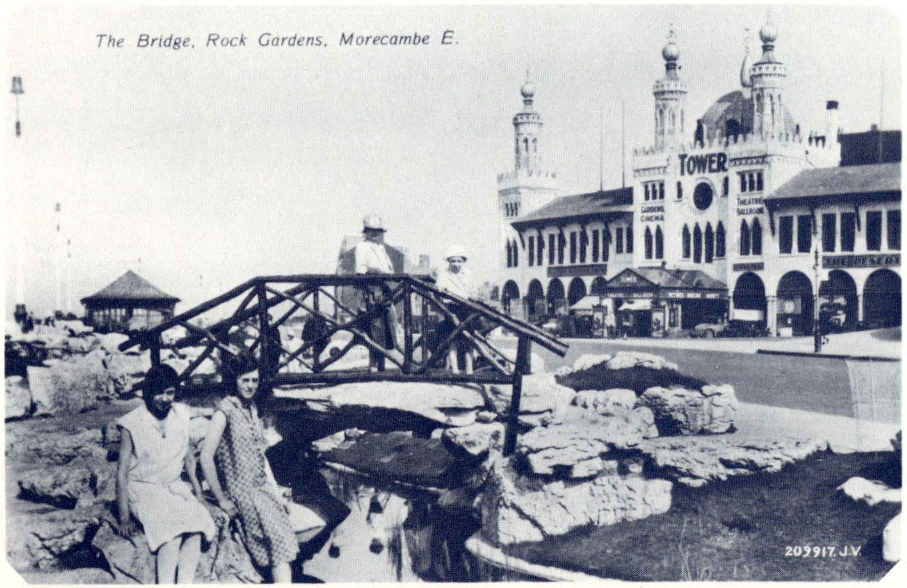


30. THE TOWER

Perhaps Blackpool's most celebrated attraction is its tower and in an attempt to meet the competition, Morecambe launched a company in 1898 to build a rival. The intention was to provide an Oriental environment with shop assistants and attendants bedecked in Arab and Moorish costume. This intention is plainly seen from the Tower buildings opened in 1909. Sadly, the Tower itself was never completed. It stood for a few years as a sawn-off skeleton before the fates openly declared their preference for Blackpool in a bolt of lightning directed at the more northerly intruder. The Morecambe Tower was eventually melted down for armament manufacture during the First World War. This card shows the Morecambe buildings, complete with theatre, cinema, ballroom and cafés. They survived until 1959.

# GENERAL INDEX

# INDEX OF PLACE NAMES